# The Architecture of Illegal Markets

# The Architecture of Illegal Markets

## Towards an Economic Sociology of Illegality in the Economy

Edited by
Jens Beckert and Matías Dewey

OXFORD
UNIVERSITY PRESS

OXFORD
UNIVERSITY PRESS

Great Clarendon Street, Oxford, OX2 6DP,
United Kingdom

Oxford University Press is a department of the University of Oxford.
It furthers the University's objective of excellence in research, scholarship,
and education by publishing worldwide. Oxford is a registered trade mark of
Oxford University Press in the UK and in certain other countries



First Edition published in 2017



Published in the United States of America by Oxford University Press
198 Madison Avenue, New York, NY 10016, United States of America

British Library Cataloguing in Publication Data
Data available

Library of Congress Control Number: 2016962767

ISBN 978–0–19–879497–4

# Acknowledgments

Illegality is a pervasive issue in market transactions but not an important topic in economic sociology, a situation that this book sets out to help change. The fourteen chapters assembled in the volume provide insights on the social organization of illegal market activities from a broad range of different settings, from financial markets to the market for illegally poached rhino horn.

The volume grew out of a research group on illegal markets that was established at the Max Planck Institute for the Study of Societies in 2010. In early 2015 we held a two-day workshop in Cologne. Many of the chapters in this volume were first presented at this workshop.

We would like to thank first and foremost Ian Edwards who was in charge of the copy-editing of the manuscript. We also wish to extend our gratitude to those who do not appear in this volume but decisively enriched our discussions: Keith Hart, Peter Reuter, Michael Levi, and Paolo Campana. Finally, we would like to thank the staff of the Max Planck Institute for the Study of Societies and Michael Böttcher for their organizational help.

# Contents

# List of Figures

# List of Tables

# List of Contributors

**Jens Beckert** is Director of the Max Planck Institute for the Study of Societies, Cologne.

**Ronald L. Breiger** is Regents' Professor in the School of Sociology at the University of Arizona.

**Matías Dewey** is a senior researcher at the Max Planck Institute for the Study of Societies, Cologne.

**Cyrus Dioun** is a doctoral candidate in the University of California Berkeley Department of Sociology and a data science fellow at the Berkeley Institute for Data Science.

**Kirsten W. Endres** is Head of Research at the Resilience and Transformation in Eurasia Department, Max Planck Institute for Social Anthropology, Halle/Saale.

**Nina Engwicht** is a researcher at the Peace Academy Rhineland-Palatinate, Academy for Crisis Prevention and Civil Conflict Management, Landau, Germany.

**Victoria A. Greenfield** is a visiting scholar at the Department of Criminology, Law, and Society, George Mason University, Fairfax, VA.

**Thomas J. Holt** is Professor in the School of Criminal Justice, Michigan State University.

**Annette Hübschle** is a postdoctoral researcher with the Environmental Security Observatory at the University of Cape Town, South Africa.

**Simon Mackenzie** is Professor of Criminology at Victoria University of Wellington and a member of the Scottish Centre for Crime and Justice Research at the University of Glasgow, where he is Professor of Criminology, Law, and Society.

**Renate Mayntz** is Emeritus Director of the Max Planck Institute for the Study of Societies, Cologne.

**Meltem Odabaş** is a PhD candidate in the School of Sociology at the University of Arizona.

**Ronen Palan** is Professor of International Political Economy at City University London.

**Letizia Paoli** is Professor of Criminology at the University of Leuven Faculty of Law.

**Vadim Radaev** is Professor and Head of the Laboratory for Studies in Economic Sociology at the National Research University Higher School of Economics, Moscow.

**Boris Samuel** is a research fellow at the Chair of Comparative African Studies, Mohamed VI Polytechnic University, Rabat and an associate researcher at Sciences Po CERI, Paris.

**Philippe Steiner** is Professor of Sociology at the University of Paris-Sorbonne.

**Robert Tillman** is Professor of Sociology at St John's University, New York.

**Donna Yates** is Lecturer in Antiquities Trafficking and Art Crime at the Scottish Centre for Crime and Justice Research, working in an interdisciplinary role across the College of Social Sciences and the College of Arts at the University of Glasgow.

# 1

# Introduction

## The Social Organization of Illegal Markets

*Jens Beckert and Matías Dewey*

Estimates place the annual revenues from market exchanges that violate the law at over 653 billion US dollars (*Economist* 2013).[1] From illegal drugs, stolen artwork, and forged trademarks, to fraud on financial markets, the phenomenon of illegality in market exchanges is pervasive. Transactions on markets that are outright illegal and illegal transactions in legal markets are economically important, have significant social and political consequences, and shape market structures in specific ways.[2]

Strangely, the field of economic sociology remains almost silent on the topic. This is despite the broad range of topics addressed in economic sociology over the past thirty years and the fact that the "architecture of markets" stands at the center of much of the sociological approach to the economy (Fligstein 2001). With few exceptions (Beckert and Wehinger 2013; Centeno and Portes 2006; Fligstein and Roehrkasse 2015; Dewey 2015; Dioun and Haveman 2016), however, the literature unquestioningly accepts the premise that the institutional structures and exchanges taking place in markets are law abiding in nature. Though some scholars have complained about this (Zelizer 2007; Sørensen 2003), illegality and crime have not been established as major fields of analysis. Economic sociology has addressed neither the consequences of the illegal production, distribution, and consumption of illegal products for the architecture of markets, nor the underlying causes or political and social

[1] Such figures are notoriously imprecise and cannot provide more than a rough estimate of illegality. Moreover, the estimate does not include illegality in markets in the form of rule violations, what we call "type 5" markets.

[2] We would like to thank Henri Bergeron, Renate Mayntz, Letizia Paoli, and Philippe Steiner for their valuable comments on an earlier version of this introduction.

concerns stemming from the infringement of the law. In the sociology of finance, to give one example, one finds much research on market devices but until now only scarce research on the prevalence of financial crime. That the illegal side of market exchanges has failed to gain attention in economic sociology seems almost ironic given the historical tradition of ground-breaking work on illegality in sociology exemplified, for instance, in the work of the Chicago School and in more recent studies such as those by Howard Becker (1963), Philippe Bourgois (2002), and Sudhir Venkatesh (2006, 2009).

Instead of being a subject area of economic sociology, the analysis of law-breaking social phenomena in economic action has developed around the notion of organized crime, an established field of research informed mainly by criminology and economic theory, and often oriented towards the policy-making process. Here, the social organization of markets—the focal point of economic sociology—has so far occupied a secondary role at best. This book is motivated by recognition that the analysis of extra-legal arenas of exchange and illegal practices in the economy can contribute to a more general understanding of markets and should play a much more prominent role in the field of economic sociology.

Our main aim is to contribute to the analysis and understanding of market exchanges under conditions of illegality from a perspective that focuses on the social organization of markets. Illegal markets can be characterized as arenas of regular exchange of goods or services for money under conditions of competition and in which the product itself or its production, exchange, or consumption violate legal stipulations (Beckert and Wehinger 2013).[3] While the first part of this definition alludes to features shared by both legal and illegal markets, it is the second that flags the specific difference and provides the particular tonality of this type of exchange: the violation of legal stipulations. The definition does not imply that necessarily *all* elements in the market are illegal. Rather, it is often the case that only certain actions are illegal, and these illegal aspects may be embedded in perfectly legal organizations, take place within legal market structures, and stem from otherwise legally operating actors.

Though there are many overlaps with the literature on organized crime and the informal economy, the definition underlines four significant elements that distinguish it from these approaches: for one, it shifts the focus onto

[3] This does not imply that conditions of perfect polypolistic competition must be given. Without any competition, however, we could not speak of a market. Steiner and Trespeuch (2015) (see also Steiner in this volume) argue that the notion of "illegal markets" is a misnomer because the transactions lack the guarantee of property rights by the legal system. They suggest "illegal exchanges." We do not follow this suggestion based on our definition of markets. However, there are clearly different degrees of "marketness" in illegal transactions. This itself would be an interesting point for empirical investigation.

market exchanges, making clear that we have entered into a social space structured around sellers and buyers. Putting market exchanges at the center of the investigation provides a different and more comprehensive perspective to the study of illegality in the economy compared with a focus on criminal organizations. This perspective takes into account the interactions between the supply and demand sides, emphasizes the demand side as the propelling force behind illegal market exchanges, stresses the interfaces between illegal and legal action, and investigates the coordination problems faced by actors when their transactions violate the law. Secondly, unlike qualifiers such as "shadow," "underground," or "black," the adjective "illegal" makes no bones about the nature of the phenomenon we are confronted with: market exchanges that stand in violation of the law. Thirdly, by including the exchange of products or services whose production, exchange, or consumption are prohibited, the approach goes beyond what is usually known as the informal economy. Research on the informal economy has been concerned mainly with the distinction between wage employment and self-employment (Hart 1973), and the avoidance of regulations (Centeno and Portes 2006: 26; Portes 2010: 134). While several contributions in this volume suggest considerable overlap of both phenomena, they are also in many ways distinct. Fourthly, the focus on markets allows for a systematic comparison between the functioning of illegal and legal markets and enables us to bring the investigation of illegality within the context of a broader debate on markets, capitalism, and the role of the state in them.

In this introduction we will develop conceptual ideas for the study of illegal markets and illegality in markets from the perspective of economic sociology. Our interest focuses on the social organization of illegal markets, including their relationship to the state, social norms, political power, and capitalist accumulation. In the course of developing these conceptual ideas we will locate the chapters of the volume and introduce them briefly.

We will start by presenting a typology of different forms of illegality in markets, followed by a discussion of the role of the state in illegal markets. Illegal markets, we argue, are illegalized arenas of exchange, which makes the state a central actor in them. This is followed by a discussion of several interfaces essential to illegal markets: the interface between illegality and informality, the interface between illegality and legitimacy, and the interface between illegality and legality. In the subsequent section we discuss the peculiarities of the social organization of illegal markets, bringing to the fore the parallels and differences in the organization of markets under conditions of legality and illegality. Finally, in the last section we discuss the connection between illegality and the capitalist economy. Illegality in markets is not simply a parasitic phenomenon at the fringes of the economy. Instead, it is an integral part of capitalist accumulation and should be investigated as such.

## Illegal Markets

Illegal markets and illegal practices within markets are multifaceted phenomena that require typological distinctions in order to be accessible for research. Though they both involve law breaking, there is a marked difference between, say, the heroin market (Paoli et al. 2009), in which the production, transportation, selling, and consumption of the product are all illegal, and the manipulation of Libor rates by banks, which involves illegal activities taking place within a legal framework of financial institutions and financial markets. The heterogeneity of phenomena within the broad category of illegal markets can be systematized in a typology that distinguishes between five types of illegality in markets (Wehinger 2011; Beckert and Wehinger 2013):

The first type refers to markets in which the traded good (or service) is itself forbidden, including its production. This is the case for drugs, child pornography, child prostitution, and so on. As a consequence of the prohibition of the good, its subsequent trade and consumption are equally outlawed. Transactions in these products form markets in their own right, which are largely segregated from the legal economy.

The second type refers to stolen products. Here the product itself is legal but has come into the possession of the person attempting to sell it illegally, making its sale and purchase (if the theft is known to the buyer) also illegal. Examples include market transactions with stolen cars, antiques, or artworks. Transactions for these products can be organized on separate markets in which the stolen products are traded or the products can be channeled into legal markets.

The third type entails products that have been falsified, counterfeited, or forged. While the act of counterfeiting products itself is often not outlawed (as is the case for the counterfeiting of art works), it is illegal to trade in these products. Counterfeit products constitute a major portion of illegal transactions in the economy, including the counterfeiting of trademarks for consumer goods and spare parts for industrial goods. Also in this category are counterfeit medicines, which may be marked with either the wrong dose of the effective substance or no dosage at all, and may thus be harmful to the patient. Falsified and counterfeited medicines are assumed to contribute between 5 and 7 percent to the global pharmaceutical market, with much higher rates in many of the poorer countries (Paoli and Feytens 2016). Market transactions can take place in separate markets or become part of the markets in which the authentic product is being sold.

A fourth type encompasses products that are themselves perfectly legal, but trading of which is outlawed. Examples of this are the trade in human organs (see the chapter by Steiner in this volume), adoptions, and surrogate motherhood (in some countries). In the latter case the illegal aspect is not the pregnancy itself, but carrying a child for another person with whom a contractual relation exists that stipulates that the child will be handed over at birth. Often, markets of this type have been described in the literature as "contested," "repugnant," or "noxious" markets (Satz 2010; Steiner and Trespeuch 2015). Even in the case of their legalization, market transactions in these products are typically seen as morally offensive. Often the transactions take place in separation from the legal economy.

Finally, in the fifth type of illegality, the production, exchange, and consumption of the products are in principle legal, but actors violate existing regulations during the production or the exchange process. Examples are the import of cigarettes in ways that evade taxation, the violation of insider trading rules on the stock market, the trading of guns without permission, and the export of diamonds without a Kimberley certificate (see the chapter by Engwicht in this volume). Much of what is known as the informal economy can be categorized under this type. Only in the case of certain commodities does widespread illegal behavior lead to the constitution of a market in its own right: alcohol (Radaev in this volume), cigarettes, and precious stones are possible examples of this. Other illegal practices in markets, such as the manipulation of diesel engines by Volkswagen engineers to falsify emissions tests, do not constitute an illegal market. This fifth type is certainly the most complex and probably also the most common because rule violation can take very different forms, and the legal and illegal aspects are most closely intertwined. Violation of regulations can refer to norms in the production process (for instance, labor laws or environmental laws), but can also refer to norms regarding product characteristics (for instance, safety standards), norms that relate to the transaction itself (the license to trade the good, for example, or rules against insider trading), or laws regarding the rights of third parties (such as tax obligations to the state, or royalties to be paid to artists).

Table 1.1 depicts the typology, showing the dimensions in which the transactions are illegal in each type. Clearly, the typology is purely analytical in the sense that, from an empirical viewpoint, a specific market transaction can be illegal in terms of more than one of the categories and products may be illegal in certain contexts but not in others. Given the complexity of the empirical phenomena in question, the overdetermination of the typology is unavoidable. This would also hold for any other typology one might develop.[4] The typology introduced here helps the researcher to become aware of, and distinguish between, different forms of illegality in markets and thus gives not only an impression of the breadth of possible violations of legal stipulations in markets, but also helps to structure the field for the researcher. It may also help

[4] See, for instance, the distinction between white, grey, black, and criminal markets often used in criminology (Paoli and Feytens 2016).

**Table 1.1.** Dimensions of illegality in the different types of illegal markets

| Type | Product illegal | Consumption/ possession illegal | Market exchange illegal | Violation of regulation | Example |
|---|---|---|---|---|---|
| Type 1 Illegal products | x | x | x | x | Hard drugs |
| Type 2 Stolen goods | | x | x | x | Stolen artworks |
| Type 3 Counterfeit goods | | (x) | x | x | Fake Rolex watches |
| Type 4 Repugnant goods | | | x | x | Organ transplants |
| Type 5 Rule violations | | | | x | Informal markets Libor manipulation |

to counterbalance the trend that much research on illegal markets has focused on type 1 markets, especially for drugs, which in reality constitute only a small part of the phenomenon of illegality in markets (Paoli and Feytens 2016).

At the same time, it should also not be forgotten that the distinction between legal and illegal is neither homogenous nor static. The assessment of specific products and transactions varies between places and changes over time. Surrogate motherhood is outlawed in Germany but not in India (Rudrappa 2015). Commercial transactions for organs for transplantation purposes are legal in Iran but nowhere else in the world (Steiner 2010). Paoli and Greenfield (in this volume) show the ambiguities between legal and illegal within one jurisdiction with regard to the "quasi-illegal" market for doping products in sport in Italy, demonstrating that legal ambiguities are a chief cause of the difficulties faced in prosecuting actors trading in doping products.

Statements about illegality thus always need to be made with reference to specific legal and social contexts. This also holds because of changes in definitions of legality over time. Products and market transactions may shift in and out of illegality. The need for a dynamic perspective can be seen in several of the chapters in this volume. Annette Hübschle analyzes the market for rhino horn after the "production" of this product became largely illegal through the international CITIES convention in the 1970s (see also Hübschle 2015 and 2016). Cyrus Dioun describes the opposite process of the legalization of marijuana in several US states since the 1990s. Making marijuana legal, however, does not mean that there has ceased to be any illegal aspect in this market. Concurrently with its legalization, the markets became strictly regulated and producers, vendors, and consumers can act in violation of these new regulations. The illegality in the states that legalized marijuana switched from type 1 to type 5.

From the sociological perspective, it also needs to be kept in mind that the knowledge of illegal conduct differs between actors. In some cases—especially in type 1 markets—the illegality of the transaction is clearly visible to all parties involved. In many other instances, the illegality of the conduct is much more covert and becomes invisible further down the value chain. A diamond turned into a piece of jewelry and offered for sale by a jeweler in Berlin has, for the buyer and the seller, probably completely lost its association with possible illegal acts at the source of production. Equally, a product that is completely legal at the beginning of the supply chain may be transformed into an illegal product later on (see the chapter by Paoli and Greenfield). In both cases, one of the chief activities of actors involved in illegality is to camouflage the fact that illegal acts have taken place. Often this is done not only to avoid prosecution, but also to maintain the value of the product. A painting known to be forged or stolen sells, if at all, for a fraction of what it would have fetched otherwise. Hence, as Philippe Steiner maintains in his chapter, one of the chief characteristics of illegality in markets is secrecy.

## States and Illegal Markets

Recognizing illegal markets and illegality in markets brings the researcher in direct contact with the state. In economic sociology today, it is a truism that it is largely the hand of the state that structures capitalist economies. The idea that market formation is part of the state-building process, however, takes into consideration only the establishing of arenas of "legal" exchange. As Philippe Steiner emphasizes in his chapter, this already holds for the treatment of the nexus between markets and states in the works of classical sociologists such as Weber and Durkheim. The addition of illegal markets expands the scope of economic sociology while holding that the state apparatus is also essential in defining and giving shape to illegal markets. After all, it is through state-devised acts that the distinction between legal and illegal is established. Illegal markets are illegalized arenas of exchange. Or, to express this in a terminology familiar to economic sociologists: illegality is an act of qualification (Bergeron and Nouguez 2014). Acknowledging the presence of the state as a key actor opens up a fruitful entry point to the study of illegal markets.

Each case study contained in this volume shows how exchanges are affected by specific constellations of the state through its numerous institutions, regulations, and enforcement agencies. This adds an additional layer to the sociological investigation of the relationship between states and markets: the significance of legal definitions (or, more precisely, their real-life consequences for the way actors exchange goods and services) depends on the concrete actions of the state apparatus behind these definitions and its capability or willingness to enforce rules.

That a particular product or behavior has been illegalized by the state must moreover be seen within the wider social and political context. Illegalization and enforcement are outcomes of moral debates, social demands, and political power. Prostitution is a pertinent example, as is the alcohol market, as shown in this volume by Vadim Radaev in the case of Russia. Shaping the boundary between legal and illegal and deciding on the enforcement of rules is also a form of governance and often a means of exercising power over marginalized groups of the population. This also points to the interface between illegality and legitimacy, to which we will return.

### *Selective Enforcement*

Rule violation in illegal markets does not make the formal rules disappear, and the state and its agents can selectively exploit the gap between economic practices and formal rules. Formal rules are devices that allow state authorities to interfere in informal and illegal practices with the intent to produce order, to establish positions of domination, or to provide benefits selectively. Referring to the law, justifying the imposition of the rule of law, selectively enforcing the law, and bargaining legality are all practices in which state authorities and economic actors interact in informal settings. Legal definitions are crucial devices in the hands of state institutions, which shape their practices and influence both the structure and the extent of illegal markets. Endres' and Dewey's chapters in this volume show just how important legal definitions are in illegal markets when it comes to the negotiation of order through webs of generalized protection rackets. Nina Engwicht shows that in illegal diamond production in Sierra Leone, the state is not simply absent but interferes for its own goals of taxation. The state benefits from the illegal activities, and minimum levels of social and economic security are assured for the communities involved in the illegal mining. As Boris Samuel stresses in his chapter on protests against the pricing of consumer goods in Guadeloupe and Mauritania, the state can pursue clientelistic strategies through the selective enforcement of laws and public campaigns against illegality. The power of the state lies in the selective and often arbitrary enforcement of its rules.

The *actual* enforcement enacted by state agencies can be used as an instrument of social control. In this, non-government organizations, as diffusors of ideologies and prohibition initiatives, can play a decisive role. The selective intervention of state agencies is an issue not only for economic transactions described as informal, but also for illegal markets of the first type; that is, markets in which the product, its distribution, and its consumption are clearly prohibited. Annette Hübschle's chapter is an in-depth portrayal of how racial divisions and the activities of civil society advocacy groups provoke selective enforcement of the law in South African wildlife parks. The typology suggested by Paoli et al. (2009: 201 ff.) for the analysis of the world opiate market also addresses this issue: While "strict enforcement of prohibitions" poses significant risks of incarceration and asset seizure, "non-enforcement" means the opposite; that is, the tolerance, or even promotion, of illegal exchanges by formal authorities. According to the authors, the intermediate possibility is "lax enforcement," under which entrepreneurs are not guaranteed complete immunity from enforcement and still risk incarceration and asset seizure. It follows that variations in the size and shape of illegal markets are closely related to these variations in the enforcement of the law.

### *Enforcement of Informal Rules*

The way state institutions are seen in the chapters of this volume recognizes the large body of empirical research accounting for the two-sided character of the state (Reno 1995; Heyman 1999; Bayart et al. 1999; della Porta and Vannucci 1999; Nordstrom 2000; Green and Ward 2004; Arias 2006b; Rodgers 2006; Auyero 2007; Auyero and Joseph 2007; Darden 2008; Briquet et al. 2010; Holland 2015; Auyero and Jensen 2015; Dewey 2015). Economic sociologists typically stress the significance of the law as applied by the state and its legal institutions for the structuring of the economy. For instance, Richard Swedberg (2003: 4) asserts in a Weberian manner that "law, in modern society, is constitutive for most economic phenomena, meaning by this that it is an indispensable as well as an organic part of them." Other economic sociologists addressing legal phenomena in the economy (Suchman 1995; Halliday and Carruthers 2009; Fligstein 1990; Beckert 2008) focus on the ordering effects of the law for economic behavior and the expectations actors hold based on legally secured property rights, contractual obligations, organizational structures, or bequests. The scholarship usually presumes the presence of an effective infrastructure of enforcement, including dedicated state officials tasked with implementing regulations.

This volume reveals the more complex role of states. The cases presented by Matías Dewey, Kirsten W. Endres, and Nina Engwicht, among others, show that the state is not the only source of rules. In connection with existing empirical evidence, centered mainly on Africa (Reno 1995; Nordstrom 2004, 2007; Hibou 2004; Bayart et al. 1999), the Americas (Arias 2006a; Reuter 1984; Bourgois 2002; Goffman 2014; Brinks 2003; Misse 2007; Dewey 2012), and Eastern Europe (Volkov 2002; Stephenson 2016), these chapters demonstrate the existence of well-functioning bodies of informal rules that are nevertheless enforced "off the books" (that is, illegally) by government actors and law enforcement agents on the ground.

By recognizing formal and informal rules, as well as the specific ways in which they are enforced, studies of illegal markets consider additional forms of regulation and alliances between legal and extra-legal actors, private companies and public agencies, or local and foreign actors. Sociological investigations of illegality in markets focus on sets of "regulations" overlooked by scholars focusing only on the realm of legal transactions. Extra-legal norms and their enforcement are often described as corruption, but to understand them as mechanisms that produce order in illegal markets opens up hitherto unexplored fields of investigation for economic sociology, especially considering its interest in the social order of markets (Fligstein 2001; White 1981; Beckert 2009). In fact, the interest in informal institutions among political scientists (O'Donnell 1993; Lauth 2000; Helmke and Levitsky 2006; Holland 2015; Darden 2008) and the interest among sociologists in extra-legal governance structures, as well as criminologists studying mafia organizations (Gambetta 1993; Varese 2004; Paoli 2003; Weinstein 2008; Campana 2011), offers fertile ground for dialogue. To grasp the operation of extra-legal institutions, scholars need to pay particular attention to the contestation of the (in many cases contradictory) rules and how they come to bear on the understanding of legality and illegality in economic practices.

## Illegality and Informality in Markets

The investigation of economic activity taking place outside legal frameworks is not new to sociology. Besides classic studies from the Chicago School and, more recently, the works of Howard Becker (1963), Philippe Bourgois (2002), and Sudhir Venkatesh (2006, 2009, 2013), among others, sociology has been investigating the operation of economic systems in which much economic activity takes place outside the formally regulated economy (see also Hart 1973; Castells and Portes 1989; Schneider and Enste 2003; Sassen 1994). Some scholars have argued that informality is a major cause of underdevelopment. An example of this can be found in Hernando de Soto's famous book *The Other Path* (1990), in which the author considers formal property rights to be cure-all remedies for developing countries that will pave the way to economic prosperity through the formalization of economic relations.

Another perspective on informality, however, has become more important. It emphasizes how local, often marginalized, populations navigate economic opportunities by sidestepping legal regulations. These activities often constitute a major portion of the economic activity in less developed countries, where they are primary generators of employment and wealth. The term "informal," as originally introduced by Keith Hart (1973), aimed to distinguish "the firm-type economy [that] consisted largely of western corporations who benefited from the protection of state law" (Hart 2008: 16) from other economies, such as those described by Clifford Geertz (1963) in Indonesia, by Lomnitz (1975), Seligmann (2004), Babb (2010), and Goldstein (2016) in Latin America, or by Hart himself in Africa. In these places, the economy functioned according to a different pattern, one that deviated from Weber's sense of rational enterprise. In this perspective on informality, the adjective "informal" leads to a distinction between unregulated self-employed earnings and wages from formal employment; that is, between the degrees of *rationalization* of the work process (Guha-Khasnobis et al. 2007: 25). In another definition, tailored more to developed countries, informality refers to all kinds of unrecorded economic activity, often motivated by an attempt to evade taxes (Adriaenssens and Hendrickx 2015). In this view, the business activities and labor practices in the informal economy often violate state regulation or tap into spaces unregulated by the law.

Although the economic activity detached from official regulations violates legal stipulations, they do not form illegal markets. First of all, informal enterprises deal mainly with legal products, implying that the defining characteristic of informality is the circumvention or avoidance of formal standards and regulations (Centeno and Portes 2006: 26–7), which we have described as the fifth type of illegality in markets. Informality comprises "economic actions that bypass the costs and are excluded from the protection of laws and administrative rules" (Portes 2010: 134). The notion of informality reminds us that an understanding of illegality needs to be sensitive not only to legal definitions, but also to the social contexts in which economic exchanges take place. This leads us to the issue of the legitimacy of illegal market conduct.

## Illegality and Legitimacy in Markets

In Chapter 2, Renate Mayntz elucidates the double sense in which we usually understand legality. On one hand, we designate an action as legal if that action shows compliance with sanctioned norms. But on the other hand, an action could be legal not because it shows compliance with existing rules, but because it does not violate any state-sanctioned norms. In other words, it exposes a gap in regulation. Parts of the self-styled "sharing economy"—including companies such as Airbnb and Uber—thrive due to their exploitation of regulatory loopholes and the blurring of the boundary between legal and illegal in the globalized economy. Legal gaps provide room for economic activities and innovation, but they may also lead to social and political contestation because they are deemed illegitimate by some market actors. The protests of taxi drivers in many cities around the globe against some of Uber's services and practices are a testament to this. The contestation may lead the state to declare the activities illegal through regulatory initiatives. However, conflicts can also remain unresolved and linger on.

Renate Mayntz also points out the opposite situation, in which an economic transaction is clearly illegal but nevertheless enjoys high social acceptance. Legitimacy is a traditional sociological topic of inquiry. As Mayntz reminds us, Max Weber defined the term "legitimate" not as an objective property, but as a subjective belief. For the analysis of illegal markets, these beliefs can be identified empirically only by investigating the assessments actors make of products, transaction practices, and rules that are formally illegal. The transactions described with regard to informal markets often fall into the category of *legitimate illegality*.

Legitimacy is not just used in the Weberian sense of a belief in the appropriateness (*Gerechtfertigkeit*) of authority and rules, but also refers to the tolerance, acceptance, or moral rejection associated with specific products and services that are offered illegally. Products can be tolerated or rejected (that is, can be legitimate or illegitimate), which is an important point for the valuation of the respective products, the pressure to prohibit exchanges, and their price (see Figure 1.1). There are products, such as child pornography, human beings, hard drugs, and protected animal species, whose exchange provokes instant moral rejection among many. In contrast, there are goods and services that provoke little rejection and may be met with tolerance, either because of their very nature, because they are embedded in tradition, or because they are considered vital for life. Examples of markets often met with tolerance are those for counterfeit garments or illegally copied music, smuggled cigarettes, and soft drugs (see Dioun in this volume).

It may be observed that the state reacts differently to transactions and products that are strongly rejected compared with those that enjoy high legitimacy despite their illegality. It should also be considered that rejection and tolerance do not arise with the same intensity across society. To understand the phenomenon, a historical and comparative perspective is needed, as well as sensitivity to diverging moral judgments between social groups, which allows a developing understanding of the shifting boundaries and the contestation of legality and illegality. The market for rhino horn described by Annette Hübschle in this volume, for instance, can be understood only if one examines the contestation of the legitimacy of this product among the different economic and social groups involved in poaching, the protection of the animal, and the consumption of the horn. It is through the investigation of value judgments that the interfaces between illegality and legitimacy and their effects on the architecture of illegal markets can be seen. With the term "interfaces," we refer to the points at which legal and illegal, or illegal and legitimate, intersect; that is, the term refers to connections through boundary spanning (see also the chapter by Renate Mayntz). If considered as a field, illegal markets change through the

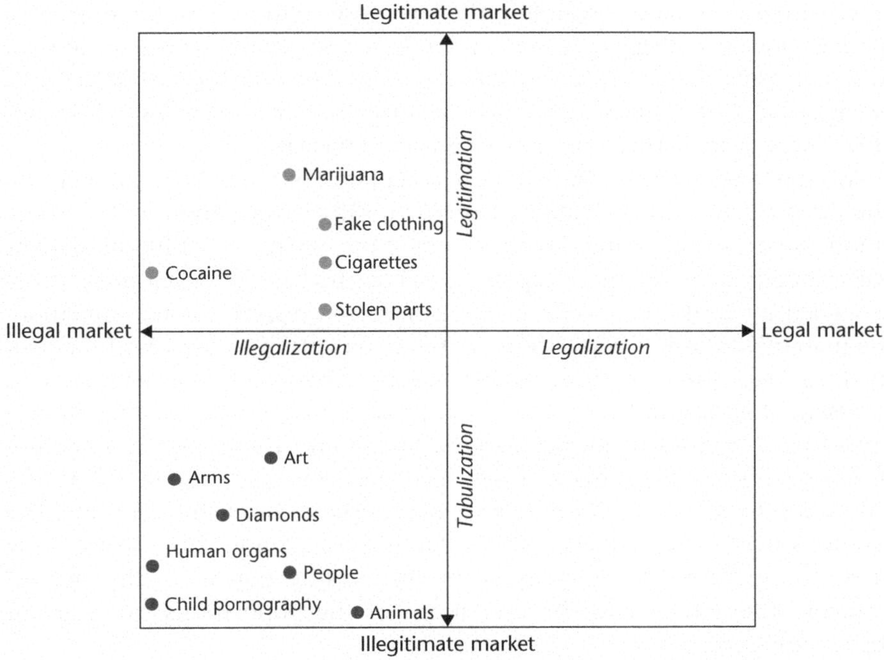


**Figure 1.1.** Dimensions of the legal/illegal and the legitimate/illegitimate

interaction of social networks, institutions, and cognitive frames, a process similar to what can be observed in legal markets (Beckert 2010).

### *Sources of Legitimacy*

But where does the legitimacy of illegal products and economic practices originate? The studies presented in this volume highlight two factors in tolerance or rejection: externalities and hope for the future.

In the case of externalities, tolerance or rejection arise as a by-product of the consequences of illegal markets. Market activities have social and economic effects that can be positive or negative. Among the negative aspects are such prominent issues as violence, interpersonal distrust, predation of natural resources, addiction, and human rights violations. There is a vast body of literature on these detrimental effects brought about by criminal groups and mafias, or by the qualities of the product traded.[5] The more these negative

[5] One needs to keep in mind that the prohibition of the legal use of certain goods can itself have negative externalities, as has often been discussed for the prohibition of drugs. The stance of prohibiting the exchange of certain goods thus does not necessarily follow a consequentialist

externalities dominate perception, the lower the legitimacy of the respective market. However, illegal markets can also generate socially accepted externalities such as work and, more generally, sources of income for significant parts of the population. This is shown, for instance, by Arias and Barnes (2016; see also Dewey et al. 2016) in the case of Brazilian favelas.

This is related to the second source of acceptance of formally illegal products and practices, namely their ability to evoke positive expectations of the future among actors in the market. It appears as if the expansion of illegal markets has gained new momentum, especially in countries in the developing world, propelled by continuous economic crises, forced displacements, migration, the marginalization of populations, extreme poverty, and persistent inequality. Illegal economic practices can become a mechanism that promises access to essential goods and services. Actors project imaginings of better futures onto their activities in illegal markets. Sometimes this is not just wishful thinking. Certain illegal markets have become economic structures that provide access to at least a minimum level of economic citizenship for some. The production of faked products, the illegal mining of diamonds, or the poaching of rhino horn need to be analyzed in close connection with (the lack of) available alternatives and the aspirations of the populations carrying out these activities.

Ironically, such positive effects are sometimes the result of the fragmentation of state authority, giving rise to the emergence of illegal markets in the first place. As pointed out by Diane Davis (2010), new informal governance structures may emerge under conditions of fragmented state sovereignty that sometimes even include non-state armed actors who take over policing functions. These actors do not necessarily operate against state authority (Davis 2010; Clunan and Trinkunas 2010; Nordstrom 2007), but by securing the functioning of illegal economic activities through, for instance, the policing of market places or the organization of the supply of resources, they are beneficial for local economic and social development. Counterintuitively, it is through the expansion of illegal markets connected to the fragmentation of state authority that actors perceive new opportunities. The state's loss of some of its influence as a sovereign power leads to a shift in governance that intertwines private and public actors in new ways (Hibou 2004; Reno 1995; Arias 2006a) and generates illegal market structures that sometimes foster civic participation.

Participation in these economies and access to goods, services, and a certain lifestyle means that some illegal markets have become mechanisms that increase people's perceived opportunities (Appadurai 2013: 115). Especially in the case of marginalized populations, illegal economic settings may expand the individual's

ethics but may entail also an ethics of conviction. We would like to thank Henri Bergeron for pointing this out to us.

aspirations and their ability to plan for future events. The market opens a door to the experience of striving to achieve; it allows actors to experience their capacity to affect change in their livelihood. Including perceptions of the future (Beckert 2016) in an analysis of the attraction of illegal market activities helps us to understand an important propelling force behind the expansion of illegal economies: the motivations of actors participating in these risky arenas of exchange. The promise of access to products, inclusion in reciprocity networks, economic citizenship, or simply a certain level of economic autonomy are strong motivators, as several of the chapters in this volume show.

### *Dialogue among Research Perspectives*

In the investigation of *illegitimate legality* and *legitimate illegality*, sociological research on illegal markets has an opportunity for dialogue with other scholarly fields interested in the legitimacy of informal institutions and illegal activities in economic exchanges. Considerable advances have been made by criminologists researching extra-legal governance structures, especially with regard to the sale of protection as the main business of mafia groups (Gambetta 1993; Volkov 2002; Varese 2004; Campana 2011). Additionally, political science offers a large body of research addressing the phenomenon of informal institutions understood as "socially shared rules, usually unwritten, that are created, communicated, and enforced outside officially sanctioned channels" (Helmke and Levitsky 2006: 5). Such informal institutions play a crucial role, for instance, in the analysis of clientelism and patrimonialism (Helmke and Levitsky 2006; Erdmann and Engel 2007; Brinks 2003; O'Donnell 1993; della Porta and Vannucci 1999; Lauth 2000), which are closely linked to research on illegal transactions (Nordstrom 2004; Reno 2009).

The investigation of the legitimacy of informal institutions and rules (that is, of one of the bases of the social structure of illegal markets) improves our understanding of illegal and informal practices. Examples of this are the understanding of the financing of criminal groups; the conventions and cultural scripts that influence the production of faked products; the reaction of the state to illegal practices; the informal norms that regulate competition among suppliers of illegal products; and the logic behind the commodification and innovation of new illegal products and services.

## Illegality and Legality in Markets

The relationship between illegality and legitimacy is just one of the interesting interfaces concerning illegality in markets; another is the interface between legality and illegality (see also the chapter by Mayntz). Only rarely do markets operate almost completely in the realm of illegality. Most prominent in this regard are perhaps the market for hard drugs and the "market" for child pornography, which are completely detached from legal exchanges in most parts of the value chain. In the latter case, secrecy is so important that the emerging structures more closely resemble reciprocal exchange rings than a market. Pornographic images are used as currency in a barter system (Wehinger 2011: 36). However, even in type 1 markets the illegal transactions are not completely separated from the legal economy. The purchase of production equipment, the selling to final consumers, and the channeling of profits into the legal money circuit are points of interpenetration where the illegal economy and the legal economy interact.

These interfaces are much more numerous and complex in the other market types demarcated in the typology. For instance, in the market for looted antiquities described in the chapter by Simon Mackenzie and Donna Yates, the stolen archaeological artifacts are often sold by fully legal and reputable galleries and auction houses trading in these objects. The final consumer does not buy the product from a "dealer" who can be clearly identified as acting illegally, but from a reputable sales person. The same holds for financial crime, which in most instances becomes possible only through its operation within completely legal organizations and market structures. Illegality takes place in a symbiotic or parasitic relationship of dependency with the legal part of markets. For the illegally operating actors, the close symbiosis with legal markets and organizations reduces the risk of detection, increases access to customers and capital, and allows the illegal conduct to be camouflaged, thus avoiding having to give illegality discounts to customers aware of the illegality of the product or service they are buying (see also Mackenzie 2005).[6] From the perspective of (otherwise) legally operating firms, the connection with illegal market activities—though risky—may lead to competitive advantages. This holds, for example, for the illegal disposal of toxic waste by industrial companies, the illegal manipulation of test results, the employment of illicit workers, and the evasion of taxes. In all these cases, the illegal conduct is carried out with the aim of reducing costs and thus offers an advantage in the market struggle.

As Renate Mayntz points out, a further interface between illegal markets and legal entities is established through the encounter with law enforcement. At first sight, it could be assumed that the relationship is purely antagonistic. After all, law enforcement has the task of fighting crime. While illegal market actors must indeed fear the destruction of their business through law

[6] Such a discount is not to be paid in type 1 markets, where all participants are aware of the illegality of the transaction.

enforcement and also personal prosecution, the relationship between the two sides is often more nuanced than it first appears. As already discussed, law enforcement has different alternatives with regard to how to interfere in illegal market activities and their destruction is often not the primary goal. The representatives of the state may also decide to benefit privately from making the enforcement of the law a tradable good (corruption) and the state may exercise power and domination through the selective and arbitrary enforcement of the law.

While the concrete gestalt of the interface between illegal and legitimate, as well as that between legal and illegal, is largely contingent, the close investigation of these interfaces is crucial to understanding the architecture of any illegal market. It is from these interfaces that the specific morphology of a market unfolds.

## The Architecture of Illegal Markets

By introducing the notion of the *architecture of markets*, Neil Fligstein (2001) aimed to develop the conceptual tools needed for an approach to markets that highlights their social organization. Markets do not just consist of technologies, competition, and rational actors, but also entail a set of rules that are indispensable for their development and reproduction. Fligstein distinguishes between four different types of rules structuring markets: property rights, the governance structure of companies, rules of exchange, and market actors' cognitive understanding of the operation of the market, which he calls "conceptions of control." The state plays the central role in reducing uncertainty and stabilizing markets through securing property rights, setting standards, and regulating firms' governance structures.

Fligstein developed this approach under the presumption of the legality of the exchanges taking place in markets. By talking about the architecture of *illegal* markets, we chime with Fligstein's interest in the social organization of markets, while also attempting to understand how the coordination of exchanges differs under conditions of illegality. The obvious source of such differences is the completely changed role of the state, which does not provide the legal infrastructure for market development, abstains from the protection of property rights, and (selectively) prosecutes market participants. The social organization of illegal markets can be understood largely as the outcome of the fundamentally different role of the state, which forces actors to overcome coordination problems in different ways (Beckert and Wehinger 2013).

One of the initial problems reflecting the different stance of illegal market activities is that actors must be willing to engage in conduct that violates legal stipulations.[7] Customers and suppliers must be ready to overcome moral scruples stemming from the illegality of the transaction, risk possible prosecution, and deal with the lack of enforcement of contracts through the legal system. The moral scruples are a variable of the social legitimacy of the product, but also, as Wikström's Situational Action Theory postulates, reflect the individual's moral engagement with a certain moral setting and their personal characteristics (Wikström 2006; Wikström and Treiber 2007; Wikström 2010).

As Sykes and Matza (1957) demonstrated, deviance-normalizing and neutralization practices play a significant role in masking illegal behavior. Such cognitive techniques are used to silence the urge to follow moral obligations, for instance through justifications that deny moral responsibility. The chapter by Mackenzie and Yates confirms the significance of such discursive tools in the market for looted antiquities that are sold in prestigious galleries. The entry of these antiquities into exclusive circuits of trade is possible in part because the dealers and buyers go to great lengths to provide justifications for violating norms, the result being that criminal acts are camouflaged and the workings of the illegal market are more easily sustained (see also Mackenzie 2005, 2013). In Annette Hübschle's chapter, the notion of *contested illegality* is used to describe similar mechanisms of justification for law-violating behavior in the context of rhinoceros poaching in South Africa. White owners of private wildlife areas justify their non-conformity with South African conservation laws for a variety of reasons: the perception that the law is unfair, cultural norms that contradict the ban, or with a politically motivated defense.

Secrecy is another core component of the architecture of illegal markets that allows both law enforcement and potential moral condemnation to be avoided. Studies show the significant role played by officially sanctioned legal mechanisms that help keep criminal practices secret (Thomas 2015). One example can be found in the laws that protect the identities of account holders in tax havens, which adds to the secrecy surrounding the banking activities connected to many illegal markets (Volkov 2011; Palan 2006; Palan et al. 2013). As Philippe Steiner shows in his chapter, secrecy as an institutionalized social mechanism also plays a significant role in the market for human organs. In France, for instance, citizens can go abroad, receive a transplant, and return for follow-up treatment in France without any obligation to declare the operation (Steiner 2010). It is through legal devices that secrecy around illegal trade is facilitated.

Closely associated with secrecy is a further structural aspect of the architecture of illegal markets: their lack of transparency. Lack of transparency is a

[7] In type 1 and type 4 markets, participation in the illegal market is the only possibility of gaining access to the good. In type 5 markets moral scruples may play a diminished role because of the high legitimacy of the activity.

limitation of competition that leads—if seen from the economic perspective—to market inefficiencies. Customers cannot compare prices and product qualities due to their lack of overview of the market supply. However, as previously shown for the cases of marijuana and illegal organ transplantation, lack of transparency is a variable rather than a fixed element. In the market investigated by Dewey—the La Salada market outside of Buenos Aires—the concentration of supply in one condensed location leads to high transparency of product quality. In the drug market, this is typically much less the case. In some contexts, such as in the market for stolen car parts, lack of transparency means a serious inhibiting of market development. It is as a direct consequence of lack of transparency that illegal markets are usually very fragmented.

The architecture of illegal markets is further influenced by the fact that the ability of these markets to create market stability (reduce uncertainty) by communicating transparently with consumers about product quality is impaired. Due to the absence of legally enforceable regulations on standards, problems emerging from the asymmetric distribution of information play a much larger role in illegal transactions, which increases the risks for the purchaser. Without a clear understanding of product qualities the problem of valuation, one of the coordination problems in markets (Beckert 2009), becomes very difficult to resolve for buyers. Fake medication is a good example of this in that the buyer has no way of knowing which active ingredients are present in the purchased substance. Odabaş, Holt, and Breiger focus in their chapter on the information asymmetries regarding the product quality of stolen credit card data. The purchaser of such data does not know in advance what quality the provided data will have. In legal markets, product warranties play an important role in overcoming market failure deriving from information asymmetries (Akerlof 1970). This instrument is not available—or only very minimally available—for illegal transactions (Wendel and Curtis 2000: 230). However, the way information about products circulates depends heavily on the commodity at stake, the market technologies (especially online markets), and the present levels of moral tolerance towards the exchange. Philippe Steiner's chapter on the market for illegal organ transplantation and Cyrus Dioun's chapter on medical marijuana are two cases in point. Whereas illegal organ transplantation provokes a strong moral reaction in most countries, leading to the creation of institutions that strictly regulate the relationships between patients, donors, and doctors (that is, a process characterized by a consolidated prohibition of exchanges outside officially sanctioned channels), the use of marijuana for medical purposes is the consequence of advocates proclaiming certain beneficial properties of marijuana consumption. In the first case, uncertainty regarding quality is huge. In the second case, acceptance leads to the free flow of information, the creation of informal institutions such as the "Cannabis Buyers' Club," and better-informed consumers.[8]

Unresolved coordination problems and the ensuing peculiarities of the organization of illegal market transactions are caused not only by difficulties in quality assessment, but also by the risks stemming from the threat of being prosecuted, the possible non-fulfillment of contracts, and the inability to secure property rights through the legal system. In more general terms, illegal markets are limited in their capacity to develop institutional trust (Beckert and Wehinger 2013). The danger of being prosecuted and the risk of asset seizure imply that long-term investment in factories and equipment becomes impossible, organizations are kept very small, networks can be only loosely coordinated, and networks are structured around kinship relations or regional ties. Illegally operating firms thus lack access to what Ronen Palan (in this volume) calls the future economy.

For the reduction of transaction risks, actors need to resort to instruments that are rather archaic compared with those in the legal economy. Three such instruments are characteristic of the social organization of illegal markets. The first is reputation through personal networks. Although personal networks also play an important role in legal markets (Granovetter 1973; Uzzi 1996), their role is much more pronounced in illegal markets, in which impersonal forms of cooperation fail to be adopted. As Gambetta stated for the case of the Sicilian mafia, personal reputation sets in as an (inferior) substitute for state-sanctioned and legally enforceable standards and regulations (Gambetta 1993). Odabaş, Holt, and Breiger show in their chapter on the governance of markets for stolen credit card data that market participants develop interpersonal trust through online communication among buyers, sellers, and the operators of the electronic platforms, which allows transactions to take place despite the impossibility of resorting to the legal system in the case of fraud. They emphasize the role of forum administrators who step in as third parties to help sellers and buyers to promote trust in the transaction partner. The investigation of such extra-legal governance structures as providers of non-state assurances for the fulfillment of contracts offers interesting perspectives for economic sociology research on illegal markets.

The second mechanism is the latent threat of violence in illegal markets. While illegal markets are not violent per se, the underlying threat of violent reactions to non-compliance is an important ordering device.[9] If suppliers fail to deliver the promised product quality, purchasers can threaten to retaliate—

[8] For marijuana consumers, for instance, web pages exist that allow users to report the prices they recently paid for the drug. See: <http://www.priceofweed.com>.

[9] A possible exception to this is type 5 markets. But also for informal markets it holds that legal protection is at best incomplete, making the threat of violence a more likely instrument to be used to enforce contracts.

as they do in the wholesale drug market—by punishing defective suppliers. Here, the connection between illegal markets and mafias as a sub-type of organized crime comes to the fore (see also the chapter by Renate Mayntz).

A third device used to resolve coordination problems and create market stability is the selective cooperation with state agents, who are allowed to benefit from the illegal economic activities either personally or on behalf of the state. In her chapter, Kirsten W.Endres describes the situation in a Vietnamese border market in which market merchants are able to smuggle goods from China by bribing customs officials. Though merchants try to avoid the bribes because they cut into their profits, it is a regular means of insuring against the risk of punishment and thus assuring their ability to bring merchandise to the market. Seen from the perspective of the social organization of markets, corruption is a means to structure competition in the market and to protect market stability by securing the state's tolerance toward the illegal activity. While the case described by Endres refers to *individuals* paying bribes, the involvement of state agents in illegal markets can also be organized on a larger scale, as Dewey shows in his chapter. Especially effective is the influencing of law enforcement by organized crime groups that can, if successful, create conditions for illegal transactions under which they can operate with little state interference. Paying bribes or protection rackets constitute at the same time barriers to entry and thus structure competition in illegal markets.

Further specificities of the social organization of illegal markets refer to the demand side. In economic sociology, much work has been done recently on the demand side of markets, especially on the question of valuation and preference formation (Beckert 2011; Aspers and Beckert 2011; Orléan 2014). However, this research considers legally produced goods and services only. Exceptions are Sandberg (2012; Hammersvik et al. 2012) and Dwyer and Moore (2009), who address the cultural dimension of cannabis consumption, and Wehinger's (2013) work on the consumption of counterfeit consumer products. He shows the importance of an imagined future that potential buyers indulge in. The lower price of the fake product allows the buyer to pretend they have a lifestyle that is beyond their current financial means. Also taking the demand side into consideration, Vadim Radaev shows in this volume that demand for illegal alcohol in Russia is related to widespread ignorance, tolerance of illegal conduct, and state pricing policies in the market for legal alcohol.

Illegal markets are, for structural reasons, especially driven by demand. Since opportunities to create preferences and brand loyalty through marketing tools are limited, market creation through the supply side is seriously compromised compared with most legal markets (Beckert and Wehinger 2013; Bergeron and Nouguez 2014). One area in which the possibilities for marketing illegal products may be increasing, however, is online purchases. As

Paoli and Greenfield show in their chapter, illegal doping products for sport are increasingly offered for sale through web pages. Another example are fake spare parts for industrial goods which become instantaneously globally available through the internet. Odabaş, Holt, and Breiger highlight in their chapter that the internet has enabled the formation of new markets for illegal goods. Despite these new online opportunities the challenges for quality assessment of illegally offered goods remain and form an important research domain for understanding the social organization of illegal markets.

Paying attention to the coordination problems of actors in illegal markets shows that market exchanges under conditions of illegality take quite a different form compared with their legal counterparts. Common problems in legal markets rapidly become acute issues in illegal markets. Propelled by the need to neutralize the enforcement of the law, problems such as building trust, avoiding risk, and gathering information lead to strategies, practices, and moral valuations that are specific to illegal markets. The study of the order of illegal markets, therefore, is tasked with confronting these particular social phenomena, including the production of secrecy, the justification of moral transgressions, strategies to cope with lack of transparency, and the practices of quality assessment.

## Illegality and Capitalism

Illegality in markets is often described using examples of economically marginal product markets and products that are unambiguously legally condemned (such as hard drugs), or with reference to socially marginalized actors and organized crime. This leaves the impression that illegal activities are relevant only at the edges of the capitalist economy, located on the periphery, and populated by actors making a living in the shadows of society. Such a picture is misleading and is at least partly an artifact of previous research on illegal markets. Often studies in criminology focus on type 1 markets such as for drugs or human trafficking. In studies of informal markets, the pervasiveness of conduct outside the confines of the law is recognized as economically important, but the locations investigated are situated mainly on the periphery of the capitalist system. Illegal activities and pushing the boundaries of legality, however, are *also* constitutive elements of the competitive struggle at the core of the capitalist economy.

Historians have often alluded to the law-violating practices that existed at the beginning of capitalist development and helped to bring it about. In his treatment of the origins of capitalism, Marx (1867) described the violent process of what he called "original accumulation," with its disregard of rights. In the enclosure process beginning in the sixteenth century, peasants in

England were violently dislocated from lands to which they had customary rights.[10] In this process of expropriation, important foundations of the capitalist economy were laid, allowing the globally operating British wool industry to emerge and creating a class of landless laborers who would eventually become the proletariat, fueling the industrialization process. Land-grabbing processes are not singular to the Industrial Revolution in England and can be observed in many countries integrating into the capitalist economy today; China and Brazil are two especially vivid examples.

### *Illegality and Economic Dynamics*

The embracing of illegal economic practices can also be found in the present as part of economic development strategies. An example of this is the tolerance and participation of Argentine state agencies in allowing the growth of an informal garment industry in which producers systematically violate legally codified labor standards through manufacture in sweatshops, and intellectual property rights are regularly impinged through the sale of counterfeit garments (Dewey 2014). As Matías Dewey describes in his chapter, the informal market "La Salada" has become one of the largest suppliers of garments manufactured in South America. The expansion of La Salada needs to be viewed in the context of the devastation of the Argentine garment industry, an important sector of the country's economy up until the 1980s. The global relocation of the textile industry, mostly to Asian countries, made tens of thousands of Argentine garment workers redundant. Some of them found new employment in the developing informal garment sector, working in sweatshops and selling products at La Salada. The emergence of an informal market relieved the Argentine state of some of the social pressures stemming from the otherwise unemployed workers, and contributed to the social integration of impoverished people through the evocation of new prospects and aspirations. Seen from a macro perspective, this trend toward illegal market activities is based on the drastic lowering of wages and the sidestepping of labor standards as a path to remain competitive in a liberalized global economy.

Illegal markets thus become visible as parts of global domination and exploitation. For this one does not even have to look at the southern periphery exclusively. Sweatshops with large pockets of predominantly Chinese migrant populations have become a prevailing phenomenon also in the textile region of northern Italy. And illegal markets for organ transplants or surrogacy typically have a structure in which demand comes from rich

[10] See also Thompson (1963: 237), who speaks of "class robbery." See also Thompson on the origin of the Black Act in the United Kingdom (Thompson 1975: chapter 2).

customers in the Global North, while supply is provided by the poor populations in developing countries.

### *Illegality in the Capitalist Core*

Competitive strategies based on the undermining of labor standards and business practices that either exploit regulatory loopholes or willingly transgress legal regulations can also be seen in the Global North. The self-styled "sharing economy" creates business models that target unregulated areas of commerce, or establishes services that violate the legal standards that apply to the industry in the country in question. Google CEO Eric Schmidt praises the internet as "the world's largest ungoverned space" (Schmidt and Cohen 2013: 3). Relying on the newest technological developments, such as apps and geo-localization, the strategy of these companies is to exploit loopholes and sometimes even to offer their services despite rule violations and to fend off legal challenges in court. The issue of legitimacy is crucial here, though in a conflicted way. In taxi markets, established taxi companies view the new competition as illegitimate and illegal. However, the story is more complicated for the users and drivers. The new service is often cheaper for consumers and it offers employment opportunities; exactly the kind of positive externalities discussed earlier. A similar claim can be made about Airbnb. While the hotel industry, among other agents, sees Airbnb as an illegitimate and in part illegal competitor whose business model is based on the flouting of regulations and evasion of taxes, consumers and suppliers focus on the benefits. For consumers the platform offers accommodation that is often cheaper and more desirable than a hotel. For private suppliers it is a means to make additional income. Airbnb exploits this legitimacy to fight its case.[11] No matter what position one takes in these struggles, it is clear that operating on the margins of legality, or aggressively exploiting regulatory loopholes, can be part of business strategies even at the dynamic heart of the capitalist economy.

In criminology, the violation of legal stipulations by the management of in themselves completely legally operating companies has been discussed since the 1930s under the heading of "white-collar crime" (see Reurink 2016). Such illegal conduct might be interpreted either as the misconduct of individuals for personal benefit or as a collective phenomenon (Calavita et al. 1997) and part of the competitive struggle of companies. While the two variants exist both alone and in combination, it is the latter—the collective phenomenon—that is of particular interest for the sociology of illegal markets.

[11] In Paris, Airbnb ran an advertising campaign in 2015 in which it claimed that people renting their apartments to tourists could realize their life goals through the money they make.

The conditions of competition and the institutionally and personally anchored incentive of high profits seem to induce companies to resort to practices that seek profits also in grey zones or in outright illegal behavior. Though anything but new (see Whyte and Wiegratz 2016), one example is the 2015 scandal involving the German car manufacturer Volkswagen. Volkswagen admitted to having manipulated millions of diesel engines by installing software that would show lower emissions when the car was at a test rig compared with the actual emissions produced when the car was on the road. What made the company cheat? In the wake of the scandal, it came out that Volkswagen had been under pressure to develop a cleaner diesel engine in order to conform to tougher emissions standards. Management handed this task to the engineers together with a clear cost target. The engineers, unable to find a technical solution within the preset cost frame, decided instead for the software option as a way to "conform" both to more restrictive emission standards *and* the management demands regarding cost. It is not fully established at what level of the managerial hierarchy this decision was actually taken. The illegal conduct is interesting from the perspective of organizational sociology (see also Vaughan 1985), but from the perspective of market sociology some important additional aspects come to light. Deviant behavior appears to be the outcome of organizational structures and ambitious market goals. Volkswagen wanted to become the world's number one car company and even resorted to illegal behavior as a means to achieve this target when it could find no legal solution to a particular technical problem.

Market pressures and institutional rules also seem to be underlying factors in some of the illegal conduct in the financial industry revealed in the wake of the 2008 financial crisis (Reurink 2016). Deutsche Bank, currently one of the global banks most beset by legal disputes (Fligstein and Roehrkasse 2015; Fouquau and Spieser 2015), set the ambitious goal in 2004 of a 25 percent return on equity. To reach internally set profit margins—and to satisfy shareholders, as well as to secure high personal bonus payments—traders, not just at Deutsche Bank, resorted to illegal practices such as the manipulation of Libor rates and the fixing of currency prices (see the chapter by Tillman in this volume).

Illegality in markets needs to be investigated in connection with the hypercompetitiveness of contemporary global capitalism and companies' self-set demands on their profitability. One means of gaining a competitive advantage is to resort to illegal practices and fraudulent behavior (see also Reurink 2016 for financial markets) Illegal behavior as a way to reduce costs and secure additional profits is by no means concentrated in car companies or the financial industry. Norm violations such as the illegal disposal of toxic waste (Massari and Monzini 2004: 293), the use of illicit labor, or the violation of environmental laws can be found across industries. But, as Robert Tillman argues in his chapter on financial fraud, financialization, the increasing subjection of politics by the financial industry, and the dramatic increase in compensation for workers in the financial sector have heightened its criminogenic tendencies. The legality of the organization that carries out such practices, the high degree of division of labor, the sometimes very high level of expertise necessary to even understand the norm violation, the high costs of internal controlling, the dependency of the state on private businesses, and the high social reputation of the actors involved help to camouflage the illegal activities. At later stages in the value chain, the violations are often no longer visible. As a consequence, "market discipline," the mechanism assumed by economic theory to drive out fraudulent and deceptive behavior from markets, is not working. Here, again, the interface between legality and illegality is crucial.

### *Tax Havens*

The possibilities available to camouflage illegal market conduct have been enormously enhanced by the legal architecture of tax havens. Tax havens are financial conduits that, in exchange for a fee, offer their own principal asset—their sovereignty—as a service to a non-resident constituency of accountants and lawyers, bankers and financiers, to minimize taxes and conceal the ownership and origin of financial wealth. They are legal entities at the center of contemporary capitalism in which legality and illegality mix. Far from being marginal or in the exotic backwater of the global economy, tax havens are an integral part of modern business practices (Palan et al. 2006, 2013; Maurer 2006; Harrington 2016). The combination of little or no income and corporate taxes, lax regulations, robust bank secrecy laws, and easy incorporation laws make tax havens a magnet for money originating in illegal markets and fraudulent schemes. Their particular legal structure provides the necessary legal blanket of secrecy that illegal businesses and organizations need for their operations (Volkov 2011). This has been shown to the wider public through the recent data leaks, the biggest of them the so-called "Panama Papers," that have exposed the practices of law firms in tax havens, making it possible to conceal illegal business activities. As Ronen Palan argues in his chapter, tax havens have the additional function of expanding illegal market actors' options by granting secure access to a large variety of financial instruments that allow profits to be leveraged against the future. Access to elaborate financial tools allows criminals to launder money and to change the nature of their business by becoming able to operate—in the same way as legally constituted companies—in "the economy of the future."

Today, there are at least fifty-six jurisdictions that are commonly identified as tax havens and connected to cases of money laundering, corruption, and tax evasion (list of tax havens: Palan et al. 2013: 40–5). Experts claim that tax havens have not only been a driver of the current European crisis (Zucman 2013), but have also led to rising inequality and human rights violations (Christensen and Kapoor 2004).

## Conclusion

The chapters in this volume all contribute to a research perspective that is nascent at best: the investigation of illegal conduct in markets from the point of view of the social organization of markets. The authors capture a wide array of social and economic settings, each providing a different perspective and portraying different actors and products. But despite the many different vantage points, the goal remains the same: to understand the functioning of illegal markets, the political reactions to them, the social consequences of their existence, and their development in connection with changes in the social environments in which they operate. The chapters show that investigating illegality in the economy from the perspective of markets provides additional insights compared with perspectives that focus on organized crime.

Research guided by the perspective of the architecture of illegal markets is sensitive to the organization of demand. It focuses on a broader set of actors, going beyond the interaction of suppliers along the value chain and the role of law enforcement. Illegal markets, as well as illegality in markets, is also seen as part of the normal operation of economic processes and is not limited to a set of actors that appear to be disconnected pariahs of an economy otherwise operating perfectly legally. The chapters in this volume convey the message that illegality in the economy can be analyzed as part of the capitalist process of accumulation, a topic that has been explored extensively by historians, but in much less detail by political scientists and sociologists interested in current configurations of the economy.

This volume cannot be more than a start. It will achieve its goal if it motivates more social scientists—and especially economic sociologists—to extend their research interests to encompass aspects of illegality in markets. It will achieve its goal, too, if the approaches pursued in the chapters provide some orientation for social scientists in forging a path through a territory that is admittedly difficult to map, but full of insights that are crucial for a detailed understanding of the contemporary economy and the relationship between economy, state, and society.

## References


Adriaenssens, Stef, and Jef Hendrickx. 2015. "Can Informal Economic Activities Be Explained by Social and Institutional Factors? A Comparative Analysis." *Socio-Economic Review* 13(4): pp. 1–23.

Akerlof, George A. 1970. "The Market for 'Lemons': Qualitative Uncertainty and the Market Mechanism." *Quarterly Journal of Economics* 84(3): pp. 488–500.

Appadurai, Arjun. 2013. *The Future as Cultural Fact: Essays on the Global Condition.* London: Verso.

Arias, Enrique Desmond. 2006a. *Drugs and Democracy in Rio de Janeiro: Trafficking, Social Networks, and Public Security.* Chapel Hill: University of North Carolina Press.

Arias, Enrique Desmond. 2006b. "The Dynamics of Criminal Governance: Networks and Social Order in Rio de Janeiro." *Journal of Latin American Studies* 38(2): pp. 293–325.

Arias, Enrique Desmond, and Nicholas Barnes. 2016. "Crime and Plural Orders in Rio de Janeiro, Brazil. "*Current Sociology*. October 13. doi:10.1177/0011392116667165.

Aspers, Patrik, and Jens Beckert. 2011. "Value in Markets." In *The Worth of Goods, Valuation and Pricing in the Economy*, edited by Jens Beckert and Patrik Aspers, pp. 3–38. New York: Oxford University Press.

Auyero, Javier. 2007. *Routine Politics and Violence in Argentina: The Gray Zone of State Power.* New York: Cambridge University Press.

Auyero, Javier, and Katherine Jensen. 2015. "For Political Ethnographies of Urban Marginality." *City and Community* 14(4): pp. 359–63.

Auyero, Javier, and Lauren Joseph. 2007. "Introduction: Politics under the Ethnographic Microscope." In *New Perspectives in Political Ethnography*, edited by Lauren Joseph, Matthew Mahler, and Javier Auyero, pp. 1–14. New York: Springer.

Babb, Florence E. 2010. *Between Field and Cooking Pot: The Political Economy of Marketwomen in Peru.* Austin: University of Texas Press.

Bayart, Jean-François, Stephen Ellis, and Béatrice Hibou. 1999. *The Criminalization of the State in Africa.* Oxford: Currey.

Becker, Howard Saul. 1963. *Outsiders: Studies in the Sociology of Deviance.* New York: Free Press of Glencoe.

Beckert, Jens. 2008. *Inherited Wealth.* Princeton, NJ: Princeton University Press.

Beckert, Jens. 2009. "The Social Order of Markets." *Theory and Society* 38(3): pp. 245–69.

Beckert, Jens. 2010. "How Do Fields Change? The Interrelations of Institutions, Networks, and Cognition in the Dynamics of Markets." *Organization Studies* 31(5): pp. 605–27.

Beckert, Jens. 2011. "Where Do Prices Come from? Sociological Approaches to Price Formation." *Socio-Economic Review* 9(4): pp. 757–86.

Beckert, Jens. 2016. *Imagined Futures: Fictional Expectations and Capitalist Dynamics.* Cambridge, MA: Harvard University Press.

Beckert, Jens, and Frank Wehinger. 2013. "In the Shadow: Illegal Markets and Economic Sociology." *Socio-Economic Review* 11(1): pp. 5–30.

Bergeron, Henri, and Étienne Nouguez. 2014. "Les frontières de l'interdit: le commerce de cannabis." In *Marchés contestés: Quand le marché rencontre la morale*, edited by

Philippe Steiner and Marie Trespeuch, pp. 121–50. Toulouse: Presses Universitaires du Mirail.

Bourgois, Philippe. 2002. *In Search of Respect: Selling Crack in El Barrio*. 2nd ed. Cambridge: Cambridge University Press.

Brinks, Daniel M. 2003. "Informal Institutions and the Rule of Law: The Judicial Response to State Killings in Buenos Aires and São Paulo in the 1990s." *Comparative Politics* 36(1): pp. 1–19.

Briquet, Jean-Louis, Gilles Favarel-Garrigues, and Roger Leverdier (eds). 2010. *Organized Crime and States: The Hidden Face of Politics*. Basingstoke: Palgrave Macmillan.

Calavita, Kitty, Henry N. Pontell, and Robert Tillman. 1997. *Big Money Crime: Fraud and Politics in the Savings and Loan Crisis*. Berkeley: University of California Press.

Campana, Paolo. 2011. "Eavesdropping on the Mob: The Functional Diversification of Mafia Activities across Territories." *European Journal of Criminology* 8(3): pp. 213–28.

Castells, Manuel, and Alejandro Portes. 1989. "World Underneath: The Origins, Dynamics, and Effects of the Informal Economy." In *The Informal Economy: Studies in Advanced and Less Developed Countries*, edited by Alejandro Portes, Manuel Castells, and Lauren A. Benton, pp. 11–37. Baltimore, MD: Johns Hopkins University Press.

Centeno, Miguel Angel, and Alejandro Portes. 2006. "The Informal Economy in the Shadow of the State." In *Out of the Shadows: Political Action and the Informal Economy in Latin America*, edited by Patricia Fernandez-Kelly, pp. 23–48. Philadelphia: Pennsylvania State University Press.

Christensen, John, and Sony Kapoor. 2004. "Tax Avoidance, Tax Competition and Globalisation: Making Tax Justice a Focus for Global Activism." *Accountancy Business and the Public Interest* 3(2): pp. 1–16.

Clunan, Anne L., and Harold A. Trinkunas. 2010. *Ungoverned Spaces: Alternatives to State Authority in an Era of Softened Sovereignty*. Stanford, CA: Stanford University Press.

Darden, K. 2008. "The Integrity of Corrupt States: Graft as an Informal State Institution." *Politics and Society* 36(1): pp. 35–59.

Davis, Diane E. 2010. "Irregular Armed Forces, Shifting Patterns of Commitment, and Fragmented Sovereignty in the Developing World." *Theory and Society* 39(3): pp. 397–413.

De Soto, Hernando. 1990. *The Other Path: The Invisible Revolution in the Third World*. New York: Perennial Library.

della Porta, Donatella, and Alberto Vannucci. 1999. *Corrupt Exchanges: Actors, Resources, and Mechanisms of Political Corruption*. New York: Aldine de Gruyter.

Dewey, Matías. 2012. "Illegal Police Protection and the Market for Stolen Vehicles in Buenos Aires." *Journal of Latin American Studies* 44(4): pp. 679–702.

Dewey, Matías. 2014. *Taxing the Shadow: The Political Economy of Sweatshops in La Salada, Argentina*. MPIfG discussion paper 14/18. Cologne: Max Planck Institute for the Study of Societies.

Dewey, Matías. 2015. *El Orden Clandestino: Política, Furzas de Seguridad y Mercados Ilegales en la Argentina*. Buenos Aires: Katz.

Dewey, Matías, Daniel Miguez, and Marcelo Fabián Sain. 2016. "The Strength of Collusion: A Conceptual Framework for Interpreting Hybrid Social Orders." *Current Sociology*. August 5. doi:10.1177/0011392116661226.

Dioun, Cyrus, and Heather A. Haveman. 2016. *The Price of Marijuana: Legal Institutions and Calculability in New and Contested Markets*. Berkeley: University of California. <http://nebula.wsimg.com/ba72e7a956c10fe8dc6aca44e51cf7fe?AccessKeyId=CEE24B7170B669FB3B55&disposition=0&alloworigin=1> (accessed March 12, 2016).
Dwyer, Robyn, and David Moore. 2009. "Understanding Illicit Drug Markets in Australia: Notes towards a Critical Reconceptualization." *British Journal of Criminology* 50(1): pp. 82–101.
*Economist*. 2013. *Illegal Markets*. News release, April 29. <http://www.economist.com/blogs/graphicdetail/2013/04/daily-chart-19>.
Erdmann, Gero, and Ulf Engel. 2007. "Neopatrimonialism Reconsidered: Critical Review and Elaboration of an Elusive Concept." *Commonwealth and Comparative Politics* 45(1): pp. 95–119.
Fligstein, Neil. 1990. *The Transformation of Corporate Control*. Cambridge, MA: Harvard University Press.
Fligstein, Neil. 2001. *The Architecture of Markets: An Economic Sociology of Twenty-First-Century Capitalist Societies*. Princeton, NJ: Princeton University Press.
Fligstein, Neil, and Alexander Roehrkasse. 2015. *The Causes of Fraud in Financial Crises: Evidence from the Mortgage-Backed Securities Industry*. IRLE working paper no. 122-15. Berkeley: Institute for Research on Labor and Employment, University of California, Berkeley.
Fouquau, Julien, and Philippe K. Spieser. 2015. "Statistical Evidence about LIBOR Manipulation: A 'Sherlock Holmes' Investigation." *Journal of Banking and Finance* 50: pp. 632–43.
Gambetta, Diego. 1993. *The Sicilian Mafia: The Business of Private Protection*. Cambridge, MA: Harvard University Press.
Geertz, Clifford. 1963. *Peddlers and Princes: Social Development and Economic Change in Two Indonesian Towns*. Chicago: University of Chicago Press.
Goffman, Alice. 2015. *On the Run: Fugitive Life in an American City*. London: Picador.
Goldstein, Daniel M. 2016. *Owners of the Sidewalk: Security and Survival in the Informal City*. Durham, NC: Duke University Press.
Granovetter, Mark. 1973. "The Strength of Weak Ties." *American Journal of Sociology* 78(6): pp. 1360–80.
Green, Penny, and Tony Ward. 2004. *State Crime: Governments, Violence and Corruption*. London: Pluto.
Guha-Khasnobis, Basudeb, Ravi Kanbur, and Elinor Ostrom (eds). 2007. *Linking the Formal and Informal Economy: Concepts and Policies*. Oxford: Oxford University Press.
Halliday, Terence, and Bruce Carruthers. 2009. *Bankrupt: Global Lawmaking and Systemic Financial Crisis*. Stanford, CA: Stanford University Press.
Hammersvik, Eirik, Sveinung Sandberg, and Willy Pedersen. 2012. "Why Small-Scale Cannabis Growers Stay Small: Five Mechanisms that Prevent Small-Scale Growers from Going Large Scale." *International Journal of Drug Policy* 23(6): pp. 458–64.
Harrington, Brooke. 2016. *Capital without Borders: Wealth Managers and the One Percent*. Cambridge, MA: Harvard University Press.
Hart, Keith. 1973. "Informal Income Opportunities and Urban Employment in Ghana." *Journal of Modern African Studies* 11(1): pp. 61–89.

Hart, Keith. 2008. *Between Bureaucracy and the People: A Political History of Informality*. DIIS working paper 27. Copenhagen: Danish Institute for International Studies.

Helmke, Gretchen, and Steven Levitsky (eds). 2006. *Informal Institutions and Democracy: Lessons from Latin America*. Baltimore, MD: Johns Hopkins University Press.

Heyman, Josiah McConnell (ed.). 1999. *States and Illegal Practices*. Oxford: Berg.

Hibou, Béatrice (ed.). 2004. *Privatizing the State*. New York: Columbia University Press.

Holland, Alisha C. 2015. "The Distributive Politics of Enforcement." *American Journal of Political Science* 59(2): pp. 357–71.

Hübschle, Annette. 2015. *A Game of Horns: Transnational Flows of Rhino*. Studies on the Social and Political Constitution of the Economy. Cologne: International Max Planck Research School on the Social and Political Constitution of the Economy. <http://pubman.mpdl.mpg.de/pubman/item/escidoc:2218357:9/component/escidoc:2262615/2016_IMPRSDiss_Huebschle.pdf> (accessed October 1, 2016).

Hübschle, Annette. 2016. "The Social Economy of Rhino Poaching: Of Economic Freedom Fighters, Professional Hunters and Marginalized Local People." *Current Sociology*, October 13. doi:10.1177/0011392116673210.

Lauth, Hans-Joachim. 2000. "Informal Institutions and Democracy." *Democratization* 7(4): pp. 21–50.

Lomnitz, Larissa. 1975. *Cómo sobreviven los marginados*. Buenos Aires: Siglo XXI editores.

Mackenzie, Simon. 2005. "Dig a Bit Deeper: Law, Regulation and the Illicit Antiquities Market." *British Journal of Criminology* 45(3): pp. 249–68.

Mackenzie, Simon. 2013. "Conditions for Guilt-Free Consumption in a Transnational Criminal Market." *European Journal on Criminal Policy and Research* 20(4): pp. 503–15.

Marx, Karl. 1867. *Das Kapital: Band 1. MEW, Bd* 23. Berlin: Dietz.

Massari, Monica, and Paola Monzini. 2004. "Dirty Businesses in Italy: A Case-Study of Illegal Trafficking in Hazardous Waste." *Global Crime* 6(3–4): pp. 285–304.

Maurer, Bill. 2006. "The Anthropology of Money." *Annual Review of Anthropology* 35(1): pp. 15–36.

Misse, Michel. 2007. "Mercados ilegais, redes de proteção e organização local do crime no Rio de Janeiro." *Estudos Avançados* 21(61): pp. 139–57.

Nordstrom, Carolyn. 2000. "Shadows and Sovereigns." *Theory, Culture and Society* 17(4): pp. 35–54.

Nordstrom, Carolyn. 2004. *Shadows of War: Violence, Power, and International Profiteering in the Twenty-First Century*. Berkeley: University of California Press.

Nordstrom, Carolyn. 2007. *Global Outlaws: Crime, Money, and Power in the Contemporary World*. Berkeley: University of California Press.

O'Donnell, Guillermo. 1993. "On the State, Democratization and Some Conceptual Problems: A Latin American View with Glances at Some Postcommunist Countries." *World Development* 21(8): pp. 1355–69.

Orléan, André. 2014. *The Empire of Value: A New Foundation for Economics*. Cambridge, MA: MIT Press.

Palan, Ronen. 2006. *The Offshore World: Sovereign Markets, Virtual Places, and Nomad Millionaires*. Ithaca, NY: Cornell University Press.

Palan, Ronen, Richard Murphy, and Christian Chavagneux. 2013. *Tax Havens: How Globalization Really Works*. Ithaca, NY: Cornell University Press.

Paoli, Letizia. 2003. *Mafia Brotherhoods: Organized Crime, Italian Style*. New York: Oxford University Press.

Paoli, Letizia, and Kelly Feytens. 2016. "The Belgian and Indian Pharmaceutical Market." Research outline, mimeo.

Paoli, Letizia, Victoria A. Greenfield, and Peter Reuter. 2009. *The World Heroin Market: Can Supply Be Cut?* New York: Oxford University Press.

Portes, Alejandro. 2010. *Economic Sociology: A Systematic Inquiry*. Princeton, NJ: Princeton University Press.

Reno, William. 1995. *Corruption and State Politics in Sierra Leone*. Cambridge: Cambridge University Press.

Reno, William. 2009. "Illicit Markets, Violence, Warlords, and Governance: West African Cases." *Crime, Law and Social Change* 52(3): pp. 313–22.

Reurink, Arjan. 2016. *From Elite Lawbreaking to Financial Crime: The Evolution of the Concept of White-Collar Crime*. MPIfG discussion paper 16/10. Cologne: Max Planck Institute for the Study of Societies.

Reuter, Peter. 1984. "Police Regulation of Illegal Gambling: Frustrations of Symbolic Enforcement." *Annals of the American Academy of Political and Social Science* 474(1): pp. 36–47.

Rodgers, Dennis. 2006. "The State as a Gang: Conceptualizing the Governmentality of Violence in Contemporary Nicaragua." *Critique of Anthropology* 26(3): pp. 315–30.

Rudrappa, Sharmila. 2015. *Discounted Life: The Price of Global Surrogacy in India*. New York: New York University Press.

Sandberg, Sveinung. 2012. "The Importance of Culture for Cannabis Markets: Towards an Economic Sociology of Illegal Drug Markets." *British Journal of Criminology* 52(6): pp. 1133–51.

Sassen, Saskia. 1994. "The Informal Economy: Between New Developments and Old Regulations." *Yale Law Journal* 103(8): pp. 2289–304.

Satz, Debra. 2010. *Why Some Things Should Not Be for Sale: The Moral Limits of Markets*. New York: Oxford University Press.

Schmidt, Eric, and Jared Cohen. 2013. *The New Digital Age: Transforming Nations, Businesses, and Our Lives*. New York: Knopf.

Schneider, Friedrich, and Dominik H. Enste. 2003. *The Shadow Economy: An International Survey*. Cambridge: Cambridge University Press.

Seligmann, Linda. 2004. *Peruvian Street Lives: Culture, Power, and Economy among Market Women of Cuzco*. Urbana: University of Illinois Press.

Sørensen, Jesper B. 2003. "Book Reviews." *Administrative Science Quarterly* 48(3): pp. 534–7.

Steiner, Philippe. 2010. "La transplantation d'organes: Un commerce entre les êtres humains?" *Revue du MAUSS* 35(1): pp. 455–62.

Steiner, Philippe, and Marie Trespeuch. 2015. *Marchés contestés: Quand le marché rencontre la morale*. Toulouse: Presses Universitaires du Midi.

Stephenson, Svetlana. 2016. "It Takes Two to Tango: The State and Organised Crime in Russia." *Current Sociology*. Unpublished manuscript.

Suchman, Mark C. 1995. "Managing Legitimacy: Strategic and Institutional Approaches." *Academy of Management Review* 20(3): pp. 571–610.

Swedberg, Richard. 2003. "The Case for an Economic Sociology of Law." *Theory and Society* 32(1): pp. 1–37.

Sykes, Gresham M., and David Matza. 1957. "Techniques of Neutralization: A Theory of Delinquency." *American Sociological Review* 22(6): pp. 664–70.

Thomas, Kedron. 2015. "Economic Regulation and the Value of Concealment in Highland Guatemala." *Critique of Anthropology* 35(1): pp. 13–29.

Thompson, Edward Palmer. 1963. *The Making of the English Working Class*. London: Victor Gollancz.

Thompson, Edward Palmer. 1975. *Whigs and Hunters: The Origin of the Black Act*. London: Allen Lane.

Uzzi, Brian. 1996. "The Sources and Consequences of Embeddedness for the Economic Performance of Organizations: The Network Effect." *American Sociological Review* 61(4): pp. 674–98.

Varese, Federico. 2004. *The Russian Mafia: Private Protection in a New Market Economy*. Oxford: Oxford University Press.

Vaughan, Diane. 1985. *Controlling Unlawful Organizational Behavior: Social Structure and Corporate Misconduct*. Chicago: University of Chicago Press.

Venkatesh, Sudhir. 2006. *Off the Books: The Underground Economy of the Urban Poor*. Cambridge, MA: Harvard University Press.

Venkatesh, Sudhir. 2009. *Gang Leader for a Day*. London: Penguin.

Venkatesh, Sudhir. 2013. *Floating City: A Rogue Sociologist Lost and Found in New York's Underground Economy*. London: Penguin.

Volkov, Vadim. 2002. *Violent Entrepreneurs: The Use of Force in the Making of Russian Capitalism*. Ithaca, NY: Cornell University Press.

Volkov, Vadim. 2011. "From Full to Selective Secrecy: The Offshore Realm after the Crisis." In *The Deepening Crisis: Governance Challenges after Neoliberalism*, edited by Georgi Derluguian and Craig Calhoun, pp. 203–20. New York: New York University Press.

Wehinger, Frank. 2011. *Illegale Märkte: Stand der sozialwissenschaftlichen Forschung*. MPIfG working paper 11/6. Cologne: Max Planck Institute for the Study of Societies.

Wehinger, Frank. 2013. "Fake Qualities: Assessing the Value of Counterfeit Goods." In *Constructing Quality: The Classification of Goods in Markets*, edited by Jens Beckert and Christine Musselin, pp. 268–87. Oxford: Oxford University Press.

Weinstein, Liza. 2008. "Mumbai's Development Mafias: Globalization, Organized Crime and Land Development." *International Journal of Urban and Regional Research* 32(1): pp. 22–39.

Wendel, Travis, and Ric Curtis. 2000. "The Heraldry of Heroin: 'Dope Stamps' and the Dynamics of Drug Markets in New York City." *Journal of Drug Issues* 30(2): pp. 225–59.

White, Harrison C. 1981. "Where Do Markets Come From?" *American Journal of Sociology* 87(3): pp. 517–47.

Whyte, David, and Jörg Wiegratz (eds). 2016. *Neoliberalism and the Moral Economy of Fraud*. London: Routledge.

Wikström, P. 2006. "Individuals, Settings, and Acts of Crime: Situational Mechanisms and the Explanation of Crime." In *The Explanation of Crime: Context, Mechanisms and*

*Development*, edited by P. Wikström and Robert J. Sampson. Cambridge: Cambridge University Press.

Wikström, P. 2010. "Explaining Crime as Moral Actions." In *Handbook of the Sociology of Morality*, edited by Steven Hitlin and Stephen Vaisey. New York: Springer.

Wikström, P., and K. Treiber. 2007. "The Role of Self-Control in Crime Causation beyond Gottfredson and Hirschi's General Theory of Crime." *European Journal of Criminology* 4(2): pp. 237–64.

Zelizer, Viviana A. 2007. "Pasts and Futures of Economic Sociology." *American Behavioral Scientist* 50(8): pp. 1056–69.

Zucman, Gabriel. 2013. *La richesse cachée des nations: Enquête sur les paradis fiscaux*. Paris: Le Seuil.

Part I

# Conceptualizing Illegal Markets

# 2

# Illegal Markets

## Boundaries and Interfaces between Legality and Illegality

*Renate Mayntz*

Illegal markets have been sadly neglected in the newly flourishing market sociology (Beckert and Wehinger 2013). But this is not specific to market sociology. Despite the focal importance of (social) norms in sociological theory and research, the dimension legal/illegal does not play an important role in most sociological sub-fields, the sociology of law being an obvious exception. While "the law" and the legal system are important concepts in sociological macro theories, legality and illegality are not. The focal analytical dimension in dealing with social norms is not their character, but whether or not they are complied with—in other words, compliant or deviant behavior. Although it is recognized that legal norms are a special category of social norms due to their formally regulated origin and their mode of sanctioning, the infringement of legal norms is not treated as a special kind of norm violation or deviance, again except in the sociology of law. In other words, in sociological theory generally, the dimension compliant/deviant is not systematically related to the dimension legal/illegal. This may be characteristic of a discipline that has developed in countries where what is legal is overwhelmingly also considered to be legitimate—that is, where legality and legitimacy are tacitly conflated. It may have been the study of failing or weak states that called attention to the frequent divergence between what is legal and what is considered to be legitimate, and has made us realize that this is an empirically consequential distinction.

The study of illegal markets thus faces the challenge of defining the "nature of the beast" or its object of cognition more clearly, so as to distinguish illegality from legality and relate both to the dimension of legitimacy. This involves establishing conceptual boundaries, and relating them to empirical phenomena—a tiresome but essential exercise because conceptual clarification concerning legality, illegality, and the interface between them is a necessary prerequisite for formulating substantive questions about the genesis and control of illegality in markets and related forms of illegal action.

## Legality and Illegality

Boundaries can be both conceptual and real. Conceptually, boundaries are definitional distinctions between different properties (for example, red/green/blue, friendly/hostile) or object categories (for example, cats/dogs, Africans/Arabs/Chinese). Where properties define objects, as skin color defines race, the two types of definitional distinction merge. Both for property and for object categories, the defining criteria are rarely given objectively, as in the distinction between atoms by the number of protons. Where the properties defining an object are continuous rather than discrete variables—as is true of hostility and centralization, as well as of temperature and weight—definition is a labeling process involving arbitrary distinctions between different degrees of the same property. Definitional boundaries, as between races or between life and death, can be drawn in different ways, and they can be more or less sharply drawn. With decreasing conceptual distinctiveness, assigning a given instance to a specific category becomes increasingly difficult.

The boundaries of *social* object categories—for example, what counts as a law, political party, or market—are likewise established by definitions. But underlying the definitions are observable facts that are used to operationalize the concepts and thus delineate "real" entities, such as the Federal Republic of Germany or the European market for dairy products. Definitional boundaries and the observable boundaries of social entities easily shade into each other. Socially accepted definitions are "performative": assigning a gesture to the category "hostile" and terrorist acts to the category "war" rather than "crime" (Daase 1999), or a market to the category "illegal," has consequences for behavior.

There is no *conceptual* ambiguity about the distinction between legal and illegal as properties of action if we define legal action as action in conformity with a legal norm, and illegal action as action that violates a legal norm. Legal norms are a sub-set of formal rules. Formal rules such as laws, regulations, a charter, or a statute are set by persons or bodies authorized to do so by law, convention, or agreement, and are typically supported by (the threat of) sanctions. This holds for constitutional authorities, as well as for the CEO of an enterprise or the International Olympic Committee. In daily speech, of course, the word "legal" often includes some substantive quality, such as being just or justifiable in moral terms; but in the study of illegal markets it makes sense to stick to a narrow concept of "legal" in order better to distinguish it from the related concepts "legitimate," "appropriate," or "moral." Where we are dealing with legal rules, it is relatively easy to say what is formally illegal. Legal rules can be prescriptions (do-rules) or proscriptions (don't-rules)—they command, or prohibit. In some fields, such as tax law, do-rules prevail, but in many fields (for example, traffic regulation, consumer protection) we find both types.

The core problem in calling an act "illegal" is the often very large room for interpretation of legal rules. All kinds of formal rules—not only legal ones—use what in German are called *unbestimmte Rechtsbegriffe* (undefined legal terms). This is less true of (regulatory) standards, a category of formal rules that typically includes quantitative, measurable terms; standards can be incorporated into law, but can also be based on agreement or convention. While existing legal rules establish what can be called "illegal," the term "legal" is used in practice in two fundamentally different ways, often not explicitly distinguished: either more narrowly to designate action in *compliance* with legal rules, or much more widely designating all actions that *do not violate* any legal rule. This is a highly important distinction, because many actions are not subject to any formal, let alone legal, rule—in other words, they are neither prescribed nor proscribed. The Ten Commandments consist of do- and don't-rules, but they cover only a very small segment of human action. To the extent that sanctioning is tied to the violation of specific legal rules, the valuation of behavior that does not violate such norms is an open question. It is here that the dimension of legitimacy comes in.

## Legality and Legitimacy

Legitimacy and a lack thereof are of paramount interest in political theory. In political theory, the term "legitimate" is used specifically in relation to authority and authority relations. However, the term is often used without definition (Suchman 1995: 572); some authors judge the legitimacy of a regime by its conformity to or violation of theoretically derived normative standards. In sociological theory, Niklas Luhmann was concerned with legitimacy (Luhmann 1983), but only in relation to "the law," as Matías Dewey points out (Dewey 2016). If legitimacy is defined, reference is made mainly to Max Weber. For Weber, a social order is legitimate if it is considered to be exemplary and binding. This applies not only to legal norms, but also to practices based on tradition, custom, or convention. Max Weber distinguished between legality and legitimacy, defining legitimacy not as an objective property, but as the subjective *belief* that a given social order or practice is exemplary and binding (Weber 1956: 26). Thus in a given market order, the observable practices of market exchange considered to be legitimate by participants need not be based (only) on compliance with *legal* norms. The concept of legitimacy has a wider scope than legality. For the analysis of illegal markets, the Weberian concept of legitimacy as belief is crucial. Legitimacy beliefs are social facts to be established empirically. The criteria (or basis) on which legitimacy is attributed to a given authority, social order, or practice vary culturally and historically; legitimacy beliefs are not universally shared in any given society.

The conceptual distinction between (formal) legality and (social) legitimacy is empirically relevant where not everything that is formally legal is deemed to be legitimate by "rule takers." Formal rules are issued by a competent authority, but authority may only be claimed by rulers, not granted by the ruled; this can hold for clan chiefs, for CEOs, and for governments. In this case, imposed sanctions are experienced as the unwarranted exercise of power/force; a certain tax may then be seen as unwarranted political expropriation. On the other hand, actions formally defined as illegal can be considered legitimate. In *both* cases, (formal) legality and (social) legitimacy diverge. If the legitimacy of a political authority is contested, or if a political authority cannot impose threatened sanctions, illegality is only formal. Where formal legality and social legitimacy diverge, legitimate illegality flourishes.

There is a conceptual overlap between the concept of "legitimate illegality"—in other words, behavior deemed legitimate, although known to be illegal—and economic action termed "informal." According to Hart, informal economic action escapes state regulation, either because it is not regulated or because, although formally regulated and possibly violating existing rules, it remains invisible to the bureaucracy (Hart 2010: 141–9). "Informal" thus covers more than "illegal." There is also a conceptual overlap between legitimacy, defined in the Weberian tradition, and what March and Olsen (2006) call "appropriate" and define as behavior that is expected and seen as natural and rightful for members of a given collectivity playing a specific role in a given situation. While there is a clear distinction between legality and legitimacy, the concepts of informal economic action and of "appropriate" market transactions gloss over the difference: informal economic action, as well as appropriate behavior, can be legal as well as illegal, which ignores the tension that exists where legality and legitimacy diverge.[1] It is the possible divergence between the dimensions legality/illegality and legitimate/illegitimate that is theoretically significant, because the resulting tension impacts on behavior. In fact, as the divergence between legality and legitimacy grows, its practical

[1] Admittedly, it is difficult to empirically separate legitimacy beliefs from beliefs about appropriate behavior, and both from moral beliefs.

relevance increases. What generates congruence or divergence between legality and legitimacy is therefore a crucial theoretical question.

## Illegal Markets and Other Kinds of Illegality

Illegality can be a property of individual acts and of different kinds of social action systems. Illegal markets are but one kind of illegal action system, which must be distinguished both from individual illegal acts, such as corruption and financial crime, and from other types of illegal action systems, such as organized crime, mafia organizations, and terrorist organizations. The elements constituting an illegal market are illegal market transactions. Market transactions can be illegal for different reasons (Wehinger 2011): because the good exchanged is illegal per se (for example, certain kinds of drugs); because it is produced illegally (for example, illegally mined diamonds); because it is illegal to trade it (for example, human organs); or because it is traded in violation of restrictive rules (for example, arms). Illegal actions need not be executed by members of an illegal (for example, mafia or terrorist) organization. Generally law-abiding citizens may participate in illegal action systems, occasionally giving shelter to a terrorist or buying counterfeit goods.

The specificity of illegal markets is best thrown into relief by trying to distinguish them from other kinds of illegality, but it is often difficult to draw a clear line between different kinds of illegality. Mafia organizations and illegal markets are closely related empirically, and corruption is a strategy also used by organized crime, mafia organizations, and in illegal markets. Conceptually, however, corruption and financial crime such as fraud and embezzlement can be distinguished from illegal markets by virtue of being specific categories of acts or interactions.

There is a vast literature on corruption (see, among others, Rose-Ackerman 1999; Transparency International 2007; Rothstein 2015) and a large, if highly dispersed literature on financial crime.[2] Corruption—the granting of official favors (for example, export licenses, public building contracts) by a legal actor in violation of formally established rules or withholding sanctions in exchange for money or other rewards—typically takes place in bilateral interaction, where the corrupting actor may be the CEO of a legal business firm, an illegal trader, a mafioso, or a member of a drug cartel. The proximate purpose of bribing may be the evasion of legal sanctions, but the main driving motive of corruption is economic gain, whether such gain simply means profit or is a condition of the

[2] A literature survey on financial fraud has been conducted at the Max Planck Institute for the Study of Societies (see Reurink 2016); in contrast to corruption, financial crime has not been a popular topic for sociologists.

corrupting actor's economic survival. Economic gain is also the driving motive in financial crime. In the typical case of financial crime, otherwise legal individuals (for example, traders in a financial institution, accountants in a corporation) commit formally illegal acts, either in their personal interest or for the benefit of their organization. Perpetrators who identify primarily with their organization will not necessarily consider their behavior to be illegitimate, even though they are conscious of the fact that they are infringing a legal rule. As is true of corruption, acts of financial crime tend to be kept secret.

Market actors may engage in corruption and commit financial crimes, but this does not constitute illegal markets. Illegal markets are systems composed of illegal market transactions. By definition, a market presupposes multiple sellers or potential buyers, and market transactions are assumed to be voluntary on the part of sellers and buyers (see Aspers and Beckert 2008: 225f.). There is a fluid boundary between voluntary and constrained engagement in legal as well as illegal market transactions, but "selling" mafia protection to enterprises is clearly extortion rather than a market transaction. The driving motive in illegal markets is generally economic; some actors may simply seek sustenance or even survival rather than profit.

The social acceptance (legitimacy) of formally illegal trades/markets varies considerably. In social contexts of contested legality, where "the law," whether because of its source or its content, is not considered legitimate, the legal/illegal boundary is only weakly drawn, and what is formally illegal may become accepted everyday practice. The more diffused the perceived legitimacy of formally illegal acts, the less is the felt need to hide them; examples are the Argentinian market La Salada described by Dewey (2012), and the Open Eye markets described by Nina Engwicht in her dissertation (Engwicht 2016).

Illegal markets can be conceptually distinguished more clearly from terrorist organizations than from organized crime and mafia organizations. Illegal markets differ from terrorist organizations in the main driving motive (economic rather than political), in the type of social order or governance (market versus organization), and in the role of physical violence. The market is traditionally associated with peaceful exchange, and contrasted to violent strife and war (for example, Hirschman 1977). Whereas violence, the spectacular murder of uninvolved people, is a defining feature of terrorism (see, for instance, Daase 2007), actual violence—in contrast to the threat of violence—is a strategy of last resort in mafia organizations, organized crime, and even more so in illegal markets. Terrorist organizations commit such crimes as extortion, kidnapping, and bank robbery, but terrorism is also considered a crime in itself. Terrorist organizations differ from organized crime in the driving motive rather than the nature of their actions. While for criminal organizations, extortion and drug trafficking are a source of profit, terrorist groups commit these criminal acts to fund their political activities.

Illegal markets and organized crime are connected in so far as criminal organizations specializing in car theft or art robbery act as suppliers to the corresponding illegal markets. In fact, the distinction between illegal markets and organized crime seems to turn mainly on a conceptual or classificatory distinction—the difference between "illegal" and "criminal." Not all illegal acts are violations of criminal law and can thus be classified as crimes; illegal market exchange is often in violation of trade law, not criminal law. Profit is the dominant driving motive in illegal markets and in organized crime, and the same kind of good can be involved. There are even similarities with respect to organization; criminal "organizations" are often much more loosely structured than the term suggests. In fact, the *Oxford Handbook of Organized Crime* has a whole section on illegal markets (Paoli 2014). But illegal market activities are more likely to be socially tolerated than the activities associated with organized crime—stealing, blackmail, and extortion are generally judged to be morally wrong.

The *Oxford Handbook of Organized Crime* also has several chapters on mafia organizations, treating them as one kind of organized crime among others; obviously these classificatory categories overlap. The distinction between mafia organizations and illegal markets is also difficult, although less for semantic than for empirical reasons. Mafia organizations typically engage in illegal market activities, but in mafia organizations the driving motive is not merely economic. Mafia organizations try to establish a monopoly over *several* types of illegal markets (drugs, prostitution, garbage, toxic waste disposal, and so on) in a *specific territory*; the driving motive is thus both economic and political.[3] The means–end relation between profit and territorial power is variable. In a given illegal system, the relative dominance (or rank order) of the economic (profit) and the political (power) motive can change, and it may be difficult to tell which is the means and which the end. It is basically the means–end relation between the two—the dependence of economic gain on territorial power and of power on money—that makes for their empirical interrelation and the fluid boundary between illegal markets, mafia organizations, and organizations involved in armed conflict in civil wars.

## Interfaces between Legal and Illegal Action Systems

All social action and action systems that are formally illegal are surrounded by, and in constant interaction with, actors complying with and actors bent on defending legal norms. Illegal markets interact with legal markets, and with

[3] There is a vast literature on mafia organizations, including excellent sociological studies (for example, Gambetta 1992; Sciarrone 2011) and documentary studies in the form of novels (for example, Saviano 2006).

official guardians of legality, in particular the police and courts. There is an important difference between these two relations: while the relation between legal and illegal (sections of) markets is at its worst one of competition, the relation to the "forces of order" is in principle repressive. However, there are cases of tolerance by the police and even by political authorities, as in the case of the Argentinian market La Salada (Dewey 2012 and in this volume) and the illegal diamond market in Sierra Leone (Engwicht in this volume). Political repression used against illegal markets varies in intensity, not only between fully developed modern nation states and so-called fragile states, but also within states; in both cases this is due to differences in the extent of divergence between legality and legitimacy. Where formal legality and perceived legitimacy diverge, or where actions are neither illegal nor considered inappropriate, non-repressive interaction between formally legal and formally illegal actors and action systems is facilitated. In such cases, legal and illegal action systems are not separated by clear social boundaries, but connected by what has come to be called "interfaces."

The concept of "interface" has not been used much in sociological writing and lacks an accepted definition. However, an "interface" between two distinct social entities presumably designates a relationship other than conflict or cooperation. "Interface" is sometimes used to refer to boundary-spanning institutions, such as notaries, brokers, and attorneys; these actors mediate between two parties or systems, belonging to neither of them. In this case, the boundaries of the two systems that are connected by a third party are clearly drawn. More relevant for the study of illegal markets is, however, a concept of interface closer to "interpenetration" (Münch 1991) than to boundary spanning, a concept referring to cases where the boundary between legality and illegality loses its distinctiveness. This happens where legality and legitimacy diverge. An "interface" between legal and illegal social systems that links, but at the same time blurs the boundary between them can take different forms.[4]

First, there are *ambivalent* phenomena, actions/actors that are *assigned* to opposed categories on the dimensions legal/illegal and legitimate/illegitimate. The resulting combination of properties—legitimate illegality and illegitimate legal action—appears contradictory, if in everyday experience these dimensions are normally correlated. If they diverge, actors are forced to choose between two different orientations, acting legally while knowing this violates an informal norm, or acting legitimately in the full knowledge of violating a legal rule. The mafia member who testifies in court has decided to violate the

[4] I do not include hybrid phenomena among "interfaces." Hybrid phenomena possess "defining" properties belonging to both categories in a dualistic pair. If legality is *formally* defined, there can be no genuine hybrids of legal/illegal.

informal norm of *omertà*, while the seller of a counterfeit Rolex watch decides to violate a legal norm.

There is, secondly, a grey zone of phenomena that *cannot be clearly assigned* to one specific category on the dimensions legal/illegal and legitimate/illegitimate. This can be due to a number of reasons. For one thing, as already underlined, there are gaps in legal regulation, where actions can be judged only by the legitimacy accorded to them, or more generally by their appropriateness. In regulated areas, legal norms are often subject to interpretation. When does "taking" become "stealing" in the legal sense, and making use of an opportunity "cheating"? However, not only the legal, but also the social definitions of cheating, stealing, and lying can be fluid and uncertain. Where actions are not legally regulated, and where the legitimacy of a legally unregulated action is unclear, the subjectively felt uncertainty is greatest.

Finally, there are *actors* who, at different times or in different situations, engage both in legal and illegal actions, who are *moving between* two worlds, acting legally and then again illegally, or the other way round. In the typical case the actors themselves are generally law-abiding citizens, but occasionally commit illegal acts. There is the honest businessman selling garments produced in mafia sweatshops in his boutique; the renowned firm that, off and on, dumps (or allows the dumping of) its waste illegally; and the law-abiding citizen giving shelter for a couple of days to a criminal on the run. Similarly, the sympathizers surrounding a terrorist organization may on occasion render active support, moving as it were between two worlds (Malthaner and Waldmann 2012). In these cases, otherwise "legal" actors act illegally. But as Nina Engwicht (2016) has shown, there is also the illegal trader of illegally mined diamonds who sells them to a legal export firm, and the seller of counterfeit goods who invests his profit in a legal business or legally buys an apartment.

The close empirical connection between illegal markets and terrorist organizations, mafia organizations, and what is called organized crime is reflected in the difficulties—evident in the third section of this chapter—involved in distinguishing between them conceptually. The conceptual boundaries between these different types of illegal action systems are fluid. Interfaces, however, are real social phenomena that can be empirically established, even where they are subjective, as are beliefs. The term "interface" can refer to phenomena (both actions and social systems) that are formally illegal, yet considered to be legitimate, or legal yet considered to be illegitimate; it also refers to phenomena whose legality and/or legitimacy is open to interpretation, and to actors participating with their actions in both a legal and an illegal system. Actors who move between two distinct social worlds serve as linking pins between them. Ambivalent phenomena force actors to make choices, blurring the hard edges of social categories. These kinds of interface bind together what is socially distinct, provide scope for innovative action, and permit flexible adaptation. Grey zones can create tension in everyday behavior; they are also a challenge for legislators, and thus a source of institutional change. Selling complex CDOs to speculate on expected losses did not infringe any legal norm and was accepted practice before the recent financial crisis, but has come to be considered illegitimate, and may become illegal in the course of regulatory reform. The boundaries between legal/illegal and legitimate/illegitimate are not stable: they shift. The observation of interfaces between legality and illegality, stimulated by the study of illegal markets, alerts us not so much to the dark side of the social world as to the many shades of grey that lie between black and white.

## References


Aspers, Patrik, and Jens Beckert. 2008. "Märkte." In *Handbuch der Wirtschaftssoziologie*, edited by Andrea Maurer, pp. 225–46. Wiesbaden: VS Verlag.

Beckert, Jens, and Frank Wehinger. 2013. "In the Shadow: Illegal Markets and Economic Sociology." *Socio-Economic Review* 11(1): pp. 5–30.

Daase, Christopher. 1999. *Kleine Kriege—große Wirkung: Wie unkonventionelle Kriege die internationale Politik verändern*. Baden-Baden: Nomos.

Daase, Christopher. 2007. "Terrorismus als asymmetrische Gewaltstrategie." In *Terrorismus und Rechtsstaatlichkeit: Analysen, Handlungsoptionen, Perspektiven*, edited by Kurt Graulich and Dieter Simon, pp. 91–9. Berlin: Akademie Verlag.

Dewey, Matías. 2012. "Illegal Police Protection and the Market for Stolen Vehicles in Buenos Aires." *Journal of Latin American Studies* 44(4): pp. 679–702.

Dewey, Matías. 2016. *The Organization of Market Expectations beyond Legality: Towards New Distinctions in Luhmann's Theory of Systems*. Unpublished manuscript. Cologne: Max Planck Institute for the Study of Societies.

Engwicht, Nina. 2016. "After Blood Diamonds: The Moral Economy of Illegality in the Sierra Leonian Diamond Market." MPIfG discussion paper 16/9. Cologne: Max-Planck Institute for the Study of Societies.

Gambetta, Diego. 1992. *La Mafia Siciliana*. Torino: Einaudi.

Hart, Keith. 2010. "Informal Economy." In *The Human Economy*, edited by Keith Hart, Jean-Louis Laville, and Antonio David Cattani, pp. 142–53. Cambridge: Polity Press.

Hirschman, Albert O. 1977. *The Passions and the Interests: Political Arguments for Capitalism before Its Triumph*. Princeton, NJ: Princeton University Press.

Luhmann, Niklas. 1983. *Legitimation durch Verfahren*. Frankfurt a.M.: Suhrkamp.

Malthaner, Stefan, and Peter Waldmann (eds). 2012. *Radikale Milieus: Das soziale Umfeld terroristischer Gruppen*. Frankfurt a.M.: Campus.

March, James G., and Johan P. Olsen. 2006. "The Logic of Appropriateness." In *The Oxford Handbook of Public Policy*, edited by Michael Moran, Martin Rein, and Robert E. Goodin, pp. 689–708. Oxford: Oxford University Press.

Münch, Richard. 1991. *Dialektik der Kommunikationsgesellschaft*. Frankfurt a.M.: Suhrkamp.

Paoli, Letizia (ed.). 2014. *The Oxford Handbook of Organized Crime*. Oxford: Oxford University Press.

Reurink, Arjan. 2016. *Financial Fraud: A Literature Review*. MPIfG discussion paper 16/5. Cologne: Max Planck Institute for the Study of Societies.

Rose-Ackerman, Susan. 1999. *Corruption and Government: Causes, Consequences, and Reform*. Cambridge: Cambridge University Press.

Rothstein, Bo (ed.). 2015. *Political Corruption*. Cheltenham: Edward Elgar.

Saviano, Roberto. 2006. *Gomorra*. Milano: Mondadori.

Sciarrone, Rocco (ed.). 2011. *Alleanze nell'ombra: Mafie ed economie locali in Sicilia e nel Mezzogiorno*. Rome: Donzelli.

Suchman, Mark C. 1995. "Managing Legitimacy: Strategic and Institutional Approaches." *Academy of Management Review* 20(3): pp. 571–610.

Transparency International. 2007. *Global Corruption Report 2007: Corruption in Judicial Systems*. Cambridge: Cambridge University Press.

Weber, Max. 1956. *Wirtschaft und Gesellschaft*. München: C.H. Beck.

Wehinger, Frank. 2011. *Illegale Märkte: Stand der wissenschaftlichen Forschung*. MPIfG working paper 11/6. Cologne: Max Planck Institute for the Study of Societies.

Part II

# Secrecy and Illegal Markets

# 3

# Secrecy and Frontiers in Illegal Organ Transplantation

*Philippe Steiner*

## Introduction

The existence of a market for organ transplants involving transactions between suppliers and patients is a central issue for both patients and institutions concerned with the ethical dimension of transplantation. It is also of relevance for current research on illegality and the market, because when human body parts—mainly kidneys—are bought and sold, this implies that human beings are, albeit briefly, treated as a commodity, providing the human resource necessary to heal another human being whose life is dramatically impaired by illness. The transformation of human beings, or parts of human beings, into commodities is treated as a political and moral threat by most legislatures, and market-like relationships of this kind generally trigger moral condemnation. However, there is extensive evidence that the commodification of human body parts occurs in many countries.

The present chapter aims at highlighting the complexities of illegal transactions when they must hide themselves among legal ones. The first part of the chapter considers how the issue of commodification was dealt with after the decision to ban the market for kidneys in the United States, which constituted the decisive political step to make this form of transaction illegal. The second part of the chapter considers the role that violence, secrecy, and the frontier between legality and illegality play in the functioning of illegal transactions. In the final section we consider three cases of illegal transactions in organ transplantation, paying attention to their organizational dimension and to the work of concealment carried out so that the frontier between legal and illegal worlds can be crossed.

## The Legal Dimension

In the 1960s and 1970s the issue of commercialization in the field of transplantation was not a matter of general concern. The first successful kidney graft between two homozygote brothers was done in a research hospital in Boston in 1957. Subsequently, the surgical technique and its associated complex postoperative procedures were progressively applied to other patients and also different organs. The turning point came at the beginning of the 1980s with the discovery and management of Cyclosporine, a new drug capable of preventing the rejection of a grafted organ by the body of the recipient. Unfortunately, medical success prompted concern about the availability of a sufficient number of organs—I shall limit myself to kidneys, which are the most important organ for transplantation and the most common organ involved in illegal transactions—for the growing number of patients waiting for a transplant (Steiner 2010: chapter 3). Until the mid-1980s there were few reasons to ban the selling of human body parts for transplantation: such operations were mostly unsuccessful, few in number, and done in research hospitals with public funding; commercialization was therefore pointless. Cyclosporine was a game changer: suddenly, kidney transplantation became a successful medical technique that could save the lives of people suffering from end-stage renal failure. Commercialization became an issue.

Two events brought the issue of commercialization to the fore in the medical and political worlds: the entrepreneurial activities of Dr. Harvey Jacobs, and the behavior of wealthy patients.

In 1983, Dr. Jacobs contacted several hospitals in the United States, offering to provide them with kidneys bought from foreign sellers by his company (Kidney International). This offer triggered an immediate response from the political world, notably from Al Gore, a congressman specializing in new technologies, who acted swiftly to bring about a ban on market transactions for the purposes of transplantation (Gunby 1983). Accordingly, the National Organ Transplantation Act was passed in October 1984, clarifying the legal status of organs and outlawing their commercialization in the United States. At about the same time, but far from Washington, significant commercialization of transplant surgery began, involving wealthy patients from the Arabian Peninsula and India. This prompted concern in the transplant community, which reacted negatively to this commercial development, and proposed ethical guidelines in major professional journals (*Lancet* and *Transplantation*, in 1985 and 1986, respectively). Major international changes to the laws regulating living transplantation in South America and Europe (USSR included) followed these developments. These legal changes demonstrate that, before 1984, specific issues related to living organ procurement and the possibility of the commodification of human body parts in transplantation were not part of the legislative framework in many countries. Only 40 percent of the legislation relating to transplantation passed before 1984 banned the commodification of kidneys. There was a dramatic shift after new US legislation was passed in 1984: 75 percent of legislation now banned the commodification of human body parts, about twice the proportion in the previous period. Countries in which there was legislative activity in both periods confirm the trend because, with the exception of Venezuela, all these countries added specific sections banning such commodification in their post-1984 legislation (Steiner 2015: 264–6). Since then, there have been important moves to extend the ban on commodification, notably the Palermo Protocol adopted by the United Nations in 2000 to "Prevent, Suppress and Punish Trafficking in Persons, especially Women and Children" and more recently, in 2008, with the Declaration of Istanbul "On Organ Trafficking and Transplant Tourism," which has been endorsed by more than 100 medical organizations to date. This illustrates the key role of the state in making illegal the market in organ transplantation and, because the ban must be international to be effective, it also illustrates the role of non-governmental organizations in producing the necessary coordination between legislative decisions.

Nevertheless, the mere possibility of organ trafficking was, and probably still is, sufficiently strong to play a part in the introduction of new legislation. The rationale is the following: "When there are so many rich patients waiting for a kidney, when there are so many poor people desperate for cash, then there is organ trafficking." In more technical terms, the spread between what the rich are ready to pay for a kidney and what the poor are ready to accept for selling their kidney is so large that trafficking can easily intervene and offer an illegal transaction to both parties, together with hefty profits to the broker and the surgeon. This narrative can be heard not only among European surgeons, but also in political discussion, as illustrated by the French parliamentary debate on the bioethical law regulating organ transplants. In his opening speech, Jean-Yves Le Déault stated that organ trafficking was a special concern for the members of the parliamentary committee examining ethical issues in advance of public debate in the French parliament. The committee stressed the necessity of suppressing this odious form of commerce;[1] but Le Déault did not give a single real example of such trafficking. The same thing happened when Bernard Kouchner, a former physician and at the time Minister of Health, warned in a speech to deputies that a central aim of the bioethical law was the prevention of a situation in which men and women were driven to sell one of their kidneys in order to make a living. Throughout these lengthy debates organ trafficking was no more than a fear or a dread, but all the same powerful

[1] *Journal Officiel, Assemblée nationale*, November 19, 1992, p. 5721.

enough to produce effective results. In this sense, organ trafficking is a fiction, a form of belief organized as a credible narrative producing legal outcomes. This is a clear example of the mechanism known as the "Thomas theorem."[2]

Nevertheless, the issue of legality must be considered, together with the issue of legitimacy: the first concerns the law, the second public opinion. In many cases, illegality and illegitimacy go hand in hand; does this apply to illegal transplantation? The answer is "yes" as far as the middlemen—or the broker, the trafficker, and so on—and the rogue surgeons are concerned, because they play the role of the villains benefiting from hopeless patients and moneyless sellers. However, not only is the behavior of patients usually not deemed criminal, but it is sometimes considered legitimate: someone suffering poor health for lack of an available human kidney for transplant. Public opinion does not condemn such persons for engaging in illegal transactions abroad, especially when these transactions take place in countries where the illegality of organ transplantation is not clearly established, or where existing legislation is easily bypassed because of rampant corruption in public administration. This legal/legitimate duality is important to bear in mind in order to understand the specific situation of a patient whose behavior is both illegal and more or less legitimate in their own country, while legitimate and legal or easily camouflaged as legal in the country visited as a transplant tourist.

## Violence, Secrecy, and Frontiers

The legal dimension is important for the functioning of a market economy and the management of profit-making activity as a regular social activity. The founders of political economy and sociological theory generally considered that their topic was the study of legal transactions and the functioning of the market under the rule of law—the major exception would be Pierre-Joseph Proudhon's account of profit making as the outcome of theft, according to his famous sentence: *La propriété, c'est le vol* (property is theft).[3] From Karl Marx's detailed study of the capitalist mode of production to Emile Durkheim's conception of the contractual underpinnings of market exchanges, the market is considered to be a social institution in which disagreements are settled through the courts. This does not prevent exploitation and injustice, but the

[2] According to Robert Merton, William Thomas asserted the following: "If men define situations as real, they are real in their consequences."

[3] Proudhon argued that capitalists secured profit for themselves because they only paid the wages of individual workers, not for the value created by workers acting together as a collective entity (a team). Profit therefore originated in the wealth created by workers as a collective group, but was appropriated by the capitalist (Proudhon 1926 [1840]: 215, 217).

social sciences treat the market primarily as a legal institution. This is also true of Max Weber's standard definition of profit making in a market economy, where there is a marked emphasis upon the *peaceful* pursuit of economic activity:

> Profit-making is activity which is oriented to opportunities for seeking new power of control over goods on a single occasion, repeatedly, or continuously. Profit-making activity is activity which is oriented at least in part to opportunities of profit-making. Profit-making is economic if it is oriented to acquisition by peaceful methods.
>
> (Weber 1920: 90–1)

This peaceful dimension is directly connected to the legal dimension, for if transactions are illegal, actors cannot rely on the law to enforce a contract, or protect themselves and their wealth.

The peaceful dimension of the market does not rule out the existence of conflict between market participants, a situation understood as *competition* over "opportunities for profit-making." However, whether it is a matter of price setting or of command over goods, economic competition is deemed to be *peaceful*: "a peaceful conflict is competition in so far as it consists in an attempt to attain control over opportunities and advantages that are also desired by others" (Weber 1920: 38). Competition as struggle has a social dimension aptly captured by Georg Simmel who, in his chapter on conflict, argues that it is an *indirect struggle*. In his view, firms competing with each other to sell their goods to consumers are not involved in a direct struggle in which one firm has to defeat its adversary; the struggle is indirect, in the sense that each competes to seduce a third party, the consumer (Simmel 1999 [1908]: 297ff.). Accordingly, the struggle between sellers and buyers, firms and consumers, does not entail direct violence in the market. If market exchange and market competition are conducted peacefully, this is legal social action, in the sense that disagreements can be settled by law and not by private or public violence, nor by any threat to use violence. I thus suggest that we follow Weber's conception that the economy is a world of struggle without violence, because violence involves the use of quite different means, implying that the adversary is to be physically eliminated (Weber 1920: 38).

By contrast, illegal transactions entail an effective or potential use of *violence* and the management of *secrecy*. Violence may arise in different aspects of illegal transactions: preventing someone's access to the market; constraining someone to sell or buy a good that otherwise they would not have done; preventing someone from getting the full benefit from a transaction; expanding one's share in the set of illegal transactions; and the use of violence to settle disputes between those involved in illegal transactions. Violence is not a new issue where market and money transactions are concerned. For example, the French Civil Code states that a contract must meet four conditions to be effective: consent, capacity to contract, object of the contract, and licit cause. Consent is considered in a series of articles (from Art. 1109 to Art. 1122) explaining what happens when consent is obtained by fraud, violence, or error. Violence inflicted upon a contracting party nullifies the contract (Art. 1109); this is also the case when violence is not inflicted by the other contracting party (Art. 1111), or when a relative of the contracting party suffers violence (Art. 1113). However, the issue of violence is far from simple, because there are different conceptions of what is meant by violence in the context of contracts.

When a market is declared illegal for a given area, illegal transactions are associated with violence (Chimeli and Soares, 2011) even if, most of the time, illegal transactions occur without actual violence (Andreas and Wallman 2009: 225–6); the ever present threat of violence is sufficient to bring about a substantial modification of the rules of exchange. Where there are no legal means of resolving disputes between transacting parties, violence, or the threat of violence, plays a central role. The level of violence may be high, as is the case with the production and distribution of drugs in Mexico, which seems to follow the lethal logic of the escalation of violence that Clausewitz identified. It may be weak, as with illegal clothing transactions on La Salada place in Buenos Aires (Dewey 2014), or the sale of stolen cars in the same city (Dewey 2012). Nevertheless, in these situations violence supports the illegal order of the exchange arena, in the form of the bribery and corruption of street-level bureaucrats and policemen.

This dimension of violence is recognized by the international institutions and conventions that regulate the procurement of human organs. According to the UN Palermo Protocol's Article 3(a), trafficking in persons is defined as:

> the recruitment, transportation, transfer, harboring or receipt of persons by means of the threat or the use of force or other forms of coercion, of abduction, of fraud, of deception, of the abuse of power or a position of vulnerability or of giving and receiving of payments or benefits to achieve the consent of a person having control over another person, for the purpose of exploitation. Exploitation shall include, at a minimum, the exploitation of prostitution of others or other forms of sexual exploitation, forced labor or services, slavery or practices similar to slavery or the removal of organs.

This is a general statement in which the issue of organ removal is only one element; it is thus useful to also consider the Istanbul Protocol, which specifically addresses the issue of organ trafficking, defined as:

> the recruitment, transport, transfer, harboring, or receipt of living or deceased persons or their organs by means of the threat or use of force or other forms of coercion, of abduction, of fraud, of deception, of the abuse of power or of a

> position of vulnerability, or of the giving to, or the receiving by, a third party of payments or benefits to achieve the transfer of control over the potential donor, for the purpose of exploitation by the removal of organs for transplantation.

Because it is illegal, trafficking necessarily involves *secrecy*.

## *Secrecy*

Secrecy is crucial here, as it is in many other illegal transactions (see particularly Palan's chapter in this volume) because the conduct of illegal transactions requires that their existence be concealed, although some aspects can be performed openly.

Secrecy means that there is a social divide between those who know that illegal transactions are being carried out and how they are carried out—to a great extent, at least. Secrecy covers a range of social relations, as exemplified by Simmel's chapter on this issue (Simmel 1999 [1908]: chapter 5). It is first of all a general form of behavior without which social life would be almost impossible, because social intercourse is made difficult if a participant provides full and open access to all information about themselves and their activities. This form of secrecy involves "fragmentary knowledge," or secrecy as "discretion." But in other cases secrecy gives rise to secret societies in which members are expected to adopt a strategy of "dissimulation," hiding from non-members their participation in secret activities, any breach of dissimulation being considered a "betrayal," putting the traitor in jeopardy. In Albert Hirschman's language, "defection" is a strategy that is difficult and dangerous to implement (Hirschman 1970). Obviously, secrecy is also present within legal markets; there is "business confidentiality," notably concerning the intangible resources contributing to the efficient functioning of a firm not protected by a patent. This last category of secrecy differs from that attached to illegal transactions, because it is possible to regulate and control the former by law, whereas the latter is regulated and controlled by the threat of violence. They also differ in the following sense: business confidentiality involves a degree of secrecy that is openly acknowledged; it may even be explicitly stated in the employment contracts of those with access to confidential information, notably in the case of a CEO who, after leaving a company, is not allowed to work for competitors for a given period. By contrast, secrecy in illegal transactions is most effective when the existence of secrecy is itself secret. In that situation the functioning of illegal transactions is a first-order secret; second-order secrecy means that the existence of illegal transactions is not known. This second-order secrecy reduces the risk of investigations, and illegal transactions are thus easier and safer to undertake. The *work of concealment* necessary to produce secrecy and, better, a secret secrecy, is thus a crucial element of illegal transactions: this work of concealment is about transgressing the legal–illegal frontier.[4]

### Frontiers

The existence of a *legal frontier* between what is permitted and what is not is linked to a *social frontier* between those who know the existence and functioning of these illegal transactions and those who do not. Different sets of people occupy this social frontier: first, there are those in charge of preventing or containing illegal activities; in the opposite camp there are members of illegal organizations or networks who secure their operations from the activities of "traitors" who jeopardize the smooth functioning of illegal activities. There are also many people moving back and forth between these two worlds on a regular basis, for illegal activities usually need to be connected to legal activities. This happens when illegal goods are to be sold—for example, drugs—or legal goods are to be obtained with illegal means (for example, smuggled tobacco) to customers who otherwise live in the legal world. This also happens when the money accruing to those who benefit from illegal transactions has to re-enter the legal world through some form of money-laundering activity. Insofar as illegal transactions are aimed at profit making, the use of money becomes almost unavoidable; and as Simmel noted, money is an absolute means: money facilitates illegal transactions because it is a compressible, abstract, and arms-length device (Simmel 1999 [1908]: 370), so that large sums can be sent to someone far away without there being any taint related to its illegal origins.

Simmel is of course right; but we need to add a qualification to gain a full picture of what happens at the frontier. In many cases, illegal transactions are conducted as a business, which means the existence not only of a secret society or network, but also the existence of some form of organization. Organizations need a great deal of information, and ways of storing that information to keep a memory of what happened in previous transactions, and/or to plan future ones. Hence there is also what I would call a *material frontier*, where things are recorded in files before being translated from the illegal world to the legal one, and vice versa. There are many things to store, hide, and translate: money, personal data, nationality, organizational records, and so on. Each item raises different issues and needs specific forms of secrecy, preventing outsiders from understanding that illegal transactions are

[4] This work is the opposite of the work that has to be done to meet the rules of exchange, one of the four institutions in accordance with which market exchanges are possible in Neil Fligstein's conceptualization (Fligstein 2001: chapter 2). The key difference is that concealment work seeks to escape the legal rules, and not to implement them; however illegal and legal markets are intertwined, both must be performed.

being conducted, while cheating in order to make these illegal transactions effective in a legal environment. Accordingly, illegal transactions should be studied at the frontier, since the way a set of persons involved in illegal transactions manages the passage through the frontier is crucial for the functioning and understanding of what is happening.

These features of illegal transactions have a quantitative consequence. Since transactions cannot be conducted openly and important parts of the process must be concealed, the price paid by the buyer varies dramatically. Data are sparse and of poor quality, but the price range given in the HOTT report devoted to patients who go abroad to pay for a transplant is so wide that it is hard to believe that prices are really set according to "supply and demand" in whatever location these illegal transactions occur (Ambagtsheer et al. 2014b). Swedish patients paid USD 10,000 to USD 13,000 for their transplant in Iran and Iraq, but one of them mentions a price of only 280 euros (10 million Iranian real). Patients from the Netherlands paid on average 7,600 euros in Pakistan, which is close to the price paid by clients from Sweden, once the 2005–6 euro–US dollar exchange rate is taken into account; the price was lower in India (5,000 euros), but higher in Columbia (11,500 euros), and three times higher in China (25,000 euros). Patients from Macedonia traveling for a transplant to India or Pakistan paid more, with an average price (travel costs not included) of 22,000 and 18,500 euros, respectively. The highest price recorded is 45,000 euros paid by a patient for a transplant in Moscow (Ambagtsheer et al. 2014b: 11, 15, 18). If the route to the illegal transaction is taken into account there is no difficulty in understanding these price differences: almost all the people interviewed became involved in illegal transplantation through a kinship or friendship network in their own country that made them aware of the possibility of obtaining a transplant abroad, and which assisted them in arranging travel and covering the costs. These transactions, spread over a large number of countries, covertly organized, on the one hand, but also through friendly and affective relations on the other, do not generate a market understood as an institution, and there is no reason to believe that prices signal a relative scarcity of resources.

To conclude these theoretical considerations, I would like to emphasize that illegal transactions are different from market transactions. The market as a social institution is one arena of exchange among many others, characterized by *peaceful, anonymous competition* for the control of economic opportunities through the "haggling of the market," where the *ability to pay* plays the central part and where disputes are settled by *law* and the "legitimate use of violence." In contrast, illegal transactions are regulated by the use, or the threat, of *violence*; they require *secrecy*, and need to transgress the *social and material frontiers* between illegal and legal worlds. It is for this reason that market theory is of little use for understanding illegal transactions in organ transplantation. These transactions are specific economic forms characterized by violence, secrecy, and the trespassing of frontiers. The next section of the chapter illustrates this approach.

## Illegal Transactions: Violence, Globalization, and the "Work of Concealment"

In the mid-1990s transplant professionals began to realize that some of their patients were going abroad to buy kidneys. This realization did not follow from police investigations, uncovering the secrecy concealing illegal transactions. It was much simpler: patients were moving from waiting lists and the dialysis program to the list of people in need of post-transplant follow-up, immunosuppressive drugs, and the complex management of the rejection episodes. There is consequently a significant literature on the medical outcomes of so-called transplant tourism originating in countries such as Canada, the United States, the United Kingdom, and many countries of Continental Europe.[5] Some of the information provided by these studies could be of use in the present inquiry; but their primary goal is to provide a medical assessment of the quality of the surgery performed, the difficulties of follow-up, and the effectiveness of these transplants compared with those performed in the home country, and so they contain little that is directly relevant to the illegal dimension of these transactions.

There is also a significant amount of literature on kidney vendors, which is of use in assessing the question of violence in this specific form of illegal transaction. There is also information provided by inquiries into the issue of transplant tourism aimed at dismantling the illegal networks that support transplant tourism. The HOTT project funded by the European Commission[6] is particularly useful for understanding the functioning of the illegal transactions in transplant tourism, notably for gauging the importance of the material frontier when those who benefit from organ trafficking are brought before a court.

[5] See for example Prasad et al. (2006) and Sajjad et al. (2008). The medical outcome of these illegal transplantations is not so significantly different from legal ones.

[6] The HOTT project (<http://hottproject.com/home.html>) was created at the initiative of the Erasmus Medical Center Rotterdam (Netherlands), Lund University (Sweden), the Bulgarian Center for Bioethics (Bulgaria), and the Academic Society for the Research of Religion (Romania). The project aims at studying "Trafficking in Human Beings for the Purpose of Organ Removal" in order to increase public awareness. The HOTT project receives financial support from the Prevention and Fight against Crime Program of the European Commission.

### *Violence*

In the case of organ transplantation, some philosophers who are influenced by a libertarian conception of freedom consider consent to be effective even when given by a man being threatened with a gun—the man would always have the option of choosing death rather than giving his consent (Taylor 2005: chapter 3). This position is rather extreme, but Taylor insists that if one accepts violence as a sufficient cause for nullifying a contract, then many workers could claim that their consent to work is tainted with violence, or the prospect of dying from starvation. This formal view of law and violence is challenged by material perspectives which distinguish illegal violence from that which is deemed legal. Contrary to the "flat earthism" of the economistic libertarian view, social conventions distinguish between a man constrained to work under the threat of hunger and a man constrained to work under the threat of a gun. Furthermore, whatever libertarian philosophers might maintain, most societies distinguish between selling one's work and selling a part of one's body.

In the present case, violence is directed mainly to the sellers. What is meant by violence here? Direct physical violence is barely mentioned; violence is more indirect since, most of the time, it is related to poverty aggravated by indebtedness in countries where there is no safety net beyond that provided by family members. Violence takes the form of duress, biased information, straightforward lies, and deductions made from the payment promised before the kidney is sold. Fieldwork done in Egypt and India has highlighted two different situations. In Egypt, where a ban on the commercialization of kidneys is not enforced because of the high level of corruption in the country, most transplants involving a living donor are tainted by illegal arrangements for compensating the donor through the extended family. Besides these illegal transactions between Egyptian citizens, illegal Sudanese migrants are coerced into selling a kidney (Coalition for Organ-Failure Solutions 2011: 7, 10). Because of their illegal situation few of them—actually twelve out of fifty-nine victims identified—agreed to testify, for fear that their participation in an illegal transaction would incriminate them. The approach taken by brokers is described by one of the sellers:

> I left Sudan after suffering from prison and torture there . . . I met a friend in Sudan who advised and helped me get to Egypt. He took care of everything in Sudan, obtaining a passport and the procedures. I flew to Cairo and met him again and stayed with him and his family in his apartment in Cairo. After some weeks his family stopped feeding me. I had no money for food and I began to fall ill. He then told me that I needed to sell my kidney to raise money for my stay and help my situation.
>
> (Sudanese seller quoted in Coalition for Organ-Failure Solutions 2011: 15)

This story, among many others, describes what can be called a *capture process*, in which the victim is initially assisted, but then channeled into a situation into which they are trapped because they have no money, no job, and a debt to the former "helper," and thus no other alternative than selling a kidney. In some other cases violence is more direct, the "helper" managing to obtain the kidney without the consent of the Sudanese migrant:

> I came to Egypt by way of smuggling. I knew an old Egyptian who brought me to Cairo . . . Our relationship increased and he treated me like a son . . . I didn't know what I could do in return for him exactly . . . Soon I began to complain about pain in my right side. He said he could send me to a clever doctor, at a pharmacy, who gave me medicine and injection drugs for the pain. One day when I was tired, he called the pharmacy doctor to come and give me the injection, and then I slept and lost consciousness and later found myself in the hospital. [Actually, he had had his organ removed.]
>
> (Sudanese seller quoted in Coalition for Organ-Failure Solutions 2011: 15–16)

In India, the capture process documented by researchers is not about single persons or illegal migrants, but overwhelmingly about poor married people whose life is overshadowed by a debt that they cannot repay. The average monthly household income of the 153 people identified as kidney sellers, 83 percent of them married, is USD 54, about 60 percent of the average Indian monthly income (Coalition for Organ-Failure Solutions 2014: 28). These debts have different origins, such as marriage, loss of job, substance abuse, children's education, being widowed, or family illness.

In both countries payment created difficulties. In Egypt the money promised ranges between USD 5,000 and USD 40,000; seven sellers received less—one received nothing—but five sellers received the full amount of the money promised, up to USD 25,000 in the case of a buyer coming from a Persian Gulf country (Coalition for Organ-Failure Solutions 2011: 19). Curiously, these prices are high, because an Egyptian seller receives, on average, USD 2,000 for a kidney. In India, some people received nothing (4 percent of the 153 people interviewed), whereas the money paid to other sellers ranged from USD 200–1,000 (58 percent) to USD 4,000 (2 percent), with an average price of USD 1,170 (Coalition for Organ-Failure Solutions 2014: 34). Price variations are not addressed in the report; however, it seems to depend heavily on the status and behavior of the buyer (for example, in the case of the buyer from the Gulf area) and, obviously, on the situation of the seller, according to the level of their debt and weak social position, for example, as a woman or a maid, as exemplified in the two following cases:

> My husband convinced me that many of our problems will be solved if I do this and we could live a happy life. He said we would receive much money so that we can make a separate house because we are two wives with him. He also told me that we would get more money for my kidney than his.

> A Malayalam [an Indian language mainly from the south of the country] lady asked me to give my kidney to her husband when I was working as a maid in her home. She gave me Rs 1 000 [about 20 US dollars] as my salary after they took my kidney.
>
> (Two women sellers in India quoted in Coalition for Organ-Failure Solutions 2014: 32)

What about the buyer? Violence is not a relevant category for them. Instead, the HOTT report devoted to the people who travel abroad to buy a kidney transplant stresses the fact that contact with a broker is barely mentioned, and none of them complained about violence (Ambagtsheer et al. 2014b). Usually buyers were told that there was a chance of obtaining a transplant abroad by their family or their friends; some of them arranged the connection with the medical facility and even helped to cover the cost. It is important to bear in mind that in a significant number of cases these buyers are returning to the country in which they were born and where they still have close family members.[7] This is the case of three Swedish patients (from the five people interviewed), one from Iraq, and two from Iran, all of whom went back to their mother country to get a transplant. This is legal for an Iranian citizen; and this is also the case with four patients from the Netherlands who went back to their mother country to get a transplant (one to China and three to Pakistan).

In order to go beyond these remarks about the violence suffered by the seller, it is necessary to consider a morphological dimension of these illegal transactions that, without exception, involve people coming from different countries. Globalization is a key element of illegal transactions in the domain of kidney transplantation.

### Globalization

The existence of illegal transactions involving actors distributed among many countries means that these transactions are global, as is the case for the majority of market exchange in our current globalized economic world. The global dimension is also evident when we consider the legal framework that could prevent or at least contain these illegal transactions (Cohen 2015), as is also the case with the legal framework necessary for the smooth functioning of market exchange—consider, for example, how complex it is to develop international laws relating to bankruptcy (Halliday and Carruthers 2009). However, it is still necessary to distinguish between market exchanges and illegal transactions.

[7] About 33 percent of the twenty-two patients interviewed are of this kind; if we add patients going to a country close to their own mother country (for example, Colombia–Curacao, Sri Lanka–India, Iraq–Pakistan), then the percentage rises to 41 percent.

In the case of illegal transplantations on a global scale, people move from one country to another in order to gain access to higher-quality medical services or just because these services are unavailable in their home country. Glenn Cohen makes clear in his comprehensive study of medical tourism that transplant tourism involves countries with different levels of regulation, so that what might be illegal in the patient's country is legal, or potentially so, in another. In this sense, globalization and legal discontinuities make it more difficult to contain illegal transactions. However, in his chapter (Cohen 2015: chapter 7) devoted to transplant tourism being cast in terms of (black) markets, Cohen misses some crucial elements of these transactions, because he focuses upon buying, selling, and brokerage; also important are the movements that make such transactions possible, because they are directly related to the transgression of legal, social, and material frontiers.

Transplantation surgery is for the most part a national affair: surgeons, patients, and the organ donor are usually all citizens of the same country; where there are comprehensive regulations concerning who can donate an organ to a relative the patient and the donor are socially close. However, this purely national situation may also arise for illegal transactions where state administration is weak, and regulations go unenforced; this latter situation is reported by the Coalition for Organ-Failure Solutions study of Indian sellers. But apart from this last case, movements across borders are a common feature of illegal transactions. Country to country movements were already apparent in the 1980s, when patients went from Saudi Arabia to the United States to obtain a (legal) transplant, because there were no transplant teams in Saudi Arabia: "South" to "North" medical tourism. Now the situation is much more complicated, because there are significant numbers of surgeons trained in transplant surgery in Europe and North America who are able to perform a kidney transplant in their own countries (India, Pakistan, Egypt, Turkey, and so on). Consequently, current flows in transplant tourism are either the other way round, with European and North American patients going to Asia and the Middle East ("North" to "South" medical tourism) or involve movements between the latter countries ("South" to "South" medical tourism).

These movements take four general forms (see Table 3.1) according to the countries (A, B, C) involved. In all cases, the surgeon—that is to say, the medical facility in which the graft is performed—is the focal point upon which sellers and buyers converge. One of the reports provided by the HOTT project (Ambagtsheer et al. 2014a) makes it possible to elaborate these cases.

In all these forms of medical tourism, the surgeon's location determines the meeting point, because medical facilities cannot be easily moved, so that

Table 3.1. Country to country movements involving countries A, B, and C

| | Case 1 | Case 2 | Case 3 | Case 4 |
|---|---|---|---|---|
| Patient–Buyer | B | B | A | B |
| Seller | B | A | B | C |
| Surgeon | A | A | A | A |

buyer and seller must come to the hospital in which the surgeon is working.[8] Case 1 is typified by the initial phase of the Netcare Case, when from 2003 to 2010 a series of illegal transactions took place where both the buyer and the seller traveled from Israel for an operation in Durban, South Africa carried out in one of the largest healthcare groups, Netcare. This was also the initial modus operandi in the Rosenbaum case. Rosenbaum was a broker who operated from 2001 to 2009, offering Israeli organ donors to patients and helping them coordinate a cover story so that they could deceive hospital staff in different parts of the United States. The second case differs from the Netcare case, in which the seller and the surgeon are from the same country, and the buyer is the only person moving back and forth. This case is not mentioned in the HOTT report. The third case is illustrated by the Rosenbaum case during its final phase, when Israeli sellers came to the United States to sell a kidney to patients from the orthodox Jewish community. The third case is certainly the most common. It is important to bear in mind the fact that people move in *and* out of the country in which the illegal transplant occurs. Brazilian sellers come back with only one kidney and several thousand US dollars which are supposed to change their lives in their home country, while the Israeli buyer returns with a grafted kidney in order to receive drugs and the post-operative follow-up, and a significant subsidy from the government and the health insurance company. Finally, the fourth case covers the Netcare case and the Medicus Clinic case (the name of a privately run clinic performing illegal kidney transplantation in Priština, Kosovo in 2008).

These cases illustrate the role of discrepancies between national legislations: Iran has had a legally regulated market for kidney transplantations since 1987, and the first Israeli law prohibiting brokerage in kidney transplantation was passed only in 2008.[9] Other countries are notoriously corrupt, offering many exploitable loopholes for brokers and surgeons eager to make money from illegal transplantations. Furthermore, this also explains how these illegal—or

[8] It can happen that a surgeon will escort one of his patients traveling abroad for a transplant, as was the case with some Israeli surgeons in the 1980s (Friedlander 2002).

[9] According to Zvika Orr this law is rather ambiguous, the prohibition being quite mild with no punishment for those who buy and sell kidneys, and fairly light punishment for the broker (maximum imprisonment of three years, or a fine of up to 44,000 euros) (Orr 2014: 43).

not fully legal in the case of Israeli patients—transactions can be tolerated. Such discrepancies seem to be vagaries in legislation, making it easier for patients to align their moral beliefs with their illegal behavior. If HOTT reports stress the difficulties that patients have in facing ethical questions about the buying of a kidney, noticing in some cases the existence of a "guilty conscience" (Ambagtsheer et al. 2014b: 12, 16, 20), the picture offered by Israeli patients is quite different, because most of the buyers interviewed were reluctant to incriminate the brokers, considering them to be "life savers" (Ambagtsheer et al. 2014a: 20).

### *Secrecy and Frontiers*

Discrepancies between legislations necessitate different levels of secrecy for conducting illegal transactions; according to one Israeli buyer, all the information was common knowledge among dialysis patients, and non-governmental organizations assisted patients through media fundraising campaigns (Ambagtsheer et al. 2014a: 20). Whatever their frequency, illegal transactions require secrecy because they transgress the legal–illegal frontier; consequently, one can consider the *specific work to be done to make the move from the legal to the illegal world possible.* This is the key point in understanding illegal transactions, and the way in which they differ from market transactions; obviously, this concealment work is not specific to illegal transplant activities, because it is also present in many other cases studied in this book (see notably Hübschle's chapter on rhino horn and Mackenzie and Yates' chapter on looted antiquities, in this volume).

The HOTT report gives sufficient information about three cases investigated by local lawyers and policemen. Here the main problem came from the social and material frontiers demarcating the medical facility involved in illegal transactions. Such transactions require the work of a significant number of people and the management of a significant amount of documents. Hence illegal transactions generate and leave behind many signs and traces that can be tracked by police investigators, and by social scientists trying to understand the social practices that are underlying these illegalities.[10] The three cases documented in the HOTT reports offer the possibility of understanding the *work of concealment* creating the secrecy necessary for transgressing the legal–illegal frontier.

[10] The features common to both groups are highlighted by the Italian micro-historian Carlo Ginsburg in his "evidential paradigm" (Ginzburg 1980; see also Boltanski 2012), which directs attention to apparently minor evidence through which the real action or the real actor lurking behind the scenes can be identified.

In the Netcare Clinic case in Durban, several whistleblowers reported illegal transplantations—a person working in the clinic acting according to her conscience, a surgeon, and a social scientist; but paradoxically, the key person was one broker who "opened a charge of theft in which he openly stated that an organ supplier had run off with money that he had received in advance, which was subsequently established to be true" (Ambagtsheer et al. 2014a: 11). Police investigators then seized computers, transplant files related to recipients, and blood bank records relating to recipients and various potential sellers. This material evidence permitted them to identify the person who had altered "non-related" to "related" on the document necessary to perform the transplant in the clinic. Other evidence came from tracking the money paid to brokers and surgeons involved in these illegal transactions. In this case, it was the breach created by a broker infuriated by the seller's absconding that broke the social frontier, revealing material evidence of the way in which illegal transactions had been transmuted into formally legal transactions.

The Medicus Clinic case is somewhat different. It was initiated by immigration officers at Priština airport puzzled by foreigners coming to Kosovo for heart treatment when their country of origin was supposed to offer treatment of higher quality. Pursuing their inquiry, they discovered that all the patients were attending the same clinic, so they decided to detain one returning to Turkey and ask him to show them his scars. The man finally admitted that his kidney had been removed in the clinic, which was subsequently found to be true. Documents needed to transgress the material frontier had not been done carefully enough.

The Rosenbaum case came as a surprise because, initially, the issue was the corruption of a public official and tax evasion within the orthodox Jewish community in New Jersey. One of the fraudulent real-estate actors involved in the financial issue became an informant; and by chance he told the police that one of his relatives was buying a kidney through a broker. The social frontier no longer functioned, and the informant agreed to arrange a series of meetings between an FBI agent and Rosenbaum, ending with the first payment for buying a kidney, upon which Rosenbaum was arrested.

In all these cases social and material frontiers were the key weaknesses of illegal transactions, which I take as proof of the central importance of the work of concealment that has to be done in order to achieve the level of secrecy necessary for conducting illegal transactions.

## Conclusion

Illegal transactions should be conceptualized as sui generis phenomena. They belong to the broad scope of the systems of relations in which resources move from hand to hand, and there is no reason to think that market exchanges should be treated as the appropriate model or benchmark for other forms of transaction (Steiner 2016: chapter 5).

Markets are characterized by *competition*, *anonymity*, and *free movement*: competition is a form of peaceful struggle between parties that concludes with a contract in which reciprocal obligations are agreed, including the fact that any future disagreement will be settled in a given jurisdiction, and involving the transfer of property rights. Exchange is conducted under a logic of anonymity, so that customers are not differentiated by their personal traits, these being irrelevant to their capacity to meet their market obligations; people may enter or leave the market at will according to the old motto of economic liberalism: "*laissez-faire, laissez passer*," once legal provisions are taken into account. Illegal transactions are organized according to a different set of characteristics: *violence*, *secrecy*, and *frontiers*. The existence of frontiers appears to be the central sociological element for understanding how illegal transactions are processed. *Concealment work* is thus necessary to the maintenance of secrecy, without which flows of resources and people cannot move from the illegal to the legal worlds, and vice versa. It is also a key element in the complex process through which illegal transactions can be linked with the legal world of exchange, as exemplified by those illegal transactions in organ transplantation that were recently documented.

## References

Ambagtsheer, Frederic, Martin Gunnarson, and Jessica de Jong et al. 2014a. "Trafficking in Human Beings for the Purpose of Organ Removal: A Case Study Report." <http://www.hottproject.com>.

Ambagtsheer, Frederic, Martin Gunnarson, and Linda van Balen et al. 2014b. "Organ Recipients Who Paid for Kidney Transplantations Abroad: A Report." <http://www.hottproject.com>.

Andreas, Peter, and Joel Wallman. 2009. "Illicit Markets and Violence: What Is the Relationship?" *Crime, Law and Social Change* 52(3): pp. 225–9.

Boltanski, Luc. 2012. *Enigmes et complots. Une enquête à propos des enquêtes*. Paris: Gallimard.

Chimeli, Ariaster, and Rodrigo Soares. 2011. *The Use of Violence in Illegal Markets: Evidence from the Mahogany Trade in the Brazilian Amazon*. Discussion paper no. 5923. Bonn: Institute for the Study of Labor.

Coalition for Organ-Failure Solutions. 2011. "Sudanese Victims of Organ Trafficking in Egypt: A Preliminary Evidence-Based, Victim-Centered Report." <http://www.cofs.org>.

Coalition for Organ-Failure Solutions. 2014. "Human Trafficking for Organ Removal in India: An Evidence-Based, Victim-Centered Report." <http://www.cofs.org>.

Cohen, Glenn. 2015. *Patients with Passports: Medical Tourism, Law and Ethics*. Oxford: Oxford University Press.
Dewey, Matías. 2012. "Illegal Police Protection and the Market for Stolen Vehicles in Buenos Aires." *Journal of Latin American Studies* 44(4): pp. 679–702.
Dewey, Matías. 2014. *Crisis and the Emergence of Illicit Markets: A Pragmatist View on Economic Action outside the Law*. MPIfG discussion paper 14/18. Cologne: Max Planck Institute for the Study of Societies.
Fligstein, Neil. 2001. *The Architecture of Markets: Economic Sociology for the 21st Century*. Princeton, NJ: Princeton University Press.
Friedlander, Michael M. 2002. "The Right to Sell or Buy a Kidney: Are We Failing Our Patients?" *Lancet* 359(9310): pp. 971–3.
Ginzburg, Carlo. 1980. "Signes, traces, pistes: Racines d'un paradigme de l'indice." French translation. *Le débat* 6: pp. 3–44.
Gunby, Phil. 1983. "Bill Introduced to Thwart Kidney Brokerage." *Journal of the American Journal of Transplantation* 250(17): pp. 2263–4.
Halliday, Terence, and Bruce Carruthers. 2009. *Bankrupt: Global Lawmaking and Systemic Financial Crisis*. Stanford, CA: Stanford University Press.
Hirschman, Albert. 1970. *Exit, Voice and Loyalty: Responses to Decline in Firms, Organizations, and States*. Cambridge, MA: Harvard University Press.
Orr, Zvika. 2014. "International Norms, Local Worlds: An Ethnographic Perspective on Organ Trafficking in the Israeli Context." In *Organ Transplantation: Ethical, Legal and Psychological Aspects: Global Issues, Local Solutions*, edited by Willem Weimar, Michael Bos, and Jan van Busschbach, pp. 39–49. Lengerich: Pabst Science Publisher.
Prasad, Ramesh, A. Shukla, M. Huang et al. 2006. "Outcomes of Commercial Renal Transplantation: A Canadian Experience." *Transplantation* 82(9): pp. 1130–5.
Proudhon, Pierre-Joseph. 1926 [1840]. *Qu'est-ce que la propriété ?* In *Œuvres complètes de P.-J. Proudhon*. Paris: Rivière.
Sajjad, Iman, L. S. Baines, P. Patel, M. O. Salifu, and R. M. Jindal. 2008. "Commercialization of Kidney Transplants: A Systematic Review of Outcomes in Recipients and Donors." *American Journal of Nephrology* 28(5): pp. 744–54.
Simmel, Georg. 1999 [1908]. *Sociologie: Études sur les formes de la socialisation*. French translation. Paris: Presses Universitaires de France.
Steiner, Philippe. 2010. *La transplantation d'organes: Un commerce nouveau entre les êtres humains*. Paris: Gallimard.
Steiner, Philippe. 2015. "Les organes humains: Du bannissement du marché au don contesté." In *Marchés contesté: Quand le marché rencontre la morale*, edited by Philippe Steiner and Marie Trespeuch, pp. 251–78. Toulouse: Presses Universitaires du Mirail.
Steiner, Philippe. 2016. *Donner . . . Une histoire de l'altruisme*. Paris: Presses Universitaires de France.
Taylor, James. 2005. *Stakes and Kidneys: Why Markets in Human Body Parts Are Morally Imperative*. Aldershot: Ashgate.
Weber, Max. 1968 [1920]. *Economy and Society: An Outline of Interpretative Sociology*. New York: Bedminster Press.

# 4

# What Is Grey about the "Grey Market" in Antiquities?

*Simon Mackenzie and Donna Yates*

## Introduction

The global market in antiquities has been described as a "grey market" in discussions by various commentators on the problem of illicit cultural property. In this contribution, we set out to examine that terminology, ultimately providing (we hope) a definitive breakdown of the meanings and implications of the idea of "greyness" as it applies to this particular illicit market. As we shall see, the term "grey market" has been applied fairly liberally by researchers working on illicit markets in cultural objects and is in danger of becoming a generic, but unrefined synonym for the interface between certain illicit practices in excavation and the public antiquities trade. It would therefore seem helpful at this point in the development of the research evidence based on illicit antiquities—and particularly in the context of the theme and other contributions in this book—to pause and reflect on what we mean when we observe greyness in this market.[1]

In general, "grey" has become a term used to suggest a liminal or hard to assess zone between two poles. Often these poles are those identified by Mayntz in her chapter in this volume: il/legal, im/moral, and/or in/appropriate. In such usage, we find the assessment of the meaning of certain forms of social action described as "a grey area": in other words, hard to judge and open to argument either way, where, for example, the law or an institutional or personal code of ethics does not seem to provide a firm basis for pronouncement. Grey areas

[1] This chapter is based on research funded by the European Research Council under the European Union's Seventh Framework Programme (FP7/2007-2013)/ERC Grant agreement n° 283873 GTICO.

such as these may be only foggy, in that a correct interpretation is possible but hard to discern, or more genuinely grey in that the law, ethics, or social normativity in fact do not provide definitive guidance.

As well as questions of interpretation of the meaning of action, greyness can be used to signify a mixing of two types of black/dirty and white/clean things; for example, grey water for recycled household use is neither clean nor entirely tainted. In a similar vein, researchers speak of a grey literature, which is neither openly published nor entirely restricted from access upon request or negotiation. This includes the internal institutional reports of bodies such as government departments or the police. Grey can thus mean "neither one thing nor the other" in the context of mixed origins of constituent parts, or in the context of residing in a social realm that is neither fully public nor private.

Finally, we should distinguish from our discussion the economic use of the term "grey market," which is the normal use of the term. In discussions of international trade, a grey market in this usual sense is a parallel market. Parallel markets are not illegal, but the objects they move are unauthorized for sale in a particular jurisdiction by their manufacturers, who have developed different versions of the product for different global markets. Grey imports of cars, for example, may produce problems for consumers who find their vehicle to be unsupported by a national network of dealers and parts providers in a jurisdiction in which the car was never intended for sale. There are other versions of grey or parallel markets along these lines, but we do not need to go into detail here as the point is simply to note that the developed use of the term "grey market" to refer to the international trade in antiquities is at odds with the usual use of the term in the literature on international trade from the perspective of the disciplines taught in business schools.

Two dimensions of the interfaces between legality and illegality in markets that the editors draw out in their introduction to this book are (i) that definitions of legality and illegality are contested in the social practices of market actors, and (ii) that the distinction between legality and illegality is complicated by the intermingling of both types of activities in markets. These propositions map roughly onto a threefold distinction, which we will argue for in this chapter in relation to understanding the illicit antiquities trade as a "grey market," building on the general observations about greyness laid out above. That distinction is between: (a) an uncertainty or contest in the ethical, legal, or normative construction of the issue, (b) the practical mixing of licit and illicit chains of supply, and (c) the changing social/market and legal classification of individual artifacts as they are laundered through multiple transactions and jurisdictions over time. In summary, then, both of the editorial's dimensions of interfaces between legality and illegality are well reflected in studies of the global antiquities market.

In respect of the first point, there is illegality at each stage of the market (at source, in transit, and in terms of trade and collection in market countries). Archaeological looting is a criminal offence in most source countries, cross-border trafficking will usually breach a number of legal provisions, and trade in the international marketplace with knowledge or serious suspicion of illicit origins will also usually constitute a crime (Prott and O'Keefe 1984, 1989). There can be no doubt that the international legal regime and its constituent domestic jurisdictional parts consider trade in illicit antiquities to be illegal. However, at all of the stages of transaction there are deviance-normalizing and neutralizing engagements with the issues exercised by the actors and constituencies involved.

Looters have in some texts been characterized as "subsistence diggers" (e.g. Matsuda 2005), drawing them directly into line with the discourse the editors of the present volume identify as "survival strategies," in respect of which they suggest tolerance has been increasing since the financial crisis. It has even been argued that we should recognize looting as a moral and human right "where there is no viable alternative economic means for subsistence diggers to access their human rights to clean water, food and medicine" (Hardy 2015). One can equally, however, find studies that debunk this construction of looters working only to put food on the table. In recent known cases it is clear that the looters were career criminals, close enough to accepted definitions of organized criminals to merit discussion in those terms (Mackenzie and Davis 2014; Felch and Frammolino 2011).

In the cross-border trafficking phase we find the value and purpose of export restrictions disputed by market-oriented "cultural internationalists" (Merryman 1986). Source states are considered "retentionist" by these neo-liberal commentators, who would like to see cultural property the subject of worldwide free trade. They consider export prohibitions to be a causal mechanism in the formation of international black markets in cultural property, since by restricting the buying pool only to national collectors, export controls create a situation where higher prices are available for antiquities or significant artworks outside the jurisdiction in which they can be legally sold (Bator 1983).

Finally, in the international marketplace, it is clear that high-end antiquities buyers contest some of the premises upon which the current legal regime is based, and engage in practices of "creative compliance," which use the letter of the law to defeat its spirit (McBarnet 2003). Less clear is whether this reflects a genuine clash of values, or something more like a process of Matzian neutralization (Matza 1964), where the general ethical and normative value structure underpinning the governance of trade in antiquities is largely accepted but traders engage in occasional moments of drift where they are temporarily dislocated from conventional normativity and open to the performance of a criminal act, using discourse/narrative as the mechanism to achieve that drift into deviance (Mackenzie and Yates 2016).

It is primarily in respect of the editors' second point—the mixing of legal and illegal supply chains in the market—that, as we shall see, the antiquities market has been considered "grey" rather than black or white. Market actors tend to refer to "the legitimate market" (the "white"), which they consider to be separate from the market in illegitimate artifacts (the "black" market), presenting a picture of an above-board trade whose reputation is sullied by criminal traffickers engaged in a parallel but separate enterprise. In the black-market paradigm, illicit trades are the province of underground private sales and if the so-called legitimate trade is found to be involved it is because either the dealer was a "bad apple" or he was duped.

As we shall see, however, the weight of research evidence suggests that analysts should reject the black-market hypothesis and work instead with a view of the antiquities trade as "grey," in the sense that what has been called the legitimate market is empirically a mix of legality and illegality at the demand end of the supply chain. Dealers, collectors, auction houses, and museums are regularly the subject of complaints about their involvement in trading illicit cultural and archaeological goods, which often result in successful repatriation claims in respect of the objects by their countries of origin. Within the grey-market paradigm, while it has been clear for some time that we are talking about a market which is in some respects dirty, it has not really been analytically clear exactly how illicit artifacts are intermixed with legal trades, in other words the mechanics by which the market is polluted. Some of our research in the Trafficking Culture project over the past few years has helped to clarify the polluting mechanism that greys the market in this sense (Mackenzie and Davis 2014).

As we shall see in the next section, the mixing type of greyness mentioned above of being neither definitively one thing nor another applies well to the antiquities trade, which is in another inflection of the term "greyness," similar to "grey literature," at once out in the open but hidden to an extent, neither fully public nor entirely private. The greyness in this sense might be summarized as meaning that the activities of the trade are slightly obscure or inscrutable to the average person.

## The Functioning of the Illicit Trade in Antiquities

The term "antiquity" is commonly used to mean a human-made object created in the past and found at an archaeological site. There is no set definition of how old an object has to be to be considered an antiquity, rather the essence of an antiquity is that it was constructed then deposited before the present.

Antiquities are a sub-set of what are termed "cultural objects" or "cultural property." Cultural property is related to ideas of heritage and experiences of cultural identity, but objects classified as cultural property need not have been made in the past or deposited at an archaeological site. Many countries legally define antiquities by clear "older than" dates: for example, anything over 100 years old is considered an antiquity. These dates vary from jurisdiction to jurisdiction. For the most part, though, antiquities are equivalent to artifacts: the terms are and will be used interchangeably.

Artifacts are the primary unit of archaeological investigation and archaeological investigation has provided a significant amount of our collective knowledge of humanity's past. Yet it is the careful observation of these artifacts within deposited strata that allow archaeologists to draw conclusions about our ancestors. Determining how an artifact relates to the surrounding matrix of other artifacts and architectural features allows an archaeologist to slowly reconstruct the sequence of cultural and environmental events that brought about its deposition. In archaeology this concept is called "context" and artifact context is vital to everything that an archaeologist does. An antiquity with context adds another piece to the complicated puzzle of understanding ancient lives. An antiquity without context, it has been argued, is archaeologically worthless.

When an archaeologist excavates a site, the majority of their time is spent recording artifact context via forms, notes, photographs, plans, drawings, and digital scanning. This is because the act of conducting archaeology destroys context: once a site is disturbed by excavation it cannot be reconstructed. Thus unprofessional excavations at archaeological sites inevitably destroy vital context which can never be recovered. In archaeological looting, then, the theft of the object from its rightful owner (usually the source country, although in some jurisdictions it may be the private landowner) is strongly associated with the destruction of the context of the find, obliterating our only window into the past. The looting of antiquities is always destructive.

This destruction extends beyond archaeology and can translate into economic loss for communities that live near archaeological sites. Many countries with rich archaeological pasts are currently economically poor. These countries depend on the cultural tourism that comes from foreign visitors to their spectacular archaeological sites. However, the very countries that outsiders most equate with intact archaeological wonders (for example Peru, Cambodia, or Jordan) are naturally hotspots for antiquities looting and trafficking. The despoliation of these sites challenges the viability of vital national tourism industries and threatens the livelihood of anyone involved (Brodie 2010).

Besides economic destruction, there are indications that the looting of archaeological sites results in challenges to community cohesion and perceptions of security. Antiquities are tangible objects but they often serve as a physical manifestation of intangible concepts that underlie the social fabric of local and descendant groups. Threats to these objects are felt as threats to culture, and the trafficking of antiquities to Western markets, especially in post-colonial situations, is interpreted as a racist challenge to indigenous sovereignty and cultural dignity. It outwardly confirms the lived experience of social inequality between the developing and the developed world.

There is incredible variation in the structure of antiquities trafficking. It can range from objects passing through numerous countries and changing hands many times before ultimately being sold to a collector or museum (for example, the Cambodian statue-smuggling networks described by Mackenzie and Davis 2014), to situations where the object passes through no hands, with the collectors themselves digging up the artifact, transporting it, and keeping it (for example, the "pothunters" who loot Native American sites in the southwestern United States). That said, it is possible to present common features seen in various antiquities trafficking networks and cases.

At source, "looters," meaning the people who actually dig antiquities out of the ground, are often poor locals with few other economic options. They may take significant risks to locate sellable artifacts: there are many cases of looters dying in cave-ins or from suffocation, and they are also the group in the trafficking chain most likely to be caught and prosecuted. For their efforts, they are paid a derisory percentage of the final sale value of the antiquities they find (Brodie 1998).

Because antiquities that come from archaeological sites are unknown before they are looted, there are no official records of their existence. That, coupled with the remoteness of many archaeological sites, makes it incredibly difficult to protect against or even detect archaeological looting. How does a country protect an archaeological site that it does not yet know exists? Furthermore, as many archaeologically rich countries are located in the developing world, the systematic and structural deficits of local and national authorities may allow antiquities trafficking networks to function. Underfunded, ineffectual, or corrupt police and customs abet all kinds of commodities smuggling, antiquities among them (Yates 2014a, 2014b).

Thus at source, the model antiquities network would be economically marginal locals digging at a nearby, poorly protected archaeological site. They would then sell their finds to an in-country broker or intermediary with connections to corrupt inspection or enforcement authorities, who could be paid to look the other way when the objects are exported.

During the transit phase of antiquities trafficking, objects follow routes based on the nature of the objects themselves and the needs of both the intermediaries and the ultimate buyers. In some cases, antiquities are moved directly from their country of origin to their country of sale: carried on flights, driven overland across a border, or shipped/posted. In other cases the objects are moved through one or more "transit ports," which physically distance the pieces from their illicit origins and, at times, result in the acquisition of import/export paperwork that supports the impression of legitimacy (Polk 2000).

Paperwork, then, is an important part of the transit stage. False customs declarations may allow shipments of antiquities to pass through customs checks. Valid paperwork for legally exportable antiquities may be used to traffic other antiquities that are not exportable (Kersel 2006). Weaker import restrictions in transit ports may result in antiquities that were illegally exported from their countries of origin acquiring legitimate export documentation as they pass through on their way to their final market. This documentation may be used later to create a false provenance narrative.

During transit, the model antiquities network would see the source end intermediary shipping the pieces through one or more transit ports on the way to the final market country. Export documentation for the pieces would list them as modern handicrafts or replicas and such replicas might be mixed in among the authentic artifacts. An official in the country of origin may have been bribed. The antiquities may seem to move in a nonsensical path (for example, from Egypt to Thailand to Dubai), but the path represents both known security weaknesses and differences in import and export regulation in each country. At each transit port, the shipment would obtain legitimate import and export documentation, which would eventually ease its transition into the ultimate market country where a suitable paper trail becomes useful in selling the item. In an alternative model a carrier might put an artifact in their cabin luggage, get on a plane, and bring it into the market country through security checkpoints that are screening for guns, not antiquities.

After the transit phase we move to the market phase, where antiquities enter the wider art market, usually in relatively wealthy developed-world countries that have either a long tradition of antiquities collecting (Western Europe, USA) or an elite class with significant spending power (China, UAE). It is at this stage that documentation acquired during the antiquities-trafficking process may be converted into a false provenance to allow for public sale. For example, a freshly looted artifact that passed through Switzerland on its way to being sold in New York might be presented to buyers as "property of an anonymous Swiss collector," with the implied understanding of "old money" selling off artifacts that were collected before restrictions were put in place. False provenance, then, is a narrative that casts a dodgy artifact as legitimate and is accompanied by the minimal amount of fraudulent or misleading paperwork needed to allow the piece to pass into the art market.

The model market end of the antiquities-smuggling chain, then, is where an artifact is exported from a transit port into a market country along with whatever paperwork it has acquired. The receiver of the piece is likely to be a high-level intermediary or dealer who may know or at least suspect the illicit origins of the piece, and who participates in the elite circles of the art market. That dealer then offers the piece for sale either quietly to private buyers or by consigning it to public auction. The dealer will say the piece was in an old family collection in a plausible foreign country, supporting this either with the available paperwork or with a persuasive but false narrative. The buyer may or may not believe this false provenance, but it will be considered sufficient for sale. The piece will be sold, sometimes along with a certificate of authenticity, but not a certificate of legality.

## Antiquities Market Features that Facilitate "Greying"

While the specifics of how the antiquities market can be considered "grey" will be discussed in the following sections, it is worth noting in preliminary observations and context for that discussion that there are several features particular to this trade that can be seen as facilitating the process of greying.

Research has identified certain individuals who, due to their position at the nexus between what might be termed the "black" and the "white" market for antiquities, allow for the functioning of the entire smuggling network. Termed "Janus figures" (Mackenzie and Davis 2014), these intermediaries are able to transition looted antiquities from their dubious origins into the high-class world of art sales through their connections on both sides. The Janus figures know at least some details about the looting and smuggling of the pieces and they know at least some details of their subsequent high-end sale: like Janus, they look in both directions.

The art market is traditionally opaque. Despite the large sums of money that change hands, the market functions on the basis of trust and reputation, not asking too many questions. This reflects an unspoken understanding that sales of art reflect the financial state of the wealthy sellers and an understanding that such financial matters are private. Thus art and antiquities sales are in effect somewhat "back-door," with no public record of the buyers and sellers that are connected through dealers. Even at public auction, both consigners and buyers are able to remain anonymous. In other words, it is an art-market tradition not to ask who is selling an antiquity, why they are selling it, or where they got it from.

There is no requirement that antiquities sale details be made public in most countries or to provide proof to buyers that an antiquities sale is legal. While there are various guidelines on good practice in codes of ethics and laws in various jurisdictions, there is no universally accepted standard for what constitutes seller or buyer due diligence when it comes to the ownership and import/export history of antiquities. The art market trains participants to not ask questions that may result in the divulging of problematic knowledge about the origins of a proposed purchase. For the most part, then, the antiquities trade relies on self-regulation of participants, which clearly does not work as there is no financial or social motivation for them to self-regulate.

Finally, the public has no access to most private antiquities collections and, in many jurisdictions, neither does the state. While some states may require collectors to register the antiquities that they own, others do not, including such collecting bastions as the United States and the United Kingdom. The opacity enveloping collections means that antiquities can disappear into the private market, not to be heard of until they surface again. The fact that the market has developed this terminology of "surfacing" highlights the routine nature of the effective disappearance of artifacts into the depths of the private collecting market.

## Use of the Concept of the Grey Market in the Literature on Illicit Antiquities

Let us revisit our threefold classification of antiquities market "greyness," mentioned above and further explicated in the following sections. We have identified greyness here as either (a) some type of normative indecipherability, (b) practical mixing, or (c) transition in individual object status/classification (and, of course, these three types are connected by an overlap in their coverage, where mixing leads to indecipherability, status transition complements general mixing, and so on). We can identify these approaches in the idea of the "grey market" with in the academic literature on the illicit antiquities trade (often implied in the context in which the term is used).

First, and most commonly, the market is described as grey to suggest that, in general or aggregate terms, streams of looted (illegal/black) antiquities are commingled with streams of recirculating (legal/white) antiquities to the point that it becomes impossible to say that the market as a whole is a legitimate or legal trade, as of course it generally purports to be. This mixing of licit and illicit produces a market that overall has the features and performs the functions of both a black market and a legal market, and so is close to the interpretation of "grey" as meaning "neither one thing nor the other" and rather displays properties of both black and white. The image is also one of pollution, where the white market is tainted by the insertion of black-market objects. One example of this polluted market imagery is references to the trade as a "murky shade of grey" (Bowman 2008: 226).

The second sense in which researchers have used the terminology of the grey market in analyses of the global trade in antiquities is on the level of the individual object, as opposed to the first sense, which applied to supply flows in the market in aggregate. Individual antiquities have been categorized as "white" (legally excavated and exported), "black" (looted and illegally exported), or "grey." In this sense grey antiquities were looted and so started out black but have become legally saleable through the operation of law. This can occur where in some jurisdictions a good faith purchase vests title to a stolen chattel in the bona fide purchaser (Redmond-Cooper 1997). It can also occur through the application of limitation periods which may bar a claim by a dispossessed owner, in this case the state from which the artifact was taken. These grey antiquities are therefore legal but, for some critics at least, still tainted ethically by the circumstances of their illicit origins, especially if a purported good faith purchase is suspected to have been a ruse in which "forum shopping" has been used to identify a soft-touch jurisdiction in which title to an object can be easily laundered.

The third sense in which the concept of a grey market has been applied to the antiquities trade considers the "grey market" to be something separate from the "legal" and the "illicit" trade (Bichler et al. 2013: figure 1). It is not clear, however, what the properties of that grey market are conceived as being if they are separate from an elision of the legal and the illicit parts of the trade. This interpretation of the grey market as a separate zone from the legal and the illicit trades seems to be at odds with all other uses of the idea of the grey market in the illicit antiquities literature. In Bichler et al.'s formulation, the grey market interfaces with both the legal and the illicit markets, but also contains transactions that are part of neither the legal nor the illicit zones of trade. The authors do not explain how that grey market is supposed to work outside both the legal and the illegal types of trade, but the model must mean that the grey market contains trades with regard to which we cannot be reasonably sure whether they are legal or illegal. On that interpretation, it is a different way of putting the first version of greyness mentioned above: the mixing of licit and illicit supply flows such that it becomes hard to tell them apart.

Fourth, and finally, there are psychological "grey areas" that have been identified in research on the illicit antiquities market and have been analyzed in terms of the techniques of neutralization that pervade market discourse. These are discursive tools that have been quite well recognized and written about in criminology and beyond (Maruna and Copes 2005), attenuating the "moral bind to law" (Matza 1964) via mechanisms of justification and excuse of illegal action in context (Scott and Lyman 1968; Mackenzie and Yates 2016).

In the following section we will review the first, second, and fourth types of greyness mentioned above, passing over the third type in the absence of a clear specification of its parameters, but in the likelihood that it is a reformulation of the first type. Then we will conclude with some thoughts about other relevant kinds of greyness beyond those explicitly discussed in the literature to date.

## Three Main Ways that the Market Might Be Considered Grey

### *Mixed Streams of Supply*

The most common proposition about the grey market in the literature is that the antiquities market may be considered to be grey based on the belief that the market is the confluence of a supply of legitimate antiquities and a supply of illegitimate antiquities that are impossible to distinguish from each other. In other words, white (licit) antiquities mix with black (illicit) antiquities to form a grey market and this grey market is allowed to flourish because of tolerance of the opaque business practices of the art market. This position implies that both looted and trafficked antiquities and legal and saleable antiquities will look roughly the same when they are presented on the market: lacking in provenance documents, import/export information, or excavation history.

Examples of this "mixed-supply" greyness proposition can readily be found in writing on the market. Mackenzie and Green write of the grey market as signifying that "the flows of licit and illicit objects are intermixed and therefore that, rather than being a market characterized by a 'clean' public trade and a 'dirty' private or underground trade, the supposedly clean public trade in antiquities is tainted 'grey' by the circulation therein of illicit antiquities" (Mackenzie and Green 2009: 154). Bowman Proulx observes that "the fact that legally obtained antiquities circulate side-by-side with illegally obtained objects further obfuscates the market and turns the issue from one of black and white to an ominous shade of grey" (Bowman Proulx 2011a). Alderman thinks "there is no distinct black market or white market for antiquities" (Alderman 2012). Visconti sees the antiquities market as "intrinsically opaque, so much so that we should think in terms of a 'grey market,' with licit and illicit dealings closely interwoven" (Visconti 2015). Brodie thinks "it is now clear that the antiquities market cannot be separated into legal and illegal components, but is better described as what criminologists call a 'grey' market. Legitimate actors and actions facilitate the trade of illegally acquired artefacts... the legal and illegal markets cannot exist apart" (Brodie 2012). Mackenzie sees a grey market in which illegitimate objects pass through the "legitimate" trade (Mackenzie 2011). Bowman Proulx has perhaps the most explicit definition of a grey market in this context, which she describes in a glossary entry in a crime handbook as follows: "Grey Market: A market that is neither definitively 'black' nor 'white' in terms of its legality. Grey markets instead exhibit dynamics of both the licit and the illicit" (Bowman Proulx 2011b).

The main problem with this interpretation of the idea of a grey market is that on this definition rarely would a market be definitively black or definitively white. It is very common for public markets in any goods to have an illicit side. Sometimes that illicit side is called a shadow or informal economy (Shapland and Ponsaers 2009), although those terms tend to describe an untaxed economy taking place outside the purview of official scrutiny rather than, as in the case of antiquities, a shadow that interfaces and ultimately merges with the formal, taxed supply chain. Criminologists, sociologists, anthropologists, and economists have produced a considerable wealth of studies of a wide variety of markets that all suggest that where there is legal trade there will be an undercurrent of illicit activity which interfaces with it and exploits the profit opportunities it presents (Naylor 2004a, 2014b, 2010; Ruggiero 1997; Passas 2003). In the present volume alone we can see plenty of examples of this in the studies of markets in diamonds (Engwicht), wildlife (Hübschle), organs (Steiner), and fake goods (Endres).

Thus a definition of greyness that places grey markets somewhere between the wholly black and wholly white is redundant, since so many purportedly legitimate markets are probably grey in that sense, although some will be more so than others. More sense and usefulness can be made of this "mixing streams" idea when we combine that type of greyness with the others covered below.

Interestingly, this argument presenting the market as grey due to mixed supply is used by both supporters of an unregulated trade in antiquities and supporters of tighter regulation or bans. Pro-market commentators often state that any given unprovenanced antiquity has a chance of being licit and because it is impossible to tell either way they should be "innocent until proven guilty." Anti-market commentators often assert that because the market is tainted by illicit objects, all unprovenanced antiquities should be treated as suspect. Either way, the idea of the antiquities market as grey because of a mixing of looted and unlooted antiquities assumes that such objects are truly indistinguishable. This will not always, and perhaps not even often, be the case.

Antiquities that left their countries of origin either via legal export or before relevant export restrictions were put in place might well have acquired documentation that proves their legitimacy. Since the seventeenth century, antiquities in private collections have been extensively published, displayed, declared on taxation and insurance forms, have appeared in wills, and have been the subject of academic study. When an object that is truly from an old European collection is offered for sale, this documentation is presented with the piece and it is immediately distinguishable from the unprovenanced antiquities surrounding it. An example of this is the sale at Christie's London of an ancient Egyptian statue depicting the scribe Sekhemka in 2014 by the Northampton Museum (UK). The statue had been in the private collection of the Marquess of Northampton who gifted the statue to the museum in 1870, placing the object firmly out of Egypt before that date. The piece sold for £15.8 million. The sale was controversial as it represented the movement of a publicly held antiquity into private hands and, ultimately, Northampton Museum lost their accreditation from Arts Council England over it. The response shows both how rare it is for a legitimate, legal antiquity to enter the market and how obvious that legality can be to observers. It is not impossible that there is a steady stream of undocumented but legal antiquities flowing from the grandmothers' attics of the world, but it does seem unlikely.

### *Changing Status of Individual Objects as They Pass through Trafficking Networks*

Another way that we might cast the market for antiquities as grey is related to the so-called "washing" of antiquities as they pass through a trafficking network. To continue the analogy, a black (illicit) antiquity is slowly cleaned as it passes through different hands; moving towards white (licit), but most likely ending up grey: not ethically clean, but legal.

This cleaning process is at the core of the antiquities-trafficking chain. Indeed, many aspects of antiquities-trafficking networks are structured as they are in order to promote this cleaning process. As previously discussed, in some cases antiquities-trafficking networks include multiple intermediaries and one or more transit ports. As the object moves farther from its illicit excavation it becomes less "hot" or less likely to be associated with a direct theft from the ground. It may be initially exported with forged paperwork or pass through transit ports where they acquire questionable export certificates or other fraudulent documentation, which creates a false provenance for the piece. It also may be held in a freeport warehouse or other location for a certain amount of time until statutes of limitation for reclamation of stolen goods have passed. We can see, therefore, that within these variants of the laundering process there are two possibilities: looted artifacts either become legalized or they become more difficult to identify as looted because they become more deeply inserted into the normal market supply chains.

Antiquities that come onto the market after this process of cleaning are bought and sold openly; however, even if they are rendered legal by good faith purchase and/or time bar, it would be hard to say they were truly clean or licit in all senses. The dubious or illegal actions that brought them to their sellable state leave them suspect; the perception that a loophole was exploited stays with the object. Thus the argument for the market as grey in this respect rests on the assertion that no amount of laundering through network and market structures can completely negate the object's illicit origins.

This understanding of greyness therefore has an object focus rather than a market focus, and in the literature in this field it is seen most clearly in statements about the legal and moral transitions made by objects as they pass through trafficking networks and into the public trade (Bowman 2008; Mackenzie 2005).

### *Neutralization and the Greying of the Moral Psychological Processes of Engagement*

One final way that we can conceive of the antiquities market as "grey" is through the moral ambiguity inherent in engaging with it. At the very least since the drafting of the 1970 UNESCO Convention, the destructive nature of archaeological looting and its clear links to the trade in antiquities have been public knowledge. Numerous repatriations and criminal cases have further increased public understanding of the link between antiquities and serious crime. Thus to participate in the market for antiquities is to some degree to participate in, or at least to benefit from, criminal enterprise and the process through which market participants justify their actions can be described as neutralizing an otherwise morally reprehensible action; greying it.

Both collectors and dealers in antiquities frame their engagement with the market in ways that portray their actions as favorable and even heroic (Mackenzie and Yates 2016). They tend to appeal to higher loyalties to justify their purchases. While many will concede that antiquities come from illicit digging and trafficking and that both of these are illegal, they assert that their actions actually save the objects; they believe that the law is wrong and that their actions are justified. These justifications validate the dealer/collector getting what they want (Mackenzie 2005).

Thus by appealing to higher loyalties, an antiquities buyer acknowledges, for example, that an ancient funerary relief was looted from a Syrian tomb, but asserts any or all of the following: that by buying it they can pay to preserve the piece properly; that Syria was obviously not caring for it or it would not have been stolen; that if it was left in Syria it would be destroyed by fundamentalists; that they will donate it to a museum someday for the public to enjoy; even that they are indirectly funneling money to poor looters who have no other job. Using these techniques they push illegal (black) acts of purchase into a grey area.

## What Does This Mean for Our Broader Understanding of Grey Markets?

To say that the antiquities trade operates as a grey market is therefore to call attention to a particular cocktail of its properties. Usually the term is used to refer to the mixing of recently looted antiquities with those that can be sold legally. Unlike in so-called black markets where purchasers will usually knowingly seek out and buy from criminals, the antiquities market is grey because of the sale of illicit objects via a public, visible, and purportedly legitimate network of dealers and auction houses. This interface is supported by the ethical greyness applying to looted objects through the effects of the passage of time and their passage through jurisdictions via multiple trades that obscure or overwrite their illicit origins. It is also supported by the active greying of the binary right/wrong distinction achieved by a neutralizing discourse that permits the purchase of illicit objects in constructed circumstances of "saving" or "preserving" artifacts.

There are also, however, other inflections to the idea of this type of grey market that we have not mentioned so far. We can, for example, observe a public disapproval but private tolerance of the issue of looted antiquities in the market among key sectors, such as the personal and institutional collecting and dealing communities, and indeed some degree of ambivalence or lack of interest among the general public. This we might call an elephantine type of greyness: a large-scale ignoring of the "elephant in the room" (Zerubavel 2006). As well as grey elephants there are grey people in the market, referred to above as Janus types. These are figures who have occupied peculiar positions in the market over decades, being simultaneously both notable collectors and dealers, supplying major institutions worldwide with high-end artifacts, and also suspected, rumored, and by some parties known, to be criminal handlers of stolen antiquities. In the grey areas these individuals occupy they have traditionally performed brokering roles important to connecting the supply and demand phases of the international trade. The apparent respectability of the dealers in question insulates those at the demand end from direct knowledge of wrongdoing at source (Mackenzie and Davis 2014).

By way of conclusion, in greyness, which at first seems a somewhat straightforward and perhaps self-evident adjective to describe the global antiquities market, closer analysis finds several layers of meaning which allude to the multiple ways in which the interface between il/legal, il/legitimate, and in/appropriate works to produce a marketplace that has so far successfully resisted most of the ethical and legal scrutiny directed at it.

## References


Alderman, Kimberly. 2012. "Honour among Thieves: Organized Crime and the Illicit Antiquities Trade." *Indiana Law Review* 45(3): pp. 601–27.

Bator, Paul M. 1983. *The International Trade in Art.* Chicago: University of Chicago Press.

Bichler, Gisela, Stacy Bush, and Aili Malm. 2013. "Bad Actors and Faulty Props: Unlocking Legal and Illicit Art Trade." *Global Crime* 14(4): pp. 359–85.

Bowman, Blythe A. 2008. "Transnational Crimes against Culture: Looting at Archaeological Sites and the 'Grey' Market in Antiquities." *Journal of Contemporary Criminal Justice* 24(3): pp. 225–42.

Bowman Proulx, B. 2011a. "Organized Criminal Involvement in the Illicit Antiquities Trade." *Trends in Organized Crime* 14(1): pp. 1–29.

Bowman Proulx, B. 2011b. "Trafficking in Antiquities." In *Routledge Handbook of International Criminology*, edited by Cindy J. Smith, Sheldon X. Zhang, and Rosemary Barberet, pp. 192–9. London: Routledge.

Brodie, Neil. 1998. "Pity the Poor Middlemen." *Culture without Context* 3(Autumn): pp. 7–9.

Brodie, Neil. 2010. "Archaeological Looting and Economic Justice." In *Cultural Heritage Management, Policy and Issues in Global Perspective*, edited by Phyllis M. Messenger and George S. Smith, pp. 261–77. Gainsville: University Press of Florida.

Brodie, Neil. 2012. "Uncovering the Antiquities Market." In *The Oxford Handbook of Public Archaeology*, edited by Robin Skeates, Carol McDavid, and John Carman, pp. 230–52. Oxford: Oxford University Press.

Felch, Jason, and Ralph Frammolino. 2011. *Chasing Aphrodite: The Hunt for Looted Antiquities at the World's Richest Museum*. New York: Houghton Mifflin Harcourt.

Hardy, Sam. 2015. "Virtues Impracticable and Extremely Difficult: The Human Rights of Subsistence Diggers." In *Ethics and the Archaeology of Violence*, edited by Alfredo González-Ruibal and Gabriel Moshenska, pp. 229–39. New York: Springer.

Kersel, Morag M. 2006. "From the Ground to the Buyer: A Market Analysis of the Trade in Illegal Antiquities." In *Archaeology, Cultural Heritage and the Antiquities Trade*, edited by Neil Brodie, Morag M. Kersel, Christina Luke, and Kathryn Walker Tubb, pp. 188–205. Gainesville: University Press of Florida.

Mackenzie, Simon. 2005. *Going, Going, Gone: Regulating the Market in Illicit Antiquities*. Leicester: Institute of Art and Law.

Mackenzie, Simon. 2011. "The Market as Criminal and Criminals in the Market: Reducing Opportunities for Organised Crime in the International Antiquities Market." In *Crime in the Art and Antiquities World: Illegal Trafficking in Cultural Property*, edited by Stefano Manacorda and Duncan Chappell, pp. 69–85. New York: Springer.

Mackenzie, Simon, and Tess Davis. 2014. "Temple Looting in Cambodia: Anatomy of a Statue Trafficking Network." *British Journal of Criminology* 54(5): pp. 722–40.

Mackenzie, Simon, and Penny Green. 2009. "Criminalising the Market in Illicit Antiquities: An Evaluation of the Dealing in Cultural Objects (Offences) Act 2003 in England and Wales." In *Criminology and Archaeology: Studies in Looted Antiquities*, edited by Simon Mackenzie and Penny Green, pp. 145–70. Oxford: Hart.

Mackenzie, Simon, and Donna Yates. 2016. "Collectors on Illicit Collecting: Higher Loyalties and Other Techniques of Neutralization in the Unlawful Collecting of Rare and Precious Orchids and Antiquities." *Theoretical Criminology*. doi: 10.1177/1362480615607625.

Maruna, Shadd, and Heith Copes. 2005. "Excuses, Excuses: What Have We Learned from Five Decades of Neutralization Research?" *Crime and Justice* 32: pp. 221–320.

Matsuda, David. 2005. "Subsistence Diggers." In *Who Owns the Past? Cultural Policy, Cultural Property, and the Law*, edited by Kate Fitz Gibbon, pp. 225–65. New Brunswick, NJ: Rutgers University Press.

Matza, David. 1964. *Delinquency and Drift*. New York: John Wiley.

McBarnet, Doreen. 2003. "When Compliance Is Not the Solution but the Problem: From Changes in Law to Changes in Attitude." In *Taxing Democracy: Understanding Tax Avoidance and Evasion*, edited by Valerie Braithwaite, pp. 229–43. Aldershot: Ashgate.

Merryman, John Henry. 1986. "Two Ways of Thinking about Cultural Property." *American Journal of International Law* 80(4): pp. 831–53.

Naylor, Robin Thomas. 2004a. "The Underworld of Ivory." *Crime, Law and Social Change* 42(4): pp. 261–95.

Naylor, Robin Thomas. 2004b. *Wages of Crime: Black Markets, Illegal Finance and the Underworld Economy*. Ithaca, NY: Cornell University Press and McGill-Queen's University Press.

Naylor, Robin Thomas. 2010. "The Underworld of Gemstones. Part 1: Under the Rainbow." *Crime, Law and Social Change* 53(2): pp. 131–58.

Passas, Nikos. 2003. "Cross-Border Crime and the Interface between Legal and Illegal Actors." *Security Journal* 16(1): pp. 19–38.

Polk, Ken. 2000. "The Antiquities Trade Viewed as a Criminal Market." *Hong Kong Lawyer* 82: pp. 82–92.

Prott, Lyndel V., and Patrick J. O'Keefe. 1984. *Law and the Cultural Heritage*, Volume 1: *Discovery and Excavation*. Abingdon: Professional Books.

Prott, Lyndel V., and Patrick J. O'Keefe. 1989. *Law and the Cultural Heritage*, Volume 3: *Movement*. London: Butterworths.

Redmond-Cooper, Ruth. 1997. "Good Faith Acquisition of Stolen Art." *Art, Antiquity and Law* II: pp. 55–61.

Ruggiero, Vincenzo. 1997. "Criminals and Service-Providers: Cross-National Dirty Economies." *Crime, Law and Social Change* 28(1): pp. 27–38.

Scott, Marvin B., and Stanford M. Lyman. 1968. "Accounts." *American Sociological Review* 33(1): pp. 46–62.

Shapland, Joanna, and Paul Ponsaers (eds). 2009. *The Informal Economy and Connections with Organised Crime: The Impact of National Social and Economic Policies*. Den Haag: Boom Juridische Uitgevers.

Visconti, Arianna. 2015. "Cultural Property Trafficking." In *Routledge Handbook of Transnational Criminal Law*, edited by Neil Boister and Robert J. Currie, pp. 264–79. Abingdon: Routledge.

Yates, Donna. 2014a. "Church Theft, Insecurity and Community Justice: The Reality of Source-End Regulation of the Market for Illicit Bolivian Cultural Objects." *European Journal of Crime Policy and Research* 20(4): pp. 445–57.

Yates, Donna. 2014b. "Displacement, Deforestation and Drugs: Antiquities Trafficking and the Narcotics Support Economies of Guatemala." In *Cultural Property Crimes: An Overview and Analysis on Contemporary Perspectives and Trends*, edited by Joris D. Kila and Marc Balcells, pp. 23–36. Leiden: Brill.

Zerubavel, Eviatar. 2006. *The Elephant in the Room: Silence and Denial in Everyday Life*. Oxford: Oxford University Press.

# 5

# Governance in Online Stolen Data Markets

*Meltem Odabaş, Thomas J. Holt, and Ronald L. Breiger*

## Introduction

The massive increase in online banking and financial transactions completed via web-based retailers has made personal information a valuable commodity, to be bought and sold by corporations for retail marketing (Newman and Clarke 2003; Peretti 2009).[1] The increased availability of information on transactions has also transformed personal information into a prime target for criminal actors who can acquire sensitive data, such as credit or debit card numbers, addresses, and other identifying details, through various means, including mass breaches of retailers' customer databases (Peretti 2009). There are now a range of stolen data markets operating via web forums, internet relay chat (IRC), and other communications platforms as an underground online economy offering for sale not only stolen credit card data and user account information, but also tools and services for hacking this information. Cybercriminals rely on these markets to acquire a wide range of goods and services: stolen email addresses for spam and phishing; credit card information for making fraudulent purchases; scans of real passports for identity theft; stolen gaming accounts for attaining vulnerable virtual items; custom malware for payment diversions and bitcoin theft; and stolen cloud accounts for hosting command and control servers (for detailed information, see Symantec Corporation 2014).

Researchers have focused on such market characteristics as the price of goods sold and the net worth of transactions conducted (Beckert 2011; Beckert and Wehinger 2013; Franklin et al. 2007; Herley and Florencio 2010; Holt and

[1] This research was supported by Grant SBE 1314631 from the US National Science Foundation.

Lampke 2010; Holt et al. 2015), as well as on the social dynamics of exchange and status in stolen data markets (Herley and Florencio 2010; Hutchings and Holt 2015; Motoyama et al. 2011; Yip et al. 2013). Few studies have considered or analyzed the governance structure of stolen data markets as a whole, however. What research has been done suggests that the illicit nature of stolen data markets keeps them beyond the reach of state intervention, leaving internal auto-regulation as the primary mode of governance (see Holt and Lampke 2010; Holt et al. 2015). Sellers and buyers appear to move in and out of the market, due in part to the public nature of advertisements. There are also various administrative forces present, depending on the nature of the market, which create a continuum of organizational sophistication ranging from no regulation to heavy management of exchanges between participants by moderators and site administrators (Dupont et al. 2016; Holt 2013).

These studies do not, however, account for the ways in which governance is directly influenced by the underlying economic imperatives and social interactions that affect the behaviors of buyers and sellers. If participants, whether buyers or sellers, desire to make money from their involvement in a market, then exchanges must be directly affected by the structure and conditions of the market. In this respect, economic sociological theory may prove invaluable in improving our knowledge of stolen data markets. For instance, "multiple markets" approaches model the distribution of goods as a set of social relations in which social networks (White 1981), cultural aspects (Reddy 1984), and economic factors interact (Zelizer 1988; Granovetter 1985).

Specifically, forums and IRC channels in which personal information is bought and sold may comprise a two-sided market because they are operated by independent groups that benefit from regulating transactions between buyers and sellers who would otherwise have difficulty in efficiently completing transactions on their own. Industrial organization theorists focusing on two-sided markets tend to consider the practices of market owners while giving short shrift to the ways in which buyers and sellers operate to affect markets' economic structures, as this literature adopts a game-theoretic rational-choice perspective. However, we argue that there may be greater value in understanding the role of online communication in creating trust and governing the market for stolen data as evident in the operation of web forums. This leads us to emphasize both regulatory and normative pillars of an institutional analysis of online stolen data markets. We focus on the regulatory strategies of market actors at the micro level to govern the market. At the same time, we identify how these micro-level actions define what roles the market owners, consumers, and sellers adopt and how this role structure increases the level of market trust. If, as Beckert (2003) suggests, the economic model of rational action focuses on how to conceive the structure of action, while the sociological concept of embeddedness tells us about the external variables that influence the action process, then our analysis combines both perspectives, thus reinforcing the link between them.

## Economic Organization of Two-Sided Markets

A two-sided market attracts two types of customer, notably sellers and buyers, just as in an ordinary market. However, what makes this type of market distinctive to economic theorists is its ownership and governance structure and the way the volume of transactions can be increased by actions taken by a third party, the owner (Caillaud and Jullien 2003; Evans 2003; Rochet and Tirole 2003; Armstrong 2006; Armstrong and Wright 2007; Rysman 2009). In legitimate credit card markets, for example, the third parties are credit card companies, such as American Express, Visa, and MasterCard, which facilitate economic transactions among retailers and their consumers when purchases are made through credit. In the advertising sector, newspapers (or other media) become the intermediary platform in which advertisements are visible to their readers. As an additional example, shopping malls are owned by a developer, an intermediary who aims to maximize profits by attracting many consumers with an ideal shop-mix of retailers (Rochet and Tirole 2003).

In all these examples of two-sided markets, sellers want the platform to attract as many buyers as possible because an increase in demand enables them to increase the price of their product and the potential surplus emerging from trade interactions. At the same time, buyers want to find as many sellers as possible as they enter the platform, in order to find products at lower prices and higher quality through product search (Nelson 1970; Stigler 1961). Therefore, an increase in the number of buyers attracts more sellers; for example, having more shoppers at a mall is a positive consideration in the location decisions of more shops. Likewise, an increase in the number of sellers attracts more buyers. This dynamic generates a duality that economists call "inter-group externalities": each potential seller (buyer) decides whether or not to enter the community by taking into account the number of buyers (sellers) already taking part in the market. The more buyers (sellers) are in the market, the more the seller (buyer) is willing to enter.

This duality is typical of any market with information asymmetries. However, emphasizing this duality among sellers and buyers is important for understanding the reason for a third actor to step in, which distinguishes two-sided market governance from that of other market types. The main reason for the market creator to also take on the role of regulator is the potential for increasing the volume of transactions—and therefore market efficiency—through specific measures to internalize the aforementioned inter-group externalities. Those externalities can also be internalized by the participants in the market (the sellers and buyers), but those actors need to act collectively in order to do so. When the contribution is voluntary, however, as Olson (1965) pointed out, it is hard to sustain the participants' collective action for cooperation. The private actor can step in where collective action among market participants either does not take place or remains limited.

The role of the platform (or market) owner is different in each market because the form of externalities also differs. In legal credit card markets, credit card companies take over the risks of consumer default that the seller firms face. This leads more firms to step in, and to turn short-term credit used for consumption purposes into a large-scale and global market. In the case of shopping malls, the mall owner creates a physical attraction point for consumers by adding extra facilities and services, such as on-site free parking, a clean and orderly environment with security guards, and amusement areas for children. Alternatively, these services could also have been provided if firms could have joined collectively to build such a large facility, and in this way they would not have needed to pay extra rent to the mall owner. However, it is not easy to overcome free-riding problems, especially when the effort costs are high. Therefore, the mall owner's role becomes more crucial in urban areas as commercial land is limited, and in suburban areas where potential shoppers are distributed across a wide area.

Turning now to online stolen data markets, the role of the market owner as a regulator in these markets appears to be the implementer of the tools to increase the level of trust as buyers and sellers strive to maintain their anonymity in an environment in which the quality of the goods is not observable before purchase. We now discuss these issues.

## Understanding Illicit Online Data Markets

Applying a two-sided market framework to an illicit economy, such as a stolen data market, is sensible given their structure and processes. In order to link the governance structure of online stolen data markets to the existing conceptualization of two-sided markets, we first describe the market characteristics of stolen data markets.

Illicit economies of any sort operate with various formal and informal risks to participants (for example, Best and Luckenbill 1994; Jacobs 2000). Formal risks are based on the likelihood of detection and arrest by law-enforcement agents, while informal risks come from various sources depending on the role of an actor within the economy. For instance, in open-air drug markets sellers may be targeted for robbery and physical violence by other dealers or by participants seeking money and drugs (for example, Jacobs 2000). Drug buyers may, however, buy a product that does not induce a sufficient high due to dilution, or one that creates a risk of overdose or death due to incorrect chemical composition (Jacobs 2000).

The development of the internet has enabled the formation of unique markets for illicit products, such as drugs (Barratt et al. 2014), malicious software (for example, Holt 2013), and personal data (Franklin et al. 2007; Holt and Lampke 2010; Holt et al. 2015; Motoyama et al. 2011; Yip et al. 2013). Research has demonstrated that these markets are structured differently from real-world markets: not only is payment accepted electronically, but there is virtually no physical interaction between the participants or knowledge of their identities (Hutchings and Holt 2015). These markets also present unique formal and informal threats to participants in the form of unscrupulous actors who are able to market goods of dubious quality or obtain payments without delivering the desired product.

In stolen data markets, participants enter into the community group in order to engage in bilateral exchanges for monetary profit. One example is the market for stolen credit card information, in which hackers and thieves sell information they have retrieved, as well as services designed to acquire data and system-level access (Bacher et al. 2005; Chu et al. 2010; Fossi et al. 2009; Franklin et al. 2007; Holt 2013). Other examples include sales and distribution of malicious software and hacking tools that enable less-skilled actors to gain direct access to services that extend their abilities (Holt and Lampke 2010; Motoyama et al. 2011; also Holt 2013).

There is a growing literature examining the presence of illicit markets emerging online to facilitate the sale of stolen personal information and services associated with identity crimes and hacking (Franklin et al. 2007; Holt and Lampke 2010; Motoyama et al. 2011; Peretti 2009; Wehinger 2011). The process of data acquisition and sale in these markets begins when a seller obtains financial or personally identifiable data through various means. This might be accomplished by using malicious software that can capture customer data at point-of-sale terminals (Peretti 2009), or through phishing attacks, whereby bank information is acquired from victims (James 2005). The data are then sold directly by the thief, or by an intermediary vendor who creates a thread in a forum that provides a detailed explanation of their products or services along with pricing information, preferred payment mechanisms, and contact information (Franklin et al. 2007; Holt and Lampke 2010; Holt 2013). Buyers then contact the seller, negotiate a final price for the information, and pay for the goods. Most market actors accept and prefer to use electronic payment systems, such as WebMoney, where vendors are able to receive payment immediately (Wehinger 2011). Buyers must then wait for delivery, which ranges from an immediate response to a few hours or days, depending on the vendor's timeline.

Once the data arrive, the buyer can then attempt to use them in order to engage in fraudulent purchases, make transfers between accounts, or work with other service providers in the market to obtain funds (Franklin et al. 2007; Holt and Lampke 2010). Because buyers expect to turn a profit from their purchase, they depend on working account information in order to maximize their return. Should an individual not receive the data purchased, or if it consists of inactive accounts or false information, or is of poor quality, the buyer has no legal recourse to offset losses (Holt 2013; Holt and Lampke 2010).

As a result, market actors' behavior is shaped by social forces intended to maximize rewards for both buyer and seller while minimizing risk of loss (Holt and Lampke 2010; Wehinger 2011). Unscrupulous sellers—known as "rippers"—can post false ads to attract customers, accept payment for data, and then provide bad data or not deliver any product (Herley and Florencio 2010; Holt and Lampke 2010). To minimize the risk of being ripped off, some markets allow buyers to post feedback and reviews of their experiences to promote trust and establish seller reputations (Holt and Lampke 2010; Motoyama et al. 2011). Such information directly affects actor position within social networks, such that sellers with more positive reviews receive a higher proportion of contacts from prospective buyers (Motoyama et al. 2011). Sellers offer customer-service mechanisms designed to attract customers and maintain a client base over time, through the use of bulk discounts, samples, and real-time customer support through various instant-messaging clients (Herley and Florencio 2010; Holt and Lampke 2010).

Additionally, some sellers offer discounted pricing schemes based on the quantity of data purchased, making it difficult to disaggregate the individual price for each item (Franklin et al. 2007; Holt and Lampke 2010). Finally, the negotiation process and purchase of data take place outside the forum or public component of the IRC channel, making it extremely difficult to know the quantity of data purchased or the final price paid for information (Franklin et al. 2007; Herley and Florencio 2010; Holt and Lampke 2010; Motoyama et al. 2011; Wehinger 2011).

Although most transactions are hidden from the public, there is evidence of attempts to purchase data or engage in transactions through feedback and reviews provided by data buyers in the forums. Customers are encouraged and expected to publicly post their experiences with a seller in their forum communication thread to characterize their encounters (Holt and Lampke 2010; Motoyama et al. 2011; Wehinger 2011). If a customer does not feel satisfied, either because the goods were not as advertised or went undelivered, the experience can be described in clear terms for all to see. In much the same way, those who were pleased with their interactions can post a comment about the seller's practices or data quality (Herley and Florencio 2010; Holt 2013; Holt and Lampke 2010; Motoyama et al. 2011). Thus, the use of feedback provides a window into the number of transactions completed by customers of a given vendor.

## Governance in Online Stolen Data Markets

As described in the preceding section, stolen data markets carry high risks as selling stolen data is a criminal act; thus sellers and buyers remain anonymous. These risks create market externalities, as described in the two-sided markets literature. In stolen data markets, as in two-sided market theorizations, forum administrators step in as a third party to regulate the market and to internalize the externalities.

Another crucial characteristic of stolen data markets, which is not addressed at all in the existing literature on two-sided markets, is the personal and public communication among buyers and sellers that helps them to measure the risks of engaging in market interaction in a particular stolen data market. Therefore, beyond arguing that the governance structure of stolen data markets can be identified as a two-sided market, we also indicate that two-sided market theories ignore the interactions among buyers and sellers. This is due mainly to the assumption that the market participants are incapable of internalizing the market externalities by themselves, and therefore the entrance of a private actor as a third party is necessary. However, as we observe in stolen data markets, second- and third-party governance can act simultaneously in a market. (Second parties are exchange partners themselves or relevant social groups to which they belong; third parties are external enforcers who neither participate in the exchanges themselves nor in the relevant networks; Ferguson 2013: 46.) Therefore, we find it fruitful to adopt a multiple-markets approach by looking not only at the interaction of economic factors but also at the communication and social interaction among market actors.

As platform owners and operators, forum administrators play an important role in increasing the level of trust among anonymous participants in the marketplace (Holt 2013; Holt et al. 2015). However, their role as market regulator is affected not only by market conditions and group characteristics, but also by the medium of communication. Traditionally in legitimate markets, platform owners serve as a regulator because there are externalities that have not yet been internalized. Communication technologies among sellers and buyers in illicit online markets enable these participants to take part as market regulators also, independently of their direct communication with the market owner. Therefore, we argue, these participants can also internalize the externalities of low levels of market trust to some extent, and forum administrators step in where communication among participants is insufficient for resolving problems. Thus, not only third- but also second-party controls (Della Porta and Vannucci 2005) are active in the self-regulation of illegal online markets.

Despite the coordination problems and accompanying issues of market trust, both the two-sidedness of stolen data markets and their online characteristics are powerful features used in solving some of the valuation- and competition-related problems frequently observed in illicit economies. In illegal markets, advertising is difficult due to the market's fragmented structure. Also, non-transparency in illicit markets limits price competition; it is difficult not only for buyers to compare prices, but also for sellers to find customers (Beckert and Wehinger 2013). The "face-to-screen" setting of online markets, however, not only brings what is "geographically distant and invisible to its participants" (Knorr-Cetina and Bruegger 2002: 907), but also enables buyers to easily screen the offers and information provided in the market. Sellers post their ads, which include information on price and method of payment, in web forums (or IRC channels), thus enabling buyers to search prices easily among a number of offers. And the two-sidedness of the market draws more potential buyers as market externalities are internalized.

The wealth of information available to prospective buyers in the market for stolen data may not, however, create a more informed actor (for example, Holt et al. 2015). The products offered by a seller cannot be examined in their entirety in advance of a purchase. Buyers must make assumptions about the structure of a data file or the amount of information available from a service provider based on information provided by sellers in their advertisements, which may often be false or misleading (Herley and Florencio 2010). As a result, there is a substantial information asymmetry regarding the quality of goods sold in data markets that is not easily overcome.

This issue is present across all manner of online markets, ranging from illicit markets to eBay and Amazon sales (Conradt 2012; Dolan 2004; Heinonen et al. 2012). Another drawback of online purchases is the sequential order of transactions. Because sellers and buyers cannot meet in a physical space, the buyer is expected to make the purchase first, and the seller is expected to deliver the good afterwards. The buyer therefore faces a risk of fraud, as the seller may not send the package after the buyer's purchase (Conradt 2012; Dolan 2004).

As a result, there is some similarity in the mechanisms to promote trust between participants in stolen data markets and legitimate online markets. In the next section we reformulate the economic perspective of research on two-sided markets by emphasizing social structures that can be effective for creating efficiency (Baker 1984; Uzzi 1996), as marketplaces are not only composed of exchanges but also dependent on governance and trust (Fligstein and Dauter 2007).

## Second- and Third-Party Trust-Creating Mechanisms

The transactional exchange of money for data and services in online stolen data markets sounds simple and mimics traditional business models. A major challenge is posed by the anonymity of online communication, however, which minimizes the ability of participants to trust one another. Sellers can decide to shirk their responsibility to the buyer and not send the information purchased after receiving payment (Herley and Florencio 2010; Holt 2013; Holt and Lampke 2010; Motoyama et al. 2011). Therefore, the platform is confronted by the question of how to create internal trust-generating mechanisms that guarantee a secure system of exchange, and in turn how to attract participants and enhance bilateral exchanges.

Buyers cannot truly assess the veracity of any seller's claim until they actually have the information or service available at their disposal (Herley and Florencio 2010). The information in any advertisement can be "cheap talk" (see Farrell and Rabin 1996), and may not affect the equilibrium result of the exchange process. Or, the buyers may not make sure that the sellers' products are of good quality before purchasing them, which creates another credibility problem (Akerlof 1970; Jullien 2000).

Thus, there are two main problems to be solved in online stolen data markets. First, it is hard for buyers to observe the level of quality of products offered by sellers, creating a condition Akerlof (1970) calls the "market for lemons" (Herley and Florencio 2010; Yip et al. 2013; Holt et al. 2013). According to this principle, if buyers in exchange markets cannot observe the quality of products before purchasing them, they might not trust the sellers, and therefore the market might not function. In a market in which there are two types of good, high and low quality, in equal numbers, there is also no way for the buyers to observe the quality before purchase; thus the buyers are willing to pay only the average of the value of high- and low-quality products. High-quality product sellers, in this case, are not willing to sell their product at a lower price than its real market value, and therefore they leave the market (Herley and Florencio 2010; Wehinger 2011). Only the low-quality products that buyers are not willing to purchase are left in the market. As a result, the market collapses due to this adverse selection problem.

The second problem is moral hazard: the seller has an incentive to shirk and not complete the transaction after receiving the money from the buyer. (For some economic applications of this concept see Arrow 1963, 1968; and Pauly 1968; also see Coyle 2007 for the specific areas in which the term is used.) Also, the anonymity of participants exacerbates these two problems due to the difficulty in tracing sellers who engage in malfeasance. Under these conditions, it is hard to generate demand from the buyers' side, leading forum administrators to decide whether it is worth implementing some trust-generating mechanisms to overcome these problems.

Communication is needed among the participants in online anonymous markets, not only because communication generates support and continuity in these groups, but also because it influences the participants' decisions on how to act (see also Fourcade 2007: 1024, on "the local understandings . . . and informal practices" that provide foundations for markets, and Beckert 2010: 609, on the "local order [that] emerges where actors develop mutual expectations with regard to each other's behavior"). Through communication, participants can identify the observable features of transactions (for example, Holt and Lampke 2010; Hutchings and Holt 2015). Therefore, through the typifying of transactions, agents eliminate Knightian uncertainty: they convert incalculable uncertainty into calculable risk (Preda 2013).

In order to solve the coordination problem that may arise due to low levels of trust a forum administrator may act as a *trust generator*. The forum administrator may employ either of two general sets of mechanisms for this purpose, which we label as "authenticator" and "mediator" procedures. In the first type, the administrator provides reward mechanisms. This can be either through second-party control mechanisms, whereby potential sellers and buyers use the platform the administrator opened to rate each other and ameliorate the difficulties of transactions involving illicit goods (see Holt and Lampke 2010; Holt 2013; Wehinger 2011), or through the administrator providing reviews about sellers' products acting as a third party. In the second type, the administrator again acts as a third party, either by intermediating the transactions between buyers and sellers, or by establishing and announcing punishment mechanisms for those who upset the otherwise trustworthy environment of the platform (Holt 2013; Holt and Lampke 2010; Wehinger 2011).

In light of the distinction between mediator and regulator procedures relevant to online stolen data markets, we now focus on five different trust-generating mechanisms, the first two of which fall under second-party and the other three under third-party controls: 1) *Rating mechanisms*, 2) *Customer services*, 3) *Escrow services*, 4) *Providing reviews of sellers*, and 5) *Banning users*. Table 5.1 relates these trust-generating mechanisms to variation in the forum administrator's role, the type of economic problem addressed, and the level of control.

*Rating mechanisms* enable the users of the platform to rate other users and provide feedback about other parties' behavior and effectiveness in easing the transaction process (Franklin et al. 2007; Holt 2013; Holt and Lampke 2010; Yip et al. 2013). That feedback provides signals for other users in deciding with whom to undertake transactions; that is, deciding whether the other user is trustworthy. Even though this mechanism is implemented in the communication platform by the forum administrator, the rating process works only

**Table 5.1.** Trust-creating mechanisms used in online stolen data markets

| | Mediation[a] | | Authentication[a] | |
|---|---|---|---|---|
| | Adverse selection[b] | Moral hazard[b] | Adverse selection[b] | Moral hazard[b] |
| Third-party control[c] | Banning | Escrow services; banning | Reviews | – |
| Second-party control[c] | – | – | Rating mechanisms; customer services | – |

*Notes: a* Forum administrator's role; *b* Type of economic problem; *c* Level of control

through the participation of platform users (Holt 2013). People are rated either by assigning reputation scores or through written reviews which provide qualitative and detailed information about sellers (Holt 2013; Yip et al. 2013). Those written reviews enable the buyers to acquire a sense of the trustworthiness of the sellers. The information usually involves comments of buyers about the efficacy of the negotiation and delivery process, whether the seller was available, and the speed of replies (Holt 2013; Holt and Lampke 2010). Such information directly affects actor position within social networks, such that sellers with more positive reviews receive a higher proportion of contacts from prospective buyers (Motoyama et al. 2011).

In a sense, using the same account or nickname enables the seller to build a reputation in the market despite the fact that their identity is kept anonymous. This mediator trust-generation process enables the evolution of reputation networks. Completing successful and trustworthy transactions increases the seller's reputation through positive feedback from the buyers, which in turn increases the seller's likelihood of being selected by other buyers (Motoyama et al. 2011; Yip et al. 2013). If those transactions are again considered to be successful by the buyers, the seller gains in reputation.

The level of *customer service* advertised by sellers may be another signal of trust and reliability. Some sellers regularly advertise dedicated customer support lines via a private messaging service (such as ICQ, pronounced "I seek you") and/or email to answer questions posed by buyers, facilitate purchases, and demonstrate their willingness to satisfy customer needs (for example, Franklin et al. 2007; Holt 2013; Holt and Lampke 2010; Hutchings and Holt 2015). Many marketplaces provide or require product-testing services, whereby the forum moderators test a sample of products for quality assurance (Holt 2013; Holt and Lampke 2010; Holt et al. 2015; Hutchings and Holt 2015). The tester posts a public review of the offered product or service to validate any claims the seller has made. Some forums verify a seller's reputation through this process, which buyers can observe as a signal of trust and reliability (Holt and Lampke 2010; Holt et al. 2015). This practice fits within signaling theory, as the seemingly wasteful action of providing a sample of data with monetary value at no cost for the purpose of verification may actually be useful to the seller (Gambetta 2009). In the long run, a good reputation, established by means of data samples, can draw in more customers, generating more profit. This practice also points up the dual role of the forum administrators as actors who facilitate (and hence engage in) illegal activity, while at the same time functioning as guarantors of the reputations of sellers of illegal services; in this sense, administrators are, to use Dewey's expression (2011: 12), from a different context, "agents who send signals in both directions."

The other three mechanisms solidify the role of forum administrators and their designated agents as regulators. *Escrow services* are useful in solving the moral hazard problem in bilateral transactions by eliminating the possibility that either party will shirk its responsibility to the other (Chu et al. 2010; Holt 2013; Holt and Lampke 2010; Wehinger 2011). When a transaction is not monitored by a third party, the buyer is vulnerable to fraud and thus might avoid making transactions, either because the buyer is risk-averse in general or does not trust the other party. The seller may either shirk at the final stage of the transaction and not send the product, or might sell a product of very low quality.

These moral hazard problems leave room for the forum administrator to act as an intermediary in an escrow process. In this instance, the administrator polices transactions in order to make sure all parties are satisfied and removes users who have had a negative impact on the overall reputation of the forum through malfeasance (for example, Holt 2013; Holt et al. 2015). The escrow mechanism consists in both the buyer and seller agreeing to use this payment system and informing the designated agent of the conditions of the sale. The buyer then forwards funds to the escrow agent, who holds those funds in reserve and contacts the seller. After notification, the seller provides the buyer with the agreed-upon product. Once the buyer confirms that the data or service is as described, the escrow agent releases funds to the seller (Fallmann et al. 2010; Holt 2013; Holt et al. 2013; Holt and Lampke 2010). Typically, a forum selects a single individual to serve as an escrow agent, which may also affect the perceived trust of a vendor if they accept this form of payment. At the same time, sellers can indicate they will accept escrow payments but are not required to use the escrow service to negotiate payment (for example, Holt 2013).

In addition to escrow services, some markets provide product checks or tests of sellers' materials to determine their reliability and provide feedback about the sellers through *reviews* (Franklin et al. 2007; Holt 2013; Holt and Lampke 2010; Yip 2011). In illicit credit card information markets, for example, administrators ask sellers for a sample of the information they received.

They will then check whether the dumps (batches of credit card data that are sold) are still active and can be used to make purchases. After the sample test, the administrator reviews the seller and the quality of the sample and publishes this information on the reviewed user's ratings (Franklin et al. 2007; Holt et al. 2013; Holt 2013; Holt and Lampke 2010; Radianti 2010; Yip 2011).

Some moderators police the performance of actors within forums to ensure that sellers' and buyers' activities do not upset the trustworthy environment of the forum (Chu et al. 2010; Holt 2013). Those who do not follow the predetermined rules of the forum may be detected by moderators or administrators who read posts and receive complaints from market actors. In turn, the moderator may either send notifications to those users or directly *ban* them from entering the web forum and block their accounts (Fallmann et al. 2010; Holt 2013; Motoyama et al. 2011). These two mechanisms contribute to the peacefulness of the platform as a social communication network, which in turn benefits the web forum by attracting more active participants (see also Chu et al. 2010).

The empirical study by Holt et al. (2013) underscores the impact of trust-generating mechanisms on the price levels of products sold in different underground markets. If higher prices can be interpreted as a signal of a higher level of trust (that is, the participants' willingness to pay higher prices in order to incur lower levels of risk), then the positive association of trust-generating factors can also can be interpreted as an indicator of successful trust generation in these underground markets. For instance, the researchers found that prices were 44 percent lower in ripping forums (where fraudulent activities are observed frequently) than in non-ripping forums (Holt et al. 2013). This supports the argument that the perception of reduced prices may draw in unsuspecting customers but increase their risk of loss.

While provision of escrow services results in a significant increase (by a factor of almost two) in the level of prices for credit card dumps, product testing has a similarly significant effect on the same dependent variable (Holt et al. 2013). Positive feedback provision has a small (3 percent) though significant negative impact on dump prices. This might be because the feedback is interpreted as "cheap talk" in the market. However, more empirical study is needed to obtain a clearer picture of how trust mechanisms are used, and how effective they are in generating a more trustworthy market with a higher volume of exchanges between sellers and buyers.

## Discussion

Both the illicit and the online properties of online stolen data markets contribute to making transactions risky. As these markets operate outside the realm of state regulation, self-regulation becomes crucial for stolen data market governance. Violence between actors is a common mechanism of self-regulation in traditional illicit markets in the real world (for example, Jacobs 2000), although the situation is more complex when state institutions overlap with illicit markets (for example, Dewey 2011; Reno 2009). With regard to online spaces of illicit activity, their anonymized nature limits the ability of actors to use offensive or retaliatory strikes to regulate market behavior.

Instead, the economic organization, communication technology used, and socialization patterns of the actors identifies the type of problems to be addressed in the online illicit market, which in turn shapes the form and level of controls. In the case of stolen data markets, controls take the form of trust-creating mechanisms, and they are implemented at both the second and third levels. Second-party controls, such as ratings and customer services, solve adverse selection problems in the market; and the entrance of a third actor as not only a market creator but also a private regulator in the market leads to the use of third-party controls, which can address moral hazard problems which the second-party controls cannot.

We have emphasized the role of communication in increasing trust in markets, with an emphasis on the introduction of trust-creating mechanisms. However, other ways in which communication plays a role in increasing or reducing trust should be analyzed in greater detail. For instance, one of the studies carried out to assess signaling in stolen data markets (Décary-Hétu and Leppänen 2013) utilizes a single forum to assess "criminal opportunities," defined as the total number of threads in which individuals indicated they were "looking," "buying," "selling," and other action verbs related to the trade of information. The authors find that performance is related to the length of time a username had been registered with a forum, the percentage of posts that were in "criminal" threads, and various measures of social ties between actors.

The situational characteristics of forums may also present signals of trust concerning potential sellers. Evidence suggests that trustworthy sellers and reliable products are offered in markets in which actors communicate with one another in Russian (for example, Holt 2013; Symantec Corporation 2014). There is also a relationship between the language used by market actors and the advertised price of data (Holt et al. 2013). Actors in these markets may be in Russian-speaking nations with difficult extradition relationships with the United States and other European nations, thereby decreasing the risk of detection and prosecution for offenders (Brenner 2011). The predominant language used in forums may directly impact the ability of individuals to participate, as those who are not fluent may be unable to communicate. While some rippers may speak the same language as genuine sellers, learning to communicate fluently in a foreign language is a difficult task for many, and not easily mimicked. Individuals may be able to partially mimic foreign language knowledge online through the use of machine translation programs, though they will be unable to use jargon and slang effectively as these terms do not translate across cultures (Holt 2010). Thus, the language used in advertisements may serve as a costly signal of trust to differentiate legitimate vendors from rippers.

The types of product sold within data markets may also broadcast their own signals regarding the trustworthy nature of a vendor. Thus, another line of future research could aim to understand whether the types of products sold in stolen data markets also have an impact on market trust. Rippers may target inexperienced buyers by creating fictitious advertisements for common products that appear competitively priced compared to legitimate vendors in the market (see Herley and Florêncio 2010). They may also provide "free samples" or "tests" of their data through posted advertisements in an attempt to attract prospective buyers on the basis that they are offering legitimate products (Herley and Florencio 2010). Less common products, such as PayPal and eBay data, may be more costly for disreputable vendors to create, as their advertisement cannot blend into a larger product category (see Holt and Smirnova 2014).

As our focus in this chapter is how web forums are governed, our analysis does not consider the impact of introducing trust-creating mechanisms on the overall market, and the effects of competition among web forums. A line of research aiming to understand this aspect of stolen data markets would demonstrate the consequences of various incentives. For instance, given that actors in stolen data markets are oriented toward making money with the least degree of risk and economic loss, the presence of rippers in a forum drives sellers with legitimate data to other venues (Herley and Florêncio 2010).

Some researchers argue that there is now a two-tiered market system (Herley and Florêncio 2010; Holt et al. 2013; Wehinger 2011). "Ripper marketplaces" comprise sellers who are trying to take predatory advantage of uninformed buyers, who may be new to the idea of buying and selling stolen data. Ripper marketplaces advertise lower prices (Holt et al. 2013), but come with greater risk to the buyer, with a reduced likelihood of obtaining data that can be used to turn a profit (Herley and Florêncio 2010).

## Conclusion

Online stolen data markets must solve trust-related problems in order to attract more people to the marketplace because the participants in the market are anonymous and the state is not a part of market regulation. These problems are solved partly by second-party control mechanisms, as buyers and sellers give comments to each other. However, we also see a private third party acting as a regulator in online stolen data markets, which leads us to define them with reference to the economists' recent conceptualization of two-sided markets. Understanding the reasons behind the formation of the market with this structure is one of our main contributions to the literature and helps us to situate illicit two-sided markets in relation to legal forms of this market type. The roles taken by the actors in two-sided markets are very much the same in legal and in illicit manifestations, whereas the problems emerging in these markets and the communication methods they incorporate tend to differ. In that sense, the online and illegal characteristics of online stolen data markets determine their governance dynamics.

In contrast to many market studies that focus only on the producer side of the market (see Zelizer 2005 and Fligstein and Dauter 2007 for an extended version of this argument), our analysis includes the dynamics among all actors in the market: forum administrator, buyers, and sellers. This approach, as is the case in many other studies focused on consumer and producer dynamics in markets (Baker 1984; Granovetter 1985; Uzzi 1996), leads us to emphasize the role of trust in online stolen data web forums. The trust-creating mechanisms in these markets solve adverse selection and moral hazard problems, either by mediation or authentication, and through either second- or third-party controls. In that regard, we expect the theoretical framework we provide in this chapter to motivate a new direction of governance studies of online and illegal markets, where the level of impact of second- and third-party controls is tested.

Our analysis draws a connection between the agency and the structure of online stolen data markets: they are both a product of social action and a platform for it (Giddens 1984). Our institutional analysis of the market underlines online communication as both a regulatory tool and a medium of trust–signal exchange. In this organizational setting, we believe that social network analyses would be useful in analyzing how reviews, positive comments, and negative comments impact individual trustworthiness and market trust, as well as the number of transactions taking place in the market. Ultimately, even though the institutional, cognitive, and social network aspects of markets can be seen theoretically as distinct, in practice they are irreducible as market processes flow from their interrelations (Beckert 2010).

Following from the above, we acknowledge that a cultural analysis of online stolen data markets is missing in this chapter. Further research is therefore needed to analyze how trust and trustworthiness are framed and perceived in these markets; what reasons the forum administrators, buyers, and sellers articulate for taking part in these markets beyond monetary benefit; and the connections between online stolen data markets and hacker sub-culture (for example, Holt 2007; Jordan and Taylor 1998; Kilger et al. 2004).

We hope also to have contributed to bridging economic models of rational action and the sociological focus on what embeddedness tells us about the external variables that influence economic action (Beckert 2003). Even though our effort here is at best a small step toward suggesting an alternative approach to rational action models—which is what Beckert (2003), among other analysts, expects scholars of economic sociology to provide—we hope to have contributed insights from the study of hacker communities that can aid in developing such an alternative.

## References

Akerlof, George A. 1970. "The Market for Lemons: Quality Uncertainty and the Market Mechanism." *Quarterly Journal of Economics* 84(3): pp. 488–500.

Armstrong, Mark. 2006. "Competition in Two-Sided Markets." *RAND Journal of Economics* 37(3): pp. 668–91.

Armstrong, Mark, and Julian Wright. 2007. "Two-Sided Markets, Competitive Bottlenecks and Exclusive Contracts." *Economic Theory* 32(2): pp. 353–80.

Arrow, Kenneth J. 1963. "Uncertainty and the Welfare Economics of Medical Care." *American Economic Review* 53(5): pp. 941–73.

Arrow, Kenneth J. 1968. "The Economics of Moral Hazard: Further Comment." *American Economic Review* 58(3): pp. 537–9.

Bacher, Paul, Thorsten Holz, Markus Kötter, and Georg Wicherski. 2005. *Tracking Botnets: Using Honeynets to Learn More about Bots*. Honeynet Project and Research Alliance. <http://www.honeynet.org/papers/bots/> (accessed April 15, 2016).

Baker, Wayne E. 1984. "The Social Structure of a National Securities Market." *American Journal of Sociology* 89(4): pp. 775–811.

Barratt, Monica J., Jason A. Ferris, and Adam R. Winstock. 2014. "Use of Silk Road, the Online Drug Marketplace, in the United Kingdom, Australia and the United States." *Addiction* 109(5): pp. 774–83.

Beckert, Jens. 2003. "Economic Sociology and Embeddedness: How Shall We Conceptualize Economic Action?" *Journal of Economic Issues* 37(3): pp. 769–87.

Beckert, Jens. 2010. "How Do Fields Change? The Interrelations of Institutions, Networks, and Cognition in the Dynamics of Markets." *Organization Studies* 31(5): pp. 605–27.

Beckert, Jens. 2011. "Where Do Prices Come From? Sociological Approaches to Price Formation." *Socio-Economic Review* 9(4): pp. 757–86.

Beckert, Jens, and Frank Wehinger. 2013. "In the Shadow: Illegal Markets and Economic Sociology." *Socio-Economic Review* 11(1): pp. 5–30.

Best, Joe, and David F. Luckenbill. 1994. *Organizing Deviance*. 2nd ed. Englewood Cliffs, NJ: Prentice-Hall.

Brenner, Susan W. 2011. "Defining Cybercrime: A Review of Federal and State Law." In *Cybercrime: The Investigation, Prosecution, and Defense of Computer-Related Crime*, edited by Ralph D. Clifford, 3rd ed., pp. 15–104. Raleigh, NC: Carolina Academic Press.

Caillaud, Bernard, and Bruno Jullien. 2003. "Chicken and Egg: Competition among Intermediation Service Providers." *RAND Journal of Economics* 34(2): pp. 309–28.

Chu, Bill, Thomas J. Holt, and Gail Joon Ahn. 2010. *Examining the Creation, Distribution, and Function of Malware On-Line.* <https://www.ncjrs.gov/pdffiles1/nij/grants/230111.pdf> (accessed April 15, 2016).

Conradt, Christine. 2012. "Online Auction Fraud and Criminological Theories: The Adrian Ghighina Case." *International Journal of Cyber Criminology* 6(1): pp. 912–23.

Coyle, Diane. 2007. *The Soulful Science: What Economists Really Do and Why It Matters.* Princeton, NJ: Princeton University Press.

Décary-Hétu, David, and Anna Leppänen. 2013. "Criminals and Signals: An Assessment of Criminal Performance in the Carding Underworld." *Security Journal*, November 18. doi: 10.1057/sj.2013.39.

Della Porta, Donatella, and Alberto Vannucci. 2005. "The Governance Mechanisms of Corrupt Transactions." In *The New Institutional Economics of Corruption*, edited by Johann Graf Lambsdorff, Markus Taube, and Matthias Schramm, pp. 152–80. London: Routledge.

Dewey, Matías. 2011. *Fragile States, Robust Structures: Illegal Police Protection in Buenos Aires*. GIGA working paper no. 169. Hamburg: German Institute of Global and Area Studies. <http://ssrn.com/abstract=1868125> (accessed April 15, 2016).

Dolan, Kyo M. 2004. "Internet Auction Fraud: The Silent Victims." *Journal of Economic Crime Management* 2(1): pp. 1–22.

Dupont, Benoît, Anne-Marie Côté, Claire Savine, and David Décary-Hétu. 2016. "The Ecology of Trust among Hackers." *Global Crime* 17(2): pp. 129–51.

Evans, David S. 2003. "Some Empirical Aspects of Multi-Sided Platform Industries." *Review of Network Economics* 2(3): pp. 191–209.

Fallmann, Hanno, Gilbert Wondracek, and Christian Platzer. 2010. "Covertly Probing Underground Economy Marketplaces." In *Detection of Intrusions and Malware, and Vulnerability Assessment*, edited by Christian Kreibich and Marko Jahnke, pp. 101–10. Berlin: Springer.

Farrell, Joseph, and Matthew Rabin. 1996. "Cheap Talk." *Journal of Economic Perspectives* 10(3): pp. 103–18.

Ferguson, William D. 2013. *Collective Action and Exchange: A Game-Theoretic Approach to Contemporary Political Economy*. Stanford, CA: Stanford University Press.

Fligstein, Neil, and Luke Dauter. 2007. "The Sociology of Markets." *Annual Review of Sociology* 33: pp. 105–28.

Fossi, Marc, Eric Johnson, Dean Turner et al. 2009. "Symantec Report on Underground Economy." *Journal of Financial Services Technology* 3(1): pp. 77–81.

Fourcade, Marion. 2007. "Theories of Markets and Theories of Society." *American Behavioral Scientist* 50(8): pp. 1015–34.

Franklin, Jason, Adrian Perrig, Vern Paxson, and Stefan Savage. 2007. *An Inquiry into the Nature and Causes of the Wealth of Internet Miscreants*. Proceedings of the 14th ACM Conference on Computer and Communications Security (CCS 2007), Alexandria, VA.

Gambetta, Diego. 2009. "Signaling." In *The Oxford Handbook of Analytical Sociology*, edited by Peter Hedström and Peter Bearman, pp. 168–94. Oxford: Oxford University Press.

Giddens, Anthony. 1984. *The Constitution of Society: Outline of the Theory of Structuration.* Berkeley: University of California Press.

Granovetter, Mark. 1985. "Economic Action and Social Structure: The Problem of Embeddedness." *American Journal of Sociology* 91(3): pp. 481–510.

Heinonen, Justin A., Thomas J. Holt, and Jeremy M. Wilson. 2012. "Product Counterfeits in the Online Environment: An Empirical Assessment of Victimization and Reporting Characteristics." *International Criminal Justice Review* 22(4): pp. 353–71.

Herley, Cormac, and Dinei Florencio. 2010. "Nobody Sells Gold for the Price of Silver: Dishonesty, Uncertainty and the Underground Economy." In *Economics of Information Security and Privacy*, edited by Tyler Moore, David Pym, and Christos Ioannidis, pp. 35–53. New York: Springer.

Holt, Thomas J. 2007. "Subcultural Evolution? Examining the Influence of On- and Off-line Experiences on Deviant Subcultures." *Deviant Behavior* 28(2): pp. 171–98.

Holt, Thomas J. 2010. "Exploring Strategies for Qualitative Criminological and Criminal Justice Inquiry Using On-line Data." *Journal of Criminal Justice Education* 21: pp. 300–21.

Holt, Thomas J. 2013. "Examining the Forces Shaping Cybercrime Markets Online." *Social Science Computer Review* 31(2): pp. 165–77.

Holt, Thomas J., and Eric Lampke. 2010. "Exploring Stolen Data Markets Online: Products and Market Forces." *Criminal Justice Studies* 23(1): pp. 33–50.

Holt, Thomas J., Yi-Ting Chua, and Olga Smirnova. 2013. *An Exploration of the Factors Affecting the Advertised Price for Stolen Data*. Proceedings of the eCrime Research Summit, San Francisco, CA.

Holt, Thomas J., and Olga Smirnova. 2014. *Examining the Structure, Organization and Processes of the International Market for Stolen Data*. Washington, DC: National Institute of Justice.

Holt, Thomas J., Olga Smirnova, Yi Ting Chua, and Heith Copes. 2015. "Examining the Risk Reduction Strategies of Actors in Online Criminal Markets." *Global Crime* 16(2): pp. 81–103.

Hutchings, Alice, and Thomas J. Holt. 2015. "A Crime Script Analysis of the Online Stolen Data Market." *British Journal of Criminology* 55(3): pp. 596–614.

Jacobs, Bruce A. 2000. *Robbing Drug Dealers: Violence beyond the Law*. New Brunswick, NJ: Transaction Publishers.

James, Lance. 2005. *Phishing Exposed*. Rockland, MA: Syngress Publishing.

Jordan, Tim, and Paul Taylor. 1998. "A Sociology of Hackers." *Sociological Review* 46(4): pp. 757–80.

Jullien, B. 2000. "Participation Constraints in Adverse Selection Models." *Journal of Economic Theory* 93(1): pp. 1–47.

Kilger, Max, Jeff Stutzman, and Ofir Arkin. 2004. "Profiling." In *Know Your Enemy: Learning about Security Threats*, edited by Honeynet Project, 2nd ed., pp. 505–56. Boston, MA: Addison Wesley Professional.

Knorr Cetina, Karin, and Urs Bruegger. 2002. "Global Microstructures: The Virtual Societies of Financial Markets." *American Journal of Sociology* 107(4): pp. 905–50.

Motoyama, Marti, Damon McCoy, Kirill Levchenko, Stefan Savage, and Geoffrey M. Voelker. 2011. "An Analysis of Underground Forums." In *Proceedings of the 2011 ACM SIGCOMM Internet Measurement Conference*, pp. 71–80. New York: ACM.

Nelson, Phillip. 1970. "Information and Consumer Behavior." *Journal of Political Economy* 78(2): pp. 311–29.

Newman, Graeme R., and Ronald V. Clarke. 2011 [2003]. *Superhighway Robbery: Preventing E-Commerce Crime*. Abingdon: Routledge.

Olson, Mancur. 1965. *The Logic of Collective Action: Public Goods and the Theory of Groups*. Cambridge, MA: Harvard University Press.

Pauly, Mark V. 1968. "The Economics of Moral Hazard: Comment." *American Economic Review* 58(3): pp. 531–7.

Peretti, Kimberly K. 2009. "Data Breaches: What the Underground World of 'Carding' Reveals." *Santa Clara Computer and High Technology Law Journal* 25: pp. 375–413.

Preda, Alex. 2013. "Tags, Transaction Types and Communication in Online Anonymous Markets." *Socio-Economic Review* 11(1): pp. 31–56.

Radianti, Jaziar. 2010. "A Study of a Social Behavior inside the Online Black Markets." In *Proceedings of Emerging Security Information Systems and Technologies, 2010 Fourth International Conference*, edited by Reijo Savola, Masaru Takesue, Rainer Falk, and Manuela Popescu, pp. 189–94. Washington, DC: IEEE Computer Society.

Reddy, William M. 1984. *The Rise of Market Culture: The Textile Trade and French Society, 1750–1900*. New York: Cambridge University Press.

Reno, William. 2009. "Illicit Markets, Violence, Warlords, and Governance: West African Cases." *Crime, Law and Social Change* 52(3): pp. 313–22.

Rochet, Jean-Charles, and Jean Tirole. 2003. "Platform Competition in Two-Sided Markets." *Journal of the European Economic Association* 1(4): pp. 990–1029.

Rysman, Marc. 2009. "The Economics of Two-Sided Markets." *Journal of Economic Perspectives* 23(3): pp. 125–43.

Stigler, George J. 1961. "The Economics of Information." *Journal of Political Economy* 69(3): pp. 213–25.

Symantec Corporation. 2014. *Internet Security Report 2014*. <http://www.symantec.com/content/en/us/enterprise/other_resources/b-istr_main_report_v19_21291018.en-us.pdf> (accessed October 15, 2015).

Uzzi, Brian. 1996. "The Sources and Consequences of Embeddedness for the Economic Performance of Organizations: The Network Effect." *American Sociological Review* 61(4): pp. 674–98.

Wehinger, Frank. 2011. "The Dark Net: Self-Regulation Dynamics of Illegal Online Markets for Identities and Related Services." In *2011 European Intelligence and Security Informatics Conference (EISIC), Proceedings, Athens, Greece 12–14 September 2011*, edited by Nasrullah Memon and Daniel Zeng, pp. 209–13. Los Alamitos, CA: IEEE/CPS.

White, Harrison C. 1981. "Where Do Markets Come From?" *American Journal of Sociology* 87(3): pp. 517–47.

Yip, Michael. 2011. "An Investigation into Chinese Cybercrime and the Applicability of Social Network Analysis." In *ACM Web Science Conference 2011*, June 14–17, Koblenz.

Yip, Michael, Craig Webber, and Nigel Shadbolt. 2013. "Trust among Cybercriminals? Carding Forums, Uncertainty and Implications for Policing." *Policing and Society* 23(4): pp. 516–39.

Zelizer, Viviana A. 1988. "Beyond the Polemics on the Market: Establishing a Theoretical and Empirical Agenda." *Sociological Forum* 3(4): pp. 614–34.

Zelizer, Viviana A. 2005. "Culture and Consumption." In *The Handbook of Economic Sociology*, edited by Neil J. Smelser and Richard Swedberg, 2nd ed., pp. 331–55. Princeton, NJ: Princeton University Press.

# 6

# Futurity, Offshore, and the International Political Economy of Crime

*Ronen Palan*

## Introduction

A report entitled *From Illegal Markets to Legitimate Businesses: The Portfolio of Organised Crime in Europe* (Savona and Michele 2015) typifies the growing awareness that the proceeds of crime find their way into the legitimate economy.[1] Following a thorough survey of seven European countries, the report concludes that the business sectors with the most cases of criminal investment are bars and restaurants; construction; the wholesale and retail trade, particularly food products and clothing; transportation; real-estate activities; and hotels. The report suggests that the favorite route for "going legit" is through the opacity provided by tax havens. The report does not ask or seek to answer one puzzling question: why do organized crime syndicates seek to go legit? Most studies suggest that criminal organizations are highly profitable. Why should they be interested in investing their capital in what appear to be much less profitable legitimate business ventures? This is the question I seek to address in this chapter: what are the incentives for business organizations to re-enter the legitimate economy and why is the offshore world the preferred route for doing so?

In effect, I am asking two separate questions: the first refers to the incentives for criminal organizations to legitimize their business (goals), and the second asks why they do so using offshore platforms (means). The conventional answer is that the incentives to launder money (or "go legit") are self-evident. The proceeds of crime are among the key pieces of evidence used by

[1] I would like to thank Matías Dewey and Jens Beckert for their helpful comments on an earlier draft of this chapter.

prosecutors and the courts to prove their cases; hence, criminal organizations have a strong incentive to eliminate such evidence. The use of offshore platforms is easily explained as well. The opacity provided by offshore jurisdictions ensures anonymity and a degree of freedom from surveillance that is not matched "onshore" (Palan 2003; Palan et al. 2010). I accept the above, but I note that it does not explain why criminal organizations reinvest in legitimate businesses.[2] To that end, I would like to add a more nuanced understanding of both the incentives and the means used by criminal organizations.

My argument in this chapter is theoretical. My approach is predicated on the proposition that the capitalist economy consists of co-habiting economies. One of these may be described as the "economy of the present." It is an economy of exchange of goods and services that is described well (or not so well, depending on one's opinion) by standard economic models. This economy is dwarfed today by an "economy of the future," or, as John R. Commons described it, "futurity." The economy of the future is an economy that trades in anticipated future earnings; it generates credit and value today on the basis of anticipated income streams.

However profitable, the organized criminal world operates largely in the economy of the present, either by trading in banned substances (including people) or the extraction of "value" out of current transactions. Organized crime cannot participate, however, in the far more lucrative economy of futurity. Organized crime business cannot trade, for instance, on its "goodwill"; it faces great barriers to extracting value—in the form of shares, bonds, or even loans—against future earning capacity and potential income streams. Organized crime is caught, therefore, in the slow lanes of the modern economy. But as many criminal organizations are run by savvy businessmen, they seek to access the economy of futurity by "laundering" not only money, but the very organizations they operate. The ease of incorporation and the opacity provided by offshore secrecy jurisdictions allow criminal organizations to appear to be legitimate businesses and thus to access the realm of futurity.

## Economies of Past and Future

The notion of economies of past and future is based on an interpretation of one of the main tenets of the school of evolutionary economics of Veblen and Commons (known otherwise as "old institutional economics," Commons

[2] Throughout this chapter I will use the term "business organization" in the same way as Diego Gambetta. Gambetta argues that the Sicilian mafia is a "specific economic enterprise, an industry which produces, promotes, and sells private protection" (Gambetta 1993: 1). The idea that criminal organizations are businesses is well established in the literature. I will therefore discuss specifically what are known as "organized crime" syndicates.

1961; Commons 1959 [1924]; Veblen 1898). The old institutional economics school stresses that every economic transaction takes place simultaneously in two realms: an exchange of goods or services, or conversely, exchange of debt and risk instruments (or financial instruments) takes place in one realm. Correspondingly, all economic exchanges are replicated in a legal realm and logged as property rights exchanges. Conventional economics is concerned primarily with actors' motives on the "real" side of the exchange and seeks to develop accounts of the systemic effects of economic exchanges based on the aggregation of individual motives and preferences in entering such contractual relationships. Old institutional economics, by contrast, pays great attention to the legal realm, believing that it shapes the dynamics of exchanges and not the other way around.

Such double exchanges serve to highlight the economic difference between legal and criminal economic activities. Property rights exchanges, or contracts, are specified in terms of time and place and are backed by a sovereign power. Sovereign power, therefore, is not only a political power but crucially also an economic power. Sovereign power provides the necessary "coding" for nearly all forms of economic exchange, defining the nature of the parties to a contract, including their rights and duties, as well as the salience of the contract itself. To achieve that, sovereign power encodes every single item or transaction located within a territorial space with its own sovereign barcode: individuals are defined as citizens, economic enterprises are licensed and follow certain rules of incorporation; social clubs or religious groups are licensed by the state and subject to rules of conduct. Every movable object, cars, airplanes, ships, or boats, must be licensed by states and display a flag or a license plate. In many countries pets and agricultural animals are numerated as well and given some sort of a passport, and so on. In this way the territorial space is populated by legally defined entities and items.

The system of coding is onerous, expansive, and fraught with ethical and normative questions of liberty and freedom. Why does it work? Sovereign power may be thought of in transaction cost terms: by providing a standardized system of coding and rules of exchange, the sovereign reduces transaction costs because most transactions are standardized. The state maintains an implicit contractual relationship with its citizens, whereby a certain degree of liberty is exchanged for economic welfare (North 1994). From this perspective the state can be seen as a "club good" in Buchanan's perspective (Buchanan 1965). The services of transaction cost reduction are explicitly withdrawn from criminal activity. "When a market is defined as illegal," write Beckert and Wehinger, "the state declines the protection of property rights, does not define and enforce standards for product quality, and can prosecute the actors within it" (Beckert and Wehinger 2013: 6). Because all economic exchanges are exchanges in property rights, transactions must be backed by some dimension of sovereign power. Criminal organizations tend to replicate certain aspects of sovereign economic power by the use of implicit or explicit coercive "privatized" power (Gambetta 1993). This renders criminal economic transactions far more expensive to maintain. The criminal organization spends considerable resources doing exactly what the sovereign does: coding the parties to the exchange and the rules of exchange as they go along, and maintaining coercive power to back up exchanges. The criminal world even maintains a certain "culture" and codes that serve to lower transaction costs.

Criminal organizations are, therefore, at a great disadvantage vis-à-vis legitimate organizations that are able to share in the lower transaction costs offered by a well-maintained polity. On the other hand, criminal organizations have certain advantages vis-à-vis legitimate businesses. Most importantly, criminal organizations typically do not pay tax towards the upkeep of the state, which amounts to an average of about 60–70 percent (or more) of a transaction, once we add up income tax, corporate tax, VAT, customs duties, and so on. Criminal organizations are able to extract, in addition, monopoly rent from their businesses which are not protected by various anti-trust legislation or other consumer-protection legislation (that is why they tend to be highly territorial). At the same time, criminal organizations "free-ride" on the sovereign by using its currency, rules of conduct that sustain other aspects of life, security, and so on. Presumably, the trade-off is beneficial, otherwise traditional criminal organizations would not exist.

Territorial states contain, therefore, two sets of economic organizations: (i) those working within the boundaries of the state-club rules, paying dues and being regulated, but benefitting from its sovereign power, and (ii) those who do not. It is noteworthy that criminal organizations tend to recruit personnel from the poorly educated, less privileged sections in society. This suggests that criminal businesses are not as lucrative as assumed.

This dichotomous picture is complicated further by the large grey area "in between," which contains legitimate organizations seeking to reduce their contribution to the sovereign, primarily to avoid and even evade tax, while remaining, overall, on the right side of the law, and criminal organizations seeking to benefit from sovereign protection but changing the apparent nature of their organizations. The offshore economy is a favorite hangout for these "in betweeners."

## Futurity and the Twilight Economy

So far I have presented an annotated description of criminal organizations as understood from a conventional economic perspective. Once we put on old institutional economics lenses, however, and examine these businesses more closely from the perspective of the dominant realm of legal transfer of property rights, a slightly different picture emerges. The legal realm of property transfer reveals a surprising divergence in the behavioral orientations of individuals and corporate entities towards wealth already accumulated and wealth to be accumulated (Palan and Mangraviti 2016). Consistent with its past orientation, standard economics is concerned, as John R. Commons argued, primarily with wealth-already-accumulated, while business, in contrast, is interested primarily in wealth-to-be-accumulated: the ownership, control, and leverage of future wealth. There are important distributional battles over wealth-already-accumulated, concerning the ownership of discrete assets, but wealth-to-be-accumulated is generated through organizations. As a result, investable assets are, strictly speaking, organizations or "going concerns" (Atkinson 2009). People invest, therefore, in organizations and not in assets. Only organizations are able to generate wealth that as yet is still to be accumulated.

Let us take an historical example that marked the development of an economy of the future. An illustration of the economic significance of intangibles can be inferred from the way the US Steel Trust was organized by J.P. Morgan and Co., and one of the largest and least liked railway barons, James Hill, largely to prevent the ruinous competition that Andrew Carnegie was about to launch with his competitors in Pittsburgh (for an additional discussion see Palan 2012, 2015).

The area around Pittsburgh was at the epicenter of the steel sector during the late nineteenth century, contributing about 80 to 85 percent to US steel production. Andrew Carnegie, a successful steel magnate, in 1899 announced his intention to build a larger plant with the latest improvements on the shore of Lake Erie. J.P. Morgan and Co. was called upon by some of Carnegie's competitors to establish, in response, a holding company that would take over all the plants and form an integrated large company to avoid this "ruinous competition" from Carnegie.

It was imperative that the new trust would buy all of Carnegie's interests in the region. The value of Carnegie's holdings on a traditional valuation of reconstruction costs was estimated at $75 million at the time. Carnegie, however, demanded and received $300 million in gold bonds as his share value in the new trust. Carnegie's explanation for the not inconsiderable difference of $225 million, recalls Ida Tarbell, was that "[b]usiness on a grand scale required special talent for organization and management, and that talent was rare... If the right men were obtained, they soon created capital; otherwise capital soon took wings" (Tarbell 1904: 9). This "talent" was described in business lingo as "goodwill." The difference in valuation, writes John Commons, could not have been ascribed "on the traditional theory of economics, as the value of the corporeal property. Nor was it incorporeal property since it was not a debt owed to Carnegie. The only other name that could be given to it was 'intangible property', the name given by the financial magnates themselves" (Commons 1961: 649–50). Carnegie charged, in effect, $225 million for his personal goodwill (Tarbell 1904).

But what exactly was the goodwill that Carnegie brought to the enterprise, considering that he henceforth withdrew from steel making? The value of his goodwill was the potential or anticipated future earnings that were to accrue to the new enterprise on the basis that Carnegie was removed from competition. Carnegie was not alone in obtaining "goodwill" money during the creation of the US Steel Trust. The establishment of US Steel was such an audacious act that overnight $700 million of "corporeal" property held by the different steel barons who made up US Steel became $1,600 million (Albion and Williamson 1944). Or to put it in different terms, the new company was capitalized at an equivalent of one fourth of US GNP at the time. J.P. Morgan and Co.'s commission alone was $150 million, or nearly 2 percent of US GNP. This amounted to a huge injection of capital into the economy. So much so that Carnegie refused to accept shares in the new trust, which he considered "water," and demanded gold bonds. The creation of so much new capital under the banner of "goodwill," in and by itself, sparked the 1903 financial crisis (Jospehson 1962). But despite its stock being "water," US steel survived and flourished.

Today according to some estimates, the goodwill value of the Standard & Poor's 500 amounts to about 80 percent of their value. The consulting firm, Ocean Tomo, estimates that for the year 2009 the relevant value for the EU was 70 percent, 35.8 percent for Japan, and 73.5 percent for China (Ocean Tomo 2009). Wealth in modern economies is largely a denomination, therefore, of goodwill.

The story of the establishment of the US Steel Trust is the story of the magic of the legitimate market. Considering that businesses seek to capture future wealth (wealth yet to be accumulated), businesses will be prepared to pay for those future income streams today, if at a certain discount. In effect, investors are betting on those organizations they believe will generate future income streams. But current investments in future income streams create a value at the present time. The organization is valued above its current assets, or replacement value, and as a result the whole is more than the sum of its parts (Palan 2012). This additional value is described by Commons as "futurity" and it is entered in the books under the category of "intangible property" or "goodwill."

Criminal organizations cannot directly access the economy of futurity. Such organizations are not formally constituted; they have no formal share ownership structure supported by the sovereign, and their business interests are not protected by the state in such a way that future income streams are secured.

Criminal organizations may be able to generate great profits today, but they are not able to leverage their profits against the future. They are stuck, therefore, in the slow lane of the economy. That is where the offshore economy comes into play.

## The Offshore Economy

By "offshore economy" I refer to a combination of jurisdictions, entities, and economic transactions that are registered through the archipelago of jurisdictions described colloquially as "tax havens" or less pejoratively as "offshore financial centers" (Hampton 1996; Palan 2003; Wigan 2013). Offshore financial centers are typically defined as financial centers that serve primarily a non-resident clientele. Non-resident clients are prepared to invest in the circuitous and often expensive route of registering through a string of "out of the way" jurisdictions, argue their defenders, because they offer superior and efficient services to their clients. Critics argue, by contrast, that offshore financial centers attract a non-resident clientele because they provide a deliberate, and legally backed, veil of secrecy that ensures that those from outside that jurisdiction who make use of its regulations cannot be identified.

Various types of crime are facilitated under such cover, including tax evasion, money laundering, embezzlement, and financing of international criminal organizations. The range of regulations that might be created by secrecy jurisdictions (a synonym for tax haven) for use by those not normally resident in their domain is wide. Such regulations might include:

- corporate laws, including those on incorporation, company residence, the types of share in issue, the use of nominees, the filing of accounts and other information on public record, and the maintenance of records themselves;
- trust law, including those on the registration and taxation of trusts, the use of nominees, the right of settlors to declare trusts for their own benefit, the filing of information and accounts with regulatory authorities, and the need to maintain records;
- banking laws, including the right to maintain bank secrecy for taxation, civil law, and criminal law purposes;
- regulations with regard to competition law, labor issues, shipping, environmental matters, health and safety, and other issues which might, either through their absence, level of obligation, or compliance obligations, give rise to a lesser burden than those commonplace in other jurisdictions;
- information-exchange agreements relating to civil, criminal, and taxation law issues;

- legal cooperation regulations, including the willingness of the jurisdiction to enforce obligations arising in other jurisdictions through its legal system;
- accounting and other information-disclosure requirements of a non-statutory nature.

In combination, these regulations cover a large range of business activity and it is this, when combined with secrecy, that provides enormous scope for abuse. A number of related initiatives have been introduced in the EU and internationally in order to lift the veil of opacity (Palan et al. 2010).

Recent research has demonstrated that these jurisdictions serve the purpose of tax evasion, avoidance, and money laundering by facilitating arbitrage techniques. Arbitrage techniques operate through linked corporate structures located in different offshore financial center jurisdictions in order to take advantage of blind spots created through differentials in law, regulations, taxation, and/or transfer pricing techniques. One way firms can utilize these assets in multi-jurisdictional tax-minimization schemes is by separating tangible sources of income, such as the sale of hardware, from the intangible sources of income embedded therein, such as the sale of patent rights or intellectual property rights associated with the hardware. This is the technique used, for instance, by Apple Inc. (Apple 2014; Palan and Mangraviti 2016; Permanent Subcommittee on Investigations 2013). Other typical arbitraging techniques in the real-estate sector operate through a series of entities owning property (typically commercial real estate) located in different countries. Vendors can avoid capital gains tax and purchaser's stamp duty simply by purchasing one of the linked companies in a foreign jurisdiction (Palan and Mangraviti 2016).

The third technique that may be facilitated by offshore financial centers (although not necessarily only through these jurisdictions) is so-called "financial engineering." Financial engineering uses sophisticated financial instruments such as derivatives and swaps in order to ensure that the issuing business in charge of final transactions, or the business that appears to gain from the final transactions and hence where "profit" is logged, happen to be located in territories that levy minimal or no taxation on such entities. Hence, for instance, most hedge funds are registered in tax havens. Another popular technique is that final transactions are structured in such a way that they are logged or registered in political platforms that levy minimal taxation on a particular form of final transaction that is used for such cases—hence tax is minimized. Businesses set up holding companies and various types of special purpose vehicles in offshore locations for that purpose. They also use financial engineering to alter the character of income subject to taxation and minimize the relevant tax contribution. A third well-known technique is that the final transaction is structured in such a way that the maturity point of the transaction that triggers taxation is deferred to some point in the future, but the future never truly materializes, and/or the transaction is structured in such a way that it takes place in a simulated realm that is not easily recognizable by the tax authorities and hence the transaction may disappear completely from their radar. That is where derivatives come into play (Palan et al. 2016).

The archipelago of jurisdictions that offer such facilities can be organized into three conglomerations. One conglomeration has coalesced around what I described in a series of publications as the "Second British Empire." It is centered on the City of London, British-dependent territories such as Jersey and Guernsey, British overseas territories such as the Cayman Islands and Bermuda, and former British colonies, such as Hong Kong and Singapore. This conglomeration accounts for roughly 40 percent of wholesale international financial transactions. The second is a European conglomeration that consists of the Benelux countries, Switzerland, and Ireland, and accounts for about 15 percent of international financial transactions. A third one, now emerging, is an Indian Ocean conglomeration that consists of the Persian Gulf states, Mauritius, and the Seychelles. It is estimated that there are in excess of $25 or even $30 trillion of financial assets registered in such locations.

## Offshore and Crime: The Conventional Story

There is a considerable literature documenting the association between tax havens and crime. Meyer Lansky, the legendary treasurer of the mob, is reputedly to have forged links from the 1930s between Switzerland, the Bahamas, and the large East Coast criminal groups. There is some debate about how precisely Lansky and Co. used tax havens, whether only for money-laundering purposes (Maillard 1998) or for general financial criminal activities (Blum 1984; Dupuis 1998; Naím 2005; Naylor 2002). There is agreement, however, that organized crime is strongly represented in some tax havens.

Maingot maintains that "some 75 percent of all sophisticated drug trafficking operations use offshore secrecy havens" (1995: 181). He also believes that drug money was the principal cause of the phenomenal growth of the Caribbean havens in the 1970s and 1980s (see also Naylor 2002). Of the criminal cases identified in Internal Revenue Service investigations from 1978 to 1983 that occurred in the Caribbean, 45 percent involved illegal transactions derived from legal income (tax evasion on otherwise legitimate trade). In the other 55 percent, illegal income was involved, and 161 cases dealt with drug trafficking. Of these, 29 percent involved the Cayman Islands, 28 percent involved Panama, 22 percent the Bahamas, and 11 percent the Dutch Antilles.

These four offshore sites alone accounted for 85 percent of the cases involving transactions of illegal income (Maingot 1995).

In late 2005, Callum McCarthy, head of the UK's Financial Services Authority, publicly declared that he had information showing that organized crime groups had infiltrated some of London's best-known financial institutions. They did so to learn logistics and mechanisms and techniques to avoid detection.

Tax havens are also associated with money laundering. The International Monetary Fund estimates the magnitude of money laundering worldwide at 3–5 percent of the world's GDP (INCSR 2008: 5), a figure larger than the US federal budget. Not all money laundering operates through tax havens. Tax havens are, in fact, a minority of the countries that appear on the list of jurisdictions defined by INCSR as "major money laundering countries" (2008: 58).

Rawlings and Unger (2005) argue that some tax havens specifically target criminal money as a developmental strategy. In 1995, the Seychelles government passed the Economic Development Act (EDA), which created a board that could give specified concessions and incentives to foreign investors. "One of these incentives was complete immunity from prosecution in criminal proceedings and the protection of assets from forfeiture even if investments were earned as a result of crimes committed outside the Seychelles" (Rawlings and Unger 2005: 5). To obtain this immunity an individual had to invest a minimum of $10 million in the Seychelles. The EDA was strongly condemned and the provision was repealed in 2000, but by then the funds were already in the Seychelles.

Pacific Island tax havens are strongly associated with money-laundering schemes. Nauru, a small Pacific atoll, was involved in the largest money-laundering case in history, the so-called Russiagate scandal of the late 1990s, which involved the Bank of New York. Victor Melnikov, deputy chair of the Russian Central Bank, stated that $70 billion had been transferred to Nauru from Russia in 1998, compared with total Russian exports of $74 billion. This is a figure remarkably close to the amount of International Monetary Fund credit advanced to Russia in July 1998 in response to the financial crisis that engulfed the country that year.

Palan et al. (2016) show that the key destinations for Russian "investment" abroad are Cyprus, the Netherlands, the British Virgin Islands, and Luxemburg. But while tax avoidance is a common drive for offshore schemes around the world, in Russia, intricate chains of offshore entities are constructed with the aim of hiding the ultimate ownership of assets. In Russian offshore "envelopes" Cyprus has historically been a popular node of initial incorporation of the offshore entity, which in turn would have financial and legal links to other financial havens in order to be able to tap into the onshore financial systems of Europe and North America.

Offshore subsidiaries of the world's premier banks are also heavily implicated in embezzlement and money laundering. Oxfam estimates that from 1993 to 1998, during the reign of Nigeria's dictator Sani Abacha, about $5 billion disappeared from state coffers, of which $2.5 billion was embezzled by the dictator and his family alone (Hodess 2004: 5). The Swiss Federal Banking Commission released the names of the banks involved in management of the money embezzled by the former Nigerian dictator in September 2000. The list contains the names of some of the best-known international banks, such as Credit Suisse, Crédit Agricole Indosuez, BNP, and Baring Brothers.

Tax havens undoubtedly facilitate tax evasion, tax avoidance, money laundering, and corruption, but no one is able to estimate the sums involved with any degree of accuracy. Consequently, no one is able to address the corruption that underpins this market.

## Offshore Crime and Futurity

Money-laundering activities are typically understood to serve the purpose of hiding the proceeds of crime. I have little doubt that this is correct. But as this chapter argues, there are additional incentives for going legit. As the report by Savona and Michele (2015) shows, European organized crime syndicates are using tax havens in order to reinvest in certain types of business. Let us recall what they are: bars and restaurants; construction; the wholesale and retail trade, particularly food products and clothing; transportation; real-estate activities; and hotels. It appears to me that these businesses possess the following characteristics:

- they are relatively uncomplicated, primarily service economy types of business that do not require complex manufacturing or technological knowhow (such as high-tech);
- they are often relatively small businesses, require relatively little initial capital, and, considering the number of such businesses that are established every day in a modern economy, offer a degree of safety in numbers from the tax authorities' scrutiny;
- they offer opportunities for further profit making through relationships with public officials, whereby additional profits could be made through the application of bribery or coercion;
- they are the typical type of businesses that offer further opportunities for tax evasion and avoidance;
- they can generate easily understandable "goodwill" value, which can be leveraged against future income streams.

That last point is least understood or discussed in the specialist literature on crime. Money is not simply laundered in order to appear legitimate; money is laundered in order to gain access to the future economy. The leverage that the future economy provides, the ability to create "goodwill" value (associated with a discrete business enterprise such as a bar, restaurant, or hotel), which can then be used either to sell on, or in order to leverage credit in the legit economy, is what organized crime syndicates are after. The great advantage of the future economy may explain the puzzling preference of criminal syndicates for turning away from supposedly highly profitable criminal business to much less profitable, and more risky, legitimate enterprises.

## References


Albion, Robert Greenhalgh, and Harold Francis Williamson. 1944. *The Growth of the American Economy: An Introduction to the Economic History of the United States*. New York: Prentice Hall.

Apple. 2014. *Testimony of Apple Inc. before the Permanent Subcommittee on Investigations US Senate*. <https://www.apple.com/pr/pdf/Apple_Testimony_to_PSI.pdf> (accessed July 25, 2016).

Atkinson, Glen. 2009. "Going Concerns, Futurity and Reasonable Value." *Journal of Economic Issues* 43(2): pp. 433–41.

Beckert, Jens, and Frank Wehinger. 2013. "In the Shadow: Illegal Markets and Economic Sociology." *Socio-Economic Review* 11(1): pp. 5–30.

Blum, R. H. 1984. *Offshore Haven Banks, Trusts, and Companies: The Business of Crime in the Euromarket*. New York: Praeger.

Buchanan, James M. 1965. "An Economic Theory of Clubs." *Economica* 32(125): pp. 1–14.

Commons, John Rogers. 1959 [1924]. *The Legal Foundations of Capitalism*. Madison: University of Wisconsin Press.

Commons, John Rogers. 1961. *Institutional Economics*. Madison: University of Wisconsin Press.

Dupuis, M.C. 1998. *Finance criminelle: Comment le crime organisé blanchit l'argent sale, coll criminalité internationale*. Paris: Presses Universitaires de France.

Gambetta, Diego. 1993. *The Sicilian Mafia: The Business of Private Protection*. Cambridge, MA: Harvard University Press.

Hampton, Mark P. 1996. *The Offshore Interface: Tax Havens in the Global Economy*. Basingstoke: Macmillan.

Hodess, Robin. 2004. *Introduction: Transparency International. Where Did the Money Go? Global Corruption Report*. London: Pluto.

INCSR. 2008. *US International Narcotics Control Strategy Report, vol. 2*. US Department of State, Bureau for International Narcotics and Law Enforcement Affairs, March.

Jospehson, Matthew. 1962. *The Robber Barons: The Great American Capitalists, 1861–1901*. New York: Transaction Publishing.

Maillard J. de. 1998. *Un monde sans loi*. Paris: Stock.

Maingot, Anthony P. 1995. "Offshore Secrecy Centers and the Necessary Role of States: Bucking the Trend." *Journal of Interamerican Studies and World Affairs* 37(4): pp. 1–24.

Naím, Moisés. 2005. *Illicit: How Smugglers, Traffickers, and Copycats are Hijacking the Global Economy*. New York: Doubleday.

Naylor, R. T. 2002. *Wages of Crime: Black Markets, Illegal Finance and the Underworld Economy*. Ithaca, NY: Cornell University Press.

North, Douglass C. 1994. "Economic Performance through Time." *American Economic Review* 84(3): pp. 359–68.

Ocean Tomo. 2009. *Components of S&P 500 Market Value*. <http://www.oceantomo.com>.

Palan, Ronen. 2003. *The Offshore World: Sovereign Markets, Virtual Places, and Nomad Millionaires*. Ithaca, NY: Cornell University Press.

Palan, Ronen. 2012. "The Financial Crisis and Intangible Value." *Capital and Class* 37(1): pp. 65–77.

Palan, Ronen. 2015. "Futurity, Pro-cyclicality and Financial Crises." *New Political Economy* 20(3): pp. 367–85.

Palan, Ronen, and Giovanni Mangraviti. 2016. "Troubling Tax Havens: Multijurisdictional Arbitrage and Corporate Tax Footprint Reduction." In *Handbook on Wealth and the Super-Rich*, edited by Iain Hay and Jonathan V. Beaverstock, pp. 422–41. London: Edward Elgar.

Palan, Ronen, Richard Murphy, and Christian Chavagneux. 2010. *Tax Havens: How Globalization Really Works*. Ithaca, NY: Cornell University Press.

Palan, Ronen, Michael Rafferty, and Duncan Wigan. 2016. "The Economy of Deferral and Displacement: Finance, Shadow Banking and Fiscal Arbitrage." In *Shadow Banking: Scope, Origins, Theory*, edited by Anastasia Nesvetailova. London: Routledge.

Permanent Subcommittee on Investigations. 2013. *Offshore Profit Shifting and the US Tax Code: Part 2 (Apple Inc.)*. Washington, DC: US Congress. <http://www.hsgac.senate.gov/subcommittees/investigations/hearings/offshore-profit-shifting-and-the-us-tax-code_-part-2>.

Rawlings, Greg, and Brigitte Unger. 2005. "Competing for Criminal Money." Utrecht School of Economics discussion paper series 05-26.

Savona, Ernesto U., and Michele Riccardi. 2015. *From Illegal Markets to Legitimate Businesses: The Portfolio of Organized Crime in Europe. Final Report of Project OCP—Organised Crime Portfolio*. Trento: Transcrime, Università degli Studi di Trento.

Tarbell, Ida M. 1904. *The History of the Standard Oil Company*. New York: Cosimo.

Veblen, Thorstein B. 1898. "Why Is Economics Not an Evolutionary Science?" *Quarterly Journal of Economics* 12(4): pp. 373–97.

Wigan, Duncan. 2013. "Offshore Financial Centres." In *Europe and the Governance of Global Finance*, edited by Daniel Mugge, pp. 156–70. Oxford: Oxford University Press.

# Part III

# The State in Informal Market Places

# 7

# State-Sponsored Protection Rackets

## Regulating the Market for Counterfeit Clothing in Argentina

*Matías Dewey*

### Introduction

The fact that illegal markets thrive is something of a puzzle to sociology. Conflict resolution, regulation of competition, and formal sources of credit—mechanisms generally seen as essential to the functioning of their legal counterparts—are all absent. Despite this lack of legal frames, new illegal markets are emerging continuously. Within them, competition exists, actors make investments, and, contrary to expectations, violence is not always a foregone conclusion of illegal activity. It follows, then, that other *informal* mechanisms are at work in illegal markets that allow them to flourish.

Analysis of these informal social mechanisms is essential for a better understanding of the internal coordination. Silence and secrecy, vital for successful illegal market exchanges, can be either institutionalized as a result of agreements with varying degrees of explicitness—as is the case for looted antiquities sold in exclusive London galleries (Mackenzie and Green 2009) and illegal organ transplantation (Steiner in this volume)—or the consequence of laws unambiguously promoting opacity and ignorance, as is the case for tax havens (Volkov 2011). For their part, scholars studying mafias have highlighted the role of the sale of private protection as a mechanism that oils social relationships, especially in environments characterized by high levels of interpersonal distrust (Gambetta 1993; Varese 2004; Volkov 2002; Campana 2011). With regard to the "banking" of illegal markets, it is not only the role of formal institutions such as tax havens, loan sharks, or even micro-finance organizations that has been stressed, but also that of informal institutions, including the "hawala" system in Arab countries (Qorchi et al. 2003) and "pasanaku," an ancient Andean group-based method for raising money and financing individual needs.

The main goal of this chapter is to dissect the role of one of these mechanisms—state-sponsored protection rackets—in the context of illegal markets. As shall be noted, protection can be a "service" provided by extra-legal organizations such as the mafia, or illegally by the state itself. Whereas in the first case protection acts as a shield against the harmful actions of some anonymous person, in the latter case (illegal) protection works as a shield against the law itself. As I argue in the next section, the latter does not exclude violent actions stimulated by servants of the state and, since it is carried out by official authorities, necessarily implies the non-enforcement of the law or a *de facto* suspension of it. The suspension of the enforcement of the law is sold as a particular illegal service and thus opens up a space of social relationships regulated by extra-legal principles.[1]

I provide evidence that such state-sponsored protection rackets are present on a massive scale at La Salada, an illegal and informal marketplace occupying eighteen hectares of a suburban area close to the city of Buenos Aires. This is a single-product marketplace in which all of the 7,822 stalls sell clothing that is for the most part counterfeit and produced in nearby sweatshops.[2] La Salada is a major supply center for these goods, the first link in the supply chain of the entire Argentine market. Smaller, satellite garment marketplaces in other provinces are stocked by buyers traveling to Buenos Aires and purchasing directly from producers, who rent a stall at La Salada in order to sell items manufactured in the sweatshops they run in the local area. As the heart of the country's illegal garment market, La Salada is where market, government, and state actors meet. The protection rackets in operation there thus affect the workings of the whole market.

The state-sponsored protection rackets at La Salada serve as an interface between the interests of garment producers and those of government: the latter indirectly imposes the payment of an informal regular fee, seeking to

[1] I am indebted to Renate Mayntz who helped me to specify the difference between mafia and state-sponsored protection rackets. Although at first sight state-sponsored protection rackets appear as a protection against the "law"—that is, not against potential violent retaliation—a closer look shows that law-enforcement agencies that provide this kind of illegal service are highly corrupt institutions and therefore have close links to criminals. This way, buyers of protection rackets pay first of all to evade capture by the law, but also, secondly, to avoid violent actions that law-enforcement agencies outsource to criminals.

[2] The author counted the stalls with the help of a manual counter in July 2013. The estimated margin of error is approximately 100 stalls and variations on this number, depending on whether new streets have been acquired by the market and filled with additional stalls.

finance local political and police activities, while the former pay a fee in order to produce garments under officially banned conditions.

Focusing on the governmental use of the selective enforcement of the law, the present chapter seeks to make a contribution on informal mechanisms fostering unlawful exchanges. In seeing structures of protection rackets such as that at La Salada as a set of unwritten, shared rules that are "created, communicated, and enforced outside officially sanctioned channels" (Helmke and Levitsky 2006), the chapter also offers novel insights into the analysis of economically relevant informal arrangements. Examining how authorities maintain them helps us to explain a political economy configuration, the most visible outcome of which is a remarkable proliferation of sweatshops and low-cost garment consumption.

This chapter is structured as follows. First, I briefly review the literature on protection rackets and analyze them from a theoretical perspective. Second, I address the political economy configuration that led to the emergence of the illegal garment market centered on La Salada and the structure of state-sponsored protection rackets in place there. After referring in the third section to the methods used during the fieldwork, I then present the empirical evidence that state-sponsored protection rackets exist at La Salada and regulate its economic activities. Lastly, the conclusion outlines the relevance of this argument for future research on the interface between state and informal or illegal markets, and its particular importance for markets of officially banned goods.

## Protection Rackets and the State

Over the years, sociology has established solid knowledge of the main business of mafia groups: the production, promotion, and sale of private protection (Gambetta 1993: 1. See also: Chu 2000; Volkov 2002; Varese 2004; Campana 2011). Informed by the idea of "sale of protection," scholars have observed similar patterns between state agencies and criminal groups, such as the state-sponsored "protective umbrellas" of gambling houses and prostitution rings in China (Gong 2002; Shieh 2005; Zhang and Chin 2008; Wang 2012, 2014) and the mafia, or "roofs," in Russia (Galeotti 1998; Volkov 2002; Stephenson 2016). In the Americas, constellations of protection rackets have mainly been observed as a problem of state capacity or willingness to enforce the law. Early studies on the gambling business in Chicago (Haller 1971; Reuter 1984) and on prostitution, gambling, and betting elsewhere (Gardiner 1970) have also underlined the role played by the legitimacy of certain banned products; that is, the "popular desire to consume such illegal services as gambling and prostitution" (Gardiner 1967: 124). In Mexico, institutions of protection established by the political elites, law-enforcement agencies, and drug-trafficking organizations can, Lupsha (1991) notes, be traced throughout the recent history of the country. "Criminals were often under the control of politicians and bureaucrats and not the other way around," asserts Flores Pérez (2013: 518), clarifying exactly who protects whom in the Mexican context. Meanwhile, in their comparison of Colombia and Mexico, Snyder and Duran-Martinez (2009) found that state-sponsored protection rackets do not necessarily breed violence, a meaningful finding when analyzing legitimacy in illegal markets. Institutions of protection have also been found in situations ranging from street vending in Mexico (Cross and Peña 2006), to drug trafficking (Arias 2006) and gambling (Misse 2007) in Rio de Janeiro.

In the particular case of Argentina, the state's response to crime has been theoretically approached as *state regulation* of (Sain 2008) or the *sale of protection* to (Dewey 2012, 2015) illegal market actors. Both perspectives consider a pattern of behavior rooted in history. According to this position, security forces and Argentine politicians at different levels of government have colluded with outlaws, with a view to either making private financial gains or else to financing political campaigns (Dinatale et al. 2005). Far from being isolated cases of corruption, this pattern shows that the selective enforcement of the law has always been an informal way to negotiate order, extract resources—economic and political—and control crime (Kalmanowiecki 2000; Sain 2008; Barreneche 2009; Bohoslavsky 2010; Amengual 2011). A brief overview of the available literature shows that state-sponsored protection rackets are an underanalyzed phenomenon. Often regarded as a problem of police officers "turning a blind eye" or as sheer corruption, studies usually fail to provide fine-grained accounts of how protection rackets work and their function in the context of illegal economies. Ultimately, such accounts are needed in order to provide a satisfactory explanation of *why*; that is, why protection rackets are deep-rooted informal mechanisms present in several illegal markets.

State-sponsored protection rackets necessarily imply the non-enforcement of the law, an action that is carried out intentionally by politicians and police forces, with the capture of economic resources as the goal. As I will discuss later, state-sponsored protection rackets also establish a new power relationship beneficial for state agents. The relevance of the non-enforcement is twofold. On the one hand, it is a valuable asset for actors exchanging officially banned goods and services: their wares are not seized and they avoid prosecution or incarceration. Hence, as the literature on corruption and organized crime extensively shows, illegal market actors are willing to pay for such non-enforcement. On the other hand, authorities might be interested in the provision of non-enforcement as a source of economic resources and power over criminal groups. Elsewhere (Dewey 2012, 2011), drawing on studies about the mafia, I defined this non-enforcement as a form of protection.

Because state servants, notably police forces, have the power to manipulate the enforcement of the law, they are able to suspend its application and to transform it into a commodity that is sold to those who need "protection" from it. Needless to say, enforcing the law rightfully remains a possibility; this constant threat means that social relationships between state agents and illegal market actors can only be asymmetrical. State actors are empowered by the possibility to enforce or suspend the law in one way or another, which affords them a certain degree of control over illegal market actors and transactions.[3]

Although some parallels may be drawn, the sale of protection should not be seen as a sale of inaction, a misunderstanding probably derived from the common phrase "to turn a blind eye." Situations of course exist in which inaction and protection do appear to be the same phenomenon: for instance, if a police officer charges a law-breaking motorist a certain amount of money in exchange for not applying the official fine, then protection from the law is offered through inaction. However, other constellations suggest that the sale of protection is a phenomenon in its own right. Examples of this can be seen when police officers refrain from taking action in order to create a specific demand for protection. A shopkeeper, for instance, might refuse to pay "additional contributions" for protection; in retaliation, they would suffer police inaction, fall victim to crime, and thus be indirectly compelled to require the previously rejected protection. Here, inaction generates a demand for protection. Put another way, protection is commonly carried out through action; it does not entail "doing nothing." Protection is, therefore, the product of organization. While the goal of state-sponsored protection rackets is to function as mechanisms for the extraction of economic resources, they also allow the control of illegal actors and exchanges.

## Methods

The case study presented here is the result of seven months of ethnographic immersion in La Salada marketplace. I forged many relationships during my time in the market: with residents of the area, informal workers in the market, and lenders at a micro-credit institution. Through snowball sampling, I came

[3] In this regard, scholars usually ask if this is a case of extortion and not of protection. In my view, we can apply Federico Varese's (Varese 2014: 350) explanation for the case of the mafia. State agents do indeed force the extraction of resources for services that are promised and delivered. Even when they might overcharge for a service and supply one of poor quality, it does not follow that the provided protection is bogus. In fact, as I will show, if the illegal market grows and outlaws freely participate in the market, it means that protection is being delivered.

to spend a great deal of time with a Bolivian family, owners of a market stall at La Salada and responsible for its day-to-day operation.

In total, I conducted 109 in-depth interviews with actors at La Salada (where permission was given, the interview was recorded. Otherwise, it was written up afterwards). Armed with these data, I was able to uncover and analyze the protection-racket structure that underlies the market and molds the expectations, behaviors, fears, and economic calculations of its participants. The existence and workings of the protection-racket structure was verified with the help of two types of data. Firstly, to establish the overall size of the marketplace I counted the number of stalls, including both those located inside the site's several warehouse-like buildings (shed markets) and the open-air stalls lining the surrounding streets. Secondly, I questioned actors from different sectors of the marketplace in order to ascertain the reach of the informal taxation system and elicit information regarding the amount and frequency of the fees paid. After cross-referencing the data with the statements of the interview subjects, it was discovered that stallholders in the shed markets and the street markets were paying fees of differing amounts. This was attributed to the existence of different "fee zones," which help to soften the blow of a period of low sales and intensify the positive impact of busy sales periods. The zones were shown to be crucial in helping stallholders decide where to rent a stall. As well as workers within the market, I also reached out to actors with high-ranking positions in government: a former principal commandant of the Argentine National Gendarmerie, two local politicians working for the local government, four shed-market managers (three current, one former), an informal fee collector, and the former advisor to a previous secretary of commerce. These interviews served to establish links between government agencies and La Salada's structure of protection rackets.

Ethnographic fieldwork stands at the center of my study of La Salada marketplace. As other scholars have already established, it is through this method alone that power structures can be properly studied and "clandestine connections" most accurately reconstructed (Auyero and Joseph 2007: 5; Kubik 2009: 31). Patterns of conduct and repeat references made by market actors can, through the standard ethnographic research practice described by Katz (2001, 2002) and Becker (1958), be assigned evidentiary value. Further standard procedures used to trace and confirm links were cross-checking and member checking. It is through these methods that the state-sponsored protection rackets and their central role in market life came to light and that beneficiaries of the collected fees could be confirmed. The latter—namely, ten state agencies at various levels of government—were explicitly named by three different interview subjects (a fee collector, an ex-manager, and a local politician) with no links to one another.

## Sweatshops and Counterfeiting: A Macro Perspective

Counterfeiting relies on the existence of sweatshops as a means of production and on the popularity of certain goods. The fact that both sweatshop production and the market for counterfeit clothing have become prolific in Argentina can be traced back to the seismic shift in the structure of the country's garment industry that followed the military coup d'état in 1976. The garment industry had previously been of considerable economic importance, but the new regime's radical free-market policies, introduced upon seizing power and in force until the 1990s, led to its decimation. Globally, the textile industry saw most production relocate to Asian countries, which led to tens of thousands of garment workers in Argentina losing their jobs. It is these structural transformations that contributed to the proliferation of sweatshop-produced and counterfeit garments: the redundant garment workers continued to use their skills by founding small, informal production units. Later waves of mostly Bolivian migrants settled throughout the suburban area of Greater Buenos Aires and established their own sweatshops, which also flouted labor laws concerning wages and worker safety and led to a generalized informalization of the whole industrial sector. A partial negative integration followed, in which specific types of sweatshops are relied on by Argentina's remaining legal garment producers, whose strategy has been to cater to the high-end niche.[4] Despite also partly depending on sweatshop production, "legal" clothing has risen in price on account of new commercialization formats such as "shopping malls" and "outlets," meaning that they are unaffordable for the majority of Argentines. The industry is currently divided in terms of both methods of production and accessibility of garments, with one side of the division operating almost fully legally and catering to middle and upper sectors, and the other side of the division oriented to mass consumption and characterized by informality and illegality. It is the focus of this chapter, La Salada marketplace, which constitutes the main supply center for the mass consumption side. Significantly, the flows of money and goods at the marketplace attract not only sweatshop producers and wholesale buyers, but also police officers and politicians.

## The Marketplace: A Brief Introduction

The demise of the textile industries and rising unemployment in the immigrant population during the 1990s had a direct impact on the area that now

[4] Interviews with sweatshop producers and workers.

hosts La Salada, which subsequently underwent a dramatic change. La Salada covers eighteen hectares of mostly flat land on the outskirts of the city of Buenos Aires and is dominated by the shed markets built to house the majority of the 7,822 market stalls that trade there. Inside the sheds, stallholders benefit from, for example, electricity and other utilities. Outside, the remaining stallholders are provided with rows of wire-mesh structures that are a permanent feature of the nearby streets. Being a single-product marketplace, nearly all the stalls sell garments: La Salada has become the focal point for a countrywide informal economy. In this case, the marketplace is the primary provider of clothing to the lower and middle classes in Argentina, as well as in neighboring countries. Three times a week, 200 long-distance buses and thousands of cars arrive at the marketplace to buy wholesale counterfeit garments branded with Adidas, Puma, Disney, and more. Even with the cost of traveling across the country to reach the marketplace, the counterfeit goods are still cheaper than the originals, a testament to the success of La Salada's wholesaling approach.

There are three key actors in this marketplace. First, there are at least three managers who own and lease a large number of stalls. Consequently, their business is essentially one of real estate. They own shopping mall-like facilities sub-divided into thousands of $2m^2$ stalls, which are rented to sweatshop garment producers. Their business, therefore, depends on the producers. If the latter are stopped by the police on the way to the marketplace and their goods are seized, or if the police enter the shed markets and confiscate their wares, the managers' business is seriously damaged. In consequence, they have established a system of money collection within the sheds in order to fund the protection rackets run by the police and political authorities. Hence, it is the police's selective enforcement of the law that is behind the creation and continued functioning of protection rackets.

Ranking second in order of importance are the sweatshop producers, both those who manufacture plain, unbranded items and those who produce counterfeits. Their position is typical of illegal markets: because they are infringing several regulations and laws and their actions are not supported by state law, they are subject to legal repercussions, such as asset seizure or arrest. In consequence, they are obliged either to evade punishment or to accept "state protection." Finally, the third relevant actors are state servants, namely, police officers and health and safety inspectors. They are not only underpaid, but also belong to institutions largely known for protecting criminals in exchange for money (Sain 2013; Dewey 2015).

As briefly depicted, the state-sponsored protection rackets are in the interests not only of the state servants, but also of the managers and producers/stallholders, demonstrating that these interests intersect. Working at this intersection, the aforementioned institutionalized protection rackets help coordinate the interests of all actors involved. By relaying the experiences of an ex-fee collector working in one of the shed markets, a sweatshop producer, one of the shed markets' former managers, a former officer of the *Gendarmería*, and a mayor's secretary, I will trace the protection-racket structure from both a top-down and a bottom-up perspective.

## Protection Rackets and the Police

Stocky, tough Rodrigo is a busy man, and it is not easy to get an interview with him. Because his father bought one of the former leisure centers that became the shed markets, Rodrigo has been able to watch La Salada's growth from a privileged position. What was once a recreational area for families to relax in saltwater swimming pools and thermal springs underwent a dramatic transformation when the economy faltered in the 1980s and 1990s. When visitor numbers plummeted and maintenance of the pools became impossible, Rodrigo reacted by reinventing the property as a well-known discotheque, and reinventing himself as a successful manager of a group of *cumbia* singers, known as *cumbieros*. His entrepreneurial streak continued in the 1990s with a further diversification into the garment market, which proved to be lucrative. By filling in the pools with rubble and other debris, Rodrigo was able to convert the space into market stalls that he, along with the managers of the other two big shed markets, still rents out to stallholders selling garments. From the late 1990s onwards, Rodrigo's business turned into one of real estate.

Despite the difficulties, I managed to meet with Rodrigo, sitting with him for three hours in the office he has had decorated with *cumbieros* posters and where every available surface is covered with piles of merchandise. "I will show you the people who visited us [at the disco]: Ricardo Darin, Susana Gimenez, all famous people, good times," he says, calling to his assistant to fetch a photo album. The album is filled with the expected images of TV stars posing for the camera, but there is far more to the story than smiling celebrities. He points to his former business partner, saying: "He was a cop [*taquero*]," before turning the page to point out some more figures, explaining that "he was a cop, we were friends, he was a doctor in the Buenos Aires police, and he was actually the manager of all the doctors [*capo medico*]. He helped me. And the guy on the left, he was also a policeman." The photo album became a symbol of what Rodrigo went on to say in our meeting: "Nobody tells me the true story. Who would? The police come and surround you . . . They come to pick it [the money collected to pay the protection rackets] up . . . Well, you [as manager] have to deal with all these things." The police behavior described by Rodrigo is common knowledge in La Salada. Officers wait at the entrances to La Salada, stopping garment producers and seizing their stock, which is the produce of sweatshop labor and often counterfeited. This impacts the managers' business by dissuading stallholders from renting a stall. To ensure the safe entry of stallholders into the marketplace and thus safeguard their "real-estate" business, managers are forced to collect money to hand over to the police. "I know who I have to give it to," says Rodrigo, referring to the final destination of the collected money, and continues by alluding to the police stations: "There are around ten of them. The Federal, and others, you have to give it to everyone. Because otherwise they stop the vans [of stallholders or buyers] when they enter [La Salada]. They took the vans when they were arriving and they really fucked me up."

That police officers fulfill the role of friend or business partner and at the same time constitute a threat that "surrounds you" appears at first to be a contradiction. Until, that is, we consider the dimension of time. Rodrigo and the police may have started with conflicting goals, but the relationship soon settled down when it became evident that they could benefit from a commercial joint venture that would allow both parties to profit from counterfeit garment producers' need for space to sell their illegal wares.

The consequence of the police's recognition of a source of income is a system of money collection in which shed-market managers impose fees on stallholders in addition to the fee for renting the stall. The managers organize the collection of the money internally before it is passed to state agencies as "compensation" to the police for suspending the enforcement of the law. The relevant regulation here is trademark law: only those stallholders displaying garments branded with famous logos pay protection rackets (according to my calculations, approximately 38.5 percent of all shed-market stalls display such counterfeit garments).[5] While counterfeiting is illegal under Argentine law, the official penalties are entirely different to the fees paid by stallholders that end up in the hands of the police. These illegal fees are known as "*marca*" (brand), and every stall must pay the racket each time they display branded items, regardless of the quality of the copy. Gradually, the collection of *marca* has evolved into a complex structure in which each shed market employs collectors described by a member of one of these groups as: "[going] through the aisles, gathering money for . . . say, Delitos y Estafas [the Crime and Fraud Agency], la Brigada de Mitre [the Mitre Police Service], Narcotráfico [the Anti-Narcotics Agency], la Distrital and the Departamental [District and Departmental Offices]." Collecting *marca* and passing the money on to the police allows the managers to guarantee some degree of protection both to their tenants renting stalls in the shed markets and to those transporting illegally produced goods to and from La Salada on the connecting routes.

[5] The total number of stalls in La Salada is 7,822 and those that exhibit counterfeited products number 3,017. The amount of the "fee" varies according to various factors. For example, the price goes up if the stalls are well located or if the managers have improved the facilities.

The managers do not want the threat of police action to discourage stallholders from selling counterfeit goods. By safeguarding the stallholders against police action, the managers safeguard their stall-rental business. From time to time, the terms of the agreement are challenged by police forces demanding a larger share of revenue, or by new departments recognizing the existence of the market and demanding a share for themselves. The dynamic changes according to the renegotiated terms.

Thanks to this structure of protection rackets, the "winners" in this dynamic are the managers and police forces, though in fact all market actors draw some benefit from the system. Managers are able to rent stalls freely to clients whose use of them contravenes official regulations, and state agencies are able to profit financially from refraining from policing the illegality.

## Protection Rackets and Politics

A dual "dirty togetherness" of market managers and police officers out for themselves cannot quite account for the huge structure of protection rackets at La Salada because it fails to acknowledge the political connection. Protection rackets are frequently connected to politics (for example, see Haller 1990 for the case of Chicago) and La Salada is no exception, revealing links between the managers, police forces, and sub-national politicians.

These links became patently clear to me during an interview with one of the shed-market managers, known as "Tony." It had been difficult to schedule a meeting with Tony, and fixing the appointment to meet him on his own had been a major achievement. However, when I entered his office, I was met with what I thought was a disappointing scene: Tony was immersed in a discussion with four other people. But then he introduced his friends: a former chief of the national gendarmerie and his son, who also happens to be Tony's lawyer; Tony's right-hand man, who accompanied the president of Argentina on a state visit to the Republic of Angola in early 2012; and the advisor to a former state secretary of commerce.

Charlie, the former chief of the national gendarmerie, met with me not long after my interview with Tony and revealed the relative transparency with which the protection rackets operate on buses bound for and leaving La Salada. He leaned in across the table in the café where we were talking and practically whispered his explanation: "But it isn't in anyone's interest [to prevent buses from getting to La Salada]! Look, it isn't convenient for any authority that buses don't come any more . . . because they regularly leave a racket. If the business is over, we are fucked." He began to imitate a senior police officer speaking with a junior officer who has stopped a bus: "I take you and tell you, 'Stupid! . . . What are you doing? I told you, stop the buses from time to time: of 20 [buses] you stop one. If you take 100 pesos from each passenger...with 50 passengers...you do the math!'" Finally, Tony did not hesitate to mention his own skills as a rackets taker: "Do you think that if I see a bus on the highway I don't know it's coming from La Salada? They even have the money ready! The passengers themselves say, 'Guys, we should put the money there.'"

## State-Sponsored Protection: A Micro Perspective

Brothers Pablo and José Luis Arequipa currently run a fully equipped workshop in the same Buenos Aires neighborhood as La Salada. The brothers' parents emigrated from La Paz, Bolivia, to Buenos Aires sometime between 2003 and 2006. They are not sure exactly when, only that it was between the births of Pablo and José Luis; the elder was born in Bolivia, the younger in Argentina. Their workshop, a sweatshop according to the definition in the literature, produces around 100 counterfeit Nike jackets per week to be sold at one of La Salada's stalls.

One morning, says my detailed field note, we were at the stall when José Luis, looking through the jackets hanging from the roof, identified the *marca* collector. "Here comes the *marca* guy [*el de marca*]," he told me and then started looking for money in the belt around his waist. Seconds later, the collector appeared. Well-presented, clean-shaven, and with a notebook in his hand, he greeted each of us in turn: first José Luis, then Pablo, and finally me, the unknown. The collector smiled slightly, as if trying to ease the situation. It wasn't necessary; José Luis already had the fee ready that was the motivation for the collector's visit, and once the money had changed hands there was no need for his continued presence. The collector moved on to the next stall. The whole scene was dominated by a vacuum that Pablo tried to fill with jokes and greetings. As the money was handed over, the only words exchanged were a shy "thanks" followed by a hasty "bye." There were neither questions about why *marca* had to be paid, nor a warning regarding the offence [José Luis and Pablo selling fake "Nike" jackets]. Nothing. Everyone was simply hoping that the situation would come to an end as quickly as possible. Nobody speaks because both parties have something to hide. Collectors are characterized by their highly groomed presence. In an eclectic commercial atmosphere, with exhausted buyers carrying bags and boxes, and sellers drained from several hours on their feet, collectors stand out a mile, dressed as if they were on their way to some glamorous party. They try to be attentive and pleasant. It is them and not the stallholders that try to create and maintain the pretense of a casual, relaxed situation. The only reason that brought them here was to collect the racket, a fee that they are able to impose only because the stallholders are ignorant and distrustful. No one seems to know what kind of offence the violation of a trademark is or what the penalties for it are. Nor is there solidarity among stallholders to be able to resist what the collectors ask for and do.

The uncomfortable atmosphere that accompanied the collector is soon broken by Pablo and José Luis's chatter as they justify their own behavior and complain about the collectors. Their reaction is something of a charade: the money that changed hands actualizes a long-standing relationship that exists between the stallholder and the collector-policeman. I talk to the brothers' mother, Susi, about this relationship: "[They] collect a lot of money from us, from robbers, from everyone," she admits, but is also quick to point out the benefits of paying *marca*. "[A branded garment] is what you sell best, because if you sell plain [*liso*, without brand logos] you can't shift anything [*no se mueve nada*]," she explains. Though Susi is aware of the risks of selling counterfeit goods, she is able to justify doing so on economic grounds: "*Marca* makes you sell more, and that is convenient in every respect." Because it is intentionally oriented toward meeting her desire for economic gains, Susi's actions, along with those of thousands of other sellers, recreate the structure of protection rackets every day.

It is not just the Arequipas who profit from this business; nor is the success of the enterprise confined to Buenos Aires. Buyers from all over Argentina travel to La Salada to take advantage of the low-price garments and wholesale character of the market. These two factors are the principal causes behind the 522 "Saladitas" (very small La Salada-like resellers) that have sprung up in 111 towns and cities throughout the country, as condemned in 2014 by the Argentine Confederation of Medium Enterprises (Confederación Argentina de la Mediana Empresa) (CAME 2014). It should be noted that there is more than money at stake: for Susi and her family, La Salada is defined in terms of "a kind of home from home." Goldstein observed the same phenomenon in Cochabamba, Bolivia (Goldstein 2016: 200).

In considering everyday routines, the effects of the protection-racket structure can be clearly seen. When the structure prevents the law from being enforced, it gives actors room for action and, over time, it allows the sedimentation of routines, giving a strict timetable of which days are used for cutting fabric and which days are for sewing, which days are for ironing and which are rest days. "The fair [*la feria*]," says Pablo, "is Monday and Wednesday; this means that for [having the jackets ready on] Monday we only have Thursday, Friday and Saturday. We are slaves because we also have to sell tomorrow, Sunday. We have only two days for resting. Tuesday? Forget it [*olvidate*]; we don't do anything." He smiles at this, adding: "Tuesday we are folding, ironing, and picking up stuff from other sewers." The sentiment is repeated during other interviews with other stallholders managing the same busy routines: the coordination of suppliers of thread, fabric, and plastic bags with the workers sewing the garments and taxi companies is no easy task. All the exchanges are made without the support of contracts or other written regulations and thus require, at the very least, a phone call to confirm. Perhaps most important in these exchanges are the involvement of, as Susi's husband Carlos puts it, "people in whom we can trust." The state, as the provider of this shield, controls the conditions surrounding the emergence of a social economic order in which formal legal principles are extremely weak. In levying *marca* from stallholders, the state has established an asymmetrical relationship in which those at the bottom of the social structure are firmly kept there. This asymmetry is all too obvious to La Salada's workers, especially those who, in April 2015, witnessed the bulldozing of market stalls at the state's command.

## Conclusion

Until recently, market sociology has focused exclusively on formal institutions to explain market dynamics. Therefore, in economic sociology, the study of the architecture of markets is the study of formal institutions. This double bias—political and legal—hampers an adequate understanding of a remarkable current phenomenon: the growth and expansion of illegal markets. The basic fact that market exchanges under conditions of illegality are not supported by state law brings to the fore social phenomena that we only partially understand. How is the coordination of actors in illegal markets possible? What are the mechanisms that allow the constitution of generalized expectations on the demand side? What causes the neutralization of law enforcement? In this chapter, by focusing on informal mechanisms, I shed light on one specific informal arrangement—an extensive state-sponsored protection-racket structure—that facilitates the reproduction and expansion of illegal market exchanges.

The case presented here draws on seven months of ethnographic and qualitative fieldwork in a marketplace for counterfeit and illegally produced clothing in Greater Buenos Aires. The origin of La Salada is closely tied to global transformations in the textile industry, a process that led to tens of thousands of garment workers in Argentina losing their jobs. The redundant garment workers continued to use their skills by founding sweatshops (small, informal production units). Nowadays, this marketplace forms the heart of an informal economy that has become the primary means of acquiring clothing for the lower and middle classes of both Argentina and its neighboring countries. At this site, the neutralization of law enforcement is effectively achieved through a complex system of protection rackets that works at the intersection of several economic interests: those of stallholders, police officers, and politicians, as well as of those who informally manage the marketplace. By targeting stallholders selling counterfeit garments, this informal mechanism decisively stimulates the unregulated production of garments, as well as the consumption of cheap and very much needed goods. Such an extensive state-sponsored protection-racket structure creates a hierarchy of power (police officers/politicians over stallholders), introduces rules that allow market actors to anticipate consequences and adapt their conduct accordingly, and more importantly, it allows the reproduction of a system of exploitation of the poor.

An important implication of considering informal mechanisms is that new phenomena appear on the radar of sociological reflection. The lack of a broad understanding of coordination in illegal markets reveals that these informal institutions are under-researched (with the possible exception of the disproportionate attention given to the market for drugs (Paoli and Feytens 2016)). In the same way, secrecy and silence, methods of camouflage that facilitate agreements, conceal practices, and keep moral reactions at bay, have been systematically overlooked. Exceptions are Thomas (2015) and Steiner in this volume. Conventions and institutionalized modes of regulating competition under conditions of illegality would not only challenge the extended "violence-thesis," but also provide knowledge about spontaneous forms of conflict avoidance. In sum, as constructs of actions oriented according to a particular intentionality, informal mechanisms are key research devices when it comes to grasping the architecture of illegal markets.[6]

## References


Amengual, Matthew. 2011. "Cambios en la capacidad del estado para enfrentar las violaciones de las normas laborales: Los talleres de confección de prendas de vestir en Buenos Aires." *Desarrollo Economico* 51(202/3): pp. 291–311.

Arias, Enrique Desmond. 2006. "The Dynamics of Criminal Governance: Networks and Social Order in Rio de Janeiro." *Journal of Latin American Studies* 38(2): pp. 293–325.

Auyero, Javier, and Lauren Joseph. 2007. "Introduction: Politics under the Ethnographic Microscope." In *New Perspectives in Political Ethnography*, edited by Lauren Joseph, Matthew Mahler, and Javier Auyero, pp. 1–14. New York: Springer.

Barreneche, Osvaldo. 2009. "Por mano propia: La justicia policial de la provincia de Buenos Aires en el primer Peronismo." *Sociohistórica* 25: pp. 123–52.

Becker, Howard S. 1958. "Problems of Inference and Proof in Participant Observation." *American Sociological Review* 23(6): pp. 652–60.


[6] I would like to thank Katherine Walker for the helpful comments and editing work.

Bohoslavsky, Ernesto. 2010. "El Brazo Armado de la improvisación: Aportes para una historia social de los policías patagónicos (1880–1946)." In *Un estado con rostro humano: Funcionarios e instituciones estatales en Argentina, (desde 1880 hasta la actualidad)*, edited by Ernesto Bohoslavsky and Germán Soprano, pp. 215–42. Buenos Aires: Prometeo.

CAME (Confederación Argentina de la Mediana Empresa). 2014. "Argentina ilegal: Ya hay 522 saladitas en 111 ciudades del país, y siguen creciendo." Press release, February 17. Buenos Aires: CAME. <http://www.redcame.org.ar/contenidos/comunicado/Argentina-ilegal-ya-hay-522-saladitas-en-111-ciudades-del-pais-y-siguen-creciendo.1076.html>.

Campana, Paolo. 2011. "Eavesdropping on the Mob: The Functional Diversification of Mafia Activities across Territories." *European Journal of Criminology* 8(3): pp. 213–28.

Chu, Yiu Kong. 2000. *The Triads as Business*. London: Routledge.

Cross, John C., and Sergio Peña. 2006. "Risk and Regulation in Informal and Illegal Markets." In *Out of the Shadows: Political Action and the Informal Economy in Latin America*, edited by Patricia Fernandez-Kelly and Jon Shefner, pp. 49–80. University Park, PA: Penn State Press.

Dewey, Matías. 2011. *Fragile States, Robust Structures: Illegal Police Protection in Buenos Aires*. GIGA working paper 169/11. Hamburg: German Institute of Global and Area Studies, Leibniz-Institut für Globale und Regionale Studien. <http://www.giga-hamburg.de/de/system/files/publications/wp169_dewey.pdf>.

Dewey, Matías. 2012. "Illegal Police Protection and the Market for Stolen Vehicles in Buenos Aires." *Journal of Latin American Studies* 44(4): pp. 679–702.

Dewey, Matías. 2015. *El orden clandestino: Política, fuerzas de seguridad y mercados Ilegales en la Argentina*. Buenos Aires: Katz.

Dinatale, Martín, Alejandra Gallo, and Damián Nabot. 2005. *La Escalera Invisible: Mecanismos de ascenso en la clase política*. Buenos Aires: Konrad Adenauer Stiftung, La Crujía Ediciones, CABA.

Flores Pérez, Carlos Antonio. 2013. "Political Protection and the Origins of the Gulf Cartel." *Crime, Law and Social Change* 61(5): pp. 517–39.

Galeotti, Mark. 1998. "The *Mafiya* and the New Russia." *Australian Journal of Politics and History* 44(3): pp. 415–29.

Gambetta, Diego. 1993. *The Sicilian Mafia: The Business of Private Protection*. Cambridge, MA: Harvard University Press.

Gardiner, John A. 1967. "Public Attitudes toward Gambling and Corruption." *Annals of the American Academy of Political and Social Science* 374(1): pp. 123–34.

Gardiner, John A. 1970. *The Politics of Corruption: Organized Crime in an American City*. New York: Russell Sage Foundation.

Goldstein, Daniel M. 2016. *Owners of the Sidewalk: Security and Survival in the Informal City*. Durham, NC: Duke University Press.

Gong, Ting. 2002. "Dangerous Collusion: Corruption as a Collective Venture in Contemporary China." *Communist and Post-Communist Studies* 35(1): pp. 85–103.

Haller, Mark. 1971. "Organized Crime in Urban Society: Chicago in the Twentieth Century." *Journal of Social History* 5(2): pp. 210–34.

Haller, Mark. 1990. "Illegal Enterprise: A Theoretical and Historical Interpretation." *Criminology* 28(2): pp. 207–36.

Helmke, Gretchen, and Steven Levitsky. 2006. *Informal Institutions and Democracy: Lessons from Latin America*. Baltimore, MD: Johns Hopkins University Press.

Kalmanowiecki, Laura. 2000. "Origins and Applications of Political Policing in Argentina." *Latin American Perspectives* 27(2): pp. 36–56.

Katz, Jack. 2001. "From How to Why on Luminous Description and Causal Inference in Ethnography (Part I)." *Ethnography* 2(4): pp. 443–73.

Katz, Jack. 2002. "From How to Why on Luminous Description and Causal Inference in Ethnography (Part 2)." *Ethnography* 3(1): pp. 63–90.

Kubik, Jan. 2009. "Ethnography of Politics: Foundations, Applications, Prospects." In *Political Ethnography: What Immersion Contributes to the Study of Power*, edited by Edward Schatz, pp. 25–52. Chicago: University of Chicago Press.

Lupsha, Peter A. 1991. "Drug Lords and Narco-Corruption: The Players Change but the Game Continues." *Crime, Law and Social Change* 16(1): pp. 41–58.

Mackenzie, Simon, and Penny Green. 2009. *Criminology and Archaeology: Studies in Looted Antiquities*. Oxford: Hart.

Misse, M. 2007. "Mercados ilegais, redes de proteção e organização local do crime No Rio de Janeiro." *Estudos Avançados* 21(61): pp. 139–57.

Paoli, Letizia, and Kelly Feytens. 2016. "The Belgian and Indian Pharmaceutical Market." Research outline, mimeo.

Qorchi, Mohammed El, Samuel Munzele Maimbo, John F. Wilson, and International Monetary Fund. 2003. *Informal Funds Transfer Systems: An Analysis of the Informal Hawala System*. Washington, DC: International Monetary Fund.

Reuter, Peter. 1984. "Police Regulation of Illegal Gambling: Frustrations of Symbolic Enforcement." *Annals of the American Academy of Political and Social Science* 474(1): pp. 36–47.

Sain, Marcelo Fabián. 2008. *El leviatán azul*. 1st ed. Buenos Aires: Siglo XXI editores.

Sain, Marcelo Fabián. 2013. *La regulación policial del narcotráfico en la provincia de Buenos Aires*. Washington, DC: Woodrow Wilson International Center for Scholars.

Shieh, Shawn. 2005. "The Rise of Collective Corruption in China: The Xiamen Smuggling Case." *Journal of Contemporary China* 14(42): pp. 67–91.

Snyder, Richard, and Angelica Duran-Martinez. 2009. "Does Illegality Breed Violence? Drug Trafficking and State-Sponsored Protection Rackets." *Crime, Law and Social Change* 52(3): pp. 253–73.

Stephenson, Svetlana. 2016. "It Takes Two to Tango: The State and Organised Crime in Russia." *Current Sociology*.

Thomas, Kedron. 2015. "Economic Regulation and the Value of Concealment in Highland Guatemala." *Critique of Anthropology* 35(1): pp. 13–29.

Varese, Federico. 2004. *The Russian Mafia: Private Protection in a New Market Economy*. Oxford: Oxford University Press.

Varese, Federico. 2014. "Protection and Extortion." In *The Oxford Handbook of Organized Crime*, edited by Letizia Paoli, pp. 343–58. Oxford: Oxford University Press.

Volkov, Vadim. 2002. *Violent Entrepreneurs: The Use of Force in the Making of Russian Capitalism*. Ithaca, NY: Cornell University Press.

Volkov, Vadim. 2011. "From Full to Selective Secrecy: The Offshore Realm after the Crisis." In *Deepening Crisis: Governance Challenges after Neoliberalism,* edited by Georgi Derluguian. New York: New York University Press, doi: 10.18574/nyu/9780814772805.003.0010.

Wang, Peng. 2012. "The Rise of the Red Mafia in China: A Case Study of Organised Crime and Corruption in Chongqing." *Trends in Organized Crime* 16(1): pp. 49–73.

Wang, Peng. 2014. "Extra-Legal Protection in China: How Guanxi Distorts China's Legal System and Facilitates the Rise of Unlawful Protectors." *British Journal of Criminology* 54(5): pp. 809–30.

Zhang, Sheldon X., and Ko-lin Chin. 2008. "Snakeheads, Mules, and Protective Umbrellas: A Review of Current Research on Chinese Organized Crime." *Crime, Law and Social Change* 50(3): pp. 177–95.

# 8

# Shoddy, Fake, or Harmful

## Smuggled Goods and Entangled Illegalities in a Vietnamese Border Market

*Kirsten W. Endres*

## Introduction

Lào Cai City, November 2010. After spending the whole morning and most of the afternoon at the Lào Cai central market, the main field site of the research underlying this chapter,[1] my assistant and I went for a stroll along the newly built riverfront promenade. Stretching from Lào Cai's historical center towards the Kim Thành trade and industrial zone, still under construction, the walkway had become a popular recreational space for walkers and joggers. On the other side of the Red River, which, together with the confluent Nậm Thi River, demarcates the border with China, an ever growing number of high-rise buildings dominate the cityscape of Hekou (Yunnan Province). For a while, we watched as a wooden long-tail boat carried three men and one woman over to the Chinese riverbank. Then a small group of wild-looking young men caught our attention. "Wanna go to China?" one of them asked in heavily accented Vietnamese. We decided that feigning naive curiosity was probably the best strategy to get some information about what seemed to be an unlicensed ferry service across the river. An official-looking Vietnamese man wearing a shirt with attached badges appeared and offered assistance. I asked him, "So the boats can go freely? We wouldn't get caught?" "Don't worry," the man answered reassuringly, "we have a guarantee on that (*có bảo*

[1] The research was carried out from October 2010 to March 2011, with follow-ups in August and September 2012, April 2013, and December 2014. All individuals mentioned in the text have been given pseudonyms to protect their privacy and anonymity.

*lãnh)."* "How much for the passage?" my assistant prodded further. "50,000 đồng[2] one way," the man said. "In fact only worthwhile if you have lots of goods to carry, or if you don't have a visa for China and just want to cross over to take a few photos," he explained. "But if you're here for longer, I'd recommend you to get a border crossing permit, it's easy to obtain and in the end it's cheaper than the ferry service."

The Lào Cai–Hekou border region is a vivid—although in no way unique—example of what Itty Abraham and Willem van Schendel (2005: 29) describe as a "zone where illegal flows are naturalized and intersect with the licit." Their terminology needs some clarification. Whereas in common usage the binary opposition of the legal and the illegal is treated as synonymous with that of the licit and the illicit, Abraham and van Schendel argue for "a more subtle approach" that distinguishes "between what states consider to be legitimate ('legal') and what people involved in transnational networks consider to be legitimate ('licit')" (2005: 4). In other words, certain practices or things that the state prohibits by law may be seen by ordinary citizens as in perfect accordance with prevailing social or moral norms. The contradictions between official (state) definitions of legality and the people's sense of legitimacy perhaps become most visible at the territorial margins of nation states (Galemba 2013: 276; see also the discussion in the Introduction to the present volume). As adjacent border towns, Lào Cai and Hekou are quite distinctive in character and appearance, but both can be described as places where "unsavory trades of smuggling and trafficking, gangs and prostitution prosper alongside the grandiose development paradigm[s] promoted by the state" (Zhang 2014: 377). In Vietnam, these paradigms have been translated into development strategies aimed at creating a "rich people, strong country, fair and civilized society" through modernization, industrialization, and urbanization (DiGregorio et al. 2003: 171). Following in the footsteps of China, Vietnam's economic reforms were launched in 1986 (known as Đổi mới) and marked the country's shift from centrally planned state socialism to market socialism. However, as Martin Gainsborough (2010: 482) and others have pointed out, these policies did not necessarily entail a retreat of the state. Instead—and this is particularly true for Vietnam's border regions and their trade—the reform era has seen the emergence of both "new forms of state regulation and gate-keeping" (Gainsborough 2010) and a range of creative ways to circumvent them (Endres 2014a: 615).

Building on Edward Aspinall and Gerry van Klinken's (2011: 11) conceptualization of "the state" as a complex relational arena "that favours certain kinds of strategic action while obstructing others, and where multiple players

[2] In 2010, the exchange rate was around VND 24,000 to the euro.

compete for influence, make alliances, and expropriate resources," this chapter shows that illegality in Vietnamese marketplaces is deeply entrenched in forms and practices of state illegality, the most common and widespread of which is corruption by government officials.[3] The vantage point of my ethnographic inquiry is the Lào Cai central market located in the city's historic center on the right bank of the Red River. According to Jens Beckert and Frank Wehinger (2013: 3), "[m]arkets are illegal if the product itself or the exchange of it violates legal stipulations." As I will illustrate, three of the four forms of illegality identified by Beckert and Wehinger (4–5) are neatly in place in the Lào Cai central market: (1) illegality due to the outlawing of specific products; (2) illegality due to product forgery; and (3) illegality due to the violation of regulatory stipulations. But can the Lào Cai central market therefore be understood as an illegal market? In strictly legalistic terms the answer might be positive. From an anthropological viewpoint, however, the issue demands a more differentiated approach that takes into account "what people actually do and say about what they do (or do not do) and say (or do not say)" (Smart and Zerilli 2014: 226).

This chapter draws attention to some of the numerous entanglements between the legal, the illegal, and the informal[4] that characterize local cross-border trade and marketplace-based commerce at the Vietnam–China border. I approach this issue from the perspective of Kinh (ethnic majority) small-scale traders in the border city of Lào Cai, whose overall participation in Vietnam's market-oriented economy is increasingly being marginalized by recent government policies geared towards modernization, industrialization, and urbanization.[5] The unevenness with which these policies and their related regulations have been implemented and enforced at various levels of (local) authority has contributed to the emergence of what Aihwa Ong has termed "zones of exception" (Ong 2006: 118). Ong originally applied the concept of the exception to neoliberal strategies of governing that rely on

[3] The term "market" is not necessarily limited to a particular gathering place devoted to trading activities, but refers in a general sense to the broader institutions and mechanisms that facilitate the exchange of commodities between buyers and sellers. In contrast, the term "marketplace" traditionally denotes a spatially bounded location where buyers and sellers engage in commercial and social exchanges. However, as Kalman Applbaum (2005: 285) argues, "the oppositional categories of empirical vs. abstract market... exist in reality on a continuum with each other and they are, in fact and in theory, converging." Market*places* are thus productive sites for considering how these two aspects of market—the empirical and the abstract—relate to one another.

[4] The term "informal economy" was originally popularized by Keith Hart (1973) to describe the "unregulated" economic activities of low-income urban dwellers in Ghana. Here, it refers to "situations where the goods and services transacted are legal, but the ways in which they are transacted are not" (Smart and Zerilli 2014: 229).

[5] In Hanoi, for example, many old-style, "traditional" markets have been demolished and replaced by upscale shopping malls or office buildings (Endres 2014b). In places throughout Vietnam, modernization and urbanization projects have also led to an increasing marginalization of farmers and workers (for example, Harms 2013; Labbé 2014).

"differently administered spaces of 'graduated' or 'variegated sovereignty'" (Ong 2006: 7), such as free-trade zones in border areas and other economic and administrative enclaves. Whereas the exception, as theorized by Agamben (1998), is most often associated with the sovereign suspension of the law and the inclusive exclusion of bare life, Ong's spaces of neoliberal exception offer certain economic opportunities to certain segments of society but not to others. In line with this conception, the Lào Cai–Hekou border gate provides small-trader and migrant citizens with opportunities for economic self-advancement that are not as easily available in Vietnam's lowland regions. In contrast to the chances offered by the neoliberal exception, however, these opportunities are only considered viable if tariff regulations and other legal provisions can be successfully circumvented, which is routinely achieved by colluding with corrupt state officials. The latter, however, amount to more than just a few bad apples in Vietnam's bureaucratic system. "By paying bribes we feed [*nuôi sống*] the tax inspectors and customs officials, and these guys in turn feed other guys," a trader named Hưng explained to me, alluding to the intricate networks of patronage that permeate Vietnamese state administrative structures (Endres 2014b; Gainsborough et al. 2009; Gillespie 2001). The "illegal" economic pursuits of Lào Cai small traders must therefore be seen as deeply entrenched in the imperatives of systemic corruption through which local state officials feel invested with the discretionary power to grant exceptions to the law in exchange for bribes. But in a state in which corruption has become the norm rather than the exception, those who inhabit the margins of a relational arena in which material and immaterial "goods pass up, down and sideways through and along the patron–client networks and alliances that pervade state institutions and that crisscross the boundary between state and society" (Aspinall and van Klinken 2011: 23), ultimately becoming trapped in a "gray space" (Yiftachel 2009) of overlap between their inclusion in the neoliberal logics of economic self-advancement and their exclusion from access to legal means of livelihood.

## Smuggling Goods across the Border

At first glance, the Lào Cai central market appeared to be a typical state-run covered market, like many others in the country. The only obvious difference was the much larger volume and variety of Chinese-produced merchandize for sale at the more than 700 stalls distributed over two separate buildings.[6] The two-story main building, where I conducted the bulk of my six-month

[6] The main building was demolished in October 2014 and has since been replaced by a more contemporary structure.

research, had been constructed in the mid-1990s as "an important step towards realizing a diversified economic development, meeting the hopes and expectations of the people" (Báo Lào Cai 1996). At that time, Lào Cai was still recovering from the ravages of the 1979 border war with China that had left the town in ruins for over a decade. The new livelihood opportunities that opened up when Vietnam and China resumed normal relations and reopened their border for trade after more than ten years of hostility (Womack 2006: 209) drew many lowland (Kinh ethnic majority) settlers to the region.[7] Mr. Thông, for example, a specialist and trader in traditional medicine from Hà Tây province, first came to Lào Cai in 1993 to explore the situation. "At that time Lào Cai was still full of mines," he reminisced, "so the state issued a new policy encouraging people to reclaim mined land. If you could clear that much land the state would give you the right to use it." In the following years, many of his relatives joined him in Lào Cai to try their luck in trading and other occupations. In common with many other lowland migrants who followed the lure of the border, they were soon able to purchase land-use rights and build houses.

Along with growing business opportunities and an increase in border tourism (Chan 2013), small-scale cross-border trade flourished throughout the 1990s and early 2000s. Around the globe, "living in a borderland provides an immense opportunity to profit from the different regimes of value that exist on either side" (Reeves 2014: 165). Lào Cai market traders not only benefited from arbitrage opportunities arising from "differences in prices and exchange rates over time and space" (Williams and Baláž 2002: 323), but also took advantage of preferential policies aimed at encouraging cross-border trade relations. Moreover, and perhaps even more importantly, many of their economic transactions fall into the realm of the "subversive economy" by challenging state attempts "to regulate the movement of people and flow of commodities" (Donnan and Wilson 1999: 88), for example by evading (or negotiating) custom duties or by smuggling goods that the state prohibits from being imported (Endres 2014a). A 2010 report by the Lào Cai provincial market control department (*cục quản lý thị trường*) indicates that the local authorities are well aware of the tricks of the small-scale traders at the Lào Cai–Hekou border gate:

> Smuggling takes place on a small but relatively complex scale. The smugglers take advantage of the fact that border residents are exempt from import duties, as stipulated in Prime Minister's Decision No. 254/2006/QĐ-TTg of November 7,

[7] Vietnam is a multi-ethnic country with fifty-four officially recognized ethnic groups, of which the Kinh (or Việt) form the majority. Although ethnic minority groups account for the majority of the population in Vietnam's northern uplands, including Lào Cai province, Lào Cai City (as well as most district towns) is now overwhelmingly dominated by Kinh lowlanders (for a detailed study of Hmong ethnic minority trade relations see Turner et al. 2015).

> 2006 on the management of border trading activities with bordering countries [amended in 2009]. The smugglers' trick is to hire porters who split the consignment into small loads before transporting them through the [international] border gate or through other border crossings in the area and legitimize them with regular sales invoices stating a purchase price that is way below the actual market value of the smuggled goods.
>
> (Sở Công Thường Tỉnh Lào Cai 2010)

According to the above-mentioned Decision No. 254/2006/QĐ-TTg, Lào Cai residents may apply for a special border-crossing permit that entitles them to import into Vietnam, free of customs duties, goods up to a maximum value of 2 million đồng per person per day.[8] This policy was originally intended to "help residents in border areas exchange goods they produce and buy essential goods for daily use and production" (TBKTSG 2015), but it created a loophole that contributed to the emergence of an intricate service network of Vietnamese trader intermediaries and transporters who take their orders from both resident and non-resident retailers. By having the goods carried across the border in small 2 million đồng batches for a per-piece or per-load fee, the latter are able to evade import taxes. Many vendors at Lào Cai central market also make use of these porter services and have goods delivered directly to their stalls. One of them is Mrs. Oanh, a 47-year-old native of Thái Bình province. She and her husband moved to Lào Cai in 1998 and have since been working as porters at the border gate. Mrs. Oanh transports goods with a special cargo bicycle that can carry a maximum load of 300 kilograms in the huge side bags attached to the handlebars (see Figure 8.1).[9] The work is excruciatingly hard. "If I carry only one load and the value is below 2 million đồng, I am exempted from import tax," she explains. "But if I make a second trip on that day I have to pay." In that case the customs official would estimate the value of the goods to assess the appropriate amount of customs duty, and Mrs. Oanh would try to bargain with him in order to get what she calls "a small reduction." In case she transports high-value goods, she has to "make law" [*làm luật*, negotiate a bribe] with the official: "For each consignment I have to line their hands [*lót tay*, grease their palms] with a few hundred thousand đồng, but that amount is still less than half the customs duties," Oanh said with a mischievous smile on her weathered face. "These are the tricks by which we can make a living [*mẹo làm ăn*] as transporters" (interview February 23, 2011).

Once the goods have reached Vietnamese territory, the transporter must be careful not to run into a market control officer in charge of enforcing trade

[8] Decision No. 254/2006/QĐ-TTg of November 7, 2006, amended by Decision No. 139/2009/QĐ-TTg of December 23, 2009. The government is currently considering cutting this amount to a total of 8 million đồng per month (see TBKTSG 2015).

[9] Since January 2014, these cargo bicycles are no longer allowed at the border gate.

**Figure 8.1.** Vietnamese goods transporters at the Lào Cai–Hekou border gate

regulations and preventing the entry of illegal goods and counterfeits. Again, the size of the bribe depends on the type and volume of goods. Mr. Hưng, for example, who supplies stall holders at Lào Cai market with Chinese-produced household items, has an arrangement with the market control team on a 400,000 đồng per month basis. The good-natured trader intermediary regards these arrangements as necessary for him and the vendors he supplies to run a reasonably profitable business. "'Making law' with customs officials and evading (import) tariffs are essential, otherwise we couldn't make enough to live on," he claimed. Mr. Hưng sees his trade in cheap home appliances as a legitimate way to make a humble living, not as a way of getting rich. "Honest people who run legitimate businesses stay poor; they just make enough for a bowl of rice," he explained. "If you want to become rich, you have to smuggle and trade in prohibited goods."

While this may well be the case for organized smuggling rings who are, for example, involved in the illegal timber and wildlife trade (To et al. 2014; Milliken and Shaw 2012), it is not necessarily true for small-scale traders and transporters who trade in contraband goods and prohibited items. Let me turn briefly to the story of a woman smuggler named Thanh who supplied Lào Cai market vendors with a variety of so-called "hot" goods (*hàng nóng*). These goods exemplify Beckert and Wehinger's (2013) category of "illegality due to the outlawing of specific products," including weapons, such as electric shock prods, tasers, knives and daggers, as well as items considered morally harmful, for example dildos, vibrators, inflatable love dolls, and other sexual-pleasure products. Like Mrs. Oanh, Mrs. Thanh hailed from a rice-growing village in the Red River delta in the late 1990s in order to explore the possibilities of making a better living at the Lào Cai–Hekou border gate. Mrs. Thanh quickly acquired the skills necessary for a flourishing goods delivery service. At first, she relied mainly on the river road for smuggling. As indicated in the introductory vignette, the unofficial ferry boats used to ply back and forth between the two river banks in broad daylight and not far from the official border crossing.[10] In order that this service could operate "freely," both the boat owner and the smuggler had to negotiate bribes with various regulatory and law-enforcement agencies. For the slender 45-year-old woman, these complicated arrangements were only worth the trouble when she wanted to transport large volumes of contraband or items that could not easily be hidden in bags or strapped to the body. "When I used the ferry boat, besides paying the ferryman, I had to pay a 'local tax' [*thuế địa bàn*] at the landing place, and I also had to 'make law' with the border patrol police, the river police, and the market department," she reminisced. She therefore decided to use the official border gate for her smuggling activities. On each of her trips she only carried small amounts of illegal items hidden under legal goods or underneath her loose-fitting clothes. If the customs officer on duty was known to be "hard to please" (*khó tính*), she would rather wait for the next shift than risk having her goods confiscated. Like Mr. Hưng, she paid a monthly 400,000 đồng bribe to the market control unit. "Of course they see me [crossing the border] every day, so they know [I smuggle things]," she said. When Mrs. Thanh delivered her goods at the Lào Cai central market, she needed to be careful and clever (*khéo léo*) as well. She remembered that one day she ran into the market's chief security guard who gave her a stern warning: "I know what kind of merchandise you're bringing into the market, I don't need to say anything; you better stop doing that, that's all I'll say."

## An Illegal Market?

Whenever I met Mrs. Thanh at the market, I was mesmerized by the swiftness and agility with which she wove her way through the maze of stalls, goods, and people. Most of the stalls lining the entrance hall specialized in selling

[10] On my visit to Lào Cai in December 2014, however, the ferry boat service seemed to have stopped working. This may not be a permanent condition, though, because such types of illegal activity tend to disappear and reappear frequently.

mobile phones, consumer electronics, fishing rods, costume jewelry, and watches. The rest of the ground floor was divided into different sections selling home appliances, Vietnamese wooden handicrafts, traditional medicinal herbs, and bags and suitcases. Outside the walls of the building, but still within the market gates, were the sections for fresh and dried fruits, children's toys, refreshments, and small souvenirs. It was the souvenir section that had become notorious among male Vietnamese shoppers (usually Kinh lowlanders on a tourist or business trip) for the easy availability of prohibited items. The vendors of these goods generally acted with caution and kept their merchandize out of sight. When a potential customer expressed interest in "hot goods" or "adult toys," the vendor first checked for signs that he was in fact an undercover police agent. Trading in illegal items is a highly risky, but ultimately extremely profitable venture. "If you want to make a lot of profit you need to trade in prohibited items," a vendor named Tâm told me. "Each item may get you a profit of 1 million đồng, so if you can sell three of these items a day and a couple of other things you may easily make a profit of 3 to 4 million đồng."[11]

Mrs. Tâm was one of the souvenir vendors at the Lào Cai central market. The goods she displayed on her stall were basically of the same kind as everywhere else in the section: Chinese-produced keyrings, manicure sets, leather purses, flashlights, thermos flasks, and hairclips, as well as Vietnamese liquor, cigarettes, and instant coffee. Unlike most of her fellow vendors in this part of the market, however, Tâm did not offer any weapons or adult toys. "I just can't do that," she explained, "my conscience does not allow me to." Whereas she saw no ethical problem in selling sex toys, Tâm regarded the sale of weapons as morally reprehensible because they were very likely to be used in criminal activities. However, probably the most important reason why the divorcee and mother of a teenage son did not engage in selling any of these items was because she was worried about the legal consequences of getting caught red-handed (Endres 2015: 228). In that case, besides issuing a hefty fine, the authorities usually closed the defendant's stalls down for up to several weeks. "I see no need to compete [with other vendors] in selling prohibited items and make my life miserable," Tâm reasoned. In contrast to Mrs. Tâm, these vendors tended to exhibit a fairly nonchalant attitude focused on profit. "I know I'm selling prohibited goods," one of the women vendors related. "But if I don't sell these things, there will always be other people who sell them." Vendors usually tried to avert raids or soften punishments by bribing

[11] Market stallholders were generally reluctant to state their monthly income. On average, their profits seemed to range from 6 to 17 million đồng per month, depending on the type of goods and seasonal conditions. In comparison, wages in Vietnam have averaged 3.6 million đồng in the past seven years, reaching an all-time high of 4.8 million đồng in 2015 (approximately 195 euros; see <http://www.tradingeconomics.com/vietnam/wages>).

the relevant authorities. Although there was no guarantee that "making law" would produce the intended results, the bribes often worked to the traders' advantage. Mrs. Mai, for example, was caught selling sex toys to a group of male tourists. Her stall was closed down, but three days later she was back to business. "I had to prepare an envelope for the [market management] director," she explained. "If not, they would have closed my stall for a whole week."

Another category of goods that violates current trade law are counterfeits or so-called mimic goods (*hàng nhái*), ranging from fake designer handbags to bootlegged DVDs and pirated software. Most of the forged products are manufactured in China.[12] Mobile phones are one example. Hardly distinguishable from authentic branded phones from the outside, fakes are available at many stalls in the entrance hall and openly displayed in glass cabinets. One of the mobile phone vendors, Mr. Duy, shared his opinion as follows: "I do not like selling Chinese phones because the quality is not guaranteed. The phones are credited with many functions but many of these functions (photographing, filming) actually don't work as advertised." According to Mr. Duy's own classification, there are three types of clients who go for the counterfeits. The first type are "childish people" (*người ấu trĩ*), that is people who like cheap goods and have no understanding of quality. The second type comprises rich people who like unusual things (*đồ lạ*) in the latest fashion, but who would only use them for a short time before throwing them away. The third type of people in Mr. Duy's classification scheme are members of ethnic minority groups who do not have much money but who like to "ape" (*học đòi*) prestigious consumer tastes. "I don't advise the buyers much," Mr. Duy said, "if they want to buy a good product I refer them to the more expensive Vietnamese-produced mobile phones, if they like something cheap they just pounce on the Chinese ones." In order to compensate for the lack of a company warranty, most mobile phone vendors provided their own return guarantee by affixing a small label to the fake phone when the deal had been sealed. Alternatively, as observed by two journalists, the vendor may allay the client's concern by stating "Rest assured. The goods here have a great reputation, what do you need papers for; in case of damage just bring it back; remembering my face is the warranty" (Hà An and Nguyễn Tuấn 2014).

Like the counterfeit mobile phones, many China-made products sold at Lào Cai market were described by the vendors as shoddy goods (*hàng đểu*) that do not stand the test of time. In fact, most of the Chinese home appliances available in the market's electronic section were of low quality (*kém chất*

[12] Fake products have long been swamping the Vietnamese market. In 1999, shoppers in Ho Chi Minh City even spoke of a "a national epidemic of false goods and consumer deception" (Vann 2006: 287).

*lượng*), unclear origin (*không rõ nguồn gốc*), and without proper warranty stamps (*không có tem bảo hành*)—all of which is in violation of regulatory stipulations, such as the Vietnamese Law on the Quality of Products and Goods (Quốc Hội 2007). Despite these shortcomings, such goods are in popular demand because they feature attractive designs and are much cheaper than, for example, Vietnamese-produced goods. As one vendor put it,

> Customers like buying cheap goods, sometimes just for the sake of buying, and when the item no longer works they just throw it away. Many people know the goods are of low quality, but they still buy them because they're so very cheap. Wherever there is supply, there is demand; where there are customers, there are also sellers.
>
> (Informal conversation, January 17, 2011)

In order to discourage vendors from importing and smuggling sub-standard electronics, the provincial Department for Standards, Metrology and Quality (*Cục Tiêu Chuẩn Đo Lường Chất Lượng*; under the Ministry of Science and Technology) conducted random inspections at the market. Often enough, however, the fines imposed for violating the regulations were little more than symbolic reminders "that there in fact is a law" (Endres 2014a: 615) as well as a government agency in charge and capable of enforcing it. The latter, however, has different implications for the traders than one might expect. "That's why the traders must treat the officials well," a middleman who supplies the stallholders with Chinese rice cookers and electric fans explained. Such treats included money envelopes, gifts, and invitations to dinner parties organized by the electronics section on special occasions (for example, International Women's Day, March 8, and Vietnamese Women's Day, October 20). Whereas bribes are usually exchanged between individual traders and relevant state officials, some of my interlocutors insinuated that the market management board also coordinated bribe negotiations with other official agencies. "Before a police raid, a tax inspection, or a quarantine check, the officials would first have to work with [the market management director]," one vendor explained. Those who had bribed the director beforehand would then receive preferential treatment from police and other law-enforcement authorities.

These arrangements, as well as the unlawful activities that they were supposed to cover up, were generally considered by Lào Cai traders to be essential in order to survive in the market. Recently, their businesses had already become less profitable than in earlier years. "Trade has become difficult," one of the women vendors said in 2010. "Three or four years ago the market was always crowded with customers, but now it is empty" (interview, December 10, 2010). Under current conditions, small-scale traders found it much harder to make a decent living without breaking the law. As one woman put it, "Nowadays, if you run an honest business, that is, you don't smuggle or do bad things, it is only enough for food and basics" (interview, February 8, 2011).

## Conclusion: "Illegal Markets" and State Illegality Intertwined

The avenues through which Vietnamese small-scale traders in Lào Cai City—be they goods transporters at the border gate or stallholders in the central market—have seized the economic opportunities at the Vietnam–China border are invariably smoothed by "greasing the palms" of local government officials. Transporters and intermediaries offer bribes in order to pass legal goods through customs without having to pay the regular taxes or duties or in order to smuggle illegal goods of all sorts across the border and onwards to the market. Stallholders who sell illegal goods in the market bribe the authorities in order to be able to go about their business unmolested. No matter whether the goods are legal (but have been transacted through illegal channels), illegal (but socially licit, such as various kinds of counterfeit and sub-standard products), or both illegal and illicit (for example, weapons), illegality in small-scale cross-border trade is commonly seen as a legitimate way of earning a living. Most traders feel that state policies and legal restrictions (including taxes, tariffs, trademark rights, quality standards, and so on) constrain their participation in the economy and regard their bribe arrangements as essential for a profitable business. Their claims on the state to their right of earning a livelihood become apparent through the rhetoric of exchange that traders use to frame their bribe arrangements with officials. As Mr. Hưng put it, "They [the officials] give us a bowl of rice, and we reciprocate with a bowl of congee [*người ta cho mình bát cơm, mình bớt lại bát cháo cho người ta*]" (Endres 2014a: 618). But this does not mean that the law is negotiated solely in the traders' interest. In Vietnam's state administration system, public offices are distributed through webs of clientelist relationships that need to be nurtured by the exchange of gifts and favors. Customs officials, market control inspectors, and police officers, among others, may all have made large financial investments in securing their positions, which they now seek to recoup by extracting bribes from below, part of which needs to be channeled upward again in exchange for further patronage. In other words, what we have here is a situation where "the state" thrives upon the proliferation of informal and illegal activities, irrespective of the loss of revenue from import duties (see Reeves 2014: 169).

In common with Ong's spaces of neoliberal exception—that is, economic enclaves and special administrative zones that are "subjected to different kinds of governmentality and that vary in terms of the mix of disciplinary and civilizing regimes" (Ong 1999: 7)—the Vietnam–China border region offers avenues for economic self-advancement to small-trader and migrant citizens. The difference is that these avenues are not officially sanctioned by the law. On the contrary, they are, in fact, restricted in scale and scope by the existing legal framework. The traders circumvent these restrictions by negotiating bribe arrangements with government officials, without which, they say, their businesses would not yield enough income to feed their families. However, these arrangements, irrespective of whether the merchandise is strictly prohibited by law or merely liable to customs duty, ultimately traps the traders within a "grey space" of uncertainty that lingers between the "light" of free trade, economic opportunity, and self-advancement, and the "darkness" of illegality, corruption, and arbitrary exercise of power.[13]

## References

Abraham, Itty, and Willem van Schendel. 2005. "Introduction: The Making of Illicitness." In *Illicit Flows and Criminal Things*, edited by Willem van Schendel and Itty Abraham, pp. 1–37. Bloomington: Indiana University Press.

Agamben, Giorgio. 1998. *Homo Sacer: Sovereign Power and Bare Life*. Stanford, CA: Stanford University Press.

Applbaum, Kalman. 2005. "Directions in the Anthropology of Markets." In *Handbook of Economic Anthropology*, edited by James Carrier, pp. 275–89. London: Edward Elgar.

Aspinall, Edward, and Gerry van Klinken (eds). 2011. *The State and Illegality in Indonesia*. Leiden: KITLV Press.

Báo Lào Cai 1996. "Khánh thành hai chợ Bắc Hà và Cốc Lếu đưa vào sử dụng [Inauguration and Turn-Over of Bắc Hà Market and Cốc Lếu Market]." *Báo Lào Cai*, December 5, 267: p. 5.

Beckert, Jens, and Frank Wehinger. 2013. "In the Shadow: Illegal Markets and Economic Sociology." *Socio-Economic Review* 11(1): pp. 5–30.

Chan, Yuk Wah. 2013. *Vietnamese–Chinese Relationships at the Borderlands: Trade, Tourism and Cultural Politics*. New York: Routledge.

DiGregorio, Michael, A. Terry Rambo, and Masayuki Yanagisawa. 2003. "Clean, Green, and Beautiful: Environment and Development under the Renovation Economy." In *Postwar Vietnam: Dynamics of a Transforming Society*, edited by Hy Van Luong, pp. 171–99. Oxford: ISEAS.

Donnan, Hastings, and Thomas M. Wilson. 1999. *Borders: Frontiers of Identity, Nation and State*. New York: Bloomsbury Publishing.

Endres, Kirsten W. 2014a. "Making Law: Small-Scale Trade and Corrupt Exceptions at the Vietnam–China Border." *American Anthropologist* 116(3): pp. 611–25.

[13] I adapted this graduation from Oren Yiftachel's concept of "gray space" developed in critical urban theory that "refers to developments, enclaves, populations and transactions positioned between the ['light'] of legality/approval/safety and the 'darkness' of eviction/destruction/death" (Yiftachel 2009: 243).

Endres, Kirsten W. 2014b. "Downgraded by Upgrading: Small-Scale Traders, Urban Transformation and Spatial Reconfiguration in Post-Reform Vietnam." *Cambridge Anthropology* 32(2): pp. 97–111.

Endres, Kirsten W. 2015. "'Lộc Bestowed by Heaven': Fate, Fortune, and Morality in the Vietnamese Marketplace." *Asia Pacific Journal of Anthropology* 16(3): pp. 227–43.

Gainsborough, Martin. 2010. "Present but Not Powerful: Neoliberalism, the State, and Development in Vietnam." *Globalizations* 7(4): pp. 475–88.

Gainsborough, Martin, Đặng Ngọc Dinh, and Trần Thanh Phương. 2009. *Corruption, Public Administration Reform and Development: Challenges and Opportunities as Vietnam Moves towards Middle-Income*. Hanoi: UNDP.

Galemba, Rebecca. 2013. "Illegality and Invisibility at Margins and Borders." *PoLAR: Political and Legal Anthropology Review* 36(2): pp. 274–85.

Gillespie, John. 2001. "Self-Interest and Ideology: Bureaucratic Corruption in Vietnam." *Asian Law Journal* 3(1): pp. 1–36.

Hà An, and Nguyễn Tuấn. 2014. "Hàng lậu chọc 'thủng' đường biên [Contraband Pokes 'Holes' into the Border]." *Thanh Nien Online*. <http://www.thanhnien.com.vn/kinh-te/hang-lau-choc-thung-duong-bien-387920.html> (accessed January 24, 2014).

Harms, Erik. 2013. "Eviction Time in the New Saigon: Temporalities of Displacement in the Rubble of Development." *Cultural Anthropology* 28(2): pp. 344–68.

Hart, Keith. 1973. "Informal Income Opportunities and Urban Employment in Ghana." *Journal of Modern African Studies* 11(1): pp. 61–89.

Labbé, Danielle. 2014. *Land Politics and Livelihoods on the Margins of Hanoi, 1920–2010*. Vancouver, BC: UBC Press.

Milliken, Tom, and Jo Shaw. 2012. *The South Africa-Viet Nam Rhino Horn Trade Nexus: A Deadly Combination of Institutional Lapses, Corrupt Wildlife Industry Professionals and Asian Crime Syndicates*. Johannesburg: Traffic. <http://www.rhinoresourcecenter.com/index.php?s=1&act=refs&CODE=ref_detail&id=1345588556>.

Ong, Aihwa. 1999. "Introduction: Flexible Citizenship: The Cultural Logics of Transnationality." In *Flexible Citizenship: The Cultural Logics of Transnationality*, edited by Aihwah Ong, pp. 1–26. Durham, NC: Duke University Press.

Ong, Aihwa. 2006. *Neoliberalism as Exception: Mutations in Citizenship and Sovereignty*. Durham, NC: Duke University Press.

Quốc Hôi (National Assembly). 2007. *Luật chất lượng sản phẩm, hang hóa, số 05/2007/QH12 ngày 21 tháng 11 2007* (Law on Products and Goods Quality, Nr. 05/2007/QH12, November 21).

Reeves, Madeleine. 2014. *Border Work: Spatial Lives of the State in Rural Central Asia*. Ithaca, NY: Cornell University Press.

Smart, Alan, and Filippo M. Zerilli. 2014. "Extralegality." In *A Companion to Urban Anthropology*, edited by Donald M. Nonini, 1st ed., pp. 222–38. Chichester: John Wiley and Sons.

Sở Công Thương Tỉnh Lào Cai (Lào Cai Provinicial Department of Industry and Trade). 2010. *Báo Cáo Tổng Kết Công Tác Quản Lý Thị Trường Năm 2010, Phương Hướng, Niệm Vụ Năm 2011; Nr. 158/BC-QLTT ngày 31 tháng 12 năm 2010* (Report Nr. 158/BC-QLTT of December 31, 2010, Summarizing the Work of the Market Control Department for the Year 2010, Directions and Tasks for 2011). Unpublished report.

*TBKTSG* 2015. "Vietnam Vows to Restrict Cross-Border Trade." *VietnamNet Online*, February 6. <http://english.vietnamnet.vn/fms/business/122662/vietnam-vows-to-restrict-cross-border-trade.html>.

To, Phuc Xuan, Sango Mahanty, and Wolfram Dressler. 2014. "Social Networks of Corruption in the Vietnamese and Lao Cross-Border Timber Trade." *Anthropological Forum* 24(2): pp. 154–74.

Turner, Sarah, Christine Bonnin, and Jean Michaud. 2015. *Frontier Livelihoods: Hmong in the Sino-Vietnamese Borderlands*. Seattle: University of Washington Press.

Vann, Elisabeth F. 2006. "The Limits of Authenticity in Vietnamese Consumer Markets." *American Anthropologist* 108(2): pp. 286–96.

Williams, Allan M., and Vladimir Baláž. 2002. "International Petty Trading: Changing Practices in Trans-Carpathian Ukraine." *International Journal of Urban and Regional Research* 26(2): pp. 323–42.

Womack, Brantley. 2006. *China and Vietnam: The Politics of Asymmetry*. Cambridge: Cambridge University Press.

Yiftachel, Oren. 2009. "Critical Theory and 'Gray Space'. Mobilization of the Colonized." *City* 13(2): pp. 240–56.

Zhang, Juan. 2014. "Remote Proximity." *HAU: Journal of Ethnographic Theory* 4(1): pp. 361–81.

# Part IV

# Shifting Definitions of Illegality

# 9

# Making the Medical Marijuana Market

*Cyrus Dioun*

## Introduction

Cannabis, commonly known as "marijuana," "pot," or "weed," is a flowering herb that has psychoactive and physiological effects when inhaled or ingested. Societies have cultivated and consumed cannabis for millennia, yet the cultural meaning and legal status of the herb have varied over time and across cultures. Cannabis was rarely consumed in the United States until the middle of the nineteenth century, when medical professionals began recommending it for a variety of ailments. Cannabis was first added to *The Pharmacopeia of the United States* (1851), a list of medicinal preparations recognized by medical professionals, at the 1850 National Medical Convention.[1] The following year the *Dispensatory of the United States*, a list of legitimate medicinal substances and preparations, described the efficacy of cannabis for "neuralgia, gout, rheumatism, tetanus, hydrophobia, epidemic cholera, hysteria, mental depression, insanity, and uterine hemorrhage" (Wood and Bache 1851).

Cannabis was sold in elixirs, tonics, and other homeopathic medicinal remedies until moral entrepreneurs and state builders pushed for its prohibition in the early twentieth century, framing cannabis as an evil plant that caused madness, criminality, and violent, depraved acts in the user (Stanley 1931; Anslinger and Cooper 1937; Rowell and Rowell 1939; Becker 1963). While *Cannabis Sativa* is the official taxonomic designation for the cannabis plant, the media and public officials popularized the term "marijuana," a slang word for cannabis used by Mexican-American farm workers, in order to tie the plant to xenophobic fears of Mexican immigrants and other minority groups

[1] Hemp, a non-psychoactive variety of the cannabis plant, had been used as a textile throughout the early history of the United States.

in the early twentieth century (Bonnie and Whitebread 1970). Cannabis was prohibited at the state and federal level in 1937 and removed from *The Pharmacopeia of the United States* in 1942.[2]

These campaigns not only successfully changed the legality, medical status, and name of cannabis (i.e. marijuana), but also transformed public perception of the flowering herb.[3] In the decades following prohibition, both prohibitionists and marijuana users primarily conceptualized marijuana as a *recreational intoxicant* used for hedonistic pleasure. This recreational intoxicant conception, still prevalent today, described the act of using marijuana as "getting high" or "getting stoned" and portrayed marijuana users as "potheads" with a "hang-loose ethic" in opposition to the laws and norms of mainstream society (Suchman 1968). Prohibitionists classified marijuana as a dangerous drug and associated marijuana users with criminal behavior and a lack of motivation (Becker 1963; Drug Free World Foundation 2013). Marijuana consumers described the herb as an intoxicant that was a safe and pleasurable alternative to alcohol (McAdory 2013). While opponents and proponents of marijuana use held diametrically opposing views, stigmatizing or valorizing marijuana's intoxicating properties, both groups viewed it primarily as an intoxicant, not a medicine, following marijuana's prohibition.

In 1970 the US government codified the recreational conception of marijuana when it enacted the Controlled Substances Act (CSA), which classified marijuana, along with heroin, LSD, MDMA, and a number of other psychedelics, opioids, and amphetamines, as Schedule 1 narcotics with "no currently accepted medical value" and "high potential for abuse" (21 USC § 812). This classification prohibited the medical use of marijuana and obstructed research into its medical applications. While the US government had prohibited marijuana use for decades, the CSA marked the beginning of the "war on drugs," in which federal, state, and local governments escalated the arrest and prosecution of producers and consumers of marijuana and other illegal drugs. In the following decades, the number of marijuana arrests in the United States increased from 59 arrests per 100,000 of the population in 1969 to 276 arrests per 100,000 of the population in 2010 (US Department of Justice 1965–2010). Economists estimate that federal, state, and local authorities spent approximately $13.4 billion in 2010 enforcing marijuana prohibition (Miron 2010).

Marijuana prohibition remained relatively unchallenged until the AIDS epidemic created a deadly crisis that pushed patients and their loved ones into the illegal market to search for ways to combat the effects of the disease. During the

[2] Proponents of cannabis prohibition were also active in the temperance movement to prohibit alcohol and the movement to ban opioids.

[3] As "marijuana" was the common term used to describe cannabis following prohibition, I will use it when describing developments and events that took place after marijuana use was federally prohibited in 1937.

height of the epidemic, many AIDS patients experienced cachexia (wasting syndrome), a complication of AIDS that diminished appetite and the ability to absorb nutrients, leading to rapid weight loss and increasing the likelihood of death. Some AIDS patients, searching for ways to cope with the disease, found that marijuana's antiemetic properties—popularly known as "the munchies"—increased appetite, helping patients retain weight and live longer (Grinspoon et al. 1995).

Marijuana's ability to alleviate some of the suffering caused by the AIDS epidemic created an opening for social movement activists and illegal marijuana sellers to construct a new conception of marijuana as a *compassionate palliative* for the seriously ill and dying. This discursive opportunity did not lead to the displacement of the recreational intoxicant conception of marijuana, but rather provided a platform for entrepreneurs and activists to append it, carving out (or layering on) an understanding of marijuana as a medical palliative for the sick and dying, even though the state did not recognize its medical use.

Marijuana's ongoing prohibition obstructed the development of formal market institutions, leading market pioneers in San Francisco, who were located at the intersection of the marijuana market and the city's gay community, to build an interface between the illegal market and the legitimate needs of dying patients. These strategic and value-rational actors constructed the foundations of what would become a multi-billion dollar medical marijuana industry by openly defying the law and constructing informal institutions, such as organizational forms (the marijuana buyers' club) and rules of exchange (proof of medical need), that were sanctioned by society, while remaining formally prohibited by the state.

Market pioneers helped legitimize and legalize these informal institutions by developing frames and targeting political opportunities at the local and state level where they could bypass lawmakers and win support for medical use through the ballot initiative, a form of citizen legislation in which the public votes on a referendum to approve or reject a law. These efforts were successful: San Francisco voters passed a ballot initiative authorizing the medical use of marijuana in 1991 and California voters followed soon after to make it the first state to authorize medical marijuana use in 1996. By June 2016, twenty-five states and the District of Columbia had enacted laws allowing the medical use of marijuana, giving rise to a $4.5 billion industry that was simultaneously state-authorized and federally prohibited (ArcView Market Research and New Frontier 2016).

## Theoretical Development

Theories of institutional change often describe how an exogenous shock, such as a war, financial crisis, or epidemic, can challenge institutional arrangements previously taken for granted and create political and cultural opportunities for the transformation of prevailing attitudes and social configurations (Baumgartner and Jones 1993; Beissinger 2002). During these unsettled times, actors seek ways to cope with the insecurity caused by the crisis at hand. This "back-against-the-wall" reaction to crisis can lead those directly affected, as well as those in the surrounding community, to reconsider accepted truths; it can also give rise to new ways of understanding the world and mobilize groups to develop support for institutions that codify these emergent conceptions (Swidler 1986; Fligstein 2001).

For example, before the AIDS epidemic there was a wide range of consumer products and related topics known to marketing professionals as "unmentionables," defined as "products, services or concepts that for reasons of delicacy, decency, morality or even fear, tend to elicit reactions of distaste, disgust, offense, or outrage when mentioned or openly presented" (Wilson and West 1981: 82). Condoms, female hygiene products, sexually transmitted infections, and homosexuality could not be mentioned in commercial advertisements because they were taboo. But the death and devastation of the AIDS epidemic made it necessary to discuss previously unmentionable topics, creating a new openness regarding the advertisement of products related to sex and the body (Wilson and West 1992).

Illegal products not only draw the stigma of society, but also the prohibition of the state. Illegal markets are, by definition, banned by the state, which obstructs the development of market institutions such as property rights, governance structures, and rules of exchange (Campbell and Lindberg 1990; Beckert and Wehinger 2013). Even if actors are successful in developing socially legitimate uses for a stigmatized product, extant institutions prohibiting the sale of that product can prevent the growth of institutions that coordinate and safeguard exchange. Thus, a crisis might change public perception of an illegal product without leading to the legalization of that product. In these cases legitimacy and legality diverge, creating an *ambivalent* interface between the illegal market for a product and its legitimate crisis-specific use.

Legitimate but illegal markets face a fundamental problem: consumers without illicit ties lack access to the market. The precarious nature of such markets pushes illegal exchange into the shadows, where informal networks allow actors to develop trust and routinize transactions away from the surveillance of the state, and where conflicts and disagreements are often adjudicated with violence (Portes and Haller 2005; Beckert and Wehinger 2013). Fearing prosecution by the state and the uncertainty of selling to strangers, dealers of illegal products sell through their personal networks, making it difficult for those without a "friend-of-a-friend" to gain access.[4] Thus, when an illegal

[4] In contrast, actors in legal markets may openly advertise and sell their wares to any qualified customer without fear of state prosecution.

product or practice suddenly becomes necessary during a crisis, law-abiding consumers with a socially legitimate claim to purchase the product may not have the chthonic connections to gain access to the illegal market.

In markets that are characterized by ambivalent interfaces and limited access, market pioneers must broker between illegal producers and legitimate consumers while also constructing informal market institutions that are aligned with the new legitimate use for the prohibited product. By creating visible and accessible institutions, market pioneers take on greater risk of prosecution than they would when operating in the shadowy illegal market, out of view of the state. Market pioneers who are willing to risk prosecution in order to create an interface between the illegal and the legitimate often resemble social movement activists in both motivations and tactics. First, actors willing to face the possible consequences of jail time by operating openly are more likely to be driven by transcendental, value-rational goals, as it is safer and still profitable to stay in the illegal market away from prosecution. Second, founders of new markets and organizational forms are likely to use social movement-like tactics and construct and deploy frames that target the state and society to develop support for market institutions (Rao et al. 2000).

Social movement activists and market pioneers can use strategic frames, "schemata of interpretation," that allow actors to "locate, perceive, identify, and label" the world around them, in order to develop support for new or contested markets (Goffman 1974: 21; see also Snow et al. 1986; Snow 2004). Strategic framing is a process of theorization in which activists use language to identify problems, express grievances, assign blame, suggest cause-and-effect relationships, propose solutions, and act as signifying agents (Benford and Snow 2000; Oliver and Johnston 2000; Weber et al. 2013). Activists and entrepreneurs construct and deploy strategic frames to influence public opinion, reshape broader cultural logics, and apply pressure to policymakers.[5]

Activists attempting to develop support for market institutions will target parts of the state that are most likely to be sympathetic to their cause. The structure of the state (federal versus unitary or open versus closed) shapes the number and type of opportunities available to social movement organizations and social movement-like entrepreneurs. For example, an open federalist state is fragmented functionally and spatially, with multiple levels and centers, creating opportunities for movement activists to win support for a market (or any other institution-building project) at one level, even while that same

[5] As Sarah Quinn (2008) notes in her study of the secondary market for the life insurance market, if "institutions act like lenses that filter, focus, and direct different cultural strands and direct and refract otherwise diffuse cultural logics," then market activists use strategic frames to "extend and transform these institutionalized logics" (797).

market or project is prohibited at another level (Schneiberg and Soule 2005). Open institutional systems provide endless opportunities for protracted conflict and the development of parallel contradictory institutions (Campbell and Lindberg 1990; Djelic and Quack 2007; Purdy and Gray 2009). Thus, even if social movement activists and market pioneers are able to resolve the dissonance inherent in an ambivalent market interface by legalizing that market at one level of the state, they may create a new form of ambivalence between institutional regimes supported by different levels or parts of the state.

In the remainder of this chapter, I will draw upon interviews with activists and entrepreneurs who helped found, legitimize, and legalize the first medical marijuana markets in California, as well as recent histories, journalistic accounts, and memoirs describing the emergence of the medical marijuana industry in order to show how marijuana became medical in the contemporary United States. In 2012, I interviewed sixteen market activists, entrepreneurs, and lawyers identified by the news media and various movement histories as influential actors in the development of the medical marijuana market in California, including the founder of one of the state's first medical marijuana buyers' clubs and the author of the state's first medical marijuana initiative (see Table 9.1 for a list of interview respondents). Most respondents' names are replaced by pseudonyms in Table 9.1, however, the interview respondents quoted in the following section have agreed to use their real names.

## The AIDS Crisis: Creating an Opening

The AIDS epidemic rocked the United States during the 1980s and early 1990s, with over 500,000 reported cases and 300,000 deaths between 1980 and 1995 (amfAR 2016). AIDS was initially described as "gay cancer" due to the disease's predominance in the gay community. San Francisco, a self-proclaimed "gay mecca," was the epicenter of the crisis with nearly twice as many cases per capita as New York City, the city with the second-highest incidence rate (Kolata 1994). The widespread death and decimation that characterized the epidemic devastated the city of San Francisco, creating sympathy for AIDS patients and political and cultural opportunities for medical marijuana market pioneers. Clint Werner, an activist and writer, describes the Castro district, the historical heart of the San Francisco gay community, during the epidemic:

> I landed here in San Francisco as a Deadhead, but I'm also a gay man, and it was 1986, which was really the beginning of the height of the peak of the AIDS epidemic... If you weren't there you can't begin to imagine what it was like in the Castro in 1986. It was a horror movie. It was like the show the *Walking Dead* [a television program

**Table 9.1.** Interview respondents

| Respondent | Description |
|---|---|
| Bill | Marijuana grower |
| Quentin | Dispensary founder |
| Amy | Researcher/advocate |
| Clint Werner | Activist/author |
| Wayne Justman | Early medical marijuana patient/activist/dispensary founder |
| Arnie | Marijuana activist |
| Jack | Marijuana activist |
| Dean | Member of marijuana club |
| Charlie | Member of marijuana club |
| Barrie | Patient advocate |
| Dennis Peron | Market pioneer |
| Deborah | Early medical marijuana patient; founder of medical marijuana co-op |
| Norm | Executive director of medical marijuana dispensary |
| Ron | Marijuana lawyer |
| Ken | Marijuana lawyer |
| David | Marijuana lawyer |

> about zombies] ... the look of the people, young people ... just emaciated, gaunt, purple, their skin discolored, their faces had welts and lesions ... and just death, death everywhere—death—and suffering and misery and despair.
>
> (Interview April 23, 2012)

The deadly nature of the crisis spurred individuals to take illegal, formerly unthinkable actions. Legal sanctions paled in comparison with the wave of death that was surging through the community. Reflecting on the rise of medical marijuana in San Francisco, Dennis Peron, an illegal marijuana dealer and gay rights activist who is widely credited as the founder of one of the first medical marijuana buyers' clubs in San Francisco, describes how the crisis compelled patients and activists to break the law and pioneer a new market: "It had to happen here. It had to happen to persons affected by the AIDS epidemic. It had to be someone who had nothing to lose" (interview May 18, 2012).

During this period, AIDS patients found that using marijuana helped mitigate the rapid weight loss associated with wasting syndrome, a complication of the illness that made it hard for patients to maintain weight. Werner describes nursing his close friend who was affected by wasting syndrome,

> So I took him in and nursed him and took care of him ... I would make really nutritious stews like one-pot meals ... and then I'd get him high. I'd give him three or four bong hits and he would be like 'Arrg arrg.' He would scarf all this food down ... I mean there are drugs out there like *compazine* that will suppress your nausea, but they don't give you the munchies, they don't make you really want to eat, you still have to sort of force yourself to eat because you have the suppression of the nausea. But cannabis is unique because it triggers that compulsion to

"ehhh" [*makes gesture like shoveling food in mouth*] . . . and so he would eat and people would eat and not waste away as quickly.

(Interview April 23, 2012)

By 1993 over 28,000 San Francisco residents were living with AIDS, representing approximately 4 percent of the city's population (Kolata 1994). Moreover, many AIDS patients were politically active and socially embedded in a community integrated by decades of organizing and activism, creating local solidarity with and sympathy for patients (Armstrong 2002). Wayne Justman, an early volunteer at Peron's first medical marijuana club, describes local awareness of and support for AIDS patients: "San Francisco was receptive to this [medical marijuana], but then again who the hell didn't see somebody that they didn't know in church or in their community, a friend, who had not acquired AIDS or was HIV positive" (interview April 30, 2012). Werner echoes this sentiment: "jurors are drawn from the voter rolls, and there's no way they could seat a jury who was going to convict a man who was selling marijuana to AIDS and cancer patients" (interview April 23, 2012).

In contrast, the federal government actively obstructed the use of medical marijuana by AIDS patients. Prior to the start of the AIDS epidemic, the federal government was forced by the courts to create a small medical marijuana program in response to a lawsuit by Robert Randall, a glaucoma patient who used marijuana to relieve eye pressure. Randall sued the government in 1976 and settled, leading to the creation of the Compassionate Investigational New Drug (IND) program, which provided government-grown marijuana to seriously ill patients.[6] When AIDS patients discovered that marijuana helped alleviate some of the complications of the disease in the late 1980s and early 1990s, Randall created the Marijuana AIDS Research Service, an organization to help AIDS patients navigate the process of applying to the IND program (Randall 1991; Randall and O'Leary 1998). Soon afterwards, the number of applications by AIDS patients to the IND program surged, leading the federal government to stop accepting new applicants in 1991. Dr. James Mason, the United States Assistant Secretary for Health, gave the following explanation for the program's demise: "If it's perceived that the Public Health Service is going around giving marijuana to folks, there would be a perception that this stuff can't be so bad. It gives a bad signal . . . there's not a shred of evidence that smoking marijuana assists a person with AIDS" (Isikoff 1991: A14; Werner 2001).

[6] The IND program, supervised by the Food and Drug Administration, was a federal program that would grow marijuana and send pre-rolled marijuana cigarettes (*joints*) every month to approximately fifteen patients suffering from serious illnesses such as multiple sclerosis and glaucoma.

Thus, the AIDS crisis did not lead to the displacement of old institutions prohibiting marijuana for medical use. It initially did just the opposite, leading the federal government to reify its prohibitory stance and shut down the IND program that could have legally provided marijuana to AIDS patients.[7] Unable to gain access to marijuana through state-authorized channels, AIDS patients were pushed to the illegal market, where medical marijuana activists and pioneers developed informal institutions to distribute marijuana for medical use, creating an interface between the illegal market for marijuana and the legitimate needs of AIDS patients.

## The Buyers' Club: Building an Interface

In 1991, Dennis Peron started one of the first openly operating medical marijuana "buyers' clubs" in the United States, dispensing marijuana to AIDS patients in San Francisco. Peron had sold recreational marijuana in the illegal market for decades, most notably maintaining a speakeasy-type shop over a restaurant in San Francisco's Castro district during the 1970s. Peron had long been an activist promoting the legalization of marijuana for recreational use and had sponsored a pro-marijuana ballot initiative with legendary San Francisco supervisor and gay rights activist Harvey Milk in 1978. Peron pursued medical marijuana legalization after his partner died of AIDS in 1990. Peron explains: "So when my lover died... I set upon a path... for people like him. He had suffered so much and marijuana helped him so much. It was my personal eulogy for him. And it was for the world, but it was to him" (interview May 18, 2012).

The creation of a medical marijuana market for AIDS patients required an interface between the illegal market for marijuana and the law-abiding AIDS patients who did not have the illicit connections to purchase it. Prior to selling medical marijuana, Peron sold recreational marijuana through interpersonal networks. To avoid the consequences of taking part in an illegal act, Peron would only sell marijuana to a new customer in the illegal market if an existing customer vouched for them. Once Peron started providing marijuana to AIDS patients, he had to create informal market institutions in order to sell to patients whom he did not know through his interpersonal networks. Peron describes this shift from networks to informal institutions:

> I sold black market pot, you know, if I knew you and you had been referred, it would be alright, I would sell to you. But I remember the first time I sold to

[7] As of January 2016, federal prohibition of marijuana remains in place, and the Food and Drug Administration still maintains that marijuana has "no accepted medical use."

> someone I didn't know at all. He had a little piece of paper that said, "I have AIDS." I signed him up and think [to myself], "I'm setting on a path I had never been on before, selling to strangers at the house." I had never done that before. I did it fully expecting to get busted.
>
> (Interview May 18, 2012)

Peron moved from the safer system of personal networks, where he would sell marijuana to a customer if they were a friend-of-a-friend, to a riskier informal institution, where a person's claim to illness, in this case AIDS, granted them the right to purchase marijuana without an interpersonal connection. While the state continued to prohibit and prosecute the exchange of medical marijuana, effectively obstructing formal market institutions, Peron and other market pioneers created an informal system in which patients gained access to the market, not based on who they knew (networks) or the support of the law (formal institutions), but through a moral claim to purchase marijuana based on physical infirmity.

Medical marijuana markets that were prohibited by the state, but socially legitimate, gave way to a "work-around" system, in which doctors would write a "recommendation" rather than a Food and Drug Administration-required prescription in order to bypass the law. This system would lay the groundwork for a quasi-legal recommendation program that became the basis for patient access in state-legal marijuana markets.[8] Peron's pioneering efforts created not only an informal set of rules guiding exchange but also a new organizational form, the medical marijuana buyers' club, to distribute marijuana to AIDS patients.

Peron's first retail store, the San Francisco Cannabis Buyers' Club, borrowed from two contemporaneous organizational forms: illegal clubs for buying experimental antiretrovirals in San Francisco and New York and marijuana coffee shops in Amsterdam.

In the late 1980s and early 1990s, AIDS patients, doctors, and nurses organized "buyers' clubs," where club members illegally imported experimental antiretroviral drugs from other countries without the approval of the Food and Drug Administration. These organizations enabled patients to test the efficacy and dosing of different experimental drugs without waiting for the lengthy federal approval process (Lindemann 1994; Epstein 1995). Werner describes how these buyers' clubs functioned:

> So what happened was gay men . . . weren't going to sit by and just die. So people started researching drugs that weren't approved for use and drugs in other countries that were approved for other things that might have anti-viral activity and might be used . . . then they would smuggle them in from other countries or would

[8] In today's medical marijuana markets, marijuana providers can sell marijuana legally under state law to patients only if the patient presents a doctor's recommendation.

> find ways to buy them... This was part of what was so incredible about it, they would bring in these drugs and they would smuggle them in, they would research and find them and they would write up... what the effects were, what people were using for dosages.
>
> (Interview April 23, 2012)

Just as AIDS patients illegally smuggled antiretroviral therapies from other countries for off-label use, an illegal but legitimate act, the first medical marijuana buyers' clubs—modeled on these self-organized, antiretroviral buyers' clubs—created an interface between the illegal product and the legitimate needs of dying patients.

The medical marijuana buyers' clubs were more than just a distribution channel, they were also a value-rational community center dedicated to helping AIDS patients in a variety of ways. They provided marijuana to the seriously ill and also helped give patients purpose and bring them out of isolation. Feldman and Mandel's (1998: 181) ethnography of Peron's club conducted in 1996 depicts this scene:

> Peron's concept was to provide not only a cafeteria of cannabis products—including marijuana of varying potencies, cannabis pastries, and smoking paraphernalia—but to create a life space where persons with life-threatening or seriously debilitating diseases could gather, relax, and consume their medications in an accepting, friendly, and colorful surrounding. Some critics referred to Dennis' place as a "circus," but considering that it was both staffed and utilized by sick and dying people, more sensitive observers might conclude that he had created a therapeutic atmosphere that encouraged relaxation, friendly interaction, laughter and healing.

Justman, the security guard at Peron's buyers' club, describes Peron's value-rational hiring practices:

> Dennis asked me... when you try to hire and replace, give people that are HIV positive the first shot. He wanted to let them have something to do in life. Get them out of the hotel. Get them out of the negative... and it was really wonderful. A lot of people pushed people with HIV/AIDS away... We wanted to help people with HIV/AIDS.
>
> (Interview April 30, 2012)

The club's value-rational ethos not only shaped hiring practices but also influenced pricing decisions. Justman describes how the club tried to cater to the poor and indigent:

> Most of the people [we served] were very low income. Tenement housing clinics... We didn't have people drive up, get out, and come in and buy a hundred fifty dollars [of marijuana]. We had people come up and get a three dollar bag or if they didn't do that we would be giving them [marijuana].
>
> (Interview April 30, 2012)

Movement activists and socially minded entrepreneurs affected by the epidemic created a new informal institution, the marijuana buyers' club, to build an interface between the illegal market for marijuana and the needs of dying AIDS patients. This change not only transformed the criteria for how one became socially qualified to purchase marijuana—shifting from interpersonal networks to medical necessity—and created a new organizational form (the marijuana buyers' club), but also affected the underlying logic of the market, moving from a market that was mainly driven by money to one that was also driven by morals.

## Framing the Market, Winning State Support

The creation of informal institutions, such as buyers' clubs, helped create a path and a place for the distribution of marijuana to the seriously ill during the AIDS epidemic, but the small medical marijuana market that developed in San Francisco would have been ephemeral without state backing. In this regard the medical marijuana market is no different from legal markets (Fligstein 2001). To create an enduring market, medical marijuana activists and entrepreneurs targeted the state to win support for the market. While the AIDS epidemic created a political and cultural opportunity in which much of the public was sympathetic to AIDS patients using marijuana, government officials by and large felt that legalizing marijuana for any use, medical or recreational, was a political liability. Thus, activists and market pioneers turned to a tool of citizen legislation, the ballot initiative, in order to win legal recognition for medical marijuana.[9]

Marijuana and AIDS activists spearheaded ballot initiatives authorizing the medical use of marijuana, first in San Francisco in 1991 and then in California in 1996. In order to develop state support for medical marijuana laws, activists abandoned the recreational intoxicant conception and recast marijuana as a compassionate palliative for the dying. Peron, a self-described "hippie," explains that he consciously decided how to (and how not to) frame marijuana:

> To get the answer you want you got to ask the right questions, you got to frame it right. So I framed it in such a way, marijuana is medicine that helps people [who are] sick and dying . . . As far as the potheads . . . too much cultural baggage . . . so my main thing was with senior citizens and doctors and nurses . . . I realized I had to

[9] In both the city of San Francisco and the state of California, citizens who collect enough signatures can sponsor ballot initiatives that are voted on by the public, bypassing elected representatives. If a ballot initiative is passed, it becomes law.

> get away from the potheads. I already got their vote...they had so much baggage that I couldn't carry them. Cultural baggage, long hair, whatever it was. I'm a hippie, but I had to, not renounce it, but I had to put it aside for the greater goals.
>
> (Interview May 18, 2012)

In contrast to the recreational intoxicant conception, the compassionate palliative conception characterized marijuana as a medicine, not a narcotic, and its users as patients, not criminals. Drawing on a framing initially pioneered by Robert Randall in the 1970s, proponents of the compassionate palliative conception described marijuana as a medicine that soothed the pain and suffering of the seriously ill and dying. AIDS, cancer, multiple sclerosis, and other serious and debilitating illnesses were cast as legitimate conditions that justified patients' marijuana use. The compassionate palliative conception not only transformed marijuana's *use*, but also reframed its intended *administrator* and *user*, shifting from an image of drug dealers selling marijuana to long-haired hippies to one of doctors recommending marijuana to senior citizens and AIDS patients.

The compassionate palliative conception was integral to gaining public support for ballot initiative Proposition P in San Francisco in 1991 and then Proposition 215 in California in 1996. A poll of California voters conducted by the National Center on Addiction and Substance Abuse weeks before the vote on Proposition 215 showed that a majority of respondents polled would support the ballot initiative only if it was framed using the compassionate palliative conception (CASA 1996).

The compassionate palliative conception did not displace the recreational intoxicant conception because it neither addressed nor disputed marijuana's use as an intoxicant. Rather, the compassionate palliative conception carved out a legitimate medical use for those who deserved compassion: the seriously ill and dying. Similarly, the rise of state-legal medical marijuana markets did not displace prohibitory institutions at the federal level, but rather led to the co-existence of contradictory institutions supported by different parts of the state. Over the next twenty years, these contradictions would intensify. By 2016, the California medical marijuana market had grown to over 700,000 patients, with the number of patients using marijuana for serious illnesses such as AIDS, cancer, and multiple sclerosis dwarfed by patients with less deadly chronic conditions such as pain, anxiety, and insomnia (Reinarman et al. 2011; Marijuana Policy Project 2016). Moreover, in these two decades, laws authorizing the medical use of marijuana spread to twenty-five states, even as the federal government maintained its classification of marijuana as a Schedule 1 narcotic with no legitimate medical use.

## Conclusion

In recent years, historical institutionalists have revisited the mechanisms underlying sudden institutional transformation, often described as a punctuated equilibrium model, in which an exogenous shock leads to the breakdown of extant institutions that are then rapidly displaced by a new set of social configurations (Mahoney and Rueschmeyer 2003; Streeck and Thelen 2005; Mahoney and Thelen 2010). Scholars have elaborated upon and complicated theories of institutional change by showing how an exogenous shock is often assisted by endogenous actors who have the material, social, and symbolic resources to help win support for one set of new institutional arrangements over others (Deeg 2005).

The case of medical marijuana markets in the United States brings to light a number of processes through which social movement activists and market pioneers can leverage an exogenous shock to build social support for informal institutions that create an ambivalent interface between the socially legitimate and formally illegal. The deadly crisis forced entrepreneurs and activists affected by the AIDS crisis to create a new, public interface, the medical marijuana buyers' club, where they put themselves at risk of prosecution and incarceration in order to supply the sick and dying with medicine. After developing this informal institution, market pioneers and social movement supporters partially legalized the market by deploying strategic frames that resonated with the public and by targeting parts of the state that were more responsive to public sentiment.

Although this exogenous shock led to the rapid displacement of institutions preventing marijuana's medical use at the local and state level, prohibitory institutions at the federal level remained unchanged. Thus, even as social movement activists and marijuana entrepreneurs were able to resolve one type of ambivalence—the construction of a socially legitimate but illegal market—by passing ballot initiatives legalizing medical marijuana at the local and state levels, their successes led to another type of ambivalence, between local and state institutions that supported medical marijuana markets and federal institutions that prohibited them. In this case, institutional transformation at the local level combined with federal intransigence created a form of oppositional and contentious institutional layering, where institutional entrepreneurs responded to a political opportunity at one level of the state in a way that directly conflicted with extant institutions at another level of the state.

Once activists gained a foothold in one state, they were able to expand their efforts incrementally to other states without the aid of an exogenous shock. Even as federal incumbents continued to block changes to institutional configurations from the top down, local and state activists and entrepreneurs developed a $4.5 billion market from the bottom up. It is likely that this diffusion process was slower than it would have been if the federal government had supported (or at the very least, no longer opposed) medical marijuana markets.[10]

Together, these findings suggest that scholars of institutional change should consider both unsettled times *and* unsettled places. An exogenous shock—even one with the global consequences of the AIDS epidemic—will not necessarily have a uniform effect across geographies. San Francisco became the first city to pass a medical marijuana initiative in response to the AIDS epidemic, in part, because its population had the highest incidence of AIDS, and because the most affected population, gay men, had developed political and social capital while fighting for gay rights and inclusion in preceding decades.

Scholars of institutional change should focus not only on the social geography of institutional change, but also on the political geography, particularly the opportunities inherent in the structure of the state. The multi-level and multi-centric structure of an open, federalist state means that even when a rupture leads to rapid discontinuous change at one level of government, extant institutions at another level of government may slow the diffusion of markets, moderating the pace of institutional change.

## References


21 USC § 812: *Schedules of Controlled Substances*. <http://www.law.cornell.edu/uscode/text/21/812> (accessed December 20, 2013).

Ackrell Capital. 2016. *U.S. Cannabis Investment Report 2016*. <http://www.ackrell.com/cannabis/> (accessed September 14, 2016).

amfAR. 2016. *amfAR: Thirty Years of HIV/AIDS: Snapshots of an Epidemic: The Foundation for AIDS Research: HIV/AIDS Research*. <http://www.amfar.org/thirty-years-of-hiv/aids-snapshots-of-an-epidemic/> (accessed January 3, 2016).

Anslinger, Harry, and Courtney Ryley Cooper. 1937. "Marihuana: Assassin of Youth." *American Magazine* 124(1).

ArcView Market Research and New Frontier. 2016. *The State of Legal Marijuana Markets*. 4th ed. Oakland, CA: ArcView Group.

Armstrong, Elizabeth A. 2002. *Forging Gay Identities: Organizing Sexuality in San Francisco, 1950–1994*. Chicago: University of Chicago Press.

Baumgartner, Frank, and Bryan Jones. 1993. *Agendas and Instability in American Politics*. Chicago: University of Chicago Press.

Becker, Howard S. 1963. *Outsiders: Studies in the Sociology of Deviance*. New York: Free Press.


[10] Ackrell Capital, a financial firm that covers the cannabis industry, estimates that a legal national marijuana market would exceed $40 billion in annual revenue (Ackrell Capital 2016).

Beckert, Jens, and Frank Wehinger. 2013. "In the Shadow: Illegal Markets and Economic Sociology." *Socio-Economic Review* 11(1): pp. 5–30.

Beissinger, Mark R. 2002. *Nationalist Mobilization and the Collapse of the Soviet State.* Cambridge: Cambridge University Press.

Benford, Robert D., and David A. Snow. 2000. "Framing Processes and Social Movements: An Overview and Assessment." *Annual Review of Sociology* 26: pp. 611–39.

Bonnie, Richard J., and Charles H. Whitebread. 1970. "The Forbidden Fruit and the Tree of Knowledge: An Inquiry into the Legal History of American Marijuana Prohibition." *Virginia Law Review* 56(6): pp. 971–1203.

Campbell, John L., and Leon N. Lindberg. 1990. "Property Rights and the Organization of Economic Activity by the State." *American Sociological Review* 55(5): pp. 634–47.

CASA. 1996. *Survey of California Voters on Proposition 215 and Marijuana Legalization.* New York: Columbia University.

Deeg, Richard. 2005. "Change from within: German and Italian Finance in the 1990s." In *Beyond Continuity: Institutional Change in Advanced Political Economies*, edited by Wolfgang Streeck and Kathleen Thelen, pp. 169–202. Oxford: Oxford University Press.

Djelic, Marie-Laure, and Sigrid Quack. 2007. "Overcoming Path Dependency: Path Generation in Open Systems." *Theory and Society* 36(2): pp. 161–86.

Drug Free World Foundation. 2013. *Marijuana: What Is the Truth?* <http://www.drugfreeworld.org/drugfacts/marijuana.html> (accessed December 20, 2013).

Epstein, Steven. 1995. "The Construction of Lay Expertise: AIDS Activism and the Forging of Credibility in the Reform of Clinical Trials." *Science, Technology and Human Values* 20(4): pp. 408–37.

Feldman, Harvey W., and Jerry Mandel. 1998. "Providing Medical Marijuana: The Importance of Cannabis Clubs." *Journal of Psychoactive Drugs* 30(2): pp. 179–86.

Fligstein, Neil. 2001. *The Architecture of Markets: An Economic Sociology of Twenty-First Century Capitalist Societies.* Princeton, NJ: Princeton University Press.

Goffman, Erving. 1974. *Frame Analysis: An Essay on the Organization of Experience.* Boston, MA: Northeastern University Press.

Grinspoon, Lester, James B. Bakalar, and Rick Doblin. 1995. "Marijuana, the AIDS Wasting Syndrome, and the US Government." *New England Journal of Medicine* 333(10): pp. 670–1.

Isikoff, Michael. 1991. "HHS to Phase Out Marijuana Program; Officials Fear Sending 'Bad Signal' by Giving Drug to Seriously Ill." *Washington Post*, June 22, Final Edition, A14.

Kolata, Gina. 1994. "AIDS in San Francisco Hit Peak in '92, Officials Say." *New York Times*, February 16. <http://www.nytimes.com/1994/02/16/us/aids-in-san-francisco-hit-peak-in-92-officials-say.html> (accessed January 8, 2016).

Lindemann, Eric. 1994. "Importing AIDS Drugs: Food and Drug Administration Policy and Its Limitations." *George Washington Journal of International Law and Economics* 28: pp. 133–70.

Mahoney, James, and Dietrich Rueschemeyer. 2003. *Comparative Historical Analysis in the Social Sciences.* Cambridge: Cambridge University Press.

Mahoney, James, and Kathleen Thelen (eds). 2010. *Explaining Institutional Change: Ambiguity, Agency, and Power.* Cambridge: Cambridge University Press.

Marijuana Policy Project. 2016. "Medical Marijuana Patient Numbers." *MPP.* <https://www.mpp.org/issues/medical-marijuana/state-by-state-medical-marijuana-laws/medical-marijuana-patient-numbers/> (accessed September 27, 2016).

McAdory, Paul. 2013. "10 Reasons Marijuana Is Better for You than Alcohol." *High Times.* <http://hightimes.com/medicinal/10-reasons-marijuana-is-better-for-you-than-alcohol/> (accessed January 13, 2017).

Miron, Jeffrey A. 2010. *The Budgetary Implications of Marijuana Prohibition.* Report of the Harvard University Department of Economics and the Criminal Justice Policy Foundation. Cambridge, MA: Harvard University.

Oliver, Pamela E., and Hank Johnston. 2000. "What a Good Idea! Ideologies and Frames in Social Movement Research." *Mobilization: An International Quarterly* 5(1): pp. 37–54.

Portes, Alejandro, with William Haller. 2005. "The Informal Economy." In *Handbook of Economic Sociology,* 2nd ed., edited by N. Smelser and R. Swedberg, pp. 403–25. New York: Russell Sage Foundation.

Purdy, Jim M., and Barbara Gray. 2009. "Conflicting Logics, Mechanisms of Diffusion, and Multilevel Dynamics in Emerging Institutional Fields." *Academy of Management Journal* 52(2): pp. 355–80.

Quinn, Sarah. 2008. "The Transformation of Morals in Markets: Death, Benefits, and the Exchange of Life Insurance Policies." *American Journal of Sociology* 114(3): pp. 738–80.

Randall, Robert C. 1991. *Marijuana and AIDS: Pot, Politics and PWAs in America.* Washington, DC: Galen Press.

Randall, Robert C., and Alice M. O'Leary. 1998. *Marijuana Rx: The Patient's Fight for Medicinal Pot.* New York: Thunder's Mouth Press.

Rao, Hayagreeva, Calvin Morrill, and Mayer N. Zald. 2000. "Power Plays: How Social Movements and Collective Action Create New Organizational Forms." *Research in Organizational Behavior* 22: pp. 237–82.

Reinarman, Craig, Helen Nunberg, Fran Lanthier, and Tom Heddleston. 2011. "Who Are Medical Marijuana Patients? Population Characteristics from Nine California Assessment Clinics." *Journal of Psychoactive Drugs* 43(2): pp. 128–35.

Rowell, Earle Albert, and Robert Rowell. 1939. *On the Trail of Marihuana: The Weed of Madness.* Nampa, ID: Pacific Press Publishing Association.

Schneiberg, Marc, and Sarah A. Soule. 2005. "Institutionalization as a Contested Multi-level Process." In *Social Movements and Organization Theory,* edited by Gerald F. Davis, Doug McAdam, W. Richard Scott, and Mayer N. Zald, pp. 122–60. Cambridge: Cambridge University Press.

Snow, David A. 2004. "Framing Processes, Ideology, and Discursive Fields." In *The Illegalwell Companion to Social Movements,* edited by David A. Snow, Sarah A. Soule, and Hanspeter Kriesi, pp. 380–412. Oxford: Illegalwell.

Snow, David A., E. Burke Rochford, Steven K. Worden, and Richard D. Benford. 1986. "Frame Alignment Processes, Micromobilization, and Movement Participation." *American Sociological Review* 51(4): pp. 464–81.

Stanley, Eugene. 1931. "Marihuana as a Developer of Criminals." *American Journal of Police Science* 2(3): pp. 252–61.

Streeck, Wolfgang, and Kathleen Thelen. 2005. "Introduction: Institutional Change in Advanced Political Economies." In *Beyond Continuity: Institutional Change in Advanced Political Economies*, edited by Wolfgang Streeck and Kathleen Thelen, pp. 3–39. Oxford: Oxford University Press.

Suchman, Edward A. 1968. "The 'Hang-Loose' Ethic and the Spirit of Drug Use." *Journal of Health and Social Behavior* 9(2): pp. 146–55.

Swidler, Ann. 1986. "Culture in Action: Symbols and Strategies." *American Sociological Review* 51(2): pp. 273–86.

*The Pharmacopoeia of the United States*. 3rd ed. 1851. Philadelphia, PA: Lippincott, Grambo, and Co.

US Department of Justice. 1965–2010. *Uniform Crime Reports. Federal Bureau of Investigation*. Washington, DC: Government Printing Office.

Weber, Klaus, Hetal Patel, and Kathryn L. Heinze. 2013. "From Cultural Repertoires to Institutional Logics: A Content-Analytic Method." In *Institutional Logics in Action, Part B (Research in the Sociology of Organizations, Volume 39)*, edited by Michael Lounsbury and Eva Boxenbaum, pp. 351–82. Bingley: Emerald Group Publishing Limited.

Werner, Clinton A. 2001. "Medical Marijuana and the AIDS Crisis." *Journal of Cannabis Therapeutics* 1(3–4): pp. 17–33.

Wilson, Aubrey, and Christopher West. 1981. "The Marketing of Unmentionables." *Harvard Business Review* 59(1): pp. 91–105.

Wilson, Aubrey, and Christopher West. 1992. "Permissive Marketing: The Effect of the AIDS Crisis on Marketing Practices and Messages." *Business Strategy Review* 3(2): pp. 91–109.

Wood, George Bacon, and Franklin Bache (eds). 1851. *The Dispensatory of the United States of America 354*. 9th ed. Philadelphia: JB Lippincott Co.

# 10

# Contested Illegality

## Processing the Trade Prohibition of Rhino Horn

*Annette Hübschle*

### Introduction

The international community declared a total ban on the trade of rhino horn in the late 1970s. Despite regulation and a variety of extraordinary conservation, protective, and security measures, the illegal killing of rhinoceroses (hereafter "rhinos") continues to plague rhino range states.[1] An average of three rhinos are poached and dehorned in the southern African bush each day. At the current rate of attrition, wild rhinos are likely to go extinct in our lifetime. The analytical focus of this chapter is on South Africa, which is the greatest African rhino range state, hosting nearly 80 percent of the continent's rhinos. This chapter shows that banning an economic exchange is not a straightforward political decision but a protracted process that may encounter unexpected hurdles along the way to effective implementation and enforcement. While political considerations informed the decision to ban all trade in rhino horn initially, diffusion of the prohibition was uneven and lacked social and cultural legitimacy among key actors affected by the ban and its impact. This chapter starts with a theoretical framing, introducing the notion of "contested illegality."[2] Important market actors thus justify their participation

[1] Range states are countries in which specific populations of wildlife occur "in the wild." South Africa, Namibia, Kenya, and Zimbabwe are the main African rhino range states.

[2] The research for this chapter derives from a doctoral research project, which followed flows of rhino horn from the source in southern Africa to illegal markets in Southeast Asia. The multi-sited ethnography included participant observations, interviews, and focus groups with more than 420 informants during fourteen months of fieldwork. The sample comprised, among others, convicted and active rhino poachers, smugglers and kingpins, private rhino breeders and hunting outfitters,

in illegal economic action involving rhino horn based on the perceived illegitimacy of the rhino horn prohibition. The chapter illustrates contested illegality with empirical examples. The conclusion hones in on the question of why the illegal market for rhino horn is difficult to disrupt in spite of the myriad measures employed to protect the animals.

## Contested Illegality

The blurring of legality and illegality is of particular interest in the study of transnational flows, with national legal jurisdictions determining the boundaries and limits of legality and illegality in their sovereign territories. Once an economic exchange moves beyond the political boundaries of the state (the exchange may occur between actors located across several different states), issues of jurisdiction muddy the waters. Many scholars rely on the state as their analytical point of departure when studying regulatory frameworks and their impact. While the state[3] delineates what it considers to be legal or illegal, there may be a disconnect between the state and society regarding such legal definitions, their interpretation, and the legitimacy of such rules. Both agents of the state and members of society might flout some rules. As observed by Renate Mayntz in this volume, there is "very large room for interpretation of formal rules." The constructed and fixed dichotomies of legal/illegal or state-approved/forbidden ignore how illegal, informal, and grey economic practices are frequently intertwined with our daily lives (Van Schendel and Abraham 2005: 4–6). While a formal political authority may have criminalized (declared "illegal") something at some point in time, actors may not agree with the label or the process. It will be argued here that actors' implicit and explicit defiance or contestation of the state-sponsored label of illegality may serve as a legitimizing and enabling mechanism, which facilitates their participation in illegal markets.

Social, moral, and cultural norms may diverge from legal rules, thus delegitimizing them. Diverse cultural frames assign moral and normative meanings to the legitimacy or illegitimacy of economic exchanges, the goods or services to be exchanged, the act of producing or exchanging the goods or services, the actor constellations involved in different segments of the supply chain, or the impact of the market (see for examples: Satz 2010: 91–114). Social legitimation

African and Asian law enforcement officials, as well as affected local communities, and Asian consumers. Court files, CITES trade data, archival materials, newspaper reports, and social media posts were also analyzed to supplement findings and to verify and triangulate data from interviews, focus groups, and observations.

[3] It is acknowledged that the state is not a unitary actor. For the purposes of this argument, the state and its different arms of governance are presented as a homogenous entity.

of some goods and services is likely to confront additional challenges: while the production, exchange, or consumption/use of such goods or services may have been declared "illegal," the commodification of such goods or services may also be considered morally or culturally contested, questionable, or even repugnant. Important actors along the supply chain thus have to overcome moral scruples, cultural hurdles, or personal inhibitions associated with transacting in illegal markets (Beckert and Wehinger 2013: 7). However, actors may find it less daunting to enter, transact in, or establish markets that are illegal but socially accepted. Levels of social acceptance of the law on the books may vary based on new information, emerging cultural preferences and trends (see also the chapter by Dioun in this volume), or politico-legal developments. Wildlife contraband (especially rhino horn) falls into what has been called a "contested market" (Steiner and Trespeuch 2013) or a "contested commodity" (Radin 1996) elsewhere.[4] As will be shown later, there are competing claims as to whether rhino horn should be a tradable good or commodity, calling into question whether the label of illegality is appropriate or necessary, or constitutes a case of ethnocentric valuation (valuation that is based on a particular cultural outlook).

The economic exchange of wildlife products was legal and legitimate until regulators declared otherwise in the 1970s. Ideally, the regulation of a formerly legal activity or product should involve a protracted process of public consultation with affected constituents, negotiation, drafting, and implementation. Illegalization per se presents a socio political process rather than a static condition, likely to lead to regulations that tend to favor the preferences of powerful political elites (Heyman 2013: 304). It is important to note the significant role of the state, regulatory authorities, and law-enforcement agencies in determining legal rules and norms pertaining to the legality or illegality of an economic exchange. The influence of professional knowledge, scientific insights, and disciplinary regimes is likewise not to be discounted in the process of legalization or illegalization (Heyman 2013: 306). A further dimension relates to the sponsors of legal rules and norms, who may be economic elites or corporations seeking to protect their economic interests. Moreover, the history of "overrule that either suspended legalities or deployed them to authorize predation and criminalize opposition" has led to continued distrust of the state and its perceived anti-poor policies among the poor and marginalized strata of post-colonial society in southern Africa (Comaroff and Comaroff 2006: 11).

[4] Steiner and Trespeuch (2013: 144) define "contested markets" as "markets in which contested commodities are bought and sold." The authors build on Radin's conception of contested commodities, which are goods whose consumption may be open to moral challenges.

What happens when the economic exchange of a good is declared illegal at a specific point in time, outlawing or banning the exchange that was legal and legitimate up until the prohibition takes effect? This state of affairs is qualitatively the opposite of the case of legalization of marijuana markets in the United States, described by Dioun in this volume. A further question is related to what happens in scenarios in which international actors (such as a multilateral treaty organization) impose a ban that lacks legitimacy at the local level? The poaching of endangered wildlife, for example, is illegal in so-called range countries, whereas trade hovers in a grey zone between legality and illegality, and consumption is socially legitimate in consumer countries even if it is illegal. Noteworthy is the partial ban of the trade in rhino horn; the sale of live rhinos and trophy hunting of white rhinos is allowed in a few jurisdictions, while a full trade ban applies elsewhere. Pre-Convention[5] processed rhino horn is traded legally in many jurisdictions and no commercial trade of post-Convention raw rhino horn is allowed in CITES (United Nations Convention on International Trade in Endangered Species of Wild Fauna and Flora) member states.

## Methods of Horn Procurement and the Demand for Rhino Horn

The most common form of rhino horn procurement involves the illegal killing of rhinos (rhino poaching) in protected areas or on private land. Typically, a group of three poachers will launch an illegal hunting party with clearly defined roles during the hunt: those of the hunter, the tracker, and the food and water carrier (who carry the horns on the return trip if the hunt is successful). Once "harvested," the horns are first taken to domestic and then international transport hubs, from where they are transferred to consumer markets. The diversion of rhino horn from legal sources such as trophy hunting, private and public rhino horn stockpiles, or live animal is another source of rhino horn. The case study in this chapter illustrates the manipulation and diversion of seemingly legally procured rhino horn into illegal markets. Gangs of thieves also steal rhino horn from private collections, state-owned or private stockpiles, museums, and galleries across the globe (EUROPOL 2011; Milliken 2014). An unknown amount of previously "harvested," even antique rhino horn, horn artifacts, and hunting trophies are either in circulation or safely stowed away. Due to the high value of rhino horn—ranging between USD 45,000 and USD 120,000/kg at the time of

[5] CITES came into force in 1977. Any wildlife products that predated the enactment of CITES can be traded in most CITES member states provided that provenance can be shown.

writing—entrepreneurs have developed fake or "ersatz" horn, for which consumers are willing to part with substantial sums of money.

The demise of the rhino is linked to tenacious demand for rhino horn in consumer markets. The two horns on the African rhino's forehead are amongst the most expensive goods in the world. Asian consumers have been using powdered rhino horn in traditional Asian medicine for more than four millennia. Carved into hilts for traditional daggers known as "yambiyas," rhino horn was also in great demand in Yemen during the 1970s and 1980s (Varisco 1989). Small pockets of demand remain in the Middle Eastern country (see for more detail: Vigne and Martin 2008); however, consumers cannot compete with the high prices offered in Southeast and East Asian markets (Vigne and Martin 2013: 324). Another centuries-old tradition relates to the legal sports hunting of rhinos, traditionally associated with affluent individuals from the Global North. The resultant hunting trophies are exported to the hunter's home country where they are kept in private collections, galleries, and museums. While these "traditional" uses endure to lesser degrees, rhino horn is increasingly employed as a status symbol, religious or cultural artifact, and gift among the upper strata of Asian societies (Truong et al. 2015; Ipsos Marketing 2013; Amman 2015a; PSI Vietnam 2015). It also serves as a speculative asset and as a criminal currency (Hübschle 2016). The horn of the three-toed ungulate counts among the most expensive goods in the world, achieving illegal market prices of up to USD 120,000 per kilogram when carved into intricate artworks and religious objects. Rhino horn has long been priced as a valuable good, which has led to unregulated and excessive hunting in Asian and African rhino range states. The following sections show regulatory regimes aimed at protecting rhinos in the wild. An important element is the demonstration of the unexpected outcomes of regulation which can be explained by way of the social land cultural legitimacy of rhino horn trade among key actors.

## Hunting and Anti-Poaching Measures in Colonial Times

After Jan van Riebeeck and the Dutch East India Company arrived at the Cape of Good Hope in 1652, the lives and fortunes of local African people and wild animals changed forever. In the process of colonization, Africans lost property and hunting rights, and systemic exploitation was instituted first by colonial rulers, and subsequently reinforced during the apartheid regime. The scales tipped towards overexploitation of the still abundant wildlife shortly after the European colonizers arrived. The first colonial administrator Jan van Riebeeck decreed the first poaching law a mere five years after landing at the Cape. He declared wild animals as *res nullius*. According to this legal principle, whoever captured or killed a wild animal, owned it (Couzens 2003: 4). Despite the restricted access to firearms, hunting dogs, as well as the withdrawal of hunting and landownership rights, African people received the blame for the annihilation of wildlife during colonial times. With historical hindsight, a confluence of destructive forces—such as agricultural transformation, modernization, and industrialization—seem to have played their role, while the hunting by the colonial landowners was equally devastating for wildlife numbers (Carruthers 1993: 13). A significant aim of the early hunting laws was the creation of an African workforce that was reliant on income from wages for their livelihoods. Many Africans had maintained their economic independence from European settlers by hunting and trading wildlife and carried on with their pastoralist and agricultural lifestyles. Through the hunting ban and other colonial measures, the colonial masters created a workforce consisting of individuals who were no longer self-sufficient and depended on income from working in mines and other industrial endeavors (Carruthers 1993: 13).

While the early wildlife-protection measures served the colonial objectives, later measures were driven by the desire to preserve wildlife for sports hunting. At the turn of the nineteenth century, game reserves were designed to provide "free from all human interference, a sanctuary in which certain species of wildlife could prosper" (Carruthers 1993: 13). The early game reserves of Transvaal, for example, were to be located on land considered barren, disease-ridden, and worthless to mining interests. Eventually these "state game farming enterprises" were to be opened to sportsmen, who would pay the state for hunting privileges (Carruthers 1993: 14). While the land devoted to game reserves was uninteresting to other industries, national and provincial parks were established on sought-after real estate. These parks entail "the utilization of an area through active management for the benefit of the ecosystem and visitors." Thus, game reserves and national parks had different aims and legal foundations. While game reserves could be established and abolished by proclamation, national parks were legally secure and economically viable (Carruthers 1993: 13). Indigenous and local African property and hunting rights, and ancestral burial grounds (which are significant cultural sites) were not considered when reserves and parks were proclaimed during the twentieth century.[6]

## Rhino Conservation during the Apartheid Regime

The National Party came to power in South Africa in 1948, which paved the way for a whole range of race laws and policies that affected all aspects of social

[6] More than half of the area of the Kruger National Park is subject to land claims by local claimants in post-Apartheid South Africa.

and political life, including nature conservation. The systematic exploitation of African people that started under colonial rule was further entrenched under the formalized system of apartheid, which benefitted the interests of the white population only. African people experienced "double exclusion" from national parks. They were denied visitor's access to the parks and systematically excluded from the governance of parks (Cock and Fig 2000: 132).[7] Parks such as the Kruger National Park (South Africa's signature national park) came to represent a mechanism of apartheid rule. The apartheid regime actively promoted the view that Afrikaners had set up national parks and the black population came to perceive parks as "manifestations of apartheid."

South Africa constitutes a special case within the southern African region because private individuals can legally own wildlife including rhinos and derive financial benefit from it.[8] Although wild animals continue to be considered *res nullius* in South African common law (see earlier section), regulators made several legal changes to encourage wildlife conservation on private land. Through these successive changes in the law, game ranchers were granted ownership over wildlife and the right to derive income from consumptive utilization, such as the hunting of wild animals for profit (Lindsey et al. 2007: 463). The Transvaal Directorate of Nature Conservation[9] initially introduced the "certificate of adequate enclosure" in 1968, which was subsequently rolled out to the other provinces. This certificate exempted landowners from regulations applicable to hunting seasons and bag limits, and wild animals thus could be hunted all year round. Landowners were invited to apply for the certificate if they could demonstrate adequate game-proof fencing (Reilly 2014).[10] In essence, game ranchers were granted ownership over wildlife and the right to derive income from consumptive utilization, such as the killing of wild animals for profit (Lindsey et al. 2007: 463). The commercial trophy-hunting industry took off in the 1960s as hunters started to pay to stalk wild animals (Scriven and Eloff 2003: 246). Trophy hunting has become a major income generator on game ranches, including rhino reserves. However, the limits of the common law position (*res nullius*) remained unsatisfactory to the private sector. The South African Law Commission protected the proprietary rights of land owners through the recommendation of the Game Theft Act

[7] Until the 1980s black visitors to the Kruger Park could only stay overnight at the rudimentarily equipped Balule tented camp. Economic deprivation through apartheid restricted access further as few Africans had access to cars and disposable income to afford vacations (Cock and Fig 2000: 132).

[8] Namibia also allows private ownership of wildlife, including white rhinos. However, black rhinos (given a global population of fewer than 5,250 black rhinos, the species is considered critically endangered) form part of a state-controlled custodian program. Communities and private individuals thus may lease rhinos from the state.

[9] Transvaal was one of the four provinces in apartheid South Africa.

[10] A multi-strand nine-foot fence designed to keep wild animals inside the game ranch constituted the minimum standard of adequate enclosure (Reilly 2014).

105 of 1991 (Glazewski 2000: 428). Upon enactment, the law further protected the landowner's rights of ownership of game in cases where game escapes or is lured away from the landowner's "sufficiently enclosed" land (Glazewski 2000: 428). Beyond fencing in wild animals and claiming ownership rights both over land and wild animals this move led to the further alienation and deprivation of rural African communities, restricting their access to land and resources. Once these property and ownership rights had been asserted, subsistence hunting on game farms was inevitably branded as poaching, and accessing private land for the purposes of seeking grazing, water, or medicinal plants was deemed to fall under the criminal offence of "trespass." The apartheid regime employed this category of crime to prevent black South Africans from moving around freely in demarcated "whites-only" areas, which included parks, private land, and towns. Dangerous wild animals were to be contained within game fences, which effectively determined "no-go areas" for local communities. If a farmer were to find an unknown black person "trespassing" on the land, the latter ran the risk of being shot on sight. The waiver of the *res nullius* principle entrenched by the new regulation also strengthened the relationship between the apartheid state and the white farming community, one of its main political powerbases.

The white rhino has an important role in the drive to privatize wildlife in South Africa. The number of white rhinos in the Hluhluwe-Umfolozi Game Reserve[11] in KwaZulu-Natal was reduced through unrestrained hunting to about fifty to seventy animals in the early twentieth century and locally went extinct elsewhere in South Africa. Through successful breeding and conservation programs within the protected area, however, white rhino numbers started to increase by the 1960s. When rhino numbers began to exceed carrying capacity, conservators feared that an outbreak of disease could halt the recovery of white rhino numbers. It was at this point that the Natal Parks Board[12] commenced "Operation Rhino," which over the course of the 1960s and early 1970s saw more than 1,200 white rhinos relocated from the Hluhluwe-Umfolozi Game Reserve to the Kruger Park, white-owned private game reserves, as well as zoos and safari parks abroad (Player 2013). The Natal Parks Board had envisaged that the provision of white rhinos at low cost to private landowners would render them effective custodians of rhinos. The first white rhinos were sold to private landowners at highly subsidized prices in 1963. To parks authorities in South Africa, the sale of live rhinos to private operators constituted (and continues to do so) a much-needed cash injection.

[11] South Africa's oldest proclaimed nature reserve is now known as the Hluhluwe-iMfolozi Park.

[12] The former province of Natal has been known as KwaZulu-Natal since the end of apartheid, and its parks authority is known as Ezemvelo KZN Wildlife, the former Natal Parks Board.

In post-apartheid South Africa, conservation authorities continue to sell rhinos and other wildlife to private individuals and entities as a fund-raising and conservation strategy. By 2016, private rhino reserves occupied an area of about 2 million hectares, incorporating about 380 separate properties, similar in size to the Kruger National Park. A total of 33 percent (or about 6,200 animals) of the national population of white rhinos and 450 black rhinos were protected on private land in South Africa at the end of 2016 (personal communication with Pelham Jones, Private Rhino Owners Association, 2016). While the privatization of rhinos has been portrayed as an unqualified conservation success story ('t Sas-Rolfes 2012; Bothma et al. 2012), the darker side is often disregarded. By virtue of the apartheid race laws, African people were legally excluded from owning commercial farming land and wild animals until the end of the apartheid regime in 1994. It needs to be stressed that private rhino breeders and farmers form part of the economic landed elite (the white farming community was one of the power bases of the apartheid state), which also points to deeper structural issues that undermine rhino conservation and facilitate illegal economic activities in the post-apartheid dispensation. The need to generate profits to run and secure rhino farms and reserves provides one point of entry for illegal economic action, partly through the exploitation of legislative and regulatory loopholes (explored later in this chapter).

## CITES: Is the International Political Regulatory Regime a Neo-Colonial Tool?

CITES provides the regulatory framework for international trade in endangered plant and animal species. It was originally signed in Washington in 1973 and entered into force in 1975. Earlier regulatory attempts to deal with the unsustainable exploitation of wildlife were unsuccessful because the international community struggled to reach consensus and broad ratification of various instruments (Sand 1997). The system of negative lists (CITES calls them "Appendices") provided the first bone of contention during the drafting process of CITES. The International Union for the Conservation of Nature had suggested that wildlife trade should be controlled or banned on the basis of global lists of threatened species to be drawn up and updated on the advice of an international committee of experts. A coalition of countries from the Global South was in favor of range states determining their lists of tradable species. The United States supported the bid, thereby paving the way for the Washington Conference, which led to CITES (Sand 1997: 20). The core approach of CITES is to subject all wildlife imports to mandatory licensing with permits issued by the exporting countries on the basis of an agreed negative listing (Sand 1997: 20). Twenty-one states signed the Convention initially, which placed 1,100 species in the Appendices. Although it was a pariah state in the international community at the time, apartheid South Africa was one of the original signatories of the treaty.

Species are considered for inclusion in or deletion from the Appendices at the Conference of Parties (CoP), held every three years. Appendix I provides a list of species threatened with extinction and thus commercial trade in wild-caught specimens of these species is illegal (CITES 2002).[13] Species listed under Appendix II are not necessarily threatened with extinction but may become threatened unless trade is subject to strict regulation to prevent extinction in the wild. International trade may be authorized by the presentation and granting of an export permit or re-export certificate (CITES 1973). Appendix III relates to species, which were listed after one state party asked other state parties for assistance in controlling trade in a specific species. These species are not necessarily threatened with extinction globally. Trade is only authorized by way of an appropriate export permit and a certificate of origin (CITES 1973). CITES allows for some room to manoeuver when it comes to the listing of species where the conservation status of a species differs across its range. So-called "split listing" refers to cases in which "different populations or sub-species are in different Appendices and [in which] a population (or sub-species) may be listed and another may not" (Willock 2004: 15). Rhinos are an example of "split listing," as white rhinos in South Africa and Swaziland were moved to Appendix II after the initial absolute trade ban.

In the early years of the Convention, CITES parties placed all rhino species in Appendix I, effectively banning international trade except under exceptional circumstances (Milliken and Shaw 2012: 44). The split listing that allowed the listing of South African populations of white rhino to be moved to Appendix II happened in 1994. With this move, CITES parties recognized the huge strides made by South Africa in terms of rhino population and range growth. An annotation confined permissible trade in live rhinos to "acceptable and appropriate destinations and hunting trophies only" (CITES 1994). While CITES regulates international trade, individual states have to transpose the CITES stipulations into national law, and regulate domestic trade of endangered species. It is thus legal for live animals and hunting trophies to be exported from South Africa to elsewhere in the world. Once live rhinos or hunting trophies leave African shores, national regulatory agencies relinquish their responsibilities to authorities in receiving countries. While passing through international airspace, waters, or transit countries, there are

[13] The trade of captive-bred animals or cultivated plants of Appendix I species are considered Appendix II specimens with the concomitant requirements (CITES 2002). In other words, so-called Appendix I species can be traded if they do not derive from wild populations.

numerous opportunities for criminal networks to manoeuver, launder, and deceive national regulatory authorities that have limited oversight beyond their national jurisdictions. The annotation of permissible trades coupled with the relatively short lifespan of the CITES prohibition have allowed for legal flows to co-exist with grey and illegal flows.

CITES offers interesting insights as to why it might be difficult to garner support for trade bans when they are imposed "from the outside world" (interview with South African environmental official, 2013) or in a different historical context. The political, social, economic, and environmental dimensions of the modern world have changed since the treaty entered into force more than forty years ago. It is, for example, noteworthy that South Africa's apartheid regime gave CITES the stamp of approval in 1975, making it one of the Convention's earliest signatories. Moreover, significant consumer countries such as Cambodia, Laos, Myanmar, Taiwan, Vietnam, and Yemen joined CITES only twenty years after its inception, allowing a massive window for uncontrolled international trade in wildlife in the intervening period.

Interviews with selected African political elites revealed sentiments that reflected negatively on the politics of CITES, the futility of trade bans, and the perceived influence of Western conservation non-governmental organizations and the animal rights movement. Meanwhile, African environmental justice movements have had no or little representation at CoPs. Falling short of calling CITES a neo-colonial institution, southern African government officials portrayed CITES as an instrument that was developed and sponsored by countries of the Global North. It is seen to reflect Western conservation philosophies and animal rights ethics while paying "little concern to the plight of African rural people and their developmental concerns" (Institute for Security Studies 2009–10). Officials also pointed to the uncontrolled "slaughter of wild animals" during the colonial period, questioning why the descendants of the colonial hunters should have any say in African conservation matters. While the "Northern" lobby at CITES is perceived to be criticizing African states, Northern countries have failed to "put their money where there mouth is" in terms of paying compensation for loss of income and implementation of new CITES determinations.[14] African and Asian delegates are frequently portrayed as corruptible when it comes to crucial votes at CITES CoPs (see for example: Amman 2015b); former African delegates reported, however, that Northern conservation organizations were attempting to influence votes to swing crucial listing decisions in their favor (interviews, 2013 and 2015). The perception that Northern countries and conservation

[14] Trade bans can lead to loss of income for public institutions, protected areas, and local communities. In addition, regulators have to transpose "downlisting" or "uplisting" decisions into local laws, which costs money, time, and resources.

organizations hold sway at CITES is supported by voting patterns at CoPs.[15] Wildlife professionals shared these sentiments. A South African law-enforcement official said:

> It is crazy that these old colonial institutions are still in place. CITES decides how much and what we can sell. We stock about 90 percent of the world's rhinos. So who are they to prescribe to us? I mean we are in a controlled area, where we manage stock. We know what we are doing and we are trying to protect them for our children.
>
> (Interview with law enforcer 3, 2013)

The significance of perceptions such as the one expressed here is that they affect the diffusion and acceptance of CITES at the local level. As will be shown in the next section, South African regulations such as the Threatened or Protected Species regulations (TOPS) and the moratorium on the domestic trade in rhino horn lack support and legitimacy among key constituencies in South Africa. In essence, the perceived unfairness of CITES as an international instrument that impacts conservation and trade also affects the legitimacy of domestic laws, ordinances, and regulations in South Africa and other range, transfer, and consumer countries.

## Diffusion to the Local Level

While the apartheid regime was one of its original signatories, it failed to honor its international obligations under CITES other than passing piecemeal regulations to ensure favorable CITES decisions (such as the "downlisting" of white rhinos from Appendix I to Appendix II). On the election of the first democratic government in 1994, a new constitution cleared the way for the transformation of laws, policies, and the apartheid bureaucracy in South Africa. Environmental rights, sustainable development, and the use of natural resources became enshrined in the new constitution (Republic of South Africa 1996: 6). The protection of the environment—and by extension, the rhino—is thus considered and guaranteed by the highest law of the land. In the period immediately following the end of apartheid, several significant events impacted the state of nature conservation, known as "environmental affairs" under the new dispensation. On the eve of the first democratic elections, the former four provinces and homelands were sub-divided into nine provinces. The new environmental affairs bureaucracy was transformed and many former public servants from the old regime opted out by accepting retrenchment

[15] European Union member states have a common position at CITES meetings and vote as a block. In July 2015, the European Union became a member of the Convention.

packages, early retirement, or job opportunities in the private sector. Beyond the institutional and staffing changes in the Department of Environmental Affairs (its name and scope of work went through several changes in the new South Africa), the criminal justice, security, law enforcement, and defense sectors were equally transformed. Transposing CITES regulations into domestic laws and regulations happened at a slow pace due to the many demands for broad-based transformation across society in post-apartheid South Africa.

Dealing with the CITES requirements had been put on the backburner in lieu of the need to draft new comprehensive legislation, culminating with the enactment of the National Environmental Management Biodiversity Act (NEMBA) in 2004 and the promulgation of TOPS in 2008. The TOPS regulations list prohibits activities involving listed species, and they regulate hunting and compulsory registration requirements. The TOPS regulations were aimed not only at bringing South African norms and standards in tune with the requirements set out by CITES but also at closing loopholes that had previously been exploited. The regulations were initially promulgated in 2008; however, due to so-called "pseudo-hunting" (which involved rhino "hunters" from Vietnam and other countries of origin atypical for trophy hunters) and the identification of additional loopholes, the regulations were amended and updated in 2013. In 2009, the former Minister of Environmental Affairs and Tourism, Marthinus van Schalkwyk, declared a national moratorium on the sale of individual rhino horns (Department of Environmental Affairs and Tourism 2009)—the domestic trade of rhino horn had never been banned and presented a loophole that criminals were readily abusing. For example, rogue wildlife professionals procured rhino horn under the guise of domestic trade and sold it illegally to Asian organized-crime networks (see next section). In 2012, a Limpopo rhino breeder started to litigate against the South African government to have the moratorium lifted. John Hume, the world's biggest private rhino owner, joined Johan Krüger in 2015. The pair argued that the government was infringing on their constitutional rights, as the right to sustainable utilization is entrenched in the constitution of South Africa (Legodi 2015). High Court Judge Legodi set aside the moratorium due to insufficient public consultation in September 2015 (Legodi 2015). The Minister lodged a notice of leave to appeal soon after the court's decision, which she lost (with costs) in May 2016. By appealing to the Constitutional Court, the Department of Environmental Affairs reinstated, possibly only temporarily, the 2009 ban (Goitom 2016).

Because the TOPS regulations apply to South Africa's national jurisdiction only, CITES processes are used to deal with "import" countries and trade that transcends its national borders. The marriage between the TOPS regulations and CITES processes has been difficult, as the channels of communication were patchy at first. For example, provincial government officials deal with national and international hunting and trophy applications and permits within their province, whereas national government officials communicate with the CITES Secretariat and its various enforcement bodies regarding international trade and export. Given the "pseudo-hunting" phenomenon, all rhino-hunting applications have to be forwarded to the national department for a recommendation. This new procedure derives from illegitimate hunters' practice of "province hopping" in order to shoot more than one rhino per year without detection by provincial permit officials, who have oversight only over what happens on their own doorstep (the permissible hunting quota is one rhino per hunter within a calendar year). Previously, provincial permit officers had no recourse for determining whether a hunter had shot rhinos in any of the other eight provinces. Once the national department has made a recommendation, the provincial permit officer may then issue or refuse a hunting permit. Although the national department has a centralized database, it is not connected to other crime or biodiversity management databases as yet.

The implementation and enforcement of the law and regulations have been riddled with problems, ranging from capacity constraints within the nature conservation bureaucracy through to practical issues linked to the geography of South Africa and locations of rhino reserves, which are spread across the country. The congruence of the nine sets of provincial ordinances is also limited. The permit system thus differs across the nine provinces, with public officials displaying varying degrees of efficiency, responsiveness, and accountability. Although the Department of Environmental Affairs had consulted various stakeholders and local communities before drafting the regulations, the final version and list of protected species were not communicated ahead of publication and implementation (Institute for Security Studies 2009–10; interview with conservator 2, 2013). Moreover, the enforcers of the regulations—provincial government officials—had neither been sufficiently informed of the new regulations nor provided with adequate training prior to promulgation (interview with provincial government official, 2013).

The TOPS regulations and the now defunct moratorium lack legitimacy among key players in the wildlife industry, who feel that they were not sufficiently consulted ahead of the promulgation while being affected by the new status quo. Resistance to regulation is also linked to a sense of deprivation of agency. Increased state intervention by way of rule making, and strict or partial implementation and enforcement of the rules, has accentuated tensions between the wildlife industry and the state in the post-apartheid period. The apartheid state facilitated the establishment of private game reserves and farms by providing farmers and wildlife entrepreneurs with support (for example, subsidies and property rights). Wildlife owners had free reign over their movable and immoveable assets, with little regulatory interference or disruption to economic exchanges. In addition to other existential threats to the preferential status quo, the post-apartheid state is associated with introducing new rules, which are believed to aim at dispossessing and emasculating white landowners. Sentiments of a loss of privilege (the right to determine what happens to their property), deprivation, and entitlement were expressed: "the government is out to get us."

## Utilizing the Legal/Illegal Interface

The focus of this section is the "production" of rhino horn on private land, which constituted the principal source of supply of South African rhino horn between the late 1960s and late 2000s. Actors capitalize on loopholes within the regulatory framework. Involved are members of the wildlife industry[16] with intimate knowledge of the product (rhino horn) and of the institutional and legislative framework governing the international trade of rhino horn. These actors belong to influential and transnational social networks with links to political and economic elites in supply, transit, and consumer countries. Different modes of horn "production" on private land share the commonality that perpetrators display detailed and extensive knowledge of the rules and how to bypass, flout, or break them, or how to exploit legal loopholes. While wildlife professionals and rhino owners tend to regard the law (NEMBA), the regulations (TOPS regulations), and the moratorium on domestic trade as responsible for the surge in poaching, the regulatory framework did not emerge from a vacuum. In fact, the first rules governing the management and specifically the hunting of wildlife were passed during colonial times. The breaking or flouting of hunting rules was seen as a minor transgression (unless it involved indigenous hunters or Afrikaners) and, in some cases, it was a rite of passage. A double morality legitimizes modern rule breaking, partially linked to a sense of entitlement and privilege, and a "silent rebellion" against the new rule makers and "their rules." A wildlife expert explains (interview, 2013):

> The way it used to work, the law was always there but nobody ever pushed it. Within 48 hours of the guy getting the horn, you had to go to nature conservation and get a chip in. And then you could apply for a permit and sell it. As you had a permit to sell and trade, they never kept track of anything. You could sell without anyone noticing or caring. And because it wasn't really checked on, if you had a permit for one horn, you could use it for weeks or months. So what a lot of people

[16] The term "member of the wildlife industry" refers to any person involved in the transporting, translocation, well-being, management, farming, breeding, hunting, or securing of wildlife on private or public land.

miss is not only the entitlement that the farmer feels and that he is truly entitled to. He just bought this, most of them come from the park.

The quotation above refers to the most common form of permit fraud prior to the implementation of stricter regulations and enforcement (interviews with law-enforcement officials and conservators, 2013). Wildlife professionals would use the same permit to shoot and dehorn multiple rhinos. Or, as was the case in some provinces—most notably in the northern Limpopo Province—wildlife professionals could use a "standing permit" for white rhino hunts on certain properties. In other words, hunting outfitters applied for a blanket permit once and thereafter they hunted without further permits and state supervision on these properties until August 2008 (Milliken and Shaw 2012: 38; interviews with wildlife professionals, 2013). The existence of legal trade channels allows for early-stage conversion of an essentially illegally harvested wildlife product to a legal export product. The ban itself is ambiguous as it only concerns international trade of rhino horn, leaving space for illegal market actors to maneuver at the national level.

A few South African court cases showcase the involvement of rhino breeders, professional hunters, veterinarians, nature conservation officials, and others in the illicit "production" and trafficking of rhino horn.[17] These actors from the formal or "legal" sector not only orchestrated poaching in private and public conservation areas and theft from rhino horn stockpiles; they were also involved in complex schemes that bypass existing conservation regulations, exploit regulatory loopholes, and use legal trade channels to export illegally obtained rhino horn. Alleged rhino poaching trafficker Dawie Groenewald and his accomplices—known as the Groenewald gang or the "Musina group"[18]—illustrate a cunning instrumentalization of the legal/illegal interface. The rhino poaching syndicate currently faces 1,736 counts of racketeering, money laundering, fraud, intimidation, and illegal hunting and dealing in rhino horns in South Africa, while a US indictment alleges that the Groenewald siblings sold illegal hunts to US trophy hunters (Grand Jury for the Middle District of Alabama 2014). According to the South African criminal indictment (compare with National Prosecuting Authority 2011), Groenewald and his accomplices were involved in intricate scams, ranging from false permit applications through to illegal dehorning of rhinos and the laundering of unregistered rhino horns. Rhinos and rhino horns were acquired through a variety of grey and illegal channels. Among Groenewald's co-accused are

[17] These "big" cases revolve around Dawie Groenewald (case study is discussed in this chapter), Hugo Ras, and Chumlong Lemthongthai.

[18] Musina is a border town in the Limpopo Province. Dawie Groenewald's farm called Prachtig is located near Musina and most of the South African wildlife professionals with direct links to his criminal network live in the town or nearby.

wildlife veterinarians, professional hunters, a pilot, farm laborers, and two wives (his own and the wife of wildlife veterinarian Karel Toet), who assisted with the permit applications and other administrative tasks. The Groenewald gang entered into business ventures with rhino farmers and wildlife professionals, many of whom were unaware that they were breaking the law at the time.

Groenewald hunted numerous rhinos illegally on his farm Prachtig in the northern Limpopo Province (the indictment alleges that he illegally hunted fifty-nine of his own rhinos) and procured live rhinos and rhino horns from other rhino farmers. It is alleged that he dehorned rhinos and sold at least 384 rhino horns over a four-year period (Jooste 2012). In terms of NEMBA, separate permit applications have to be tendered to dehorn a rhino, to transport rhino horns, as well as to possess rhino horn. According to Colonel Jooste's affidavit (Jooste 2012: 14),[19] the Groenewald gang flouted these rules on numerous occasions. The carcasses of rhinos that were illegally hunted, killed, and dehorned on Prachtig were either sold to a local butcher,[20] buried, or burnt (Jooste 2012: 11). Socially embedded in the southern African wildlife industry with strong business connections to the consumer market (Vietnam), as well as extensive knowledge of legal market processes and loopholes, Groenewald was in an excellent position to procure high volumes of rhino horn through grey and illegal channels. Many horn-procurement methods crossed the fine line between legality and illegality. Although it was illegal to hunt and dehorn rhinos without the required paperwork, the gang portrayed their criminal and grey activities as legitimate business enterprises. Moreover, the privatization of rhinos and the entitlement to do "as you please with your own property" allowed many criminal and grey activities to go undetected for several years. The outcome of the Minister's constitutional appeal to reinstitute the domestic moratorium may affect the outcome of the court case. If the Constitutional Court were to dismiss the moratorium, then Groenewald could argue for charges involving domestic trade exchanges of rhino horn to be dropped from the charge sheet.

Pseudo-hunting, illegal hunting of rhinos on private land, rhino horn laundering, and grey traffic were the primary modes of rhino horn supply until rhino poaching took off in national and provincial parks, as well as in private game reserves in South Africa in the late 2000s. Essentially, grey traffic paved the way and laid the transport routes for the high volumes of rhino horn leaving southern African shores for Asian markets. Groenewald and his ilk had access to wide-ranging social and professional networks that facilitated illegal and grey transnational trade with Asian partners. The displacement of

[19] Colonel Johan Jooste heads the Endangered Species Unit at the Directorate for Priority Crime Investigations, South Africa's organized crime fighting unit.

[20] Thirty-nine carcasses were sold to a local butcher between 2008 and 2010.

grey traffic is partially explained by tougher conservation regulations, as well as the private sector "out pricing" itself. Essentially, it became cheaper and more efficient to pay local hunters to poach rhinos in protected areas than to orchestrate pseudo-hunts or pay market-related prices for rhino horn derived from private sources.

## Conclusion

The illegalization of the trade in rhino horn commenced in the late 1970s when the multilateral environmental treaty CITES entered into force. Prior to that, economic exchanges involving rhino horn were either legal or undetermined. The diffusion of the trade ban to the domestic level in range, transit, and consumer countries has succeeded to varying degrees.

The chapter highlights how important actors at the source do not accept the law on the books for a variety of reasons, including the perceived unfairness of the ban, divergent social or cultural norms that clash with the ban, and for politico-historical reasons. This sentiment is replicated further along the rhino supply chain. Dioun's chapter on marijuana markets in the United States shows that the process of legalization is protracted, encountering many institutional hurdles. In the case of rhino horn, the process of illegalization is an ongoing negotiation with divergent views among producers and regulators concerning whether trade in rhino horn should be illegal in light of its economic contribution to the private and public sectors in South Africa, as well as the social and cultural legitimacy of its use among key market participants (for more details about the cultural and social legitimacy of rhino horn consumption, see Hübschle 2016).

The chapter also shows that apartheid state actors facilitated the economic valuation of rhino horn on the supply side by facilitating the privatization of white rhinos. While current narratives focus on rhino poaching within conservation areas such as the embattled Kruger National Park (which hosts 40 percent of the world's remaining rhinos), rogue elements within the wildlife industry "set up the rhino horn pipeline to Asia" (interview with organized crime investigator, 2013). Bolstered by sentiments of contested illegality, wildlife professionals have no qualms about exploiting or bypassing regulatory loopholes (as shown in the Groenewald case). The interface between legality and illegality thus relates to agents of the state facilitating illegal flows, the existence of legal and illegal means of horn supply, and legitimate and illegitimate uses of rhino horn. The appropriation of legal trade channels (for example, hunting trophies) and exploitation of legal loopholes (domestic trade) suggests not only an interface between legal and illegal markets for rhino horn but that illegal economic activities are firmly embedded in legal markets. These findings suggest the need for a nuanced conceptualization of illegal, grey, and legal markets. Similar to findings in the antiquities sector (see Simon Mackenzie's contribution), illegal rhino horn markets are firmly embedded in legal trade chains, with industry actors featuring prominently in production, procurement, distribution, and trade.

## References

't Sas-Rolfes, Michael. 2012. *The Rhino Poaching Crisis: A Market Analysis*. <http://davidschmidtz.com/sites/default/files/files/tSas-Rolfes.pdf>.

Amman, Karl. 2015a. *Characteristics of Rhino Horn Trade along Vietnam's Northern Borders*. Conservation Action Trust, April 15. NABU International.

Amman, Karl. 2015b. *The CITES Permitting System and the Illegal Trade in Wildlife*. Kenya. <http://www.karlammann.com/pdf/cites-permiting-system.pdf>.

Beckert, Jens, and Frank Wehinger. 2013. "In the Shadow: Illegal Markets and Economic Sociology." *Socio-Economic Review* 11(1): pp. 5–30.

Bothma, J. du P., H. Suich, and A. Spenceley. 2012. "Extensive Wildlife Production on Private Land in South Africa." In *Evolution and Innovation in Wildlife Conservation: Parks and Game Ranches to Transfrontier Conservation Areas*, edited by Helen Suich, Brian Child, and Anna Spenceley, pp. 147–61. London: Earthscan.

Carruthers, Jane. 1993. "'Police Boys' and Poachers: Africans, Wildlife Protection and National Parks, the Transvaal 1902 to 1950." *Koedoe* 36(2): pp. 11–22.

CITES. 1973. *Text of Convention on International Trade in Endangered Species of Wild Fauna and Flora*. Washington, DC: CITES. <http://www.cites.org/sites/default/files/eng/disc/E-Text.pdf>.

CITES. 1994. *Resolution Conference 9.14: Conservation of and Trade in African and Asian Rhinoceroses*. Washington, DC: CITES.

CITES. 2002. *Resolution 12.10: Registration of Operations that Breed Appendix-I Animal Species in Captivity for Commercial Purposes*. Washington, DC: CITES. <http://www.cites.org/eng/res/12/12-10R15.php>.

Cock, Jacklyn, and David Fig. 2000. "From Colonial to Community Based Conservation: Environmental Justice and the National Parks of South Africa." *Society in Transition* 31(1): pp. 22–35.

Comaroff, Jean, and John L. Comaroff. 2006. "Law and Disorder in the Postcolony: An Introduction." In *Law and Disorder in the Postcolony*, edited by Jean Comaroff and John L. Comaroff, pp. 1–56. Chicago: Chicago University Press.

Couzens, Edmund. 2003. "The Influence of English Poaching Laws on South African Poaching Laws." *Fundamina: A Journal of Legal History*. <http://reference.sabinet.co.za/webx/access/electronic_journals/funda/funda_n9_a4.pdf>.

Department of Environmental Affairs and Tourism. 2009. *Government Notice on National Moratorium on the Trade in Individual Rhinoceros Horns*. No. 148. Pretoria: Republic of South Africa, Department of Environmental Affairs. <http://www.environment.gov.za/sites/default/files/gazetted_notices/nemba_memorarium_g31899gon148.pdf>.

EUROPOL. 2011. *EUROPOL and Ireland Identify Organised Crime Group Active in Illegal Trading of Rhino Horn*. Den Haag: EUROPOL. <http://www.europol.europa.eu/content/press/europol-and-ireland-identify-organised-crime-group-active-illegal-trading-rhino-horn-9> (accessed July 7, 2011).

Glazewski, Jan. 2000. *Environmental Law in South Africa*. Durban: Butterworths.

Goitom, Hanibal. 2016. *South Africa: Moratorium on Domestic Trade in Rhino Horn Temporarily Re-instated*. Washington, DC: Global Legal Monitor, Library of Congress. <http://www.loc.gov/law/foreign-news/article/south-africa-moratorium-on-domestic-trade-in-rhino-horn-temporarily-re-instituted/> (accessed September 28, 2016).

Grand Jury for the Middle District of Alabama. 2014. *Indictment: United States of America versus Dawie Jacobus Groenewald, Janneman George Groenewald, and Valinor Trading CC, d/b/a Out of Africa Adventurous Safaris*. Montgomery: Grand Jury for the Middle District of Alabama. <http://www.fws.gov/southeast/news/pdf/RhinoIndictment.pdf>.

Heyman, Josiah McC. 2013. "The Study of Illegality and Legality: Which Way Forward?" *PoLAR: Political and Legal Anthropology Review* 36(2): pp. 304–7.

Hübschle, Annette. 2016. *A Game of Horns: Transnational Flows of Rhino Horn*. Cologne: International Max Planck Research School on the Social and Political Constitution of the Economy. <http://pubman.mpdl.mpg.de/pubman/item/escidoc:2218357:9/component/escidoc:2262615/2016_IMPRSDiss_Huebschle.pdf>.

Institute for Security Studies. 2009–10. *Annual Review of Organized Crime in Southern Africa*. Unpublished research report.

Ipsos Marketing. 2013. *Consumer Research on Rhino Horn Usage in Vietnam*. Ho Chi Minh City: WWF and TRAFFIC.

Jooste, Johan. 2012. *Supporting Affidavit*. 000089. Pretoria: Directorate for Priority Crime Investigations (March 22, 2012).

Legodi, J. 2015. *In the Matter between Krüger Johan, Hume John and the Minister of Water and Environmental Affairs, Wildlife Ranching South Africa, the Private Rhino Owners Association*. Case No: 57221/12, High Court of South Africa. Pretoria: Gauteng Division.

Lindsey, P. A., P. A. Roulet, and S. S. Romañach. 2007. "Economic and Conservation Significance of the Trophy Hunting Industry in Sub-Saharan Africa." *Biological Conservation* 134: pp. 455–69.

Milliken, Tom. 2014. *Illegal Trade in Ivory and Rhino Horn: An Assessment Report to Improve Law Enforcement under the Wildlife TRAPS Project USAID and TRAFFIC*. Cambridge: TRAFFIC International.

Milliken, Tom, and Jo Shaw. 2012. *The South Africa–Viet Nam Rhino Horn Trade Nexus: A Deadly Combination of Institutional Lapses, Corrupt Wildlife Industry Professionals and Asian Crime Syndicates*. Johannesburg: TRAFFIC.

National Prosecuting Authority. 2011. *Die Staat teen Dawid Jacobus Groenewald en 10 ander. Akte van Beskuldiging*, Vol. 1. Polokwane: Musina Regional Court.

Player, Ian. 2013. *The White Rhino Saga*. Cape Town: Jonathan Ball.

PSI Vietnam, Research and Metrics. 2015. *Rhino Horn Use among Urban High-Income Men in Hanoi and Ho Chi Minh City, Vietnam*. Summary Report. Hanoi, Vietnam: TRAFFIC and PSI Vietnam.

Radin, Margaret Jane. 1996. *Contested Commodities*. Cambridge, MA: Harvard University Press.

Reilly, B. 2014. "Game Ranching in South Africa." *Wildlife Society News*.

Republic of South Africa. 1996. *Constitution of the Republic of South Africa*. Republic of South Africa. <http://www.thehda.co.za/uploads/images/unpan005172.pdf>.

Sand, Peter H. 1997. "Commodity or Taboo? International Regulation of Trade in Endangered Species." In *Yearbook of International Co-operation on Environment and Development*, edited by Fridtjof Nansen Institute, pp. 19–36. Lysaker: FNI. <http://citeseerx.ist.psu.edu/viewdoc/download?doi=10.1.1.459.9801&rep=rep1&type=pdf>.

Satz, Debra. 2010. *Why Some Things Should Not Be for Sale*. Oxford: Oxford University Press.

Scriven, Lisa, and Theuns Eloff. 2003. "Markets Derived from Nature Tourism in South Africa and KwaZulu-Natal: A Survey of the Sale of Live Game." In *Nature Tourism, Conservation and Development in KwaZulu-Natal*, edited by Bruce Aylward and Ernst Lutz, pp. 245–86. Washington, DC: World Bank.

Steiner, Philippe, and Marie Trespeuch. 2013. "Managing Passion and Constructing Interest: Online Gambling, Human Body Parts and the Market." *Revue Française de Sociologie* 54(1): pp. 143–66.

Truong, V. Dao, Madelon Willemsen, Hoai Nam Dang Vu, and Colin Michael Hall. 2015. "The Marketplace Management of Illegal Elixirs: Illicit Consumption of Rhino Horn." *Consumption Markets and Culture*: pp. 1–17.

van Schendel, Willem, and Itty Abraham. 2005. "Introduction: The Making of Illicitness." In *Illicit Flows and Criminal Things: States, Borders, and the Other Side of Globalization*, edited by Willem van Schendel and Itty Abraham, pp. 1–37. Bloomington: Indiana University Press.

Varisco, Daniel Martin. 1989. "Beyond Rhino Horn: Wildlife Conservation for North Yemen." *Oryx* 23(4): pp. 215–19.

Vigne, Lucy, and Esmond Martin. 2008. "Yemen's Attitudes towards Rhino Horn and Jambiyas." *Pachyderm* 44: pp. 45–53.

Vigne, Lucy, and Esmond Martin. 2013. "Demand for Rhino Horn Declines in Yemen." *Oryx* 47(3): pp. 323–4.

Willock, Anna. 2004. *Administrative and Monitoring Implications of Listing and Downlisting of Commercially-Exploited Aquatic Species, Including the Implications of Annex 4 of Resolution Conf. 9.24*. Paper prepared for the FAO Expert Consultation on "Implementation Issues Associated with Listing Commercially-Exploited Aquatic Species on the CITES Appendices," Rome, May 25–8. <http://www.cites.org/sites/default/files/eng/news/meetings/IFS-05/IFS05-TRAFFIC-paper.pdf>.

# 11

## "We Are the Genuine People"

### Legality and Legitimacy in the Sierra Leonean Diamond Market

*Nina Engwicht*

#### Introduction

When we talk about the legality or illegality of markets we usually rely on several assumptions regarding the nature of statehood in relation to the economy. In particular, we assume that a coherent body of laws and policies determines which type of economic actions are legal and which are illegal. We furthermore assume that the institutions of the state are both willing and able to implement the law and sanction its infringement. In short, the study of legal and illegal markets usually works on the implicit assumption of "strong" or "consolidated" statehood. This is surprising in the sense that the strong state, modeled after the liberal-democratic welfare state, is far from being the norm and is rather the exception internationally (Risse and Lehmkuhl 2007). This leads us to the question of how we can understand legality and illegality in markets in situations in which the nation state does not hold the "legitimate monopoly of violence" (Weber 1922: 29). How are legality and illegality of economic action socially defined under conditions of limited statehood and what does this mean for the way illegal markets work in these situations?

This chapter attempts to answer these questions by providing insight into the illegal diamond economy in post-war Sierra Leone. Post-conflict states are by definition cases of "fragile statehood," as their current context is shaped by the violent contestation of territory, nation, or legitimate authority in the recent past. The Sierra Leonean diamond market gained notoriety as a symbol of a criminal economy in the absence of formal state control in the course of a fourteen-year civil war that ended in 2002. In an effort to end the trade in Sierra Leonean "blood diamonds" the country's diamond sector has since been extensively reformed. However, the illegal production, trade, and export of Sierra Leonean rough diamonds persists, albeit on a significantly smaller scale.

The survival of the illegal diamond market in the post-conflict society is not surprising given that fragile, and in particular post-conflict societies, are hardly ever able to implement the law and sanction illegal action effectively and coherently. However, it does raise the question of the social organization and definition of legal and illegal economic action in a context in which "the law" does not play the role of a powerful and consistent regulator of the economy. This is particularly relevant in a social and political context in which a variety of actors (national and international, state and private) strive for tangible change of market governance with the aim of abolishing the illegal trade and its perceived harmful externalities. How does this context of imperfect, yet increasing statehood affect the social structure of the illegal market? How do illegal market participants navigate their business between long-lasting practices of trade and changing market governance?

The findings presented here are the result of six months of field research in Sierra Leone, conducted in 2012 and 2013. During field trips to four regions of the country I interviewed legal and illegal diamond miners, traders, and exporters, as well as state agents, national and international non-governmental organization staff, and journalists. In addition to single and serial in-depth interviews with a variety of market actors I conducted open, non-participant observation at artisanal diamond mines, buyers' offices, illegal market places, and police checkpoints on border routes.

Based on the data collected during the field research this chapter argues that illegality under conditions of limited statehood cannot be understood without studying the social meaning and, in particular, norms of appropriateness, attributed to illegal market action (see also Mayntz in this volume). The argument brought forward here is threefold: contrary to conventional wisdom about illegal economic action in fragile states, I will show that in the case of the illegal diamond market in Sierra Leone, the lack of law enforcement cannot be explained solely by the weak capacity of actors tasked with implementing the laws and regulations governing the diamond sector, but, more importantly, by a lack of willingness. This lack of willingness is particularly notable and influential at the local level of state governance where state actors largely pursue a laisser-faire approach toward illegal market action that defies the formal regulation of the market. Contrary to common conceptions about the nature of weak statehood in Africa, the toleration of illegal action cannot be explained primarily by corruption of enforcement agents. Instead, the relationship between the illegal market and the state is shaped decisively by norms of appropriateness according to which a large part of illegal economic activity in the Sierra Leonean diamond market is socially legitimate. This social legitimacy of illegal action can be traced back to six sources: (i) the right to subsistence, (ii) the duty of the state to care for its citizens, (iii) piecemeal legality, (iv) symbiosis with the legal market, (v) the contribution of illegal market activities to state revenue, and finally (vi) the authority of social orders that compete with the monopoly of the state.

In the first part, I will suggest how legality can be understood conceptually under conditions of limited statehood. The second part of the chapter provides an analysis of the illegal diamond market in Sierra Leone. It briefly outlines the political, normative, and institutional developments that led to the current regulation of the diamond economy and details the conditions under which market action is illegal according to the law. After explaining the *de jure* regulation of the illegal diamond market it illustrates its *de facto* governance by a formal state that largely rules the market non-formally.

## Defining Legality and Illegality under Conditions of Weak Statehood

Studies of illegal markets, particularly those rooted in criminology, commonly work on the implicit assumption that what is legal and what is illegal can be definitively and unambiguously identified: illegal economic actions are those that are prohibited by the law. The law, in this understanding, refers to a coherent and clear set of legal rules enacted by the legislature and implemented by the executive and judiciary authorities of the state. Furthermore, the study of illegality regularly operates on the premise that the law is developed and implemented in a context of legitimate statehood.[1] While the rightfulness of singular legal norms may be questioned, even under conditions of consolidated statehood, the legitimacy of the legal system as such is not usually an issue of contestation. Finally, as the law is thought to be the impartial system of rules governing *all* inhabitants of a state's territory it claims to trump all other social rules of behavior. In short, the study of illegal markets usually relies on a thoroughly positivist understanding of legality and illegality that is derived from a normative conception of a modern, Weberian state exercising its legitimate monopoly of violence. None of these

[1] This can be observed clearly in the study of organized crime and transnational illegal trade. Although plenty of studies examine illegal phenomena in weak and illegitimate states, they do not usually take into account the nature of statehood, conceptually or in their policy recommendations. With the exception of studies that stress the need to protect precarious livelihoods, this strand of literature largely still pursues a law enforcement-oriented approach, regardless of the state of the security institutions, the judiciary, or the prison system in question. In such a "rigorous" understanding of legality and the rule of law, non-enforcement and informal state control are viewed as pathological (Schuppert 2011: 40).

assumptions are particularly useful for the study of legal realities under conditions of limited statehood (Kötter 2009: 657); in other words, in a context in which the nature of state territory, nation, and legitimate authority are contested.

The dominance of a positivism of the written law in the study of crime constitutes a considerable problem for the analysis of illegal markets under conditions of limited statehood. As theorists of law and statehood have pointed out, legality not only empirically but also conceptually depends on legitimate authority, which is usually assumed to be the authority of the state (Schmelzle 2011; Kötter 2008, 2009). If an act is prohibited by the letter of the law, but non-compliance is never sanctioned, this act is only de jure and not "effectively illegal" (Paoli et al. 2009). However, the blatant illegitimacy of a regime (whether attributed from an empirical or a universal moral standpoint) can also call the validity of its legal rules into question. This is evidenced, for example, by decisions by German courts that retroactively declared void several laws of the GDR and National-Socialist regimes (Kötter 2011).

In order to conceptualize legality in contexts in which the state's legitimate authority and implementation capacity are severely limited, it is thus useful to revert to literatures that take into account the formal law, the "law in action," and the political system in which laws are created and implemented. The proposed concept of legality draws on two literatures. First, theories of law that distinguish between the formal, the empirical, and the ethical dimensions of law (Geiger 1987; Alexey 1994; Kötter 2011). In this understanding, a legal norm is *juridically* valid if it is codified in the applicable body of law. In contrast to this purely normative dimension, the *social* validity of a legal norm refers to the effectiveness of the law. Effectiveness is derived from compliance (based on the morally motivated or self-interested validity-beliefs of the addressees) and the sanctioning of deviance. In other words, the *social* or *empirical* dimension of the law concerns the "legal culture" of a society from a sociological, historical, or anthropological perspective (Alexey 1994; Kötter 2008, 2009; Tamanaha 2014). It specifies not whether a norm *should* be, but whether it *is* followed and enforced. In addition to the direct *outcomes* of legal norms their complex and broader *impact*—for example on the behavioral motivations of legal and non-legal actors—is of interest to researchers of the empirical reality of law (Wrase 2013). Lastly, the *moral* validity of the law concerns whether a legal norm is legitimate from the standpoint of moral philosophy.

Second, the chapter draws on the literature of "informal markets" that have long pointed to the divergence between legally and socially legitimate economic practices (Hart 1973; Webb et al. 2009). Studies of the market–state relationship in this field have pointed out that formally illegal economic activity in contexts of limited statehood (i) is often employed as a coping strategy to ensure survival in the absence of other employment opportunities or a basic welfare system; (ii) is often characterized and regulated by close social relations and norms of kinship, religious, ethnic, or village community; (iii) often enjoys a high degree of social legitimacy; and (iv) often takes place within a political framework in which the state is itself "informalized" and depends on the proceeds of the informal economy (Roitman 1990; Rasanayagam 2011; Dewey 2012). The study of informal markets contributes to the sociology of illegal economies in contexts of limited statehood by providing empirical insight into the social structure of markets operating outside the legal sphere, in particular in the Global South. It often suffers, however, from a lack of clarity concerning the concept of informality. Following early research on informal economies that took a societal perspective (in contrast to a state-oriented perspective) on unregulated economic activities the term is still most commonly understood as referring to activities that take place "outside" formal state regulation (de Soto 2002; Hart 2010). In other conceptions, informal markets are conflated with socially legitimate markets (Webb et al. 2009). This is misleading in several ways. Many activities that are commonly characterized as informal are clearly prohibited by the law. Against their own definition, researchers of informality often use the term not only for activities for which no regulatory framework exists, but also for formally illegal, but common activities. This vagueness muddies the waters of the concept as it obfuscates *why* these activities are so widespread. Is the formal law not enforced because these activities are hidden from the state? Because a state that is itself "informalized" profits from these markets in the form of corruption? Or because they are socially defined as legitimate, and if so by whom and with what consequences? In other words, what studies of informal markets often fail to address are the concrete ways in which these markets interact with the (informal) state and are related to social norms of legitimacy.

## The Sierra Leonean Diamond Market

During the civil war years, the Sierra Leonean diamond market repeatedly made the news as a largely criminal and violence-fueling economy. All warring factions were at some point accused of having a stake in the illegal diamond economy. Sierra Leonean rough diamonds were smuggled and traded in exchange for weapons and supplies. Because they could be used as an alternative currency, Sierra Leonean diamonds attracted money launderers, organized crime groups, and terrorists. The public outrage that followed successful media campaigns by international human rights organizations denouncing the trade in Sierra Leonean and Angolan "blood diamonds" induced regulation of the trade in rough diamonds on a global scale. Since its creation in 2003, nearly all diamond-producing countries have become members of the Kimberley Process Certification Scheme (KPCS), a global regulatory regime that requires its members to prove the source of rough diamonds via state-issued certificates of origin.

The Sierra Leonean civil war ended in 2002 after a robust international intervention drove the rebels out of the mining territories of Kono. Sierra Leone became a member of the KPCS in 2003. In line with the stipulations of the KPCS and with considerable support from international donors, the country took significant action to legalize the market. In addition to the introduction of unforgeable KP export certificates, it undertook reforms of the state institutions governing the diamond sector. These include the establishment of a National Minerals Agency (NMA), the creation of several specialized law-enforcement units, the professionalization of border controls at Lungi International Airport, and the introduction of a rotation system of independent international diamond valuators at the Government Gold and Diamond Office (GGDO). The regional offices tasked with overseeing diamond mining and trading in the diamondiferous territories, as well as the GGDO, now fall under the auspices of the newly founded NMA, instead of the Ministry of Mines, hereby separating the implementation of mining regulation from its development.

## By the Book: What Is Legal and What Is Illegal in the Sierra Leonean Diamond Market?

At first glance, there seems to be little ambiguity regarding de jure legality and illegality in the Sierra Leonean diamond market: an action is legal if the actor has acquired and paid for a license permitting it and pays the required fees, royalties, and taxes.[2] Any market activity that may lead to the extraction or sale of diamonds requires a license entitling its holder to engage in, respectively, exploration, mining (small-scale artisanal or large-scale industrial) for diamonds on a specified territory, diamond dealing, or exporting (Government of Sierra Leone 2009a, 2009b). Any diamond production, trade, or export that is conducted without a valid license is illegal. Any handling of diamonds without a valid license constitutes "unlawful possession of precious

[2] The annual cost of an artisanal diamond mining license is 250,000 leones (63 USD at the time of writing) per acre, excluding monitoring and environmental rehabilitation fees; a trading license costs 1,500 USD per year for Sierra Leonean citizens and 2,000 USD for Economic Community of West African States citizens; an exporter's license costs 35,000 USD. In addition to the formal costs of acquiring a license, market participants are usually required to give "handshakes"—bribes—to government officials and chiefs at various points during the licensing process.

minerals" and carries a mandatory minimum prison sentence of three years (Government of Sierra Leone 2009a: 128). The smuggling of diamonds requires a minimum prison sentence of five years. Illegal practices in the diamond market can hence refer to two different things: first, we can speak of illegal action if a person works entirely outside the legal framework—for example, a miner produces diamonds without a valid license, or a smuggler exports diamonds illegally; second, legally operating market actors can engage in illegal practices—for example, if a dealer buys diamonds from illegal sources or if a licensed exporter smuggles diamonds.[3]

The state furthermore regulates which transactions along the value chain are lawful and which are not. According to the Diamond Trading Bill, diamond miners are allowed to sell diamonds only to licensed dealers, exporters, and exporter agents, or to export their goods directly (provided they possess a valid export license). However, the governance of diamond trading shows a regulatory gap that is not uncommon for post-conflict states. The "Bill Entitled the Diamond Trading Act of 2009" has (as of May 2016) not been passed by the Sierra Leonean Parliament. However, the Ministry of Mines has communicated the core provisions of the Diamond Trading Bill regarding licensing and trading as the applicable rules of diamond marketing to implementing agents and market actors. Core provisions regarding diamond mining and trading are furthermore codified in a small-scale and artisanal mining and marketing policy (Ministry of Mines and Mineral Resources 2013) that currently acts as a substitute for the legal regulation of diamond trading in the absence of a diamond trading law. With regard to the value chain of minerals the policy specifies that miners must sell their proceeds only to licensed dealers or exporters, while dealers are required to sell exclusively to licensed exporters. Specifically, miners are prohibited from selling to other miners and dealers to other dealers.

It becomes clear that even when we disregard the question of whether the formal law is implemented, what actually constitutes the formal rules governing the diamond market is itself unclear. When we talk about the divide between formality and informality in post-conflict states, it is thus useful to remember that even the formal rules are not always clear cut. In the Sierra Leonean diamond market, what state and market actors consider "the formal rule" is not definitely and exclusively defined by the law. Rather, institutional actors come to a consensus about what constitutes "the law of the diamond market."

[3] Apart from the illegal production and sale of diamonds, legal and illegal market actors can break the law regulating the diamond market in a number of other ways, for example by violating legal stipulations concerning labor law, environmental as well as health and safety standards, or the prohibition of child labor. These practices, while illegal, will however not be considered part of the illegal market, as they occur in every market.

## The Interface between Legality and Illegality in the Sierra Leonean Diamond Market

The "formal" rules of the Sierra Leonean diamond market stipulate that diamonds must be traded only between legal market participants—from licensed miner to licensed dealer to licensed exporter—and that sales must be documented, so as to create a legal and transparent value chain. The reality deviates quite far from this ideal. Not only are Sierra Leonean diamonds still illegally mined, traded, and smuggled on a considerable scale;[4] in addition, the legal and the illegal diamond markets are closely interwoven, making it in many cases impossible to determine the source of a diamond.

Legal dealers and exporters buy diamonds from illegal miners and dealers all the time. As diamonds are a scarce resource, legal market actors will try to buy them, if given the chance, regardless of the source. In fact, it is a broadly understood norm, explained by legal buyers and state agents alike, that illegally sourced diamonds must be bought by legal dealers and exporters so as to prevent smuggling. If they are not absorbed by the legal market, so goes the reasoning, they will leave the country illegally, thereby depriving the Sierra Leonean state of much needed tax income. This way, the vast majority of diamonds that have been illegally produced or traded find their way into legal market channels and are ultimately exported as legal diamonds. While it is understandable that dealers buying illegal diamonds seek to justify their actions, interestingly, this practice enjoys considerable support among state agents who argue that turning a blind eye to this practice is a necessary evil, because diamonds from the illegal market would otherwise be smuggled out of the country.

As market actors are supposed to document their transactions by recording the characteristics of the goods and the license numbers of buyers and sellers, the legalization of illegal diamonds usually requires the falsification of records. In particular, buyers need to acquire a license number for diamonds that come without documentation. License numbers for illegal diamonds can be sourced in a number of ways: if the buyer is in possession of one or several mining

[4] The scope of illegal economic activity is, by its very nature, impossible to measure. The drastic increase in diamond exports in the post-war period from a value of 26 million USD in 2001 to 163 million USD in 2012 suggests a significant decrease in diamond smuggling. Small-scale illegal mining and trading are associated mainly with the artisanal mining sector that still comprises about 50 percent of diamond production and provides a livelihood for around 500,000 Sierra Leoneans (Government of Sierra Leone 2013). Nevertheless, evidence suggests that large-scale illegal activities may be strongly connected to legal corporations, which are able to smuggle large quantities of diamonds, hide their proceeds, and bribe enforcement agents with ease. This became apparent in interviews with international businessmen in the mining sector and is supported by recent reporting about the involvement of the owner of Sierra Leone's biggest diamond-producing company in corruption and tax evasion in the Sierra Leonean and Guinean mineral sector (Sharife and Gbandia 2016).

licenses they will, upon purchase, use one of their own license numbers, thereby recording the diamond as a product of their own mine. Alternatively, they can use a mining license number from a friend or colleague, usually in exchange for a small "commission." One dealer reports that he regularly receives lists of artisanal mining license numbers from the regional mines office, which he uses to legalize illegal diamonds, supposedly unbeknownst to the owner of these license numbers.[5] However, several legal exporters also report the existence of a "gentleman's agreement" between legal exporters and the Ministry of Mines, which allows them to leave a blank space where they would have to record the license number of the seller when presenting their goods for exportation at the Government Gold and Diamond Office in Freetown. This agreement is viewed as a compromise that allows legal actors to buy illegal diamonds without "cheating" the state.[6] Especially for smaller gems (which represent the vast majority of Sierra Leonean exports),[7] the state-tolerated legalization of illicit diamonds through integration into the legal market constitutes the norm.

The crucial figures that connect the legal and the illegal segment of the diamond market are the "*banabana*"—also called "*jula*" or "*njeko-njeko*" (Levin and Gberie 2006). The *banabana* are middlemen who buy diamonds from miners or dealers, both legal and illegal, and sell them on to legal and illegal dealers and exporters. Often strapped for cash, they also broker deals between sellers and buyers for commission. While they sell to legal and illegal buyers alike, most of their sales are to legal buyers. The vast majority of artisanally mined diamonds pass through the hands of *banabana* before they leave the country. Since *banabana* are unlicensed dealers, the diamonds they trade become untraceable, regardless of the legality or illegality of their extraction. While most *banabana*, especially those living in the provinces, are impoverished, some brokers trade goods of high value and acquire considerable wealth.

Most of the time transactions between the legal and the illegal market involve the legalization of formerly illegal diamonds, though in some cases

[5] If illegal diamonds are not legalized in Sierra Leone, but smuggled to a neighboring country or overseas, they can also be channeled into the legal diamond market in the receiving country. Legal and illegal market actors unequivocally report the ease of selling illegal diamonds to legal buyers on the international market, including in Antwerp, the most important turning wheel for rough diamonds from all over the world.

[6] However, this agreement was contested. In early 2013 the newly founded National Mineral Agency tried to abolish the practice by letting local diamond dealers know they could no longer present diamonds without record of the source at the GGDO. Consequently, the biggest Lebanese exporters arranged for a meeting with a senior representative of the Ministry of Mines to protest the new rules. Their objection was, as one of the participants explained, successful in preventing a change to the informal rule.

[7] Around 80 percent of Sierra Leonean gem-quality diamonds falls into the "Melee" category, which classifies diamonds weighing under 0.15 carat (Government Gold and Diamond Office 2012).

formerly legal diamonds are sold into illegal channels, if they promise to be profitable. In particular, money launderers, outsiders, and newcomers to the Sierra Leonean diamond market—such as tourists or professional or non-professional diamond buyers from overseas—often agree to buy diamonds far above their local market price. In these cases, it is again the *banabana* that usually facilitate the deal. In contrast to the legalization of illegal diamonds, the illegalization of formerly legal diamonds is widely viewed as unacceptable. It is condemned by state agents and taboo even among market actors.

While the cooperation between the legal and the illegal market will hardly be surprising to students of illegal economic activity, their interrelations seem unusually close in the Sierra Leonean case. Not only is their relationship highly symbiotic, but the legalization of illegal diamonds is also widely tolerated by law enforcement. Studies on security institutions in areas of limited and post-conflict statehood usually explain this "failure" to enforce the law with a lack of institutional capacity and the pervasiveness of corruption. The capacity argument is frequently invoked by representatives of all levels of law enforcement who lament that those tasked with governing the market are underfinanced and undertrained, making it impossible for them to effectively monitor the market. Mines monitoring officers and mines wardens employed by the regional branches of the NMA to oversee diamond mining and trading activities complain about a general lack of financing preventing them from traveling to remote mining locations, policing borders, and calling for backup. While these factors certainly impede effective law enforcement in the diamond market, they are not the primary factors preventing prosecution of illegal action in the diamond sector. Far from being unable to detect illegal market activities, law-enforcement agents frequently encounter illegal practices in their day-to-day work, which they choose to tolerate. In other words, it is not that institutional actors *cannot*, but that they *will not* enforce the law. This tacit approval of illegal market action concerns a majority of illegal activities in the Sierra Leonean diamond market, in particular illegal artisanal diamond mining and illegal diamond dealing. While corruption does play a role in the toleration of illegal activities, it is not its single most important explanatory factor. In order to understand the large-scale toleration of illegal diamond production and trade by enforcement agents we need to take into account the social legitimacy of illegal activity. A large part of illegal activity in the Sierra Leonean diamond market falls well within the bounds of appropriate social behavior. To be clear, the argument put forward here is not that corruption and weak institutional capacity do not matter, but that they alone cannot explain the lack of law enforcement of the Sierra Leonean diamond sector. This has important implications for state building as it would suggest that *even if* law-enforcing institutions were better equipped to detect illegal activity and corruption were prosecuted, illegal market practices would still be tolerated as long as they are commonly regarded as rightful.

In the remainder of this chapter, I will outline six sources of legitimacy of illegal action in the Sierra Leonean diamond market and explain how they directly lead to state agents' eschewal of rule enforcement.

## Sources of Legitimacy in the Sierra Leonean Illegal Diamond Market

### *The Right to Subsistence*

When talking about illegal artisanal diamond mining, mines wardens and mines monitoring officers tasked with the supervision of diamond production frequently evoke the right of illegal miners to earn a living. Illegal artisanal mining is largely a subsistence-based activity conducted by impoverished rural and migrant populations.[8] Contrary to the often expressed view that mining lures people away from their farms with promises of high proceeds, farmers often dig for diamonds part time and seasonally in order to supplement subsistence farming with cash income (Maconachie et al. 2006). Farming provides food and mining provides money for market actors living on the fringes of the cash economy (Bürge and Cartier 2011). Many illegal miners are otherwise unemployed and unskilled. They often have received little, if any formal education and have no work experience outside mining and subsistence farming as many started mining for diamonds as children or young adults. Although many of them find gems on a regular basis, they often sell them for only a few dollars per piece. Many diggers describe diamond production as an undesirable economic activity, taken up out of need and for lack of a better alternative. In this context, diggers often depict illegal mining as honest and legitimate labor that allows them to earn a modest living. Local enforcement actors who seldom, if ever,[9] arrest illegal miners often share this interpretation of illegal diamond digging as a form of self-led poverty alleviation. As one illegal digger explains: "The MMO [mines monitoring officers] always

[8] This type of mining is commonly identified as "informal mining" in the academic literature. This is misleading in the sense that there is no conceptual ambiguity about the legality and illegality of diamond extraction in Sierra Leone. The term is often used in a performative sense that aims to decriminalize impoverished miners by avoiding stigmatizing language. This is informed by the assumption that referring to people as "illegal miners" depicts them as deviant and as such illegitimate. The concept of informality, as it is often used, is in itself shaped by notions of legitimacy and illegitimacy.

[9] While interviewed enforcement actors sometimes claimed to have arrested illegal diamond diggers, none of the interviewed miners reported having ever been arrested and tried in recent years. Consistently, interviews with police and justice personnel in Kono did not corroborate even a single case in which illegal mining had been tried in the regional Magistrate Court.

visit us. But we talk to them and they forgive us—because we have nothing." State actors at the local and regional level of law enforcement corroborate this active toleration of illegal diamond mining for humanitarian reasons. Considering the dire living conditions of illegal miners, they stress the need to exert their power of "discretion" and not submit illegal miners to cruel punishment. As one mine warden explains:

> I greet them in the mining field. Sometimes I talk to the poor people just to encourage them to work. Although I have rules and regulations that nobody is allowed to mine without a license. But sometimes I can help them, to allow them to work. They are thieves. But as a human being, I leave them to do their job. Because they are poor people. They don't have money for their living. I will never arrest them. My duty is to arrest but I just use my brain, just to help them.

More broadly, state agents frequently depict illegal mining as a tool to deal with rampant unemployment, especially among the rural youth in the mining regions. Unemployment and dissatisfaction among the young have frequently been the cause of social tensions and have threatened the political stability of the country in the past. In this sense, state actors justify the toleration of illegal mining as a tool to ensure political stability by allowing the poor to earn a living and to share the country's resource wealth.

The same holds true, though to a lesser degree, for illegal diamond dealing by small-time traders in the mining territories and in illegal marketplaces, so-called Open Yai markets.[10] Contrary to the miners, whose struggle for survival has long been acknowledged by both researchers and policymakers, illegal dealers are often depicted as illegitimate market actors, especially by protagonists of international state building and sector reform. Policy briefs, consultancies, and internationally driven development projects generally strive to "cut out the middleman" from the diamond value chain, namely the illegal trader whose involvement is thought to unnecessarily drive up the price and muddy the track of Sierra Leonean diamonds. On the local level, however, market and state actors often equate illegal diamond dealing with unemployment. Traders spend their day sitting at the Open Yai waiting for customers because "it's better than sitting idly at home." In fact, dealers are often also miners who are seasonally or temporarily out of work. Like illegal diamond production, dealing is more often than not a subsistence activity in which actors engage to earn a modest income.

[10] The term "Open Yai" (meaning "Open Eye" in the Sierra Leonean lingua franca Krio) refers to public market places where diamonds are illegally dealt. At the same time, it refers to the association of unlicensed dealers selling diamonds at these illegal market places. Open Yai markets exist in all of the diamond-yielding territories of Sierra Leone. Equivalent market places also exist for illegally mined gold.

### *The Caring State*

Secondly, illegal economic action derives social legitimacy from law-enforcement agents' interpretations of their role in a modern and liberal state. When asked about their reaction to the discovery of illegal activities—be it in the form of illegal mining and dealing, faulty bookkeeping, or attempted smuggling—government agents frequently illustrate their relation to market actors in contrast to the defective pre-war state. In particular, they assert their duty to "protect and serve" and "not harass" Sierra Leonean citizens.[11] This includes illegal market actors. Agents tasked with law enforcement describe their duty as one of facilitating, instead of disrupting, economic activity. To this aim they tolerate illegal mining, but "advise" miners to acquire a license as soon as they can; turn a blind eye to illicit dealing as well as faulty and incomplete documentation of sales in legal dealers' offices; support those that aim to legalize stones that were illegally mined or smuggled into the country; and refrain from arresting foreign citizens lacking the necessary documentation to export Sierra Leonean diamonds. The bottom line in the treatment of these occurrences is the assumption that these are trivial offenses, most likely rooted in honest mistakes, and hence do not call for harsh punishment,[12] but gentle correction. In this sense, one could conclude that state-building efforts have been successful in that they have instilled normative values of liberal statehood into enforcement actors. As a consequence, they usually abstain from a "law and order" approach to law enforcement. As explained by one mines engineer, the head of a regional office of the National Minerals Agency with regard to illegal diamond mining: "We make arrests but we don't take people to court. Because we are just from the war. We need to create freedom. We need to create a good working environment. We need friendship. These are our customers."

### *Piecemeal Legality*

Researchers of informal and illegal markets have highlighted that the line between legal and illegal action is often nearly impossible to draw. In the case of the Sierra Leonean diamond market one of the main reasons for the blurriness of the border between the legal and illegal spheres is that illegal market actors often fulfill a part of the formal requirements of legal market

[11] Although it is safe to assume that these answers are at least somewhat influenced by social desirability, this understanding of the nature of the post-war state was reiterated by market actors and is reflected in the empirical actions of enforcement agents vis-à-vis citizens in the researched context.

[12] One interviewed state agent observes that it would constitute cruel and unusual punishment to put illegal market participants into Sierra Leone's horrific prison system for comparatively minor offenses, such as illegal mining.

participation.[13] This is particularly true for illegal miners who often obtain the approval of the chief—who according to Sierra Leonean land law serves as the custodian of land—for their mining operation and pay him a (non-formal) surface rent. Both steps are part of the process of obtaining a legal mining license (Government of Sierra Leone 2009a; Ministry of Mines and Mineral Resources 2013). While the chiefs are thus integrated into the formal regulation of the mining sector, they also frequently appear as informal agents of market governance. In other cases, illegal miners produce diamonds in verbal, but not formalized agreement with the respective license holder. Obtaining the approval of authorities that are part of the legal process of obtaining a license can lead to a situation in which market participants themselves are unable to tell whether their activities are legal or illegal. Conversely, government actors imitate the legal process of law enforcement when they non-formally "fine" illegal market participants.

### *Symbiosis with the Legal Diamond Market*

One of the most important sources of legitimacy of the illegal diamond market in Sierra Leone is its symbiosis with the legal diamond market. The vast majority of illegally mined and traded diamonds are bought by legal dealers and exporters. As a result, legal dealers and exporters largely view the illegal market as integral to the functioning of the legal economy. Illegal artisanal miners extract even the smallest gems from dispersed deposits that would often be too costly to work for more industrialized legal mining operations. They produce goods that are in high demand on the legal market largely at their own expense. Illegal dealers act as brokers that connect producers and dealers, on the one hand, and illegal and legal dealers, on the other. Even state agents stress their importance in the market. As a senior official of the National Minerals Agency in Freetown explains: "They are necessary. They have to be there. They go around, catering for stones and these stones either end up with dealers or exporters ... That's why we call them facilitators." Illegal miners and even more so illegal traders are acknowledged as professionals at the core of the market and as part of a long-standing community of "diamond people." This distinguishes them from illegal actors at the fringes of the market, such as overseas buyers, who are deemed unprofessional and unreliable, or scammers. A Freetown broker portrays the unlicensed dealers as steady, and hence trustworthy, market actors: "We are the genuine people. All over Sierra Leone we do business the same way." As a result of this reciprocal relationship between the two market spheres, legal market actors

[13] Van Bockstael (2014) observes the same in the Liberian mining sector.

will often help their illegal counterparts when needed. When shortly after the war Sierra Leonean police forces frequently raided illegal marketplaces in the city of Koidu in an effort to end illegal diamond trading, the *banabana* enlisted the help of the chairman of legal diamond dealers for the region. His negotiation with law enforcement resulted in an agreement between the police forces, the mining authorities, and market participants that the authority to control *all* diamond-related activities lies solely with the regional mines office and not with the police, and that illegal traders would largely be left to conduct their business at the Open Yai markets. Similarly, when an illegal broker was arrested in a Freetown hotel, the authorities released him after a Lebanese exporter declared that he was brokering diamonds on his orders. The entanglement between the legal and the illegal market is exacerbated by the high degree of actor mobility between the two spheres. On one hand, many participants in today's legal diamond market started out as illegal miners or traders; on the other hand, legal market actors can easily spiral back into the illegal market if they cannot afford to renew their licenses. Since they are commonly acknowledged as part of the legitimate market, illegal market actors are even able to rely on the help of the state when cheated by business partners. When a diamond was stolen from the Open Yai market in Zimmi, its members not only called on the chairman of the legal dealers associations in the closest diamond-trading centers to alert legal dealers of the stolen diamond, they also dispatched people to police checkpoints in the region to watch out for the thief together with the stationed officers.

### *Contribution to State Revenue*

Arguably, the most important criterion that determines the moral value of economic activities in the Sierra Leonean diamond market is their contribution to tax income. State and market actors divide illegal market activities into two categories: those that contribute to state revenue and hence to the public good, and those that do not. Illegal mining and trading are commonly justified because—while they deprive the state of revenue through royalties and income tax—as diamonds are channeled into the legal market they are legally exported and subject to export taxes. According to one mines engineer: "Even if the diamond comes from illicit mining, we exonerate them, because they go to the office and the dealers have a legal license to buy diamonds." This judgment is also reflected in the actions of illegal miners who consistently state that, while it is acceptable to sell smaller stones to unlicensed dealers, it is morally imperative to sell valuable diamonds to licensed dealers so as to contribute to public revenue. As one illegal miner explains: "It is better to carry it to a licensed dealer. He is paying taxes. That's the main reason why we carry it there. Development is very important to me."

In contrast, smuggling is commonly characterized as "stealing from the government" and taboo, even among illegal market actors. While illegal traders will openly engage in and discuss illicit diamond mining and trading, respondents were reluctant to talk about smuggling and depicted it as a shameful activity that they would hide even from their peers. Just how much the social legitimacy of illegal market activity depends on whether it enhances or diminishes state revenue becomes obvious in the distinct ways actors judge the smuggling of diamonds *into* or *outside* Sierra Leone. Only the latter is considered morally wrong, even by law-enforcement agents who will help diamond dealers legalize goods that have been smuggled in from neighboring countries. The causal link between social legitimacy and contribution to the public good holds up in the case of the legal market economy. Market, state, and civil society actors frequently describe the activities of the largest legal diamond mining operation in the country, Koidu Holdings/Octea, as "criminal" and cite the low tax payments, insufficient corporate social responsibility, and lack of economic and human development in the mining region of Kono as evidence.

### *Competing Social Orders*

Finally, illegal market activities derive social legitimacy from adhering to obligations of alternative social orders that compete with the legitimate authority of the formal state. These can be norms that bind market and state agents to traditional institutions and customs, or to their family and friends, village communities, or patronage networks.

In many instances, the legitimacy of illegal action can be explained by "traditional authority" (Weber 1922: 137) taking precedence over the claims of the formal state. When a chief permits illegal mining activities or powerful political and economic figures ("big men") back illegal operations, enforcement agents will often forgo the implementation of the formal law.[14] One example of the competition between legitimate custom and formal rule is the giving of "kola"—a gift symbolizing friendship and unity, which traditionally takes the form of kola nuts, but can today also be given in the form of money (Ferme 2001)—that would often be clearly identified as corruption from the perspective of modern statehood. At one research site, illegal dealers frequently gather to "greet" the local mine officers with a cash gift that roughly equals an officer's monthly wage. Such a ceremonial greeting is also arranged

[14] It should be noted, however, that traditional legitimacy is linked to traditional power structures that inhibit enforcement agents' ability to enforce the law regardless of their respect for traditional authority. Powerful economic agents are usually backed by institutional actors in the capital, which often makes it impossible for local law-enforcement agents to determine and establish authority.

when senior officials from the regional or national mining authorities—whom the illegal dealers refer to as "elders"—visit. State agents tasked with the enforcement of regulation in the diamond market—in particular, mines monitors and mines wardens in the mining territories—are frequently referred to as part of the community of diamond people. As such, they are bound by social norms of obligation and reciprocity that integrate them into the diamond market and alienate them from their principal, the Sierra Leonean state. This is particularly true in peripheral mining regions where the central state is far off and many interviewed agents had not received their salaries in over nine months at the time of research. Their income is paid not by the state, but by the market for services rendered. While this practice would clearly lend itself as an example of the "rampant corruption" that is so often attributed to Sierra Leonean state institutions, in the local context of the Sierra Leonean diamond economy, paying money to impoverished state agents as "help" or a sign of gratitude is part of a "moral economy of corruption" (de Sardan 1999). Material motives are clearly a crucial factor explaining the leniency of enforcement agents toward illegal market actors. At the same time, the toleration of illegal activities also conforms to commonly held beliefs about legitimate social action.

The toleration of illegal activities has led to what many regard as a customary right of illegal practices. In particular, illegal dealers depict their activities as permitted by the formal state. One illegal broker even describes his dealings as perfectly legal: "We have our rights to move with diamonds. Although we have no legal document, the government gives us the right.... You can quote me because everything I do is legal." In addition to conflicts between formal and traditional mechanisms of governance, illegal practices gain legitimacy through their integration in social networks governed by norms of benevolence and reciprocity. Illegal market actors and state agents may be part of the same kin group, village, or religious community, patronage network, or secret society. This can be exemplified by the friendship between a mine monitoring officer and an illegal miner, each one present during the other's interview, which in the latter case took part at his workplace.

## Conclusion

The study of legality and illegality in markets usually works on the assumption of "consolidated" statehood in which legal and illegal economic practices are distinguished from each other by a coherent set of laws designed and implemented by legitimate and capable state institutions. In these situations, illegality is strongly associated with illegitimacy and, if exposed, prosecuted by the state. If state agents connive at illegal economic activity this can usually be explained by corruption. This raises the question of how illegality is socially defined and enacted in social contexts in which statehood is limited; that is, when the legitimacy, capability, and willingness of political authorities to develop and enforce a coherent body of laws is restricted.

Analyzing social interactions in Sierra Leone's illegal diamond market, I have argued that in order to understand illegality in situations of limited statehood it is crucial to take into account how illegal economies and their relation to the legal sphere are shaped by social norms of legitimacy. I have shown that large parts of the formally illegal market enjoy considerable approval by both the legal market and the institutions of the Sierra Leonean state. This approval is rooted in legitimacy-beliefs held by state and market actors about what types of illegal economic activities are acceptable, and should hence be tolerated, and which are unacceptable, and thus punishable by law. These social norms are prominent enough to generate considerable certainty for those market actors engaged in illegal, but legitimate market action. This is particularly true for illegal diamond production and trade, which are widely regarded as socially appropriate and thus defended by legal market actors and tolerated by law enforcement. As a result, illegal market actors in these fields are largely able to conduct their business openly and without fear of arrest. Their actions are formally illegal but quasi-legal. Corruption of state officials does figure in the creation of state connivance, though not in the unidimensional way that common wisdom about the state in the Global South suggests, by simply incentivizing state agents to turn a blind eye to illegal activities in exchange for payment. Rather, non-formal fines and cash gifts to government officials are themselves embedded in social norms of appropriate behavior, and thus form part of illegal, yet legitimate market relations. Far from lacking the capacity to rule, the Sierra Leonean state does act as a governing authority in the illegal diamond market. Its engagement with the illegal market is, however, largely non-formal. State agents' response to uncovering illegal activity is not determined by the formal law, but instead by widely accepted norms of appropriateness.

## References


Alexey, Robert. 1994. *Begriff und Geltung des Rechts*. Freiburg: Alber.

Bürge, Michael, and Laurent E. Cartier. 2011. "Agriculture and Artisanal Gold Mining in Sierra Leone: Alternatives or Complements?" *Journal of International Development* 23(8): pp. 1080–99.

de Sardan, Olivier J. P. 1999. "A Moral Economy of Corruption in Africa?" *Journal of Modern African Studies* 37(1): pp. 25–52.

de Soto Polar, Hernando. 2002. *The Other Path: The Economic Answer to Terrorism*. New York: Basic Books.

Dewey, Matías. 2012. "Illegal Police Protection and the Market for Stolen Vehicles in Buenos Aires." *Journal of Latin American Studies* 44(4): pp. 679–702.

Ferme, Mariane C. 2001. *The Underneath of Things: Violence, History, and the Everyday in Sierra Leone*. Berkeley, CA: University of California Press.

Geiger, Theodor. 1987. *Vorstudien zu einer Soziologie des Rechts*. Berlin: Duncker and Humblot.

Government Gold and Diamond Office. 2012. *Gold and Diamonds Exports Report 2012*. Unpublished report. Freetown: Government of Sierra Leone.

Government of Sierra Leone. 2009a. *The Mines and Minerals Act*. Freetown: Government of Sierra Leone.

Government of Sierra Leone. 2009b. *Diamond Trading Bill, 2009*. Freetown: Government of Sierra Leone.

Hart, Keith. 1973. "Informal Income Opportunities and Urban Employment in Ghana." *Journal of Modern African Studies* 2(1): pp. 61–89.

Hart, Keith. 2010. "Informal Economy." In *The Human Economy*, edited by Keith Hart, Jean-Louis Laville, and Antonio David Cattani, pp. 142–53. Cambridge, MA: Polity.

Kötter, Matthias. 2008. "Rechtsordnung und Regelungsstrukturen: Der Beitrag einer entscheidungs- und wirkungsorientierten Rechtswissenschaft zur Governanceforschung." In *Transdisziplinäre Governanceforschung: Gemeinsam hinter den Staat blicken*, edited by Sybille de la Rosa, Ulrike Höppner, and Matthias Kötter, pp. 211–29. Baden-Baden: Nomos.

Kötter, Matthias. 2009. "Die Legitimation von Normen in Räumen begrenzter Staatlichkeit: Ein Governanceprozess jenseits des Staats." In *Governance als Prozess: Koordinationsformen im Wandel. Schriften zur Governance-Forschung* 16, edited by Sebastian Botzem et al., pp. 653–81. Baden-Baden: Nomos.

Kötter, Matthias. 2011. "Recht." In *Politische Theorie: 25 umkämpfte Begriffe*, edited by Gerhard Göhler, Mattias Iser, and Ina Kerner, pp. 309–24. Wiesbaden: VS-Verlag.

Levin, Estelle A., and Lansana Gberie. 2006. *Dealing for Development? A Study of Diamond Marketing and Pricing in Sierra Leone*. Report for the Diamond Development Initiative. Ottawa: Partnership Africa Canada, Diamond Development Initiative.

Maconachie, Roy, Tony Binns, Paul Tengbe, and Reynold Johnson. 2006. "Temporary Labour Migration and Sustainable Post-Conflict Return in Sierra Leone." *GeoJournal* 67(3): pp. 223–40.

Ministry of Mines and Mineral Resources. 2013. *Details of Policy Measures Relating to Small Scale and Artisanal Mining and Marketing of Precious, Industrial and Sand Based Minerals*. Freetown: Government of Sierra Leone.

Paoli, Letizia, Victoria A. Greenfield, and Peter Reuter. 2009. "The Theoretical and Practical Consequences of Variations in Effective Illegality." In *The World Heroin Market: Can Supply Be Cut?* Edited by Letizia Paoli, Victoria A. Greenfield, and Peter Reuter, pp. 201–34. New York: Oxford University Press.

Rasanayagam, Johan. 2011. "Informal Economy, Informal State: The Case of Uzbekistan." *International Journal of Sociology and Social Policy* 31(11/12): pp. 681–96.

Risse, Thomas, and Ursula Lehmkuhl. 2007. "Regieren ohne Staat? Governance in Räumen begrenzter Staatlichkeit." In *Regieren ohne Staat? Governance in Räumen begrenzter Staatlichkeit*, edited by Thomas Risse and Ursula Lehmkuhl, pp. 13–37. Baden-Baden: Nomos.

Roitman, Janet L. 1990. "The Politics of Informal Markets in Sub-Saharan Africa." *Journal of Modern African Studies* 28(4): pp. 671–96.

Schmelzle, Cord. 2011. *Evaluating Governance: Effectiveness and Legitimacy in Areas of Limited Statehood*. SFB-Governance working paper series 26. Berlin: Freie Universität Berlin, DFG Research Center (SFB) 700.

Schuppert, Gunnar Folke. 2011. *Der Rechtsstaat unter den Bedingungen informaler Staatlichkeit: Beobachtungen und Überlegungen zum Verhältnis formeller und informeller Institutionen*. Baden-Baden: Nomos.

Sharife, Khadija, and Silas Gbandia. 2016. "Panama Papers: Flaws in Sierra Leone's Diamond Trade." *Times Live*, April 4. <http://www.timeslive.co.za/africa/2016/04/04/Panama-Papers-Flaws-in-Sierra-Leone%E2%80%99s-diamond-trade> (accessed May 8, 2016).

Tamanaha, Brian Z. 2014. *Insights about the Nature of Law from History*. Legal Studies research paper series, no. 14-05-08. St. Louis, MO: Washington University in St. Louis, School of Law.

Van Bockstael, Steven. 2014. "The Persistence of Informality: Perspectives on the Future of Artisanal Mining in Liberia." *Futures* 62(A), Special Issue: *The Futures of Small-Scale Mining in Sub-Saharan Africa*, pp. 10–20.

Webb, Justin W., Laszlo Tihanyi, R. Duane Ireland, and David G. Simon. 2009. "You Say Illegal, I Say Legitimate: Entrepreneurship in the Informal Economy." *Academy of Management Review* 34(3): pp. 492–510.

Weber, Max. 1922. *Grundriß der Sozialökonomik, III: Abteilung, Wirtschaft und Gesellschaft*. Tübingen: Mohr.

Wrase, Michael. 2013. *Wie wirkt Recht? Überlegungen zur Rechtswirkungsforschung unter den Bedingungen konsolidierter und begrenzter Staatlichkeit*. SFB-Governance working paper series 57. Berlin: Freie Universität Berlin, DFG Research Center (SFB) 700.

# 12

# A Crooked Mirror

## The Evolution of Illegal Alcohol Markets in Russia since the Late Socialist Period

*Vadim Radaev*

### Introduction

The sociology of markets has obtained a dominant position in contemporary economic sociology (Fourcade 2007; Fligstein and Dauter 2007). Illegal markets involving illicit products and transactions have been largely ignored by economic sociologists, despite their significance in various economies (Beckert and Wehinger 2013). Sharing the view that economic sociology should turn to a more active investigation of this important area, we explore the structure and evolution of illegal alcohol markets in Russia from the late Soviet period to the present.

The chapter seeks to contribute to the research on illegal markets in three ways. First, it focuses on dynamic aspects of heterogeneous illegal markets that adjust flexibly to a changing environment. Three illegal markets within the domain are selected: for homemade alcohol, counterfeit alcoholic beverages, and illegally manufactured and sold original alcohol. A variety of statistical sources is used to demonstrate that the compositions of these markets have developed through four different stages, following the constellation of the political, legislative, and economic arenas. At each stage, some of these markets become dominant, whereas others are undeveloped or show a downward trend.

Second, the core argument of this chapter is that markets for illegal alcohol tend to grow in periods of exogenous political or economic stressors, whereas in periods of relative economic stability or growth, these markets shrink or remain at the same level.

Third, we demonstrate that changes in the structure of illegal markets are backed by a continuous reclassification of products, organizations, and transactions when the boundaries between legality and illegality are contested and moved. At the same time, some illegal activities retain their legitimacy due to the ignorance or tolerance of enforcement agencies and final consumers. Boundaries between legitimate and illegitimate activities are blurred and move slowly.

## Classification of Illegal Alcohol Markets

Illegal markets should be distinguished from unrecorded and unreported markets that circumvent statistical reporting and fiscal rules. A large part of the unrecorded economy, defined as the informal economy, involves licit products and transactions, whereas illegal markets involve products and transactions that are illicit (Feige 1990; Portes 2010).

Unrecorded alcohol in Russia accounts for between one quarter and one third of total alcohol consumption (World Health Organization 2014; author's estimate). Unrecorded alcohol is normally divided into four categories: (i) illegally manufactured or smuggled alcohol; (ii) alcohol brought into the country through cross-border shopping; (iii) non-beverage surrogate alcohol that is not officially intended for human consumption; and (iv) artisanal (homemade) alcohol (Rehm et al. 2010; Lachenmeier et al. 2011). In this chapter, we specify this classification and focus on three illegal markets: (a) homemade alcohol; (b) illegally manufactured original alcohol; and (c) counterfeit/falsified alcohol. These markets are not frequently examined in the literature, particularly in post-communist countries (Lachenmeier et al. 2011).

Homemade alcohol is produced by non-registered actors (households) using primitive distillation technologies (Zaigraev 2004; Rehm et al. 2010; Radaev 2016). In contrast to organizations that may use the same technology, home production is not separated from the household economy. One part of homemade alcohol is legally produced for the purpose of in-house consumption. It is also used in barter exchanges as a widely accepted money surrogate, particularly in remote rural areas in which monetary revenues are scarce (Rogers 2005). One can legally obtain primitive equipment for samogon distillation for less than USD 100. Ready-made kits for wine making are also for sale. Another portion of homemade alcohol is illegally sold in markets, primarily through local networks.

Alcoholic beverages can be produced illegally both by legal and illegal organizations. Moreover, both legally and illegally manufactured original alcohol can be smuggled and/or illegally sold through non-licensed stores and eateries. These activities are not declared to the state, primarily for the purpose of tax evasion.

We add "counterfeiting" as the third illegal market. Counterfeiting refers to the production and distribution of goods with unauthorized placing (forgery) of trademarks as a means of commodity differentiation for the purpose of consumer deception (Radaev et al. 2008; Rutter and Bryce 2008; Kotelnikova 2011). Counterfeits are rarely produced by households. Most are carried out by legal or illegal organizations. Infringement of registered trademarks is illegal, although the sale of counterfeit alcohol may be officially recorded.

We exclude cross-border shopping from consideration here. This type of imported alcohol is not registered in the country where it is consumed, but the transactions are legal if they comply with established quotas. Moreover, cross-border shopping presents a problem in only a small part of the world, primarily in high-income countries such as the European Union (Rehm et al. 2014: 884), whereas in Russia it does not play a significant role.

One more market for illicit alcohol that includes non-beverage alcohol, such as lotions or liquid glass cleaners, is not registered as part of alcohol consumption but is legally produced and distributed for purposes other than drinking (Gil et al. 2009; Solodun et al. 2011). This market was particularly important in the 1990s. However, because no systematic reliable data are available on this market, alcohol surrogates are not considered in this study.

## Conceptual Background

Illegal markets are heterogeneous (Beckert and Wehinger 2013). Their illegality derives from various dimensions, including violation of the ban on the market exchange of certain products (sales of homemade alcohol), non-compliance with intellectual property rights (production and distribution of fakes and lookalikes), and tax evasion (non-declared production and sales).

The illegality of organizations, products, and transactions is not necessarily linked. *Organizations* can be legal (registered) but involve illegal products and transactions, whereas legal products can be marketed by illegal (non-registered) organizations. *Transactions* can be illegal for various reasons. The sale of the product is prohibited by law (for example, homemade and counterfeit alcohol); the organization does not have a license to sell alcohol; the organization does not comply with restrictions imposed on transactions (for example, selling alcohol to underage customers); and the transaction is unreported by the seller, or the actual market value of the products is concealed. *Products* can be legal, illegal (falsified or counterfeit), and legal but misused, as in the case of non-beverage alcohol not intended for human consumption.

Illegal markets may also produce divergent *effects*. The quality of homemade spirits for in-house consumption could be even higher than the quality of legally manufactured spirits (Rehm et al. 2014), whereas commercial homemade alcohol produced for the illegal market and aiming to ensure intoxication might expose consumers to higher risks, be more harmful to health, and damage the public interest through tax avoidance (Nemtsov 2009). Counterfeit goods could also be hazardous to health and harm corporate interests by violating the intellectual property rights of organizations making investments and conducting research and development (Radaev et al. 2008; Kotelnikova 2011). Illegal manufacturing involves defrauding the state through tax evasion, which is detrimental to the public interest and welfare provision. Above all, illegal activities are associated with unfair competition, seizing a part of the market from bona fide actors (Radaev 2005).

First, we need to specify and decompose illegal markets. Second, we should analyze divergent combinations of these interrelated markets and investigate how their compositions change over time. We focus on dynamic aspects and argue that Russian illegal alcohol markets have developed through four main stages since the 1980s, with substantive shifts in the character of products, organizations, and transactions and the main factors affecting illegal markets. These stages are: (i) late socialism and Gorbachev's anti-alcohol campaign (1980–91); (ii) liberal reforms and economic collapse (1992–2000); (iii) state consolidation and economic growth (2001–7); and (iv) economic recession and new anti-alcohol reforms (2008–today).

Looking at the economic, political, and legislative factors affecting illegal alcohol markets, such markets tend to grow in periods of exogenous political or economic stressors, such as anti-alcohol campaigns or economic crises, whereas in periods of economic stability or growth they tend to shrink or remain at the same level.

We assume that economic growth and the increase in real disposable income lead to an increase in legal alcohol consumption and the shrinking of illegal alcohol markets. A large corpus of literature has established that price is inversely related to the consumption of legal alcohol (Wagenaar et al. 2009), although this effect on high-intensity drinking is limited (Byrnes et al. 2013). The effect of prices on unrecorded alcohol is less clear. However, where homemade or other unrecorded alcohol was readily available, its consumption was likely to increase as a result of price increases in the legal market (Haworth and Simpson 2004). This result derives from a substitution effect, when consumers respond to higher prices by switching to cheaper beverages (Andrienko and Nemtzov 2005).

Restrictive policy measures that reduce the availability of legal alcohol may lead to a reduction of legal alcohol sales and stimulate the use of illegal alcohol (Andrienko and Nemtsov 2005), although the experience of Scandinavian countries with a similar "northern" drinking culture demonstrated that a resurgence of illegal alcohol did not necessarily result from restrictions (Lindström 2005). The size of illegal markets could be sensitive to the level of legal sanctions against offenders but is even more affected by the effectiveness of the state and company enforcement practices against illegal dealers.

Shifts in cultural perceptions might also produce changes in consumption patterns by stimulating substitution effects. For example, in the 2000s, younger people in Russia increasingly turned from vodka to beer, and more educated people turned from vodka to wine (Denisova 2010; Roshchina 2013). These changes could develop according to inner rules that are driven by long-range indirect network ties and produce recurrent cycles, each lasting ten to twenty years (Skog 1986). We admit that cultural factors might be influential, but their influence is beyond the scope of this study.

Normally, legal and illegal markets are viewed as communicating vessels affecting each other (Thamarangsi 2013). However, their interrelations are more complicated. Illegal markets can be viewed as a crooked mirror that may provide changeable and erroneous reflections of legal markets; in other words, in some stages, certain illegal markets may move in the opposite direction from legal markets, whereas in other stages they may move in parallel with them.

Sharing the view that illegality does not necessarily indicate illegitimacy (Van Schendel and Abraham 2005; Introduction to this volume; Dioun, in this volume) and that consumers of illegal products can be deceived or can use them knowingly (Grossman and Shapiro 1988), we differentiate between two important reasons for maintaining the legitimacy of illegal activity. The first reason is ignorance (lack of understanding), and the second is tolerance (willingness to accept).

## Data Sources

The examination of divergent illegal markets requires a variety of data sources. We use diverse official statistics to calculate the volume and dynamics of illegally produced original and counterfeit alcoholic beverages, and the level of activity of brand owners and state agencies aimed at eliminating the illegal production and distribution of alcohol and protecting intellectual property rights. Statistics were collected by the author from the databases of several state agencies.[1]

[1] These agencies include the Russian Federal State Statistics Service (Rosstat), the Federal Service for Alcohol Market Regulation (Rosalkogolregulirovanie), the Russian Federal Service for Surveillance on Consumer Rights Protection and Human Wellbeing (Rospotrebnadzor), the

Survey data are also used to examine changes in beverage preferences. These data were collected from the Russian Longitudinal Monitoring Survey, RLMS-HSE, established by Demoscope and the Carolina Population Center, University of North Carolina at Chapel Hill, and conducted together with the Higher School of Economics. RLMS-HSE includes a series of annual nationally representative panel surveys. The data represent the adult population in all regions of Russia and all types of residence from 1994 to 2014. Self-reports on the incidence of the consumption and purchase of alcoholic beverages (including homemade samogon), the volume of drinking, and beverage preferences are the main reporting measures.[2]

For the analysis of homemade and counterfeit alcohol, we use data collected from the 2014 RLMS-HSE round from 14,968 adults (15+). We are aware that final consumers have limited capacities to distinguish between legal and illegal products and transactions, and their knowledge typically depends on the type of illegal market. Consumers are generally not able to distinguish between legally or illegally offered alcoholic beverages if the products are similar, although a much lower price for the same product could indicate to the consumer the use of illegal goods and transactions.

In some cases (but not all), consumers are able to detect counterfeit products, particularly if they deviate in taste or other quality characteristics, and indeed, identification frequently follows the consumption of these products. At the same time, consumers easily recognize homemade alcoholic beverages when purchasing these products in their localities. Thus, population surveys may provide relevant data on the use of homemade alcohol, which are absent from official and business statistics.

## First and Second Stages of Evolution of Illegal Markets

The *first stage*, that of late socialism (1980–91), was characterized by economic stagnation accompanied by restrictions on the availability of legal alcohol. Gorbachev's severe anti-alcohol reform of 1985–7 brought about significant alcohol price increases, restrictions on alcohol sales, the destruction of vineyards and hop plantations, and heavy penalties for alcohol-related offenses. As a result, the use of legal alcohol was abruptly cut by more than 50 percent. This collapse was compensated partially by the increase in illegal alcohol

Russian Federal Service for Intellectual Property, Patents and Trademarks (Rospatent), the Federal Customs Service of Russia, and the Judicial Department under the Supreme Court of Russia.

[2] The RLMS-HSE study met the standards for the ethical treatment of participants. It was approved by the Institutional Review Boards of the University of North Carolina at Chapel Hill, No. 96-0478, Monitoring the Social Safety Net in Russia, renewal approved June 2, 2014.

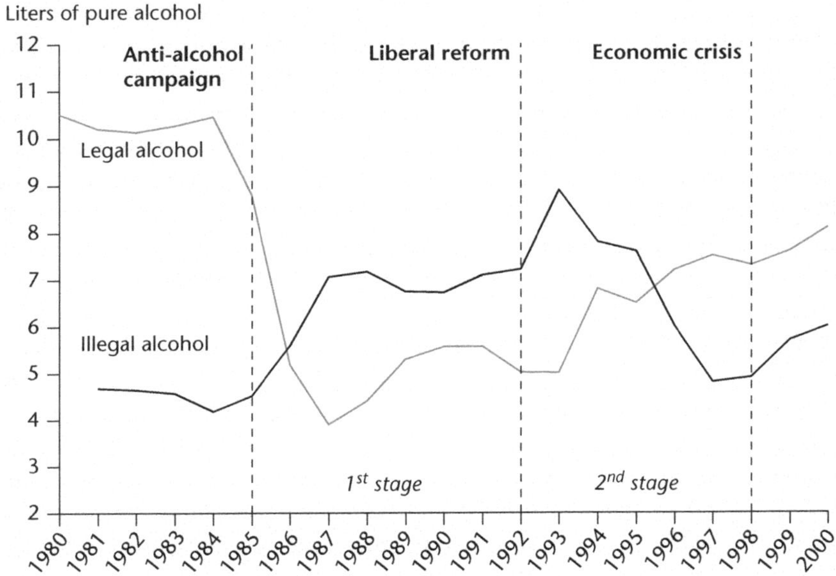


**Figure 12.1.** Per capita consumption of legal and illegal alcohol in Russia, 1980–2000
*Source*: Nemtsov 2009

consumption (see Figure 12.1). At that time, homemade distilled spirits (samogon or moonshine) were a major illegal product, whereas markets for counterfeit and illegally manufactured alcoholic beverages were undeveloped due to the strict state control over organizations. Because control over household activities was not effective and the population's tolerance for homemade alcohol remained high, samogon consumption increased by 80 percent from 1985 to 1987, accounting for 64 percent of total alcohol consumption in 1987. At least one half of the diminishing recorded alcohol was replaced by unrecorded alcohol (Vroublevsky and Harwin 1998; Nemtsov 2009). After the dissolution of the anti-alcohol campaign in 1988, legal alcohol became more available, and its consumption started to grow again, whereas samogon consumption remained at the same level until the second stage (Nemtsov 2002, 2009).

The *second stage* (1992–2000) began with the radical liberal economic reforms in 1992 that led to the legalization of private entrepreneurship, trade liberalization (including cross-border transactions), an abrupt economic collapse, and weakening state control over markets (including the removal of a state monopoly on alcohol production).

With the start of liberalization reform, samogon was largely substituted by manufactured alcohol. However, the sharp increase in manufactured alcohol was explained primarily by the increasing amount of cheap domestic and imported spirits, including pure ethanol and counterfeit and falsified products. Many of these low-quality products were detrimental to human health (Nemtsov 2002, 2009). The same inflow of imported alcohol of dubious quality was observed at that time in other Eastern European countries (Moskalewicz and Simpura 2000). Numerous legally registered and non-registered firms were involved in a mix of legal, semi-legal, and illegal transactions. A significant part of smuggled and illegally manufactured alcohol was missing from official statistics.

A large part of cheap and low-quality alcohol was imported using "grey" (tax-evading) business schemes (Radaev 2005). The process of "grey" imports was organized in the following way: a retail company had a chain of affiliated firms, starting with an offshore company that bought goods at market price from a global vendor abroad. "Independent" import dealers bought the goods from an offshore company at a drastically reduced price to minimize the amount of customs duties and VAT paid at the state border. Only a small part of legal duties was paid officially through customs brokers who received informal kickbacks for their "grey" services. Then, the merchandise was sold to "one-day" firms (*odnodnevki*) registered for one transaction or a few transactions conducted within three months. These fictitious "one-day" firms resold the goods at a high price to a wholesale trader and extracted significant revenue. Then, these firms disappeared before reporting tax. Their illegal revenue was transferred through a bank providing "grey" services back to the affiliated offshore company, whereas "cleared" goods were supplied by the wholesale trader to the retail company at a regular market price (see Figure 12.2).

The production and distribution of counterfeit alcohol flourished in the second stage, although it is difficult to find reliable systematic data. Legislation on intellectual property rights in general and the protection of registered trademarks in particular was undeveloped, although a special federal law "On Trademarks and Service Marks and Appellations of Origin of Goods" was adopted in 1992. The enforcement of this legislation was even less effective given that the courts were largely ignorant of the intellectual property rights issues. As a result, Rospotrebnadzor of Russia reported that 30–40 percent of alcohol checked during field inspections was of inadequate quality and/or dangerous for health in the mid-1990s. This was particularly true for imported alcohol. Most counterfeit alcohol was illegally produced or smuggled for legal sale on the domestic market. An increased rate of mortality attributed to heavy drinking and alcohol poisoning might serve as indirect evidence of the expansion of illegal alcohol markets (Leon et al. 2009). The second stage ended with the financial crisis in 1998 when the ruble lost 75 percent of its value. Under these conditions, the import of alcoholic beverages became less efficient and a resurgence of samogon consumption was observed for several years (Nemtsov 2009).

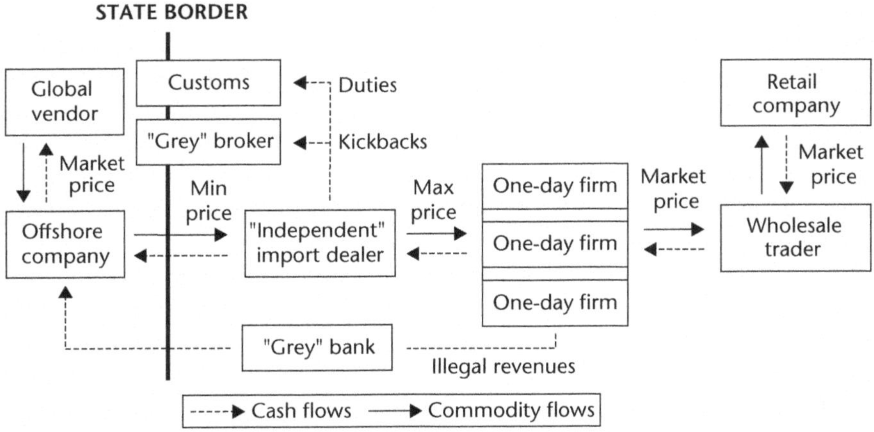


**Figure 12.2.** Organization of "grey" business schemes with a chain of affiliated firms

## Third and Fourth Stages of the Evolution of Illegal Markets

The *third stage* (2001–7) was distinguished by economic growth. Annual GDP growth rates and real disposable income reached 7 percent and 10 percent, respectively. Economic growth was accompanied by a decrease in the relative prices of legal alcoholic beverages. For example, the number of standard bottles of vodka (0.5 L) that could be bought in retail stores for an average monthly wage increased by 3.7 times from 51 to 189 units in 1998–2011, implying that vodka became much more affordable. Toughening state control over alcohol markets contributed to a decrease in illegal alcohol.

The *fourth stage* was marked by the financial crisis of 2008–9 and the economic recession of 2012–14, when the annual GDP growth rate declined to 1 percent. Average real disposable income growth rates dropped from 10 percent to 3 percent in 2008–13 and became negative in 2014.

Moreover, an active phase of pervasive anti-alcohol reform in Russia started in 2009, when Rosalkogolregulirovanie was established. A wide range of additional regulations were imposed on the manufacturing and sale of alcoholic beverages. Restrictions on alcohol availability included bans on off-premises sales of alcoholic beverages in the evening and at night. Points of sale had to be located at a safe distance from educational, medical, sports, and cultural facilities. A ban on alcohol consumption in public settings was added. Step-by-step limitations and ultimately a total ban on above-the-line advertising of alcoholic beverages through television, radio, and press were enacted.

New fiscal measures prescribed an accelerated growth of alcohol excise taxes and minimum unit retail prices on vodka. Alcohol excise taxes increased by 30 percent in 2011–12 and by 80 percent in 2013–14. The minimum unit prices on vodka were raised by two and a half times (from 89 to 220 RBL per 0.5 liters) during 2010–14. The resulting retail price of vodka increased by 77 percent between 2010 and 2013, whereas the real disposable income of the population increased by only 15 percent. Objectively, these measures created additional incentives for the production and purchase of unrecorded alcohol and tax-evading behavior.

### *Rise and Fall of Samogon*

To analyze the dynamics of homemade alcohol consumption vis-à-vis manufactured alcoholic beverages, we turn to the RLMS-HSE survey data.[3] We observe that the percentage of drinkers of vodka and other legal spirits during the previous thirty days declined during 1995–2007, stabilized in 2008–11, and decreased further in 2012–14. The percentage of beer drinkers increased between 1996 and 2000, stabilized in 2001–5 at a high level, and slightly decreased after 2006. The percentage of wine drinkers after a downward trend from 1995 to 2000 changed to an upward trend in 2001–8, with stabilization afterwards.

We observe that the consumption of recorded and unrecorded spirits moves in the same or in opposite ways again. The percentage of samogon drinkers grew rapidly, starting from a relatively low level from 1996 to 2000 and replacing the declining recorded spirits. Then, increasing real disposable income and the availability of legal alcohol led to a gradual decline in homemade alcohol consumption. Starting in 2001, we observe a downward trend from 19 percent to 5 percent of drinkers, which was largely supported by the reluctance of younger generations to drink samogon (see Figure 12.3). This trend implies that self-reported unrecorded samogon consumption declined in parallel with recorded manufactured spirits (partially replaced by the consumption of beer and wine) in the third stage. Remarkably, in the fourth stage, since 2010 this downward trend was interrupted.

Self-reported data from the 2014 round of the RLMS-HSE survey showed that 10.5 percent of respondents who drank alcoholic beverages during the previous thirty days consumed homemade alcoholic beverages. Homemade alcohol constituted 9.6 percent of the overall volume of consumed alcohol, measured in grams of pure ethanol. Samogon was prevalent, accounting for 83.7 percent of the overall volume of homemade alcohol.

[3] This part of the study was supported by an unrestricted grant for academic research from the International Alliance for Responsible Drinking. All conclusions and interpretations offered in the chapter are those of its author alone and are not necessarily those of IARD or its sponsor companies.

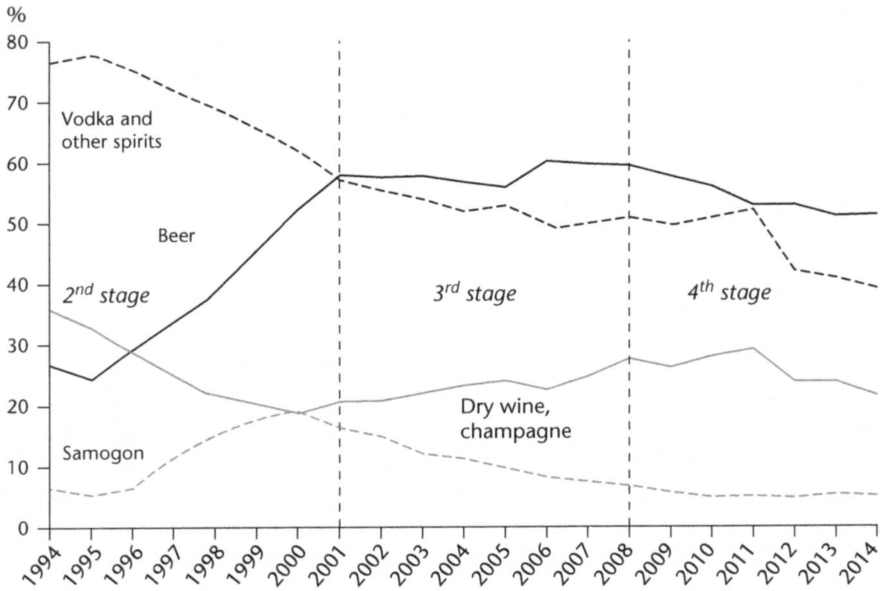


**Figure 12.3.** Percentage of recorded alcohol and samogon drinkers during the thirty days preceding the survey in 1994–2013

*Note*: RLMS data were not collected in 1997 and 1999

*Source*: RLMS-HSE data

Artisanal producers are reluctant to report on market sales of homemade alcohol because they are prohibited by law. However, self-reports on the purchase of homemade alcohol can be more effective and the illegal market for commercial homemade alcohol can be investigated by survey methods on the demand side. A total of 6 percent of alcohol buyers reported that they had purchased homemade alcoholic beverages during the previous thirty days; most of the alcohol they purchased was samogon (90 percent). This finding implies that the illegal market for homemade alcohol still exists, although its size is small.

## *Combating Counterfeit Goods*

Turning to counterfeit goods, RLMS-HSE self-reported data from 2014 showed that 5.7 percent of drinkers had consumed counterfeit (fake) alcoholic beverages during the previous thirty days. Moreover, 5.6 percent of alcohol buyers purchased alcoholic beverages that were identified as counterfeit during or after the purchase. Of course, we should treat this evidence cautiously given the limited capacity of customers to distinguish between original and counterfeit products.

Survey data on counterfeit alcohol from previous years are not available. However, from a series of in-depth expert interviews we know that the counterfeiting situation improved during the third stage in the 2000s due to serious changes in state policies regarding the merchandisers of counterfeit goods (Radaev et al. 2008). Legislation became more effective in 2002, when important amendments were added to the federal law on trademarks. All special laws that earlier regulated relations in the field of intellectual property rights were consolidated in Part 4 of the Civil Code of Russia in 2008 and there was also a serious tightening of liability for intellectual property rights infringements.[4]

A legal possibility arose to liquidate infringing merchandising companies or to suspend the activities of unscrupulous individual entrepreneurs. Equipment, other facilities, and materials used or intended to commit infringements could be confiscated, and seized counterfeit goods could be destroyed.

More importantly, the enforcement of legislation protecting intellectual property rights was improved considerably during the third stage of development. Previously ignorant of counterfeiting issues, the Federal Customs Service became much more responsive to the requests of brand owners (Radaev et al. 2008). The number of legal cases initiated against infringing companies increased more than ten times from 2004 to 2006. Approximately 10 million units of goods on average were seized by customs annually starting in 2007, with some fluctuations over the years. In the fourth stage, both the number of opened administrative cases and the amount of seized counterfeit goods initially decreased during the financial crisis of 2008–9 and then stabilized (with the exception of the outlier in 2012).

Court practices also changed dramatically in favor of brand owners in the 2000s. The number of arbitration court trials regarding the illegal use of trademarks increased more than tenfold from 2004 to 2010 and stabilized during the fourth stage from 2011 to 2013 at a much higher level than previously.

Criminal liability for dealing with counterfeit products was tightened during the third stage of development. The number of market dealers convicted for the illegal use of trademarks increased eighteen fold from 2004 to 2010, according to Supreme Court data. Afterwards, the number of criminal sentences decreased from 2011 to 2013, which could be explained by a new legislative amendment redefining the criteria of serious crimes in the field of

[4] In the Criminal Code of Russia (Article 180, Part 1), infringements of intellectual property rights and the use of trademarks in particular were reclassified to the category of serious crimes, with a maximum criminal punishment of six years in prison and penalties of up to RUB 500,000 (USD 20,000). In the Code of Administrative Offences of Russia (Article 14.10), the maximum penalty for an organization was fixed at RUB 40,000 (USD 1,600) with the confiscation of counterfeit goods. In the Civil Code of Russia (Part 4), the maximum amount of compensation was increased to RUB 5,000,000 (USD 200,000) or double the price of the goods on which the trademark was unlawfully placed.

the illegal use of trademarks in 2010. The criteria of "large-scale damage" and "particularly large-scale damage" were raised from RUB 250,000 (USD 8,300) and RUB 1,000,000 (USD 33,300) to RUB 1,500,000 (USD 50,000) and RUB 6,000,000 (USD 200,000), respectively. Thus, it became much more difficult for enforcement agencies (the police) to collect sufficient evidence. Nonetheless, the number of dealers convicted for the infringement of registered trademarks from 2011 to 2013 remained at a level twelve times higher than in 2004.

Brand owners also changed their policies as the Russian consumer market became increasingly attractive. Companies started to protect their trademarks more actively through available legal mechanisms. The number of applications submitted by the companies to Rospatent to register and protect their trademarks increased more than 150 percent from 2004 to 2013. The number of trademarks registered in the Customs Register for the Objects of Intellectual Property increased by 7.5 times from 2004 to 2013, encouraging customs to stop and check an increasing amount of goods of suspicious origin during customs clearance.

The more active protection of alcohol brands by the state and brand owners led to a decrease in the production and distribution of counterfeit alcoholic beverages. The dynamic of infringement in the quality and chemical composition of alcoholic beverages may serve as an indirect measure of this change. Starting with a high level of 30–40 percent in the mid-1990s, the amount of alcoholic beverages of inadequate quality and/or dangerous for health was decreasing, with some fluctuations during the third stage, and reached 5 percent or even less by the end of this period. During the fourth stage, starting in 2008, the amount of revealed low-quality and falsified alcohol containing dangerous substances stabilized at a historically low level (see Figure 12.4).

### *Illegal Manufacturing and Sales of Original Alcoholic Beverages*

The decline in the production of counterfeit and homemade alcohol was accompanied by the expansion of the third type of illegal markets: tax-evading illegal production and the sale of original alcoholic beverages. This type of illegal activity, practiced by many legally registered enterprises producing non-registered vodka during night shifts, became particularly important in the fourth stage of development in the 2010s. This type of illegal alcohol market became dominant. Falsified tax stamps and non-licensed stores were used for the illegal sale of non-declared products.

It is not easy to obtain reliable data on illegally produced alcohol. Using a balance method and calculating the difference between official retail sales and the official production of alcoholic beverages, Rosstat claimed that 36.5 percent of vodka and other spirits was produced illegally in 2011. This difference was explained by legal manufacturers' non-reporting of the actual production

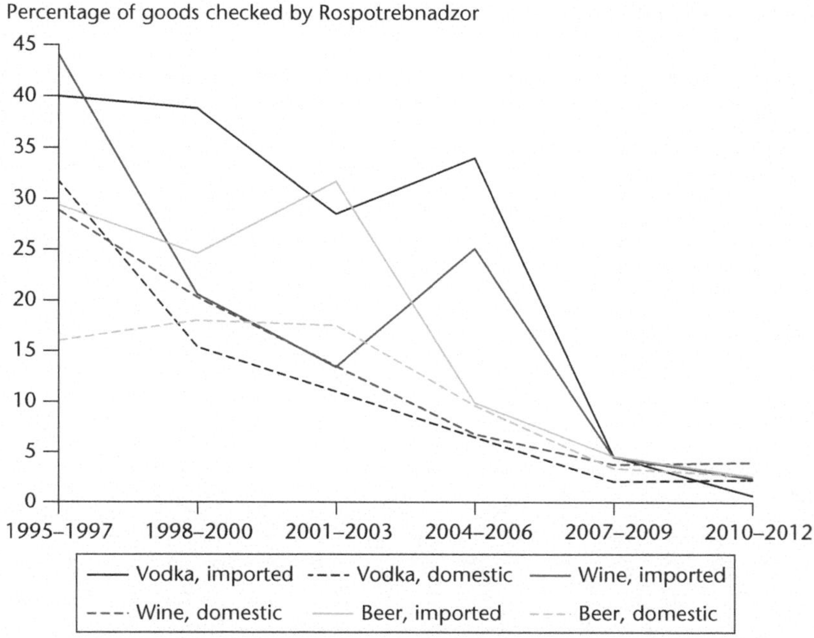


**Figure 12.4.** Inadequate quality and/or health dangers of vodka and other spirits, wine (excluding champagne), and beer from 1995 to 2012

*Notes*: We took six time intervals each comprised of three years to eliminate excessive fluctuations and make the trends more perceptible

*Source*: Rosstat Central Statistical Database, <http://www.gks.ru/dbscripts/cbsd/dbinet.cgi#1> (accessed January 13, 2017)

volume. Rosalkogolregulirovanie challenged the Rosstat calculations and indicated a smaller volume of illegal production of vodka that accounted for 23 percent of retail sales. Regardless, the size of the illegal market remains significant.

One more way to use a balance method is to calculate the difference between the level of retail sales and the level of official imports if the alcoholic beverage is not produced within the country legally. For example, retail sales of whiskey exceeded the volume of imported whiskey by 18–23 percent from 2010 to 2012, implying that illegal sales of whiskey (smuggled or counterfeit) accounted for 16–19 percent of total sales (Rosstat and Federal Customs Service data) (Puzyrev 2014).

It should be taken into account that balance calculations do not include illegal sales through non-licensed retail outlets. Some empirical evidence on these types of sales was provided by the research agency Infoline, conducting a survey of retail stores in ten cities of Russia in 2014. They compared the registers of all retail outlets with the registers of outlets obtaining licenses for

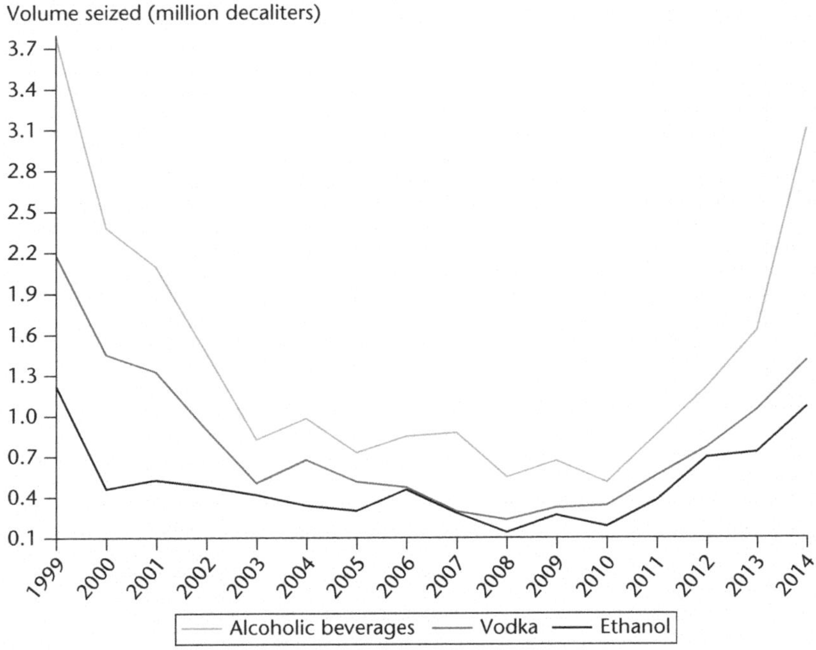


**Figure 12.5.** Amount of alcoholic beverages, vodka, and ethanol seized by state protection agencies during inspections in Russia, 1999–2013

*Source*: Rosstat Central Statistical Database, <http://www.gks.ru/dbscripts/cbsd/dbinet.cgi#1> (accessed January 13, 2017)

the sale of alcoholic beverages. It was revealed that 16 percent of almost 24,000 retail outlets sold alcoholic beverages without a license.[5]

Given the scarcity of direct empirical evidence on the amount of illegally manufactured alcohol, we use Rosstat data on the amount of illegally produced alcoholic beverages seized during police raids. The data demonstrate that this amount was at its highest level at the end of the 1990s. During the third stage, it fell and stabilized. The fourth stage started with a decline in this indicator during the crisis of 2008, and finally, it grew again rapidly from 2011 to 2014. Vodka accounted for one to two thirds of seized alcoholic beverages. Remarkably, the amount of seized pure ethanol was similar to that of vodka in most years (see Figure 12.5). Because ethanol serves as a major ingredient for producing illegal vodka, the latter is dominant in the total volume of suspicious alcohol going through illegal market channels.

In sum, a resurgence of illegally manufactured alcohol is observed in the fourth stage in the 2010s. This can be explained by several complementary

[5] These data were presented by Infoline at a business conference in Moscow in May 2014.

factors. First, a special newly established state agency (Rosalkogolregulirovanie) started to take control over the alcohol markets in 2009. Second, excise tax rates and minimal unit prices on legal vodka were raised significantly from 2011 to 2014. Resulting from the new alcohol policy, the illegal production of alcoholic beverages rose as a by-product of restrictive measures. Third, the creation of the Single Customs Union of Russia with Belarus and Kazakhstan in 2011 encouraged an increasing inflow of cheap, unregistered alcohol from Kazakhstan to Russia (Radaev et al. 2010). Fourth, the economic recession followed by the slowdown of real disposable income starting in 2012 forced customers to look for less expensive goods, and their propensity to buy products of unknown origin increased.

## Main Stages and Factors of the Evolution of Illegal Markets

The empirical evidence leads to the following general conclusions. First, illegal alcohol markets tend to grow in periods of exogenous political or economic stressors, including the anti-alcohol campaign of 1985–8, the liberal economic reform of 1992–3, the financial crisis of 1998–9, and the recession of 2012–14. In periods of relative economic stability and growth, illegal alcohol markets shrink or remain at the same level.

Second, in some periods, legal and illegal alcohol consumption moved in opposite directions (1980–92, 1996–7, and 2001–7), whereas in other periods they moved in parallel (1993–5 and 1998–2000).

Third, at different stages, exogenous political or economic stressors stimulated different types of illegal alcohol market. Regularities in the dynamics of illegal alcohol markets and the influence of the main factors can be observed in Table 12.1.

During the first stage of late socialism and Gorbachev's anti-alcohol campaign (1980–91) homemade alcohol (samogon) prevailed, in particular when the availability of legal alcohol decreased. Increasing sanctions against samogon producers did not work due to the ineffectiveness of law-enforcement agencies and public tolerance of illegal products. Markets of counterfeit and illegally manufactured alcoholic beverages were undeveloped due to the strict state control over organizations.

In the second stage of liberal reform and economic collapse (1992–2000) samogon was largely substituted by manufactured alcohol. However, the market was filled by an increasing amount of cheap domestic and imported spirits, including illegally produced, smuggled, and falsified products. The production and distribution of counterfeit alcohol was flourishing. In conditions of a weak state, numerous market sellers used "grey" (tax-evading)

**Table 12.1.** Main stages and factors of the evolution of illegal markets

| | Main stages | | | |
|---|---|---|---|---|
| | Late socialism, anti-alcohol campaign (1980–91) | Liberal reforms, economic downfall (1992–2000) | State consolidation, economic growth (2001–7) | Economic recession, anti-alcohol policy (2008–) |
| *Illegal markets* | | | | |
| Homemade alcohol | ↗ | → | ↘ | → |
| Counterfeit alcohol | – | ↗ | ↘ | → |
| Illegally manufactured alcohol | – | ↗ | ↘ | ↗ |
| *Factors* | | | | |
| Population real disposable income | → | ↘ | ↗ | → |
| Availability of legal alcohol | ↘ | ↗ | ↗ | ↘ |
| Sanctions against illegal dealers | ↗ | ↘ | ↗ | ↗ |
| Effectiveness of protection agencies | ↘ | ↘ | ↗ | ↗ |
| Legalization of market sellers | → | ↘ | ↗ | ↘ |
| Tolerance of illegal products | ↗ | ↗ | ↘ | → |

business schemes. A decrease in real disposable income explained the tolerance for cheaper illegal products.

At the third stage of state consolidation and economic growth (2001–7) real disposable income increased and legal alcohol became more affordable. Consumers became less ignorant and less tolerant towards illegal products. At the same time, liability for non-compliance with the law was seriously tightened and the enforcement of legislation was considerably improved. It resulted in the progressing legalization of market sellers and decline of all types of illegal alcohol markets.

Finally, in the fourth stage of economic recession (2008–) average real disposable income growth rates fell. At the same time, an active phase of pervasive anti-alcohol reform started in 2009, with a wide range of restrictions imposed on the manufacture and sale of alcoholic beverages. All major trends of alcohol consumption were interrupted or even reversed at this stage. Legal alcohol in total and imported alcohol in particular, since the devaluation of the ruble in 2014, became less affordable. Consumers started to look for cheaper alternative products. Despite tightening state control, a resurgence of illegally manufactured alcohol was observed, while the use of homemade and counterfeit alcohol stabilized at a relatively low level.

Along with the evolution of illegal alcohol markets, the character of the market actors involved was changing in terms of their status and role within the Russian economy. Homemade alcohol (particularly samogon) was produced and consumed mainly by households from lower classes and rural areas. The inflow of counterfeit alcohol came from the numerous small and medium-sized firms acting as "grey" dealers in the shadow economy. With the resurgence of illegally manufactured alcohol, which is chemically similar to original legal alcoholic beverages, large legal enterprises and licensed stores and horeca companies appeared in the market. Being an integral part of the legal economy, they mixed legal activity and illegal tax evasion.

## Legality and Legitimacy

The evolution of illegal alcohol markets through four delineated stages is backed by continuous reclassifications when products, organizations, and transactions are put into different categories. Two boundaries are continuously contested and changed. The first draws a distinction between legality and illegality, whereas the second distinguishes between legitimacy and illegitimacy.

Starting with the question of the legality of homemade alcohol, the manufacture, sale, and purchase of samogon were outlawed and subject to criminal liability for most of the Soviet period. At the end of the Soviet era, however, criminal liability for samogon production was removed and replaced by administrative liability in 1987. The latter was removed in 2001, when production for personal use was allowed, but sales remained prohibited. Since that time, homemade alcohol has been deemed not illegal if it is consumed at home; it becomes illegal only when it is sold on the market. Remarkably, the consumption of samogon did not grow after the removal of legal constraints, showing that legislative provisions were not a highly influential factor.

The legal definition of counterfeiting was also contested. For example, the illegal use of trademarks was specified in 2002, including not only the application of the protected trademark on products but also the distribution of products with infringed trademarks.

The classification of legal and illegal alcohol sales has changed due to changes in legal definitions of trade premises allowed to sell alcohol. For example, alcohol sales have been prohibited in children's centers, in educational, sports, athletic, and cultural facilities, and on public transport since 2006. Premises have been required to be of a certain size (no less than $50m^2$ in urban areas and $25m^2$ in rural areas) and to remain at a certain distance from educational, medical, sports, athletic, and cultural facilities since 2012. Since 2006, sale of products containing 15 percent pure alcohol and more has not been permitted in non-stationary outlets (kiosks), by individuals, from automobiles, and in other places not properly licensed and set up for such sales. Since 2014, alcoholic beverages of any kind cannot be sold in kiosks. Legal transactions are also reclassified when time restrictions are moved. For example, regular retail sales of all types of alcoholic beverages containing 5 percent pure alcohol and above, including beer, between 11 p.m. and 8 a.m. were outlawed in 2012.

To use a more recent example of product requalification, all beverages with an alcohol content exceeding 0.5 percent, including beer and alcopops, were reclassified as alcoholic beverages and became subject to the same practices of control as other alcoholic beverages in 2012.

Illegality with reference to the letter of the law does not necessarily indicate illegitimacy defined by social perceptions of activities defined as illegal (Van Schendel and Abraham 2005; Dioun in this volume). Shifts from legality to illegality and the reverse can occur overnight due to changes in legislation, whereas legitimacy is gained or lost very slowly due to changes in cultural perceptions. We differentiate between two important interrelated but autonomous reasons for maintaining the legitimacy of illegal activity. The first is ignorance (a lack of understanding), and the second is tolerance (willingness to accept).

(i) People may tolerate the production and sale of homemade alcohol, perceiving it as a survival strategy of the poor and/or as a cultural tradition even if it is banned by law.

(ii) Customers may be ignorant with regard to counterfeiting given a lack of competence to distinguish between original and fake products. They may also tolerate the infringement of intellectual property rights but not tolerate the falsification of alcohol and other food products if they are dangerous to health.

(iii) Customers might not distinguish between legally or illegally manufactured alcohol if they buy beverages of the same taste and quality. They may be ignorant of the falsified tax stamps and tolerate the fraud of the state by tax-evading organizations. At the same time, people may expect that illegal products are sold at a lower retail price and perceive sales at a regular price as an illegitimate deception.

All these propositions, summarized in Table 12.2, could be treated as testable hypotheses for future research.

The boundary between legitimacy and illegitimacy is normally blurred and differs with regard to product categories. The level of legitimacy is also subject to change over time, although this change can be slow to manifest itself. For instance, the production and distribution of counterfeit products that flourished in the 1990s was banned, but tolerated by final consumers and even by

**Table 12.2.** Reasons for the retention of legitimacy of illegal activities in social perception

| Illegal activities | Perceived as illegitimate | Perceived as legitimate | |
|---|---|---|---|
| | | Ignorance | Tolerance |
| Homemade alcohol sale | | | (+) |
| Falsification of alcoholic beverages | (+) | | |
| Infringement of intellectual property rights (illegal use of trademarks) | | (+) | (+) |
| Illegal manufacturing (use of falsified tax stamps) and non-licensed sale of alcohol | | (+) | |
| Deception of customers (selling illegal alcohol at a regular retail price) | (+) | | |
| Defrauding the state (selling illegal alcohol at a lower retail price due to tax evasion) | | | (+) |

major brand owners, whereas violations of the law were largely ignored by enforcement agencies due to their inability to identify counterfeit products (Kotelnikova 2011; Khramova 2012). During the 2000s, however, counterfeiting lost much of its legitimacy. As described in the previous section, more articulate legislation protecting trademarks was adopted in 2002 and 2008. Imported counterfeit products were increasingly seized and confiscated by customs, and arbitration courts increasingly issued verdicts in favor of brand owners. Simultaneously, brand owners became more active in combating fakes and lookalikes and in cooperating with state protection agencies (Radaev et al. 2008, 2010). However, despite positive trends, public opinion remained ambiguous concerning counterfeiting. Final consumers expressed a low level of tolerance with regard to the falsification of food products hazardous to their health, but they perceived deceptions in the area of intellectual property rights as harmless and even favorable, given that counterfeit goods were sold at much lower prices. Moreover, although some consumers are deceived by product originality, others knowingly buy counterfeit goods (Grossman and Shapiro 1988).

## Conclusions

Illegal alcohol markets are diverse and their illegality is based on different dimensions, including the violation of relevant prohibitions, non-compliance with intellectual property rights, or tax-evading behavior. Legal and illegal activities are frequently intertwined. Counterfeit goods can be sold by legally registered firms through recorded sales. Standardized products with their original trademarks can be illegally manufactured by legally registered firms that do not declare these products to the state for the purpose of tax evasion. Legally manufactured goods can be sold through non-licensed trading outlets by retailers bypassing the law.

The composition of illegal alcohol markets in Russia developed through four different stages, following political, legislative, and economic changes. At each stage, some of these markets became dominant, whereas others were unchanged or demonstrated a downward trend. In the first stage of late socialism, homemade alcohol was dominant. In the second stage of liberal reform, it was partially replaced by smuggled and counterfeit alcoholic beverages. In the third stage of state consolidation and economic growth, illegal alcohol markets shrank. Finally, in the fourth stage, positive trends were interrupted, and illegally manufactured alcohol became a dominant form of illegal alcohol market.

Changes in the structure of illegal markets are backed by a continuous requalification of products, organizations, and transactions when the boundaries between legality and illegality are contested and moved. Illegal status can be gained or lost overnight due to legislative changes, whereas boundaries between legitimate and illegitimate activities are blurred and slow-moving. Many illegal activities maintain their legitimacy due to the ignorance or tolerance of enforcement agencies and final consumers.

The obtained data show that illegal alcohol markets tend to grow in periods of exogenous political or economic stressors, whereas in periods of relative economic stability and growth, illegal alcohol markets shrink or remain at the same level.

The size of illegal markets is not very sensitive to the level of legal sanctions against offenders; it is more affected by the effectiveness of state enforcement practices. The size of the market is inversely related to the inclinations of leading market sellers to comply with the law and to protect their property rights but is positively related to the ignorance and tolerance of final consumers towards illegal products.

More restrictive policies normally reduce legal alcohol sales, whereas illegal alcohol markets have their own dynamic that requires further investigations. Like a crooked mirror, illegal markets may provide changeable and erroneous reflections of legal markets. At some stages, illegal markets may move in parallel with legal markets, whereas at other stages, they may move in the opposite direction.

## Acknowledgments

This work was supported by the Program for Basic Research of the National Research University Higher School of Economics.

We thank the participants of a seminar on illegal markets at the Max Planck Institute for the Study of Societies, members of the Laboratory for Studies in Economic Sociology, and in particular Zoya Kotelnikova, Irina Kratko, and Yana Roshchina for their valuable comments on the draft of this chapter.

## References

Andrienko, Yuri, and Alexander Nemtsov. 2005. *Estimation of Individual Demand for Alcohol*. EERC working paper series 05/10. Kyiv: Economics Education and Research Consortium.

Beckert, Jens, and Frank Wehinger. 2013. *In the Shadow: Illegal Markets and Economic Sociology*. MPIfG discussion paper 11/9. Cologne: Max-Planck Institute for the Study of Societies.

Byrnes, Joshua, Shakeshaft Anthony, Petrie Dennis, and Christopher Doran. 2013. "Can Harms Associated with High-Intensity Drinking Be Reduced by Increasing the Price of Alcohol?" *Drug and Alcohol Review* 32: pp. 27–30.

Denisova, Irina. 2010. *Consumption of Alcohol in Russia: Effect on Health and Mortality*. CEFIR/NES Analytical Reports and Papers 31 (in Russian).

Feige, Edgar L. 1990. "Defining and Estimating Underground and Informal Economies: The New Institutional Economics Approach." *World Development* 18(7): pp. 989–1002.

Fligstein, Neil, and Luke Dauter. 2007. "The Sociology of Markets." *Annual Review of Sociology* 33: pp. 105–28.

Fourcade, Marion. 2007. "Theories of Markets, Theories of Society." *American Behavioral Scientist* 50(8): pp. 1015–34.

Gil, Artyom, O. Polikina, N. Koroleva et al. 2009. "Availability and Characteristics of Nonbeverage Alcohols Sold in 17 Russian Cities in 2007." *Alcoholism: Clinical and Experimental Research* 33: pp. 79–85.

Grossman, Gene M., and Carl Shapiro. 1988. "Foreign Counterfeiting of Status Goods." *Quarterly Journal of Economics* 103(1): pp. 79–100.

Haworth, Alan, and Ronald Simpson. 2004. *Moonshine Markets: Issues in Unrecorded Alcohol Beverage Production and Consumption*. New York: Brunner-Routledge.

Khramova, Yekaterina. 2012. "Ambivalence of Consumer Attitudes to Counterfeiting." *Journal of Economic Sociology* 13(4): pp. 116–54 (in Russian).

Kotelnikova, Zoya. 2011. "Goods with Fake Faces: Why Owners of Trademarks Contribute to Counterfeiting." In *Economy in Changing Society: Consumption, Markets, Organizations and Social Policies*, edited by Maria Nawojczyk, pp. 91–113. Cambridge: Cambridge Publishing.

Lachenmeier, Dirk W., Benjamin J. Taylor, and Jürgen Rehm. 2011. "Alcohol under the Radar: Do We Have Policy Options Regarding Unrecorded Alcohol?" *International Journal of Drug Policy* 22: pp. 153–60.

Leon, David A., Vladimir M. Shkolnikov, and Martin McKee. 2009. "Alcohol and Russian Mortality: A Continuing Crisis." *Addiction* 104(10): pp. 1630–36.

Lindström, Martin. 2005. "Social Capital, the Miniaturisation of Community and Consumption of Homemade Liquor and Smuggled Liquor during the Past Year: A Population-Based Study." *European Journal of Public Health* 15(6): pp. 593–600.

Moskalewicz, Jacek, and Jussi Simpura. 2000. "The Supply of Alcoholic Beverages in Transitional Conditions: The Case of Central and Eastern Europe." *Addiction* 95: pp. S505–22.

Nemtsov, Alexandr V. 2002. "Alcohol-Related Human Losses in Russia in the 1980s and 1990s." *Addiction* 97(11): pp. 1413–25.

Nemtsov, Alexandr V. 2009. *Alcoholic History of Russia: The New Times*. Moscow: Librocom (in Russian).

Portes, Alejandro. 2010. *Economic Sociology: A Systematic Inquiry*. Princeton, NJ: Princeton University Press.

Puzyrev, Denis. 2014. "Russians Spent Billions of Rubles on Illegal Whiskey." *RBC Daily* 20 (in Russian).

Radaev, Vadim. 2005. "Informal Institutional Arrangements and Tax Evasion in the Russian Economy." In *Networks, Trust and Social Capital: Theoretical and Empirical Investigations from Europe*, edited by Sokratis Koniordos, pp. 189–203. Aldershot: Ashgate.

Radaev, Vadim. 2016. "Divergent Drinking Patterns and Factors Affecting Homemade Alcohol Consumption (The Case of Russia)." *International Journal of Drug Policy* 34: pp. 88–95.

Radaev, Vadim, Svetlana Barsukova, and Zoya Kotelnikova. 2008. "Markets for Counterfeit Goods in Russia." *Analytics of Laboratory for Studies in Economic Sociology* 2. Moscow: National Research University Higher School of Economics (in Russian).

Radaev, Vadim, Svetlana Barsukova, Zoya Kotelnikova, and Alexandr Kurakin. 2010. "Major Trends in the Markets for Counterfeit Goods and an Impact of the New Customs Union." *Analytics of Laboratory for Studies in Economic Sociology* 7. Moscow: National Research University Higher School of Economics (in Russian).

Rehm, Jürgen, Fotis Kanteres, and Dirk W. Lachenmeier. 2010. "Unrecorded Consumption, Quality of Alcohol and Health Consequences." *Drug and Alcohol Review* 29: pp. 426–36.

Rehm, Jürgen, S. Kailasapillai, E. Larsen et al. 2014. "A Systematic Review of the Epidemiology of Unrecorded Alcohol Consumption and the Chemical Composition of Unrecorded Alcohol." *Addiction* 109: pp. 880–93.

Rogers, Douglas. 2005. "Moonshine, Money, and the Politics of Liquidity in Rural Russia." *American Ethnologist* 32(1): pp. 63–81.

Roshchina, Yana. 2013. *To Drink or Not to Drink: The Microeconomic Analysis of Alcohol Consumption in Russia in 2006–2010*. Working paper WP BRP 20/SOC/2013. Moscow: National Research University Higher School of Economics.

Rutter, Jason, and Jo Bryce. 2008. "The Consumption of Counterfeit Goods: 'Here Be Pirates?'" *Sociology* 42(6): pp. 1146–64.

Skog, Ole Jorgen. 1986. "The Long Waves of Alcohol Consumption: A Social Network Perspective on Cultural Change." *Social Networks* 8: pp. 1–32.

Solodun, Yuriy V., Yulia B. Monakhova, Thomas Kuballa et al. 2011. "Unrecorded Alcohol Consumption in Russia: Toxic Denaturants and Disinfectants Pose Additional Risks." *Interdisciplinary Toxicology* 4(4): pp. 198–205.

Thamarangsi, Thaksaphon. 2013. "Unrecorded Alcohol: Significant Neglected Challenges." *Addiction* 108: pp. 2048–50.

Van Schendel, Willem, and Itty Abraham. 2005. *Illicit Flows and Criminal Things: States, Borders, and the Other Side of Globalization*. Bloomington: Indiana University Press.

Vroublevsky, Andrei, and Judith Harwin. 1998. "Russia." In *Alcohol and Emerging Markets: Patterns, Problems, and Responses*, edited by Marcus Grant, pp. 203–22. Philadelphia, PA: Brunner and Mazel.

Wagenaar, Alexander C., Matthew J. Salois, and Kelli A. Komro. 2009. "Effects of Beverage Alcohol Price and Tax Levels on Drinking: A Meta-Analysis of 1003 Estimates from 112 Studies." *Addiction* 104: pp. 179–90.

World Health Organization. 2014. *Global Status Report On Alcohol and Health*. Geneva: World Health Organization.

Zaigraev, Grigory. 2004. "The Russian Model of Noncommercial Alcohol Consumption." In *Moonshine Markets: Issues in Unrecorded Alcohol Beverage Production and Consumption*, edited by Alan Haworth and Ronald Simpson, pp. 29–38. New York: Brunner-Routledge.

# Part V
# Illegal Practices in Legal Markets

# 13

# The Supply of Doping Products and the Relevance of Market-Based Perspectives

## Implications of Recent Research in Italy

*Letizia Paoli and Victoria A. Greenfield*

### Introduction

This chapter is concerned with the nature of the supply of doping products and the relevance of market-based concepts, with specific reference to conditions in Italy. We define doping products as a combination of doping substances and doping methods. Athletes use doping substances—ranging from anabolic steroids to stimulants and from erythropoietin to growth hormones—to enhance their performance or evade detection, a practice referred to as "doping" and prohibited under sporting rules since the 1960s (for example, Waddington and Smith 2009).[1] Some of these substances are also used by non-competitive sportspeople for broader lifestyle or psychoactive purposes, such as growing muscle, reducing fat, or boosting aggressiveness, and are also known as performance- and image-enhancing drugs (for example, Graham et al. 2009). Doping products also include performance-enhancing methods, such as blood transfusions. The trade and distribution of doping products is subject to state restrictions and prohibitions, at least in elite sport, in most European countries, the United States, and elsewhere (Houlihan and Garcia 2012).

In recent years, a number of high-level international sports officials have spoken out on the growing presence of the underworld in sport.[2] For example,

[1] For a formal definition of doping, see WADA 2015.
[2] Hoberman (2012: 2–3) reports several quotations.

David Howman, the former Director General of the World Anti-Doping Agency (WADA), has denounced "the ever-increasing advance of the underworld into sport," adding that "the same people who were making a lot of money out of the trafficking of prohibited substances were also making money out of illegal betting and general corruption around the fringes of sport" (WADA 2010). Operations against the trade in steroids carried out by the US Drug Enforcement Administration (US DEA 2007) and other law-enforcement agencies (for example, Bundeskriminalamt 2011) have also been well publicized.

Notwithstanding the pronouncements of criminality and enforcement activity, relatively little is known about the supply of doping products.[3] Only a small number of studies has focused on suppliers or framed doping in market-based terms (for example, Koert and van Kleij 1998; Donati 2007; Kraska et al. 2010; Fincoeur and Paoli 2014; Paoli and Donati 2014; Lowther 2015) and criminology, as a discipline, has only recently "discovered" the topic of doping (Paoli 2012).

Against this backdrop, we analyze the supply of doping products by revisiting and building on the central findings of an empirical study of supply and demand in Italy (Paoli and Donati 2014) and argue, first, that supply and demand come together to form a "market"; second, that this market should be conceptualized as "quasi-illegal"; and third, that this conceptualization can help inform policymaking, not just in Italy, but more broadly, and might have a bearing on research in criminology and sociology. We endorse the term "market" because doping substances, if not methods, are regularly produced and exchanged—that is, distributed through complex chains and sold to end users—under competitive conditions.[4] The market can be described as "quasi-illegal" because an exchange or transaction involving a doping product can be fully legal, fully illegal, partly legal and illegal, or open to question and challenge, depending on the context, including the location of the event or characteristics of the final users. At one end of the spectrum, the distribution and use of doping products are criminalized; at the other end, some of the same products are prescribed, sold, and used for legitimate, even life-saving purposes. In-between, the legal status of products and transactions can be unclear and variable.

[3] By contrast, the use of doping products has been well researched and reveals a substantial demand in the Western world. Several studies have attempted to estimate the prevalence of the use of doping substances among specific types of users, such as elite athletes (Striegel et al. 2010), and at the national level (Paoli and Donati 2014). McCabe et al. (2007), Kokkevi et al. (2008), and others have conducted epidemiological studies and Pope et al. (2000), Hoberman (2005), Waddington and Smith (2009), and others have considered reasons for use.

[4] See Beckert and Wehinger (2013) for a discussion of the market concept that we have brought to this analysis. This and other market concepts do not require "perfect" competition; indeed, a market can be dominated by a supplier or purchaser.

Our recognition of the quasi-illegality or the often unclear, variable, and thus sometimes disputable legal status of exchanges involving doping products also suggests a need for a more thorough reflection on the concept of "illegal markets" in criminology and a better understanding of market players' shifting positions vis-à-vis legal status.

The chapter is structured as follows: the first section describes the research design and data collection; then the main characteristics of the suppliers of doping products in Italy are identified and a typology developed based on their profession or occupation; this is followed by an analysis of the distribution chains of doping products and the relationships suppliers build with each other and with users, including their use of violence and corruption; the next section singles out a unique characteristic of the elite segment of the market that is typical of the recent past, namely, the once-common protection—and, occasionally, direct involvement—of civil servants and government representatives, active in national sports bodies; this analysis is then used to conceptualize the doping market as a quasi-illegal market; the final section briefly discusses the policy and research implications of this conceptualization.

## Research Design and Data Collection

In this chapter, we rely on the same sources of data that Paoli and Donati (2014) analyzed for the completion of their study *The Sport Doping Market: Understanding Supply and Demand, and the Challenges of Their Control*, much of which was collected in close collaboration with the Carabinieri Command for Health Protection. This unit is still known—and will be referred to here—by the acronym NAS from its original name, Nuclei Anti-Sofisticazione.

The first source is the "NAS Investigations Database," which includes summary data for the eighty major anti-doping investigations conducted by NAS between 1999 and 2009. These investigations represent the vast majority of the anti-doping criminal investigations and the related criminal proceedings initiated in Italy.

The second source is a set of official documents related to forty-six different criminal investigations, thirty-six of which were carried out by NAS and were thus included in the NAS Investigation Database and ten of which were conducted by other police forces and were thus new. In some cases, the documents were extensive summaries of investigations written by NAS officers and submitted to the Prosecutor's Office; in other cases, they were charges pressed by the prosecutors, arrest warrants issued by the judges for preliminary investigations, or first-, second-, or third-degree verdicts. We refer to these cases generically as "investigations" (from NAS's perspective) or "proceedings" (from a judicial perspective) or with the specific name of the document (for example, verdict, charges).

The third source is a set of interviews with twenty-six NAS officers, seven prosecutors, one policymaker, and one other expert on anti-doping testing.[5]

Paoli and Donati also worked with various other published and unpublished materials. Among the former, they examined the annual reports of Italy's main anti-doping commission (for example, Ministero della Salute and Istituto Superiore di Sanità 2012) and the seizure statistics of the Italian customs agency and tax police. Lastly, they conducted an extensive review of the three main Italian news agencies'—*Ansa*, *Agi*, and *Adnkronos*—doping-related media reports for the period January 1998 through February 2012.

We note that one challenge facing research on doping-related matters in Italy is that many activities are alleged but, at least as a matter of process, few allegations lead to convictions. In a number of cases, for example, we found that delays in proceedings triggered the statute of limitations, so that charges were dismissed irrespective of the merits of the evidence, be it direct or circumstantial. On that basis, we can paint only a highly suggestive picture of the involvement of individuals and institutions in the supply of doping products, but cannot claim to have proven or disproven their involvement. To strengthen our conclusions, we follow Paoli and Donati (2014) and triangulate findings from the different sources, including, as noted, an extensive media analysis.

## A Typology of the Suppliers of Doping Products

In this section we outline the general characteristics of suppliers on the basis of the foregoing sources and use the analysis to develop a typology of suppliers.

The illegal suppliers of doping products in Italy appear to be mostly male, Italian citizens and rarely appear to have criminal records. With few exceptions, such as the hijackers who steal doping substances from trucks, most suppliers also appear to have a legitimate profession or occupation (see Table 13.1).

On the basis of the most relevant professional and occupational delineations and rankings in the NAS Investigations Database, as shown in Table 13.1, and all the criminal proceedings, we, like Paoli and Donati (2014), have identified ten main types of illegal suppliers of doping products in Italy and grouped them in five overarching categories (see Table 13.2).

[5] Paoli and Donati (2014) refer to these interviews with the following codes: Int-NAS-1 to 26 for the NAS officers, Int-Proc-1 to 7 for the prosecutors, and Int-Oth-1 and 2 for the two others. We use the same codes here.

**Table 13.1.** Leading professions or occupations of suspects (N = 744, 1999–2011)

| Profession | Number of suspects reported | Other suspects reported, number unspecified |
|---|---|---|
| Gym owners or managers and body-building instructors | 158 | Yes[a] |
| Veterinary physicians, breeders, horse drivers | 140 | Yes[b] |
| Owners or managers of dietary supplement shops | 64 | No |
| Pharmacists | 20 | Yes[c] |
| Physicians | 17 | Yes[d] |
| Staff members of cycling teams | 12 | Yes[e] |
| Sports federation officials | 10 | No |
| Law-enforcement and military staff | 10 | No |
| Hospital employees | 10 | No |
| Employees and salesmen of (para-)pharmaceutical companies | 6 | Yes[f] |
| Staff of private security companies | 2 | No |

*Notes*: *a* in ten other investigations; *b* in another investigation; *c* in five other investigations; *d* in three other investigations; *e* in two other investigations; *f* in one other investigation. If we were to consider team and federation affiliates as a single "organized sports" category, as we do in the "The Role of National Sports Bodies" section, they would rank ahead of pharmacists and physicians.

*Source*: adapted from Paoli and Donati (2014), drawing data from reports in the NAS Investigations Database.

## *Gym*

"Gym" consists of "gym owners or managers and body-building instructors," and "owners or managers of dietary supplement shops." These individuals usually function as retailers, selling doping products to gym patrons. Some of these individuals are also wholesalers, selling to retailers, who are often other gym managers, instructors, or body builders. The manager of a gym in Forlì, for example, supplied anabolic steroids and other drugs to visitors to his gym and the managers of at least four other gyms (Tr-FO 2009: 16–19).

On a larger scale, the diary of a former gym owner, the so-called "'big father' of national and international trafficking in anabolic steroids" (NAS Bologna 2000: 233), referenced seven Italian pharmaceutical companies, two pharmacies, and a private hospital, as likely sources, and revealed contacts with pharmaceutical companies across Europe and in Latin America and with numerous international couriers. In the late 1990s, he supplied two other substantial suppliers and had direct contact with at least twenty-seven other gyms throughout Italy (NAS Bologna 2000: 243–4 and 267–72). Concerning the longevity and magnitude of his involvement, he was arrested in 2011 in Ancona for the illegal import of doping products, valued at over 1 million euros, which had been manufactured in clandestine laboratories in Spain, the Netherlands, and the United Kingdom (*Cronache maceratesi* 2011).

**Table 13.2.** Types of suppliers of doping products in Italy

| Category | Type |
|---|---|
| Gym | Gym owners or managers and body-building instructors; owners or managers of dietary supplement shops |
| Health care | Pharmacists<br>Physicians<br>Hospital employees<br>Employees, sale representatives of (para-)pharmaceutical companies |
| Organized sports world (human) | Staff members of sports teams; staff members of sports federations |
| Horseracing | Veterinary physicians, breeders, jockeys, and drivers |
| (Semi-)professional sportspeople | Elite athletes and their family members<br>Hard-core body builders, including law-enforcement, military, and private security company staff and their family members |
| Other | People with no distinctive profession or occupation |

*Source*: adapted from Paoli and Donati (2014), drawing data from reports in the NAS Investigations Database, criminal proceedings, and media sources

### *Health Care*

"Health care" consists of pharmacists, physicians, hospital employees, and employees or sale representatives of pharmaceutical and para-pharmaceutical companies.

Pharmacists usually function as retailers of doping products, but also occasionally as producers of doping substances (for example, Tr-BO 2004) and even more rarely as wholesalers (NAS Brescia 2011; Int-Pro-4; Ryan 2011). They may also be involved in the sale of performance-enhancing drugs without being aware of the purchasers' illegal intentions. Most frequently, these "unwitting" pharmacists sell doping drugs on the basis of either false or stolen prescriptions or prescriptions written by accommodating or corrupt physicians (for example, Tr-RV 2004: 122, Int-NAS-17 and 19).

Several NAS investigations point to the role of physicians in the supply of doping products, though few criminal proceedings ended with convictions. Here, we summarize the story of Professor Franceso Conconi, both as a high-profile example of a physician's alleged involvement with doping products and as a means of exploring the chronology (see Figure 13.1) of doping prohibitions in sports rules and Italian law.[6]

Legal records and other official documents suggest, but without associated convictions, that Conconi began providing doping products to Italian elite athletes, primarily in track and field, cycling, swimming, pentathlon, rowing,

[6] Professor Francesco Conconi has been a professor of biochemistry at the University of Ferrara since 1967 and is the current head of its Centro di Studi Biomedici applicati allo Sport. See his webpage at <http://docente.unife.it/francesco.conconi/curr>.

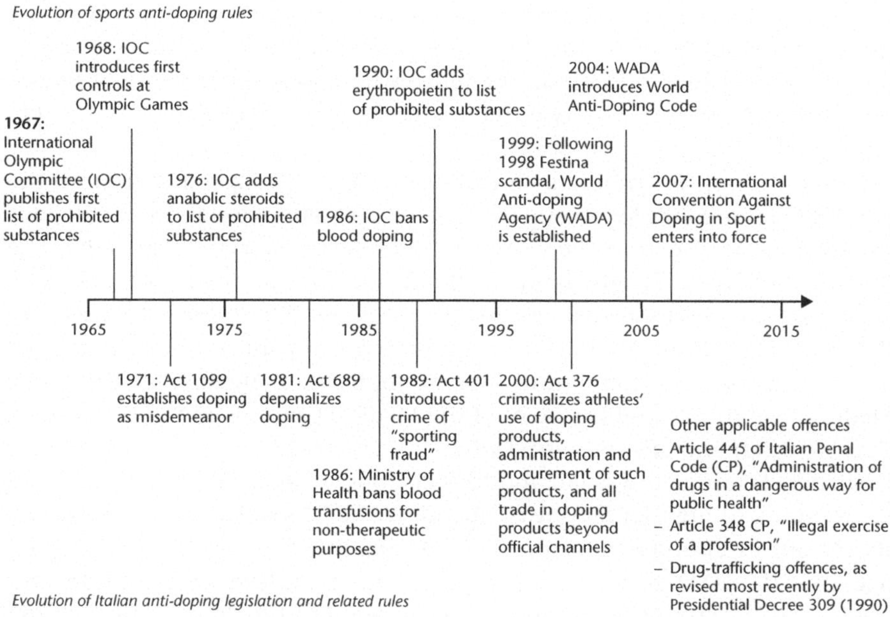


**Figure 13.1.** Chronology of doping prohibitions

and ski sports, with the tacit support of the Italian Olympic Committee (CONI; Tr-FE 2003; Pr-FE 2000), in the late 1970s.

Such activities would have violated the prohibitions and controls that the international community had introduced about a decade earlier (Gleaves and Hunt 2015) and might have violated Italian law. With Act 1099 of 1971, athletes' use of doping substances and the administration of such substances to athletes were criminalized, albeit as a misdemeanor, not a felony. These offences were depenalized in 1981 and a new specific bill on doping was not adopted until 2000 (Arioli and Bellini 2005). In the interim, other provisions of Italy's penal code and special statutes might have been applicable. Of particular relevance, we cite "administration of drugs in a dangerous way for public health" (Article 445 of the Italian Penal Code, hereafter CP) and "sporting fraud," which was introduced with Act 401 of 1989. Over time, the latter has been used to prosecute crimes related to doping, albeit in a partially controversial manner (see Paoli and Donati 2014: 153–4).

Conconi eventually faced charges in a trial conducted in 2002–3 and was named in a related proceeding in 2000, but neither event resulted in a conviction. In the trial, Conconi was charged with sporting fraud (Tr-FE 2003) and, in the proceeding, Conconi and three high-ranking CONI officials were charged with criminal association for the purpose of distributing drugs in a manner dangerous to public health (article 445 CP) (Pr-FE 2000). In both instances, however, the statute of limitations required dismissal. Whether these cases would have resulted in convictions had they continued is, obviously, unknowable. In the trial, the judge who applied the statute of limitations stressed "the seriousness and convergence of all the evidence" until 1995 (Tr-FE 2003: 46).

The records of the Tribunale di Ferrara (Tr-FE 2003) suggest that, until the late 1980s, Conconi's involvement centered on "blood doping" or analogous transfusions and that, in the early 1990s, he began working with EPO. The Italian Ministry of Health banned blood transfusions for non-therapeutic purposes in early 1986 (Donati 2012: 46–8); the IOC followed closely on that action in the same year. During this period, Conconi was well entrenched in the international community, for example, as a member of the IOC's Medical Committee and President of the Medical Commission of the Unione Cycliste Internationale (see also, Donati 2012: 129–77).

Michele Ferrari, a physician and former Conconi associate who specialized in attending to high-level cyclists, including the US cyclist Lance Armstrong, stands out as another protagonist. As documented in the US Anti-Doping Agency's (USADA) decision and reported by Hamilton in Hamilton and Coyle (2012), Ferrari was the alleged mastermind of the doping and training programs followed by Lance Armstrong, who was stripped of his seven Tour de France titles for doping, and some of his team colleagues: "Ferrari was our trainer," Hamilton recalls, "our doctor, our god... Lance mentioned Ferrari constantly, almost annoyingly so. Michele says we should do this. Michele says we should do that" (Hamilton and Coyle 2012: 102).

Several investigations and related proceedings also document the involvement of hospital, health clinic, and nursing home employees in the supply of doping products. Low-level health-care employees may engage in theft, whereas private health clinics may provide illegal doping methods to elite cyclists (for example, Pacifici and Donati 2011: 45).

Employees and sales representatives of pharmaceutical and dietary supplement companies, who might work independently or on behalf of a company, can also play a part in the supply of doping products. Among such individuals, employees of drug distributors have been implicated in the diversion of legitimate drugs with potential doping effects from the storehouses or trucks of their companies; their involvement occurs through either suspicious disappearances or thefts (Int-NAS-9 and 26).

### *Organized Sports World (Human)*

The "organized sports world" consists of sports teams and federations.

The large-scale raids conducted by the NAS branch offices at the Giro d'Italia, which is a major annual cycling event, and in other circumstances, and the considerable amount of drugs seized in some of these raids, strongly suggest that cycling team staff members were not only aware and tolerant of the illegal doping practices of their athletes but were also actively involved in such practices (for example, Int-NAS-16, NAS Firenze 2002). These findings also seem to be applicable to other countries, as shown by the USADA's (2012) investigations of Lance Armstrong and his US team, numerous doping scandals involving teams from different countries (for example, Dopingkommission 2009), and recent academic research (for example, Fincoeur and Paoli 2014).

Staff members of teams outside cycling have also been implicated. An investigation of the Turin Judicial Police and Prosecutor's Office found evidence of widespread illegal doping practices at the football club Juventus Turin from 1994 to 1998, years in which the team won three Italian Championships, the Champions League, the Intercontinental Cup, and Italy's Cup. Italy's Supreme Court (Corte Suprema di Cassazione 2007) concluded that the two main defendants, who were the manager and chief sports physician of the team, had committed sporting fraud by purchasing and administering illegal performance-enhancing substances, such as corticosteroids, but the statute of limitations precluded sentencing (see also Kistner 2015).

The line between the staff members of sports teams and the officials of sports federations is sometimes thin, but we believe the distinction is analytically important because the latter belong to sports ruling bodies. Several proceedings based on NAS investigations and other sources (for example, Donati 1989, 2012) report the involvement of sports federation officials in doping, both as direct suppliers and as "protectors"(for the latter, see the section below on the role of national sports bodies). The role of suppliers, for example, is well documented in the detailed diaries of Daniele Faraggiana, which became public in 1986. Faraggiana was then a sports physician on the payroll of both Italy's Athletic and Weightlifting Federations. In his diaries, he listed the names of all the athletes he doped (among them, a 1984 Olympic champion), the substances administered, the respective dosages, the negative effects on the athletes' health, and each athlete's performance. Faraggiana also listed the transfers of doping substances to coaches and other physicians, including Professor Conconi, with details about the types and quantities and the dates of each transfer (Donati 1989: 78).

### *Horseracing*

"Horseracing" includes breeders, veterinarians, and drivers. We combine these three types of suppliers because the NAS Investigations Database and other sources do not provide specific information on each. Several investigations, both in southern and northern Italy, have shown that numerous veterinary physicians, breeders, jockeys, and drivers exchanged doping products and administered them to horses to "fix" the results of official competitions and win bets (for example, Fazzo and Mensurati 2002; *Repubblica* 2008).

### *(Semi-)Professional Sportspeople*

"(Semi-)professional sportspeople" consists of elite athletes and hard-core body builders, including law-enforcement, military, and private security company staff, and, in some instances, their family members. NAS investigations, other criminal proceedings, and media reports indicate that some elite athletes and hard-core body builders do not just use doping products to improve their own performance but they or their closest family members also engage in the import and distribution of doping substances. Some of these individuals purchase doping products for their own consumption, but then sell additional amounts, to finance their consumption or supplement their incomes.

Given frequent trips abroad, elite athletes may be ideally positioned to import doping substances, especially from countries, regions, or localities with less-restrictive regulations or relatively lax enforcement. Exploiting differences in national, regional, or local regulations and enforcement, they also may be able to buy doping products legally or without detection or risk of penalty.

### *Other Illegal Suppliers*

The final category of illegal suppliers consists of persons who do not fit into any of the preceding categories. Most of them have a legitimate profession or occupation, ranging from salesman to student, but the NAS database does not enable quantification. In this residual category, we also find a few suppliers who are active in thoroughly illegal segments of the market for doping products, for example, as producers of doping substances in clandestine laboratories, thieves, truck hijackers, or operators of specialized websites. To illustrate with a particular case, an unemployed former nurse produced anabolic steroids and marketed them through a website on behalf of an international criminal organization (Int-NAS-9).

## Distribution Chains and Market Relationships

After classifying the suppliers of doping products, we identify the sources and distribution levels of the different doping products, distinguishing between doping substances and methods and among different doping substances. This exercise allows us to assess whether a "market" exists for either doping substances or methods.

*Doping Substances*

The existence of multiple and competing distribution chains, connecting producers and end users, is highly suggestive of market-like activity, even if money does not change hands in every final transaction (for example, when team employees are suppliers).

The distribution chains differ by length, depending on the substances and quantities traded and the degree of entrepreneurship of the end users, and by legal status, depending partly on some of the same factors (see Figure 13.2).

The legal status of the particular exchanges and transactions along a distribution chain might also vary by context. Some substances, especially steroids, are produced exclusively for doping purposes in pharmacies or in illegal laboratories, in Italy or abroad. A large but imprecisely known share of the doping substances sold in Italy appears to have been produced by legitimate drug manufacturers located in Italy or abroad and to have been diverted at some stage from the legal distribution chain. As Italian anti-doping investigations indicate, the diversion can take place at different levels of the distribution chain. Employees or managers of the Italian or foreign drug manufacturers or their distributors may decide to divert some of the legal production to the illegal market. Drugs might also be stolen from the storehouses or trucks of drug distributors or from hospitals or, more rarely, pharmacies by staff members or unaffiliated thieves in Italy and abroad. Italian and foreign pharmacists also might sell doping products intentionally, but still be unaware of the non-therapeutic purposes for which some of their customers buy and then sell the products, either on the basis of a prescription written by a corrupt physician or of a false or stolen prescription. In some non-Italian countries, pharmacists may be allowed, under domestic laws, to sell doping products, the sale and use of which are restricted in Italy.

Given the variety of doping products available in the market and the fact that, within each class of products several products can be functionally equivalent, users can engage with a variety of retailers, each representing the final link of an alternative distribution chain characterized by different combinations of legal statuses. Moreover, the availability of doping products has increased tremendously with the spread of websites selling steroids and other pharmaceuticals in an unregulated space. Internet sales have made it possible for users in Italy—and elsewhere—to bypass domestic distribution chains by ordering doping products online and having them delivered by mail at home.

Unlike illegal drug traffickers or dealers, the majority of the suppliers of doping products can hide their illegal transactions and their relationships with their "doping partners"—their own suppliers, collaborators, and customers or patients—behind the legitimate roles they play in their businesses, organizations, or professions. The embeddedness of doping-related

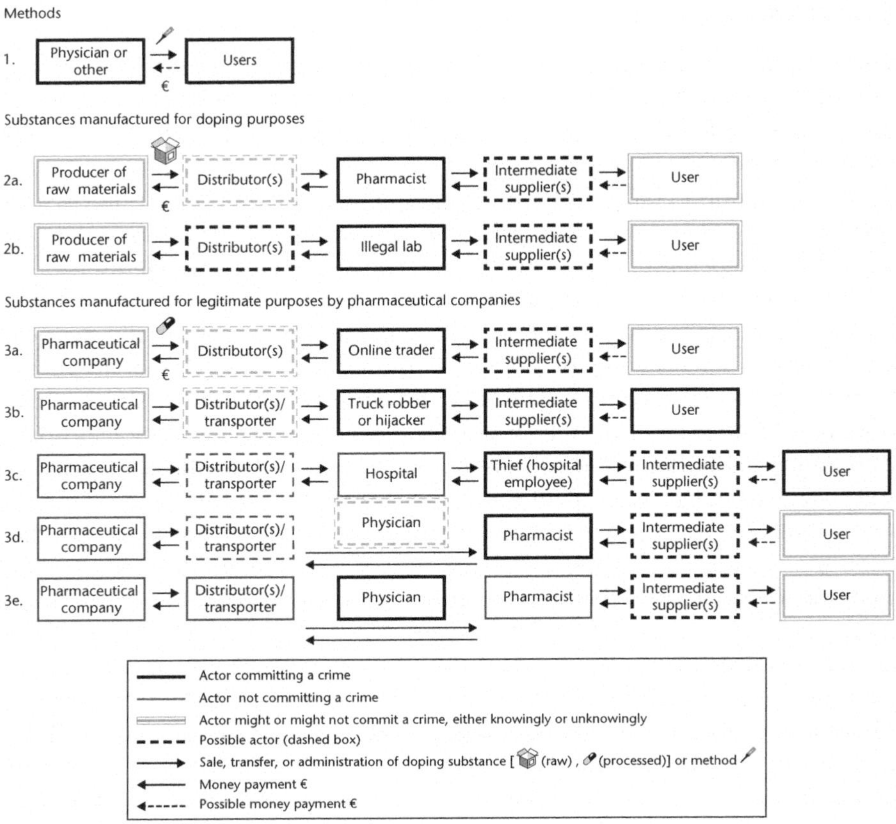


**Figure 13.2.** Illustrative distribution chains for doping products and methods

supply-side activities in legitimate professions, roles, and institutions often makes the development of separate illegal enterprises to run these activities unnecessary. That embeddedness is also suggestive of white-collar crime (Sutherland 1983), and the related and partially overlapping concepts of occupational, corporate (Clinard and Quinney 1973), and organizational crime (Schrager and Short 1978): these range from employees' thefts and other low-level crimes to high-level crimes and violations on behalf of or against organizations.

However, some illegal suppliers cannot find a professional cover to hide the production, import (smuggling), and/or wholesale distribution of doping products outside the regular channels or the product diversion from these channels. At the higher levels of the market—that is, closer to the point of production—and especially for steroids, illegal enterprises thus sometimes look similar to those operating in illegal drug markets (for example, Reuter 1985 and Pearson and Hobbs 2001).

The evidence does not suggest a major role for organized crime, as most typically construed, in the supply of doping products in Italy. The analysis of the criminal proceedings and the expert interviews indicate a very limited involvement of southern Italian mafia groups in the production and distribution of doping products in Italy. Thus far in this analysis, we can trace only one specific type of supplier back to southern Italian mafia-type organized crime groups: the hijackers who steal doping substances from trucks and are often associated with Neapolitan Camorra groups. Members of some Camorra groups also play an important role in fixing horse races, which can be achieved by doping horses (Int-NAS-26 and Marino 2001). These practices lend narrow support to WADA's assessment that the same underworld people who trade in doping substances also undermine the integrity of sport through illegal betting.

The evidence on violence and fraud in the supply of doping products suggests little of the former and an abundance of the latter. Reflecting the white-collar background of many or most suppliers, the suppliers of doping products in Italy, other than truck hijackers, are rarely reported to use physical violence. In contrast, fraud by means of counterfeiting appears to occur often, particularly in the non-elite segment of the market (Di Giorgio 2011), but we have no data with which to estimate the relative shares of counterfeited drugs, on the one hand, and diverted or stolen drugs, on the other.

The evidence on corruption is mixed, depending partly on how one defines corruption. We found almost no evidence of bribery but found ample evidence of "abuse of public or private office," albeit not necessarily "for personal gain" (OECD 2008: 22). Particularly in elite sports, different types of suppliers—for example, physicians, pharmacists, coaches, and sports federation officials—appear to abuse their positions and the athletes' and the latter's parents' trust by prescribing, selling, or administering the athletes' doping products and convincing them of the necessity and harmlessness of doping products (see also the next section). However, these abuses typically do not occur "for personal gain"—or at least not fully so—but in the name of a misconceived public or team good.

### *Doping Methods*

We found little or no evidence of a market for doping methods. Doping methods are administered on an ad hoc basis to elite athletes by a limited number of physicians and private clinics using legitimate and often banal medical instruments. Whereas there is a legitimate market for such instruments entailing multiple and competing distribution chains, there are no regular exchanges for doping methods. However, final users can, to a large extent, functionally substitute the most frequent doping method—blood transfusion—with doping substances, specifically erythropoietin.

## The Role of National Sports Bodies

The once-common "protection" provided by officials and staff members of sports authorities, such as CONI, and key sports federations is a startling attribute of the elite segment of Italy's market for doping products (Paoli and Donati 2014). As described above, some officials and staff members have served as outright suppliers, but perhaps as importantly, some have passively or actively provided cover to those engaging in doping. We might point, for example, to the aforementioned criminal proceedings against Conconi and CONI officials who appear to have served as protectors—or more—over a period of at least a decade, spanning the 1980s. The statute of limitations necessitated the closure of the case in October 2000,[7] but the Prosecutor argued that Conconi had set up a "criminal organization" (Article 416 CP; Pr-FE 2000: 42) with three CONI senior officials, including two CONI presidents. In the absence of a verdict, we cannot claim proof of individual or institutional involvement, but the Prosecutor's depictions suggest high-ranking participation to a degree plausibly consistent with institutional complicity.

In recent years, sports federations' lack of collaboration with law-enforcement agencies and their record on testing suggest a lack of interest in a thorough fight against doping (Paoli and Donati 2014: 37, 116–19; CONI 2012).

Past and ongoing scandals involving top athletes, national sports federations, and anti-doping agencies in other countries—such as Finland (Doping Enquiry Taskforce 2001; Hahn and Häyrinen 2008), Austria (IOC 2007), the former East Germany (Berendonk 1992; Spitzer 2013), West Germany (Spitzer et al. 2013), and Russia (Independent Commission 2015) as well as in international federations such the UCI (Cycling Independent Reform Commission 2015) and the International Association of Athletics Federations (IAAF, Independent Commission 2015)—raise the suspicion that other governments and sports bodies have behaved similarly over the years.

## A Quasi-Illegal Market

The previous analysis leads us to conceptualize the doping market as "quasi-illegal." Others have also applied the term to this and related environments (see, for example, Lowther 2015; Hawken et al. 2013; and *Japan Times* 2015) and we argue that the term is fitting and deserves closer inspection.

We stress that the legal status of doping products suffers from the ambiguity of contextual specificity; that is, in some contexts, the products—including

[7] See the related discussion in the section "A Typology of the Suppliers of Doping Products" in this chapter.

their supply—are legal and in others they are not. In that way they are more like other diverted or stolen pharmaceutical products, and less like cocaine or heroin. By and large, society treats the latter as inherently illegal: most countries prohibit the trafficking and possession of cocaine and heroin for non-personal use because, with few exceptions, these drugs have been deemed dangerous to public health and lacking therapeutic value. Instead, most doping products are also legitimate, well-established pharmaceutical products.

Moreover, the legal status of many supply-side doping-related activities varies along the distribution chain and by location.

A drug may begin its "life" as a legal product at one end of the supply chain and conclude its "life" as an illegal product at the other (see Figure 13.2). Many drugs that are used illegally as doping products are produced by legitimate pharmaceutical companies that might not meet the regulatory requirements of developed Western countries but can operate lawfully in their own countries.

Given the lack of harmonization of the relevant criminal law legislation within the EU let alone across more disparate borders, the same supply activities can or are likely to have different legal statuses in different countries. Body builders in Germany can legally obtain anabolic steroids through regular physicians and pharmacies (Striegel et al. 2006), whereas physicians and pharmacists cannot legally prescribe or sell the same drugs to body builders in Italy. In a comparative perspective it is also necessary to ascertain the effective degree of enforcement of the existing regulations and prohibitions.[8] Numerous observers (for example, Hoberman 2011: 100) complain that the existing sports rules and criminal law provisions have not always been implemented effectively.

Even within the same country, some doping products, with very restricted therapeutic uses, may be "more" illegal—at least from the point of view of criminal justice rather than sports authorities—than others. Nandrolone is a good case in point. In 2010, the Italian Ministry of Health added nandrolone, an anabolic steroid, to the list of psychoactive substances to be controlled under Italian drug law (DPR 309/1990 and later amendments), sharply reducing the possibility of legal transactions and allowing a whole range of special investigation methods (for example, controlled delivery) that Italy's anti-doping act does not allow (Ministero della Salute 2010).

Under Italian law, many actors frequently involved in the supply of doping products—such as physicians or pharmacists—may or may not commit a crime depending on the therapeutic needs of their customers and clients. The legality or illegality of their decisions and actions depends partly

[8] For the concept of "effective illegality," see Paoli et al. (2009).

on whether their customers and patients are athletes consuming certain products "in order to improve [their] competitive performance" (Article 9 of Act No. 376/2000). At one extreme, prescribing or materially supplying a performance-enhancing product to an athlete who is taking part in competition always constitutes a crime; at the other extreme, supplying the same product to a patient, including an athlete, who needs it for therapeutic reasons never constitutes a crime. Between these extremes resides an ambiguous continuum along which legality or illegality might depend on the relevance of other offenses and the medical assessments of attending physicians. As became apparent in our overview of the cases involving Conconi and the more systematic analysis of NAS investigations and related criminal proceedings conducted elsewhere (Paoli and Donati 2014: 179–87), the prosecution of doping-related activities can occur under a variety of statutes and codes, not all of which are specific to doping.

In fully illegal markets, both parties in a transaction are usually aware of the illegal nature of the exchange, even if, as might occur in Italy, the drug user does not necessarily commit a criminal offense if buying drugs solely for personal consumption. In the case of doping, one of the parties to a transaction involving doping products may be ignorant of any illegality or rule breaking, reflecting the embeddedness of doping exchanges in legitimate social networks and professional activities. This is, for example, the case for a pharmacist who sells a doping product on the basis of a fraudulent or stolen prescription.

As a result of the unclear, variable, and sometimes disputable illegality of many doping transactions, most of the suppliers of doping products, including retailers, differ greatly from the stereotypes of members of criminal organizations or enterprises or undocumented migrants selling wholly illegal drugs on the street.

The quasi-illegality of many doping exchanges also reduces the risks to suppliers and, as a consequence, their compensation. As only a single illegal lab has been seized in Italy, we have no direct data to assess the profits of the producers of doping substances, but we have a small amount of data on revenues of importers, collected before the rise of internet-based commerce. Working as consultants in a criminal investigation, Donati and Magrì (2001) estimated that two of the largest-scale suppliers of doping substances among gym patrons each raised about 2 billion lire (approximately 1 million euros) annually at the turn of the twenty-first century. At year-2000 prices (UNODCCP 2001: 213), the same sum could be generated with the sale of less than 30 kilograms of cocaine. However, a few individuals in Italy might be able to draw considerable incomes from doping-related activities. The physicians who treat super-elite athletes with performance-enhancing products, such as Michele Ferrari, come to mind (Int-Pro-3; Int-NAS-10; USADA 2012).

## Concluding Remarks

Framing the doping market as "quasi-illegal" might shift the discourse on anti-doping policy (Lowther 2015) or suggest new avenues for controls, but the market is not entirely unique in covering the spectrum of legality and illegality with some amount of ambiguity. This market has its own peculiarities, including a history of high-level government involvement, and might be more ambiguous than others, but many other markets could be—and sometimes have been—described as "quasi-illegal." They, too, involve goods and services that are not fully prohibited but can, under some conditions, be sold, bought, and used legally. Consider, for example, the differences between the "white," "grey," and "black"[9] components of the markets for cigarettes, weapons, gambling, and, most notably in the context of doping, painkillers and medical cannabis.

Notwithstanding the temptation to look to the well-explored heroin and cocaine markets for policy insight, they, as wholly criminal markets, might present weak analogies for a study of the supply of doping products. Thus, anti-doping policymakers and researchers might need to find different analogies, including those pertaining to other quasi-illegal markets and, possibly, to white-collar crime, to draw out the implications of variations in legality for anti-doping policy.

Our findings on the quasi-illegality of the doping market in Italy could also have broader implications for research in criminology and, perhaps, other disciplines, such as sociology. Over the decades, criminologists[10] have tended to use the word "crime" loosely, disregarding the distinction between "criminality" and "illegality." This disregard is particularly evident in the literature on organized crime and illegal markets. In the early 1970s, when US criminologists revolted against the ethnically loaded and highly formalized official understanding of organized crime, they proposed the concept of "illegal enterprise" (Haller 1990) as an alternative. Although originally meant to replace "organized crime," the phrase "illegal enterprise" has with time become a synonym for organized crime (van Duyne 1997), thus further conflating the

[9] The terms "white," "grey," and "black" are not subject to strict definitions (see OECD 2002 and Feige 1990 on ambiguities), but for our purpose, which is to draw attention to the gradations of legal status across fora, we follow the commercial literature (for example, Restani 1987) and make the following distinctions: "white" markets are wholly legal; "grey" markets violate terms of distribution, but neither the channels nor products are illegal, per se, as in the case of branded electronic or cosmetic products that are distributed through channels which, while legal, are unofficial, unauthorized, or unintended by the original manufacturer; and "black" markets involve illegal trade, but not necessarily illegal products. Others (for example, Karp 1994: 178) are less specific.

[10] Including the authors of this chapter.

differences between criminality and illegality (see Paoli and Vander Beken 2014, for an overview).

Because of the conflation of criminality and illegality and the focus on heroin and cocaine in empirical research, criminologists and, to a lesser extent, other social scientists have not yet fully explored the nuances and implications of legal status. Nor have they appreciated that players and products can shift across market segments that are characterized by different legal statuses, or can violate different criminal and non-criminal legislation simultaneously and as a result of those shifts. Even in studies of illegal rather than fully criminal markets—such as those for cigarettes (von Lampe 2011), weapons (Feinstein and Holden 2014), and gambling (Spapens 2014)—criminologists have often treated these markets as a separate "criminal" appendix to a larger legal market.

Economists have been more active in this arena, both in the conduct of case studies and the development of formal models, and some publications across disciplines have attempted to typify markets with illegal characteristics (for example, Reuter 1985; Castells and Portes 1989; Feige 1989; Naylor 2003; Beckert and Wehinger 2013). However, the foregoing assessment of the Italian doping market suggests that, to varying degrees, products, transactions, and suppliers and consumers might defy easy classifications in quasi-illegal markets and thus require careful handling under any research paradigm. At least some market players might be willing and able to get in and out of the different legal, illegal, variable, and disputable market segments, possibly adjusting their modus operandi and profit expectations as they move among them. Criminologists—and other social scientists—are called not only to weave together the literatures of their different disciplines but also to systematically investigate market players' shifts and adjustments to form a more complete picture of the implications of the shades of legal status.

## Acknowledgments

This work was supported by the World Anti-Doping Agency pursuant to a 2010 Research Funding Agreement for the project "The Trafficking of Doping Projects and the Challenges of Supply Reduction: An Examination of Italy's Experience."

## References

*Adnkronos*. 1998. "Commissione Grosso: Doping, 'Federcalcio Corresponsabile.'" <http://www.adnkronos.com/Archivio/AdnAgenzia/1998/10/14/Sport/COMMISSIONE-GROSSO-DOPING-FEDERCALCIO-CORRESPONSABILE_172900.php>.

Arioli, Giovanni, and Vincenza Bellini. 2005. *Disposizioni penali in materia di doping*. Milan: Giuffré.

Beckert, Jens, and Frank Wehinger. 2013. "In the Shadow: Illegal Markets and Economic Sociology." *Socio-Economic Review* 11(1): pp. 5–30.

Berendonk, Brigitte. 1992. *Doping: Von der Forschung zum Betrug*. Hamburg: Rowohlt.

Bundeskriminalamt. 2011. "Operation 'Sladge-Hammer' und 'International Pharmaceuticals.'" <http://www.bmi.gv.at/cms/BK/presse/files/2_2_2011_Operation_Sladge_Hammer_und_intern_Pharmaceuticals.pdf>.

Castells, Manuel, and Alejandro Portes. 1989. "World Underneath: The Origins, Dynamics, and Effects of the Informal Economy." In *The Informal Economy, Studies in Advanced and Less Developed Countries*, edited by Alejandro Portes, Manuel Castells, and Lauren A. Benton, pp. 11–37. Baltimore, MD: Johns Hopkins University Press.

Clinard, Marshall B., and Richard Quinney. 1973. *Criminal Behavior Systems: A Typology*. 2nd ed. New York: Holt, Rinehart and Winston.

CONI, Comitato Olimpico Nazionale Italiano. 2012. "Dati statistici." <http://www.coni.it/index.php?dati_statistici>.

Corte Suprema di Cassazione. 2007. *Sentenza sul ricorso proposto dalla Procura Generale presso la Corte d'Appello di Torino e dal difensore dell'imputato A.G. avverso la sentenza emessa dalla Corte d'Appello della stessa città in data 14 dicembre 1985*. Sentenza n. Reg. Gen. N. 19255/06.

*Cronache maceratesi*. 2011. "Traffico di anabolizzanti: un arresto a Pesaro." August 24. <http://www.cronachemaceratesi.it/2011/08/24/traffico-di-anabolizzanti-un-arresto-a-pesaro/95217/>.

Cycling Independent Reform Commission. 2015. *Report to the President of the Union Cycliste Internationale*. February. <http://www.uci.ch/mm/Document/News/CleanSport/16/87/99/CIRCReport2015_Neutral.pdf>.

Di Giorgio, Domenico. (ed.). 2011. *Farmaci contraffatti: Il fenomeno e le attività di contrasto*. Milan: Tecniche Nuove.

Donati, Alessandro. 1989. *Campioni senza valore*. Firenze: Ponte alle Grazie.

Donati, Alessandro. 2007. *World Traffic in Doping Substances*. <https://wada-main-prod.s3.amazonaws.com/resources/files/WADA_Donati_Report_On_Trafficking_2007.pdf>.

Donati, Alessandro. 2012. *Lo sport del doping: Chi lo subisce, chi lo combatte*. Torino: Gruppo Abele.

Donati, Alessandro, and Luciana Magrì. 2001. *Stima degli importi complessivi delle cessioni*. Report prepared for the Procura della Repubblica presso il Tribunale di Bologna.

Doping Enquiry Taskforce. 2001. *Report of the Doping Enquiring Task Force*. May 23. <http://www.minedu.fi/export/sites/default/OPM/Julkaisut/2001/liitteet/opm_57_doping_en.pdf?lang=fi>.

Dopingkommission. 2009. *Abschlussbericht der Expertenkommission zur Aufklärung von Dopingvorwürfen gegenüber Ärzten der Abteilung Sportmedizin des Universitätsklinikums Freiburg*. <http://www.uniklinik-freiburg.de/presse/live/abschlussbericht/Abschlussbericht.pdf>.

Fazzo, Luca, and Marco Mensurati. 2002. "Doping, la rotta della camorra così si riforniscono atleti e cavalla." *La Repubblica*, June 1: p. 48. <http://ricerca.repubblica.it/repubblica/archivio/repubblica/2002/06/01/doping-la-rotta-della-camorra-cosi-si.html>.

Feige, Edgar L. 1989. "The Meaning and Measurement of the Underground Economy." In *The Underground Economies: Tax Evasion and Information Distortion*, edited by Edgar L. Feige, pp. 13–56. Cambridge: Cambridge University Press.

Feige, Edgar L. 1990. "Defining and Estimating Underground and Informal Economies: The New Institutional Economic Approach." *World Development* 19(7): pp. 989–1002.

Feinstein, Andrew, and Paul Holden. 2014. "Arms Trafficking." In *The Oxford Handbook of Organized Crime*, edited by Letizia Paoli, pp. 444–59. New York: Oxford University Press.

Fincoeur, Bertrand, and Letizia Paoli. 2014. "Des pratiques communautaires au marché du dopage: Evolution de la distribution des produits dopants dans le cyclisme." *Déviance et Société* 38(1): pp. 3–27.

Gleaves, John, and Thomas Hunt (eds). 2015. *A Global History of Doping in Sport: Drugs, Policy, and Politics*. Abingdon: Routledge.

Graham, Michael R., P. Ryan, J. S. Baker et al. 2009. "Counterfeiting in Performance- and Image-enhancing Drugs." *Drug Testing and Analysis* 1(3): pp. 135–42.

Hahn, Thomas, and Raiko Häyrinen. 2008. "Doping im finnischen Skisport: Die schmutzigen Neunziger." *Süddeutsche Zeitung*, June 25. <http://www.sueddeutsche.de/sport/doping-im-finnischen-skisport-die-schmutzigen-neunziger-1.203060>.

Haller, Mark H. 1990. "Illegal Enterprise: A Theoretical and Historical Interpretation." *Criminology* 28(2): pp. 207–35.

Hamilton, Tyler, and Daniel Coyle. 2012. *The Secret Race: Inside the Hidden World of the Tour de France: Doping, Cover-ups, and Winning at All Costs*. London: Bantam Press.

Hawken, Angela, Jonathan Caulkins, Beau Kilmer, and Mark Kleiman. 2013. "Quasi-legal Cannabis in Colorado and Washington: Local and National Implications." *Addiction* 108(5): pp. 837–8.

Hoberman, John M. 2005. *Testosterone Dreams: Rejuvenation, Aphrodisia, Doping*. Los Angeles: University of California Press.

Hoberman, John M. 2011. "'Athletes in Handcuffs?' The Criminalization of Doping." In *Doping and Anti-Doping Policy in Sport: Ethical, Legal and Social Perspectives*, edited by Mike McNamee and Verner Møller, pp. 99–110. London: Routledge.

Hoberman, John M. 2012. "Doping, Gambling, and the Decline of the IOC." *Georgetown Journal of International Affairs* 13(2): pp. 135–42.

Houlihan, Barrie, and Borja García. 2012. *The Use of Legislation in Relation to Controlling the Production, Movement, Importation, Distribution and Supply of Performance-Enhancing Drugs in Sport (PEDS)*. August. <http://www.unesco.org/shs/sport/addbase/media/docs/doc-506aac23e2af9.pdf>.

Independent Commission. 2015. *The Independent Commission Report #1: Final Report*. November 9. <https://wada-main-prod.s3.amazonaws.com/resources/files/wada_independent_commission_report_1_en.pdf>.

IOC, International Olympic Committee. 2007. *Summary of the IOC Disciplinary Commission Recommendations Regarding the National Olympic Committee of Austria (Österreichisches Olympisches Comité—ÖOC)*. <http://www.olympic.org/Documents/Reports/EN/en_report_1183.pdf>.

*Japan Times*. 2015. "Number of Quasi-legal Drug Cases up Fivefold in First Half of 2015." September 3. <http://www.japantimes.co.jp/news/2015/09/03/national/crime-legal/number-quasi-illegal-drug-cases-fivefold-first-half-2015/#.VkY9Qj-FMdU>.

Karp, Aaron. 1994. "The Rise of Black and Gray Markets." *Annals of the American Academy of Political and Social Science* 535: pp. 175–89.

Kistner, Thomas. 2015. *Schuss: Die geheime Dopinggeschichte des Fußballs*. Munich: Droemer.

Koert, A. W. A., and Rens van Kleij. 1998. *Handel in doping: Een verkennend onderzoek naar de handel in dopinggeduide middelen in Nederland*. Nieuwegein: Arko.

Kokkevi, Anna, Anastasios Fotiou, Anina Chileva, Alojz Nociar, and Patrick Miller. 2008. "Daily Exercise and Anabolic Steroids Use in Adolescents: A Cross-National European Study." *Substance Use and Misuse* 43(14): pp. 2053–65.

Kraska, Peter B., Charles R. Bussard, and John J. Brent. 2010. "Trafficking in Bodily Perfection: Examining the Late-Modern Steroid Marketplace and Its Criminalization." *Justice Quarterly* 27(2): pp. 159–85.

Lowther, Jason. 2015. "Effectiveness, Proportionality, and Deterrence: Does Criminalizing Doping Deliver?" In *Routledge Handbook of Drugs and Sport*, edited by Verner Møller, Ivan Waddington, and John M. Hoberman, pp. 337–49. New York: Routledge.

Marino, Giovanni. 2001. "Marino, Giovanni. 2001. I farmaci della camorra." *La Repubblica*, May 23: p. 24. <http://ricerca.repubblica.it/repubblica/archivio/repubblica/2001/05/23/farmaci-della-camorra.html>.

McCabe, Sean Esteban, Kirk J. Brower, Brady T. West, Toben F. Nelson, and Henry Wechsler. 2007. "Trends in Nonmedical Use of Anabolic Steroids by US College Students: Results from Four National Surveys. *Drug and Alcohol Dependence* 90: 243–51.

Ministero della Salute. 2010. "Decreto 11 giugno 2010: Aggiornamento e completamento delle Tabelle contenenti l'indicazione delle sostanze stupefacenti e psicotrope relative a composizioni medicinali, di cui al Decreto del Presidente della Repubblica 9 ottobre 1990, n, 309, e successive modificazioni ed integrazioni con l'inserimento dello steroide anabolizzante nandrolone." *Gazzetta Ufficiale*, 145, June 24. <http://www.normativasanitaria.it/jsp/dettaglio.jsp?id=34277>.

Ministero della Salute and Istituto Superiore di Sanità. 2012. *Reporting System Doping Antidoping 2011*. <http://www.salute.gov.it/imgs/C_17_pubblicazioni_1732_allegato.pdf>.

NAS Bologna, Comando Carabinieri per la tutela della salute. Nucleo Antisofisticazioni e Sanità di Bologna. 2000. *Procedimento penale a carico di S. M. + altri. Atti relativi all'indagine delegata sul commercio clandestino di sostanze ormonali e a effetto anabolizzante destinate al doping umano. Informativa conclusiva*. Rif. Proc. Pen. n. 1701/99–21 RGNR. June 21.

NAS Brescia. 2011. *Comando Carabinieri per la tutela della salute. Nucleo Antisofisticazioni e Sanità di Brescia. Informativa finale sull'esito delle indagini effettuatenei confronti di G. N. + altri.*

NAS Firenze. 2002. *Comando Carabinieri per la tutela della salute. Nucleo Antisofisticazioni e Sanità di Firenze. Informativa finale sull'esito delle indagini effettuate: Operazione Quadrifoglio.*

Naylor, R. Thomas. 2003. "Towards a General Theory of Profit-Driven Crimes." *British Journal of Criminology* 43(1): pp. 81–101.

OECD. 2002. *Measuring the Non-Observed Economy: A Handbook*. Paris: OECD.

OECD. 2008. *OECD Glossaries—Corruption: A Glossary of International Standards in Criminal Law*. Paris: OECD.

Pacifici, Roberta, and Alessandro Donati. 2011. *Consulenza tecnica nel procedimento penale 5876/08 Procura della Repubblica presso il Tribunale di Mantova*. Mimeo.

Paoli, Letizia. 2012. "Doping and Anti-Doping: Neglected Issues in Criminology." *European Journal of Crime, Criminal Law and Criminal Justice* 20(3): pp. 231–8.

Paoli, Letizia, and Alessandro Donati. 2014. *The Sport Doping Market: Understanding Supply and Demand, and the Challenges of Their Control*. New York: Springer.

Paoli, Letizia, and Tom Vander Beken. 2014. "Organized Crime: A Contested Concept." In *The Oxford Handbook of Organized Crime*, edited by Letizia Paoli, pp. 13–31. New York: Oxford University Press.

Paoli, Letizia, Victoria A. Greenfield, and Peter Reuter. 2009. *The World Heroin Market: Can Supply Be Cut?* New York: Oxford University Press.

Pearson, Geoffrey, and Dick Hobbs. 2001. *Middle Market Drug Distribution*. London: Home Office Research, Development and Statistics Directorate.

Pope, Harrison G., Katherine A. Phillips, and Roberto Olivardia. 2000. *The Adonis Complex: The Secret Crisis of Male Body Obsession*. New York: Free Press.

PR-FE, Procura della Repubblica presso il Tribunale di Ferrara. 2000. *Richiesta di archiviazione parziale. Procedimento penale control Pescante Mario + 13 altri*. N. 893/99/21 R. G. notizie di reato/Mod. 21.

*Repubblica, La*. 2008. *Corse truccate, cavalli dopati—Nuova tegola sull'ippica italiana*. <http://www.repubblica.it/2008/12/sezioni/sport/ippica-indagine/ippica-indagine/ippica-indagine.html?ref=search>.

Restani, Jane. 1987. "An Introduction to the Gray Market Controversy." *Brooklyn Journal of International Law* 13(2): pp. 235–47.

Reuter, Peter. 1985. *The Organization of Illegal Markets: An Economic Analysis*. Washington, DC: National Institute of Justice.

Ryan, Barry. 2011. "Italian Judge Set to Decide if 32 Named in Mantova Doping Investigation Should Go on Trial." <http://www.cyclingnews.com/news/italian-judge-set-to-decide-if-32-named-in-mantova-doping-investigation-should-go-on-trial>.

Schrager, Laura Shill, and James F. Short, Jr. 1978. "Toward a Sociology of Organizational Crime." *Social Problems* 25(4): pp. 407–19.

Spapens, Toine. 2014. "Illegal Gambling." In *The Oxford Handbook of Organized Crime*, edited by Letizia Paoli, pp. 402–18. New York: Oxford University Press.

Spitzer, Giselher. 2013. *Doping in der DDR: Ein historischer Überblick zu einer konspirativen Praxis. Genese—Verantwortung—Gefahren*. Köln: Strauss.

Spitzer, Giselher, Erik Eggers, and Holger J. Schnell. 2013. *Siegen um jeden Preis—Doping in Deutschland: Geschichte, Recht, Ethik 1972–1990*. Göttingen: Werkstatt.

Striegel, Heiko, P. Simon, S. Frisch et al. 2006. "Anabolic Ergogenic Substance Users in Fitness-Sports: A Distinct Group Supported by the Health Care System." *Drug and Alcohol Depend*ence 81(1): pp. 11–19.

Striegel, Heiko, Rolf Ulrich, and Perikles Simon. 2010. "Randomized Response Estimates for Doping and Illicit Drug Use in Elite Athletes." *Drug and Alcohol Dependence* 106(2–3): pp. 230–2.

Sutherland, Edwin H. 1983[1949]. *White-Collar Crime: The Uncut Version*. New Haven, CT: Yale University Press.

Tr-BO, Tribunale di Bologna. 2004. *Sentenza nei confronti di Ferrari Michele + 3*. October 1. No. 2997/97 RG notizie di reato.

Tr-FE, Tribunale di Ferrara. 2003. *Sentenza nei confronti di Conconi Francesco + altri*. No. 893/99 RGNG. November 19.

Tr-FO, Tribunale di Forlì. 2009. *Ordinanza di custodia cautelare nei confronti di V.M. + altri*. No. 3870/07 RGNR.

Tr-RV, Tribunale di Ravenna. 2004. *Ordinanza applicative di misure cautelari nei confronti di M.A. + 73*. N. 619/2003 21 RGNR.

UNODCCP, United Nations Office for Drug Control and Crime Prevention. 2001. *Global Illicit Drug Trends*. New York: United Nations.

USADA, US Anti-Doping Agency. 2012. *Report on Proceedings under the World Anti-Doping Code and the Usada Protocol: United States Anti-Doping Agency, Claimant, v. Lance Armstrong, Respondent. Reasoned Decision of the United States Anti-Doping Agency on Disqualification and Ineligibility*. <http://cyclinginvestigation.usada.org/>.

US DEA, Drug Enforcement Administration. 2007. *DEA Announces Largest Steroid Enforcement Action in U.S. History*. <http://www.justice.gov/dea/pubs/pressrel/pr092407.html>.

van Duyne, Petrus C. 1997. "Organized Crime, Corruption and Power." *Crime, Law and Social Change* 26(3): pp. 201–38.

von Lampe, Klaus. 2011. "The Illegal Cigarette Trade." In *International Criminal Justice*, edited by M. Natarajan, pp. 148–54. New York: Cambridge University Press.

WADA, World Anti-Doping Agency. 2010. *Minutes of the WADA Executive Committee Meeting. November 20*. Montreal: WADA. <https://www.wada-ama.org/en/resources/governance/executive-committee-meeting-minutes>.

WADA, World Anti-Doping Agency. 2015. *World Anti-Doping Code*. Montreal: WADA. <https://www.wada-ama.org/en/resources/the-code/world-anti-doping-code>.

Waddington, Ivan, and Andy Smith. 2009. *An Introduction to Drugs in Sport*. Abingdon: Routledge.

# 14

# Illegal Prices

## The Social Contestation of High Living Costs in Guadeloupe and Mauritania

*Boris Samuel*

Between 2005 and 2010, Mauritania and Guadeloupe both faced massive social mobilizations against the high cost of living. Political discontent was directed against the fact that some leading economic actors were accumulating profits considered illegitimate and excessive, while appearing to be responsible for the high prices of some of the most important consumer goods, such as imported food and energy. The widespread use of illegal practices, breaching commercial, fiscal, or public finance laws, was blamed for the unjust pricing. At the same time, the state's responses to high living costs and illegality had met with limited success, both because market transactions could scarcely be controlled and because the state was going easy on powerful economic actors, who were or might become allies. The public debate about price formation in Guadeloupe and Mauritania thus became a tense sociopolitical conflict over inequality and its administration. This chapter will seek to shed light on this situation in order to portray the interfaces between legality and illegality in markets in specific historical situations, and to question their role in shaping social and political relations. How did legality and illegality intertwine in the formation of basic commodity prices in Mauritania and Guadeloupe? To what extent did the existence of illegality in markets contribute to the establishment of legitimate social and political orders?

To answer these questions, I will focus on a specific object, the two states' interventions against high prices, which I will explore in two directions. First, looking at the 2009 social mobilization against high living costs in Guadeloupe, I will describe how a wave of audits responded to the social demands for transparency and the unveiling of illegal practices. Auditing practices and the debates they generate are a fruitful entry point to analyze the way market practices are labeled illegal, and the institutional and sociopolitical processes by which their denunciation occurs. Their analysis also helps in identifying the conditions in which the presence of illegal practices may lead to sanctions or, on the contrary, be tolerated. My observations suggest that in Guadeloupe illegalities remained largely unsanctioned, enabling the continued coexistence of legality and illegality in price formation.

Second, dealing with Mauritania, I will focus on so-called "emergency plans" aimed at giving the population wide access to low-price commodities all over the country in case of severe price hikes. Studying these plans is useful for questioning the ambivalent relationships the state apparatus has maintained with illegal transactions in markets. In Mauritania, public interventions were necessary to contain the dramatic social and political consequences of price hikes. But circumvention of the rules was also so common in the public administration, as well as collusion and straddling positions of power and positions of accumulation (Bayart 2009), that illegal market transactions and wide use of fraudulent practices characterized the implementation of such social programs, too. They even became one of the means by which the government organized redistribution in ways that would also ensure gains for a number of powerful actors.

Examining these cases will thus give me the opportunity to examine the multifaceted and sometimes contradictory relationships between public administration and state regulation and illegality in markets. In Guadeloupe illicit activities are so pervasive and linked to the activities of powerful actors that they remain unsanctioned even when they are under the scrutiny of transparency programs. In Mauritania, the pervasive presence of illicit activities, while generating protests, may also ensure redistribution, and consolidate state authority and legitimacy. Both illustrate a certain type of "legitimate illegality" and show that, while trying to regulate or limit illegality, a state's actions may also rely on it. Unlike some of the usual interpretations of the roles of illegality in so-called "developing countries," which consider that circumvention of legal rules and corruption are so pervasive that the formal state is of no significance in social life (Chabal and Daloz 1999; Mkandawire 2013; Reno 1995), the empirical cases presented in this chapter will show that illegality may contribute to the formation of states, in line with the argument put forward by Bayart et al. (1999). The Mauritanian case will even suggest that illegality may become instrumental for the regime in building political support. The main theoretical contribution of this chapter will thus be to show that the state may govern the economy by selectively enforcing laws and regulations: in both empirical cases, the regulation of food and oil markets offers opportunities to favor a range of actors, nurture clientelistic relations, and, when needed, to respond to social contestation.

In terms of methodology, studying social dynamics and debates around prices entails investigating the interactions between a variety of social actors: consumers, firms, political parties, state services, trade unions, heads of businesses associations. For contemporary economic sociology, and most particularly in the words of the French convention school, price determination engages social conventions and institutions that mediate disputes and establish compromises between parties and actors with diverging understandings and interests (Beckert 2011; Boltanski and Thevenot 2006; Storper and Salais 1997). The present chapter will build on this framework, but will also depart from some of its usual methods and assumptions. By addressing the role of illegality and abuses in price disputes, it will shed light on situations in which compromise is difficult to reach, leading to recurring conflicts and instability (Thévenot 2015). To describe these dynamics, the chapter will rely on a Weberian approach to political economy, by studying the "constellations of interests" emerging around illegality in markets (Hibou 2011, 2015; Weber 1978). Such a framework will allow us to discuss the establishment of what Jens Beckert calls the "social order of markets" (2009) when prices are massively illegal, and to question the role of the interface between legality and illegality in stabilizing this order, or provoking dynamics of change.

## Guadeloupe: Illegality in Markets as a Cause of Political Protest and Demands for Transparency

In Guadeloupe, a forty-four-day general strike in early 2009 was led by the group *Lyannaj Kont' Pwofitasyon* ("alliance against *pwofitasyon*" or LKP). The concept of *pwofitasyon* describes a situation in which firms occupying a dominant market position make huge profits at the expense of consumers. Knowing that some of the main economic actors on the island are the heirs of settler families who have shifted into the large-scale retail and import/export business, *pwofitasyon* is also seen as a sign of continued domination after the colonial period, built on inequality in status and race. High prices are thus the starting point for a radical political critique.

During the strike, the island was completely paralyzed by roadblocks manned by LKP activists, and radical trade union factions clashed violently with police, even leading to shootings. But audits and economic analyses were also major weapons. The state-administered prices of petrol at the pump were suspected of hiding abusive profits for several local economic actors. Various violations of competition law were suspected in the retail sector as well, because the high prices of many basic products remained unjustified (such as imported food, hygiene or health products, electronic devices, and so on). The protest led to a wave of audits, which revealed abuses and delegitimized state regulation. Even though no sanctions followed, the conduct of these audits transformed the role of illegality in markets and reshaped social and political relations around illegal prices.

### *Opacity of Oil Prices as a Starting Point for a Large Protest and the Role of Audits in Unveiling Illegal Practices*

The 2009 social conflict in Guadeloupe was triggered by an unexplained rise in fuel prices. In the first half of 2008, international oil prices rose sky high, and so did prices at the pump. But while prices declined on international markets after July, the prices paid by consumers in Guadeloupe continued to rise for more than three months, until October. At that time the opacity of this sector had been criticized for many years. In the overseas departments, unlike mainland France, fuel prices are under government control. In 2005 an association of fishermen conducted investigations and denounced the opacity of the formula used by the administration (the Departmental Directorate of Consumer Affairs, Competition and Repression of Fraud) to fix prices (France Antilles Guadeloupe 2006). In 2007, the case was taken up by one of the leading wholesale importers on the island, Didier Payen, a member of the local branch of the movement representing the heads of French business. He produced a very detailed study, which was worthy of a professional audit firm despite it having been conducted on his own initiative and with no institutional support. The figures showed that the monopoly of the oil company SARA (*Société Anonyme de Raffinerie des Antilles*) had resulted in an additional cost of about 40 cents per liter, one quarter of the price paid by Guadeloupean consumers (Payen 2009).

The social movement in 2009 took place in this context. Demonstrations and strikes against high prices started in November 2008. The state reacted quickly. Oil prices were frozen and two official audits were commissioned at the end of 2008, one by the *Inspection générale des finances*, the auditing body of the Ministry of Finance, and another by the *Autorité de la concurrence*, the French body in charge of competition regulation (Bolliet et al. 2009; Autorité de la concurrence 2009a). Several other studies were produced during the same period, either by unions (the Brissac report) or by public bodies. While each report unveiled some specific aspects of the procurement policy, all confirmed that there were large irregularities and frauds in oil prices formation: for example, the Payen report showed that some taxes were being counted twice (tax on waste oils) in the official formula; the Brissac report identified some massive frauds by the SARA company, which used very basic trickery to cheat the customs authority (Brissac 2009). These practices, which enabled actors in the sector to accumulate unjustified profits, shocked the public in Guadeloupe and Martinique.

However, the audits also drew a very ambivalent and complex picture of the various factors at play and interests at stake in oil price determination. High prices, in fact, were not only due to abuses by oil firms. First, on the 40 cents surcharge identified by unions and businessmen, it appeared that only 8 cents were due to irregularities and fraud. The rest was explained mainly by the size and remoteness of the market—which entailed high fixed costs—and the lack of competition (Bolliet et al. 2009; Autorité de la concurrence 2009a). Second, in addition to oil companies, many other actors were benefitting from high oil prices. The local authorities were benefitting, because the calculation method for customs duties ensured them additional revenues (Payen 2009). The report by the Competition Authority also revealed that a consistent share of the excess oil prices was due to the high number of employees at gas stations, following an agreement between trade unions and distributors (Autorité de la concurrence 2009a). Thus, the level and opacity of oil prices were indeed hiding abuses and illegalities, but they also resulted from the existence of a complex social and political compromise between firms, administrations, and trade unions.

With the escalation of the conflict, this compromise could no longer be maintained. At the beginning of the movement, the state adopted emergency measures: in December 2008, fuel prices were frozen for three months and a decrease of 0.31 euros per liter on lead-free and 22 cents on diesel was decided (*20 Minutes* 2008).[1] The state also provided a transfer payment to SARA to compensate for the loss entailed by these lower prices. The latter decision was the starting point of the forty-four-day general strike: the LKP opposed such a transfer payment because the collective's main target was the illegitimacy of the oil company's profits, its "*pwofitasyon*." Oil prices then became the object of a series of negotiations, held under the auspices of the *Observatoire des prix* (price observatory). Although the state adopted a new pricing formula in summer 2010, taking into account the various claims and irregularities identified by the audits, unions and consumer associations considered that state services had avoided an open debate on prices and were imposing their views, thereby feeding into the suspicion of collusion and hidden arrangements with the oil corporations.

The regulation of oil prices continues to generate controversies and struggles. In 2014, for example, the government tried to ban several financial arrangements between gas station owners and international distributors (the latter paying large sums to the former to ensure exclusivity), considering they

[1] A full description of the negotiations described in this paragraph is provided in Samuel (2013).

were violating competition law, but the resistance of these powerful actors forced the state to step back.

The legitimacy of state power was thus contested through condemnation of the opacity of state-administered oil prices. A range of actors (including unions, state services, or corporations) had conducted audits and inquiries to challenge the legitimacy of prices and unveil abuses, illustrating what has recently been called "statactivist" uses of quantification (Bruno et al. 2014). But illegalities could only be partly contained. The diversity of economic interests and the power relations involved in oil price setting have made it impossible to eliminate the sources of illegitimate profits and reach consensus.

### *The Large-Scale Retail Sector: Unsanctioned Illegalities and the Reproduction of Domination*

In the large-scale retail sector, too, government audits conducted in 2009 and 2010 revealed pervasive violations of competition law, which enabled some firms to build dominant market positions and impose high prices on Guadeloupian consumers. They remained unsanctioned, however, enabling the reproduction of an unequal social and political order.

At the time the conflict started, the economic analysis of price formation had been neglected for years by the public administration. There had been no study to measure price differences between Guadeloupe and mainland France since 1992, although the French national statistical department, INSEE, was supposed to produce such a study. There were several reasons for this neglect. My interviews suggest that the administration (the Prefect, as well as local state offices) feared the consequences of publishing studies about prices.[2] On the one hand, pointing to an increasing price gap could focus the public debate on growing inequalities and nurture the perception that importers and retailers were accumulating abusive profits, with the risk of provoking protests. The abusive commercial margins are perceived on the island as a perpetuation of the exploitative colonial order.[3] Descendants of settler families, whose ascension was largely associated with state-sponsored programs in the 1960s, 1970s, and 1980s, own the largest retail companies.[4] On the other hand, finding a narrowing price gap compared with the mainland also ran the risk of provoking protests. Such a result could be seen as an attempt by the

[2] Interviews with INSEE officials, Guadeloupe, October 2010, and France, November 2012.

[3] On the links between historical imagination and price formation see Berry 2007, Boltanski and Esquerre 2015, Bonnecase 2013.

[4] Since the 1970s, to avoid an economic collapse and compensate the decline of the agricultural sector, the state has saved many settler families from bankruptcy by distributing large and often poorly targeted public subsidies. The 2009 conflict expressed the resentment such a situation had provoked: the Bernard Hayot Group and the Huygues Despointes Group, which are examples of such groups, were particularly targeted during the social movement.

state to undermine the social gains of the overseas departments, where, since 1953, civil servants have received special bonuses (known as *sur-rémunérations* which reach 40 percent in Guadeloupe), officially justified by the price differences with mainland France (Samuel 2013; Pied 2010).[5]

The LKP was thus targeting a controversial issue by putting transparency and price analysis at the center of its broad platform of protest.[6] As in the oil sector, the social conflict provoked a wave of audits and economic analyses. The report of the Competition Authority "dealing with import and distribution mechanisms of large consumption goods in the overseas departments" (Autorité de la concurrence 2009b) drew up an impressive list of violations of competition law. It showed, for example, that the small size of the market favored the establishment of highly dominant positions for very few players, who used illegal means to curb competition. Importers and distributors were integrating vertically to exclude competing products and brands from the market and to impose higher price levels. Exclusive contracts were signed between mainland brands and importers in order to eliminate competitors and make it impossible for independent newcomers to enter the retail sector. Some more invisible barriers were also protecting dominant players: land access, for example, is very limited on the island, allowing the old landowner families to control the development of the new commercial sites. It was clear to the Competition Authority that the huge price differences with the mainland could only be explained by the existence of these abuses. Among a sample of seventy-five products the Competition Authority examined, the price differences compared with mainland France were above 55 percent for more than half the sample. This was well beyond the plausible impact of the additional costs due to the remoteness and small size of the market.

For the trade unions and the LKP, the publication of this report was a major victory. In their view, it confirmed that the former "colonial forces" were still extracting profit from the population by illegal means (UGTG 2009). Nevertheless, almost no sanctions followed: sanctions would have required a major administrative effort to gather proof of misconduct (Doligé 2009). This can be interpreted in various ways. First, as Jens Beckert argued (2009), competition generates conflicts of interest between economic actors which can threaten the "social order of markets." In the Guadeloupian situation, however, unsanctioned illegal practices were able to develop under the eyes of the regulator, and these illicit practices, even if largely disapproved of and contested, could not be seriously threatened. Such a situation confirms that the regulation of competition not only mediates struggles in markets, but also

[5] In 1997, the publication of a price comparison had triggered a "revolt of civil servants" on the island of Réunion (Conan 1997) for these very reasons.

[6] For a description of the platform of protest, see Samuel (2013: 259–69).

makes complicity possible (Le Roy 2004). The existence of collusion and fraud at the heart of a market should not be a surprise: patrimonial and legal forms of domination are easily enmeshed in concrete historical situations, which are always of a hybrid form between ideal types (Weber 1978; Hibou 2015). Second, the limits between legality and illegality remain blurred (see Mayntz, in this volume). For many local actors, given the small size and peripheral character of the market, competition law is even considered to be non-applicable in Guadeloupe.[7] While this could have merely given discretionary (or even arbitrary) power to administrative institutions—the boundaries between tolerated and non-tolerated illegality being subject to a lot of subjective assessment on the part of administrators—the actual mechanisms of price formation indicate that the blurred boundaries between legality and illegality favored the perpetuation of existing hierarchies and power relations (Beckert 2011; Bourdieu 2005). The existence of unsanctioned illegalities can be interpreted even as a continuation of the long-term inequalities of colonialism, as argued by the LKP. In a Braudelian interpretation, illegality in markets appears as a contemporaneous means of capitalist appropriation, used by the dominant actors (Braudel 1985; Wallerstein 1983).

### *Toward New Practices of Judgment and Denunciation of Abusive Pricing*

The second report was produced after a "senatorial information mission" that took place in Guadeloupe and other French overseas territories between April and June 2009 (Doligé 2009). It showed that the audits could change the social and political roles illegality played in Guadeloupe, although they remained unsanctioned.

The report was a thorough diagnosis of the island's economy. Full of facts, it proved the existence of abuses: for example, it showed that the observed price gaps varied so dramatically between departments, products, and shops that it would have been impossible to find objective factors explaining the differences (such as the costs of shipment or storage) (Doligé 2009: 124). But the most striking feature of the report lay in the new language it used to discuss the issue of prices. The evidence of abuses was now investigated in great detail. The price of chocolate Nesquik, which many kids have for breakfast, for example, was the object of much attention: "The price of 'Nesquik,' an imported product, is much higher in the overseas departments: by 42% on the island of Réunion, by 75% in Martinique (although it was on sale by the time of the survey), by 128% in Guadeloupe and 142% in Guyane" (126). The shift this reflected was not ephemeral: individual prices were now considered

[7] Interviews with heads of businesses and state officials, Guadeloupe, August–November 2010.

to be social and political "events" (Boltanski and Esquerre 2015), subject to political and moral responsibility. Hidden abuses were to be found in prices for individual products, and mere details could raise suspicion.

This new moral perspective on prices and illegality could be found throughout the report: for example, the retail sector oligopoly was described and denounced with explicit reference to the families owning the largest corporations, in a naming and shaming exercise (Doligé 2009: 131). The authors also took a stand against public companies, such as the monopolistic French company CMA-CGM—an international sea shipping giant—or Air France, whose fares were deemed excessive. The emergence of this new language, aimed at denouncing price illegalities, was also a broader phenomenon: for example, a phone hotline was established during the conflict to allow individuals to immediately report to the competition authority any "abusive prices" observed in a shop. The use of this new language was not limited to official institutions, either. During the negotiations it held with large-scale retailers between April and June 2009, the LKP could force retailers to lower prices, at least temporarily, by accusing them publicly of practicing abusive prices. The main weapon used by the collective in these negotiations was a series of rough and unverifiable estimations of abusive margins on a list of specific products (Samuel 2013: 303–11; 2014). The LKP had also proposed to set up "price brigades" and a "*bureau d'études ouvrières*" (worker's research unit) in charge of conducting surveys to identify and publicize abuses, and help the state to control prices on the island. Such practices could not change the long-term dynamics of inequality, but they demonstrate the change in the political meanings attached to illegality.

After 2009, the illegal practices were increasingly stigmatized, contested, and considered illegitimate by citizens, the administration, and political groups. New legitimate ways of judging and publicizing price levels emerged, together with new practices of denunciation (Boltanski et al. 1984; Boltanski and Thevenot 2006). These new practices could be found in mundane operations, such as the use of new numeric scales to appreciate the fairness of prices and indicating the possible existence of illegalities in price formation; a high price level indicated commercial abuse and legitimated denunciations. The 2009 social movement in Guadeloupe therefore led to a transformation of disputes concerning illegality in markets. At the same time, as explained above, no sanctions were taken by public authorities against large-scale retailers. Although illegality was de facto tolerated, conflicts around prices, or a changed assessment of the interface of legality and illegality, could induce significant social and political transformations. Therefore, understanding in detail the functioning of the interface between legality and illegality is critical to appreciate the sociopolitical effects of illegality in markets.

## Mauritania: Illegality at the Heart of Social Policy

Turning to the Mauritanian case, I will both show the value of a comparative perspective in studying the politics of illegality in price formation and shed light on additional ways in which illegality in prices can shape social and political relations. In Mauritania in the 2000s, high prices were also the starting point of a radical political critique; the fight against high costs of living stood at the center of a political controversy. Since the international food price hikes in 2007, popular protests accused the political regime of not fighting against inflation and of complicity with the dominant importers who were seen as responsible for inflation. But in the Mauritanian situation, illegality was not only impossible to eliminate, or just tolerated, as in Guadeloupe: it had clearly become a tool of governance. The state maintained collusive relationships with the main businesses and certain social groups through its unorthodox and illicit regulation of markets. Those relationships were instrumental in enabling the regime to generate political support and hold together a constellation of various interests to secure its power. As in Bayart et al.'s (1999) account of the "criminalization of the state in Africa," criminal and illicit activities contributed to the formation of state power.

### *From Inflationary Pressures to Repression*

In 2004, Mauritanian inflation peaked at 16 percent per year. Price increases reached 30 percent for certain food products (bread, cereals, and meat). Inflation was triggered by fluctuations of international markets (oil prices in particular) and a series of bad harvests, which pushed food prices upwards. Inflation also had political causes. After twenty years in power, the regime of President Maaouya Ould Taya was in decline and clientelistic policies, corrupt practices, and circumvention of the rules of public finance were at a peak. Extrabudgetary and unreported public spending reached about 40 percent of the official budget in 2004 (10 percent of GDP). The central bank's foreign currencies were also looted, nurturing speculation on informal exchange markets.[8] The exchange rate on the parallel market thus deteriorated significantly, increasing import prices. Taya's regime fell in 2005, allowing an easing of economic and sociopolitical tensions, but at the end of 2007 and in 2008, during a short-lived period of internationally sponsored democratic transition, fluctuations on international oil and commodities markets again

[8] The central bank's currency reserves were not the equivalent of twelve months of imports, as officially declared, but only two weeks, as later audits revealed (Islamic Republic of Mauritania 2006). For a description of the Mauritanian macroeconomic fiction and its links with international organizations such as the International Monetary Fund, see Samuel 2015.

provoked strong inflation. In 2010 also, after a new coup d'état in August 2008, international markets were once again the cause of high inflation.[9]

Facing the social and political tensions caused by inflation, the various governments' first reaction was to resort to repression. In 2004, for example, small, informal currency resellers were imprisoned (Horizons 2004; Samuel 2013). This may seem paradoxical, because these vendors were only intermediaries earning small commissions and had no influence on the market and the deterioration of the currency. But since the speculations of Mauritanian banks, linked to powerful tribal groups, were not controllable by the state, the Mauritanian government had invented an enemy, the small resellers. At the end of 2007, repression was directed against demonstrators: the massive social unrest of December, which denounced the multiple unjust price hikes and led to police shootings and the killing of a demonstrator. And after General Mohamed Abdel Aziz took power in August 2008, the regime began to accuse business people prominent under the previous regime of mismanagement and fraud in relation to the food emergency plans: inflation and accusations of illegal practices on markets became an excuse for the regime to imprison some of its fiercest rivals.[10] Each time tensions have arisen about inflation in Mauritania during the past ten years, the government has reacted by repression and shows of authority. Although they were incapable of stopping inflation,[11] the government established various target groups and used the presence of illegality in markets as a justification to enable the promotion of disciplinary (and sometimes violent) policies, thereby consolidating their power.[12]

### *When Social Policies Exploit and Nurture Illegality*

Nevertheless, the political and social turmoil caused by inflation forced the Mauritanian government to react through social policy interventions. They managed the social conflicts triggered by severe price hikes through "emergency plans."[13] The plans had a twofold objective: to give the population access to low-price commodities and to contain the discontent by distributing resources. However, these plans provoked widespread use of illegal transactions, for two main reasons.

[9] A description of the inflation path in Mauritania can be found in Samuel (2013: 537–76).

[10] For example the so-called "rotten rice" affair (Quotidien de Nouakchott 2011).

[11] This can be compared to the way the French colonial power had engaged in repression against traveling merchants in Central Africa many decades earlier, as described by Janet Roitman (2004). This did not help to reduce inflation, but French administrators used price-related "disorders" as an argument to legitimize the establishment of a colonial political order.

[12] For other illustrations of this link between order and prices, see Dumez and Jeunemaître (1989), Roitman (2004), and Stanziani (2007). I also studied it in the Guadeloupian case; see Samuel (2014).

[13] Emergency plans were implemented in 2004, 2007/2008, 2009, and 2011.

First, because they were one of the government's most salient priorities, such "emergency plans" accounted for a substantial share of government spending. In 2008, for example, the plan accounted for nearly 200 million dollars, the equivalent of 30 percent of the annual budget (ISFP 2010). But the government financed these plans via exceptional public finance procedures, often extra-budgetary (IMF 2008; Targui 2010), arguing that price movements were unpredictable, and thus required emergency procedures that were incompatible with the rigid regular budget framework.[14] Hence, these policies led to the informal and illegal use of public funds and favored massive corruption (Samuel 2013: 579–95; Calame 2008).

Second, they encouraged state-sponsored illegal transactions on the food markets. The main instrument used to contain price hikes and give access to food commodities were the so-called "solidarity stores" (*boutiques solidarité*). These shops, present all over the country, sold subsidized basic food products (such as rice, flour, cooking oil, and sugar). But the distribution mechanism was only moderately successful. It provoked endless queues[15] and the subsidized products were said to be of poor quality.[16] Above all, the "solidarity stores" provided myriad opportunities for small-scale trafficking for many actors, ranging from shop owners to local "big men" or state representatives. The owners could easily sell the subsidized products at normal prices, thereby increasing their margins; they could sell large quantities to people who were not entitled to them, such as local notables, in order to obtain favors in return; they could also keep the wares for their own families and get access to more of the subsidized products. The selection of shops was also an opportunity for clientelistic games: the advantages were numerous for the selected shops because their owners were granted a comfortable monthly income (80,000 ouguyia, the equivalent of the salary of a state executive). A whole bureaucratic apparatus also had to be established, hiring many well-paid unemployed young people to, supposedly, control the stores and the implementation of the program. These jobs, as well as all the procedures which were used to institute and run this market, were opportunities for the exertion of influence, clientelism, and fraudulent practices. The "emergency plans" thus enabled the state to build a nation-wide commercial and sociopolitical network of supporters. They put fraud and injustice at the heart of what was supposed to be social policy.

The state benefited from the extension of illegal practices in the markets for the most consumed food items. Illegality was instrumental for the government,

[14] Interviews with officials, Nouakchott, November–December 2011.

[15] The products were distributed according to predefined rules: each household was entitled to a limited daily quantity, and the products were sold according to a well-defined daily schedule.

[16] Interviews on these issues were held with state officials, shop owners, citizens, party representatives, and international actors in Nouakchott in November–December 2011.

helping it to build a "constellation of interest" around the state's interventions against high prices. There was thus an apparent contradiction between the social goal of the policy—giving access to basic products and improving living standards—and some of its main effects, namely promoting illegal access to resources and cooptation. In such a situation, should not illegality be considered a source of political legitimacy? Studies of Mauritanian society support such a conclusion. As shown by Ould Ahmed Salem (2001), there is a moral economy of trickery in Mauritania, which confers social recognition to the skillful use of circumvention and deceit, and contributes to social order.

### *Legality as a Repertoire of Collective Action*

This does not mean, however, that illegality and mismanagement on those markets do not provoke protests. Indeed, since 2010, some opposition parties have firmly protested against the links between importers and the regime, particularly the President. The *Union des Forces de Progrès* (UFP), an influential left-wing opposition party, has for example accused the regime of unfair regulation of the food market (UFP 2011). It is well known that the market has been oligopolistic since 1993: structural adjustment policies have led to the privatization of the state monopoly on imports and established a pool of importers. These importers continue to control the market, representing some of the biggest economic powers in the country and among the most influential actors in politics. But according to the UFP, the Aziz regime has used the licensing of the import market to give access to substantial economic rents to its closest allies. As the party has shown (UFP 2011), the market shares of two import companies rose particularly rapidly within a very short period of time, in particular the one belonging to the President's cousin (Ehel Ghadde). The UFP also identified the way these dominant positions were built up: in particular, very generous custom tax exemptions, access to foreign currencies at cheap rates, and priority access to the harbor enabled these importers to attain a competitive advantage, a point confirmed in the interviews I conducted in Nouakchott. Finally, the UFP also accused the government of using the "emergency plans" to reinforce the dominant position of these importers (UFP 2011). Between 2008 and 2011, there were not even public bids for the provision of food products to the "solidarity shops," which enabled the regime to assign the contracts on a discretionary basis. When public bids were established in 2011, unsurprisingly the regime's closest ally (Ehel Ghadde) was the cheapest bidder, probably by taking advantage of his special fiscal treatment and access to currencies (Quotidien de Nouakchott 2011). The interaction between illegality and social policies thus turned these emergency plans into an artful technology of governance, albeit favoring inequality and an unjust political order.

According to my interviews, the state administration was very nervous when the UFP document was published. Some high-ranking officials I interviewed were quite embarrassed by the figures on price formation it contained. Since no official statistics on price formation existed in Mauritania, there was no way for state services to disprove UFP's accusations. On the one hand, this was UFP's weak point: the figures were very speculative. But on the other hand, in facing a state apparatus that acted through illegal and undocumented procedures, using a formalized and legal-rational language to formulate protests could in itself be a very challenging, if not subversive, political means.[17] Faced with UFP's accusations of widespread illegal management of food markets and emergency plans, the state officials denied the accusations, but they were far less persuasive than UFP's detailed figures and tables. In addition, UFP's criticism itself was devastating for the government: denouncing illegality in food markets meant that the "emergency plans" and more generally the public regulation of food markets could be portrayed as illegitimate. To some officials I interviewed, this argument was unfair: the state itself was obliged to deal with the massive use of circumvention in the economy and with the existence of powerful oligopolistic importers.[18] Anyway, UFP's action shows that legalism, representing the normative perspective that law should be respected, became a collective action repertoire (Tilly 1986; Offerlé 2008). Noticing the existence of a "demand for legalism" in such a context is very important from an analytical point of view. It proves that, even when there is no serious prospect of reducing illegality, and when illegality seems in many ways legitimate, the call for legality can be mobilized by social and political actors to protest against the existing "social order of markets." This occurs especially when this order is perceived by some parts of society as unjust.

## Conclusion

The first main conclusion that can be drawn from the preceding analysis is related to the interpretation of the roles of illegality in so-called developing countries, and particularly in Africa. For the neo-patrimonialist school, corrupt interests drive economic and social life, as well as the action of public

[17] On the rhetorical power of economic language, see Gudeman (2009).

[18] This argument has to be taken seriously. For example, my interviews showed that the relationships between the state and importers were in favor of the latter. Because of the state's urgent need to distribute large quantities of food, the importers have the ultimate power to fix the prices and determine payment conditions.

institutions (Chabal and Daloz 1999; Mkandawire 2013). In some paradigms, such as the concept of the "shadow state" developed by William Reno (1995), circumvention of the rules, trafficking, and illicit modes of action are so pervasive that the formal state is of no significance in social life.

The empirical cases presented in this chapter depart from this point of view. In Guadeloupe, for example, the attempts to enforce legal rules and contain illegalities do not succeed, but they confer new social and political meanings on abuses and favor the social demand for legalism. In Mauritania, formal public policies use illicit channels as means of action. Illegality and circumvention not only coexist with formal institutions and legalism, but both appear to interact closely with each other, creating interdependent and joint dynamics (Hibou 2015; Samuel 2013). The state selectively enforces laws and regulations to consolidate its power and legitimacy. Such a conclusion is in line with the argument put forward by Bayart et al. (1999), who argued that criminal activities may contribute to the formation of states rather than undermining it, as all normative theories of fragile or failing states argue (see also Engwicht, in this volume).

The second conclusion is more methodological: it is possible to study contexts in which the circumvention of legal rules is pervasive by observing formal economic practices and conventions. Paraphrasing Keith Hart, illegality and legality are "two sides of the coin" (1986). To study economic laws and rules in action and the social dynamics they produce, the interactions between licit and illicit activities need to be taken into account, and they are a fertile entry point. Such a position is not so common: the French convention school, for example, has long been reluctant to engage in an in-depth investigation of the forms of circumvention, fearing to overstate the importance of fraud in the development of a critical sociology of institutions, and to forget the social consistency of economic conventions and collective rules (Thévenot 2015). However, formalized administrative and technical objects resulting from the use of a legal-rational set of techniques may be the matrix of various—and sometimes contradictory—modes of action that can be legal or illegal (de Certeau 2011; Hibou 2015; Samuel 2013). "Formal legality" and "social legitimacy" of illegalities (Mayntz, in this volume) generate a variety of intertwined social processes, and contribute to shaping the social world.

The third conclusion is related to the importance of studying the interface between legality and illegality. My investigations showed that social change can be induced by the transformations of this interface and its inner tensions. In Guadeloupe and Mauritania, there are periodic protests against illegal transactions, making them appear illegitimate and as a reason to call for reforms. Dynamics of change also arise from the difficulty of applying official legal rules, which forms the background of their de facto circumvention.

Periodic readjustments of the boundaries between legality and illegality therefore occur. In addition, both of my case studies show how the sense of injustice arises from these rooms to maneuver, which create the possibility of discretionary decisions when economic rules and regulations are employed. Multiple dynamics may thus be created by the presence of illegality in markets, which can stabilize economic conventions, as well as create pressures for the emergence of new "social orders of markets" (Beckert 2009).

## References


*20 minutes*. 2008. "Guadeloupe: Un accord sur la baisse du prix du carburants déclenche la levée des barrages." December 11.

Autorité de la concurrence. 2009a. *Avis n° 09-A-21 du 24 juin 2009 relatif à la situation de la concurrence sur les marchés des carburants dans les départements d'outre-mer*. Paris.

Autorité de la concurrence. 2009b. *Avis n° 09-A-45 du 8 septembre 2009 relatif aux mécanismes d'importation et de distribution des produits de grande consommation dans les départements d'outre-mer*. Paris.

Bayart, Jean-François. 2009 [1993]. *The State in Africa: The Politics of the Belly*. 2nd updated ed. Cambridge: Polity Press.

Bayart, Jean-François, Stephen Ellis, and Béatrice Hibou. 1999. *The Criminalization of the State in Africa*. Woodbridge: James Currey Publishers.

Beckert, Jens. 2009. "The Social Order of Markets." *Theory and Society* 38: pp. 245–69.

Beckert, Jens. 2011. "Where Do Prices Come From? Sociological Approaches to Price Formation." *Socio-Economic Review* 9(4): pp. 757–86.

Berry, Sara. 2007. "Marginal Gains, Market Values, and History." *African Studies Review* 50–2.

Bolliet, Anne, Thomas Cazenave, Thibaut Sartre et al. 2009. *Rapport sur la fixation des prix des carburants dans les départements d'Outre-mer*. Inspection générale des finances. Paris, March.

Braudel, Fernand. 1985. *La dynamique du capitalisme*. Paris: Flammarion.

Brissac, Jean-Marie. 2009. *Rapport complémentaire au rapport du CESR sur le prix des produits pétroliers en Guadeloupe*. Basse-Terre, April.

Bruno, Isabelle, Emmanuel Didier, and Tommaso Vitale. 2014. "Statactivism: Forms of Action between Disclosure and Affirmation." *Partecipazione e conflitto* 7(2): pp. 198–220.

Boltanski, Luc, Yann Darré, and Marie-Ange Schiltz. 1984. "La dénonciation." *Actes de la recherches en sciences sociales* 51.

Boltanski, Luc, and Arnaud Esquerre. 2015. "Critique, valeur, prix." Paper presented at the Seminar Valeur, Prix Politique, Ecole Normale Supérieure de Cachan, mimeo.

Boltanski, Luc, and Laurent Thévenot. 2006 [1991]. *On Justification: Economies of Worth*. Princeton, NJ: Princeton University Press.

Bonnecase, Vincent. 2013. "Politique des prix, vie chère et contestation sociale a Niamey: Quels répertoires locaux de la colère?" *Politique Africaine* 130.

Bourdieu, Pierre. 2005. *The Social Structures of the Economy*. Cambridge: Polity.
*Calame*. 2008. "Brèves de la Semaine du Calame: PSI hors la loi ..." July 10.
de Certeau, Michel. 2011. *The Practice of Everyday Life*. London: University of California Press.
Chabal, Patrick, and Jean-Pascal Daloz. 1999. *Africa Works: Disorder as Political Instrument*. Bloomington: Indiana University Press.
Conan, Eric. 1997. "Réunion: Les dessous du volcan." *L'Express*, August 7.
Doligé, Eric. 2009. *Rapport d'information au nom de la mission commune d'information sur la situation des départements d'outre-mer*. Paris: Editions du Sénat.
Dumez, Hervé, and Alain Jeunemaitre. 1989. *Diriger l'économie: L'État et les prix en France, 1936–1986*. Paris: L'Harmattan.
*France Antilles Guadeloupe*. 2006. "Les pêcheurs exigent de la transparence." August 18.
Gudeman, Stephen (ed.). 2009. *Economic Persuasions*. New York: Berghahn Books.
Hart, Keith. 1986. "Heads or Tails? Two Sides of the Coin." *Man* 21–3: pp. 637–56.
Hibou, Béatrice. 2011. *Anatomie politique de la domination*. Paris: La Découverte.
Hibou, Béatrice. 2015. *The Bureaucratization of the World in the Neoliberal Era*. Basingstoke: Palgrave Macmillan.
*Horizons*. 2004. "La spéculation des devises, une opération de sabordage de notre économie nationale." Nouakchott, 3739, June 9.
IMF. 2008. *Mauritania: 2008 Article IV Consultation and Third Review under the Three-Year Arrangement under the Poverty Reduction and Growth Facility*. Washington, DC, May 5.
ISFP, Initiative sur la flambée des prix agricoles. 2010. *Mission de consultation avec le gouvernement et les partenaires au développement et identification préliminaire d'un plan d'actions—Aide-mémoire*, June.
Islamic Republic of Mauritania. 2006. *Rapport sur la révision des données macroéconomiques 1992–2004*. Nouakchott, June.
Le Roy, Frederic. 2004. "La concurrence: Entre affrontement et connivance." *Revue française de gestion* 158: 149–52.
Mkandawire, Thandika. 2013. "Neopatrimonialism and the Political Economy of Economic Performance in Africa: Critical Reflections." Working paper, Institute for Futures Studies, 1, Stockholm.
Offerlé, Michel. 2008. "Retour critique sur les répertoires de l'action collective (XVIIIe–XXIe siècles)." *Politix* 81: pp. 181–202.
Ould Ahmed Salem, Zekeria. 2001. " 'Tcheb-tchib' et compagnie. Lexique de la survie et figures de la réussite en Mauritanie." *Politique africaine* 82: pp. 78–100.
Payen, Didier. 2009. *Rapport sur les prix des produits pétroliers en Guadeloupe: Version définitive du 10/01/2009*. Observatoire des prix de la région Guadeloupe/Conseil économique et social régional, Basse Terre.
Pied, Henri. 2010. "Martinique méconnue... la grève de 1953." *Antilla*, September 2–9.
*Quotidien de Nouakchott*. 2011. "Où sont passés les 48 millions de dollars de la BCM?" January 12.
Reno, William. 1995. *Corruption and State Politics in Sierra Leone*. Cambridge: Cambridge University Press.
Roitman, Janet. 2004. *Fiscal Disobedience: An Anthropology of Economic Regulation in Central Africa*. Princeton, NJ: Princeton University Press.

Samuel, Boris. 2013. *La production macroéconomique du réel: Formalités et pouvoir au Burkina Faso, en Mauritanie et en Guadeloupe*. Thèse de doctorat en science politique, SciencesPo, Paris.

Samuel, Boris. 2014 "Statistics and Political Violence: Reflections on the Social Conflict in 2009 in Guadeloupe." *Partecipazione e Conflitto* 7(2): pp. 238–57.

Samuel, Boris. 2015. "Economic Calculations, Instability and (In)formalization of the State in Mauritania, 2003–2011." In *Measuring African Development: Past and Present*, edited by M. Jerven, pp. 77–96. London: Routledge.

Stanziani, Alessandro. 2007. "Spéculation." In *Dictionnaire historique de l'économie-droit, XVIIIe–XXe siècles*. Paris: LGDJ, pp. 195–211.

Storper, Michael, and Robert Salais. 1997. *Worlds of Production: The Action Frameworks of the Economy*. Cambridge, MA: Harvard University Press.

Targui, Mohamed. 2010. "Décret d'avance budget 2010: L'autre manière de régulariser les extras." *Biladi*, December 5.

Thévenot, Laurent. 2015. "Certifying the World: Power Infrastructures and Practices in Economies of Conventional Forms." In *Re-Imagining Economic Sociology*, edited by Patrik Aspers and Nigel Dodd, pp. 195–223. Oxford: Oxford University Press.

Tilly, Charles. 1986. *The Contentious French: Four Centuries of Popular Struggle*. Cambridge, MA: Harvard University Press.

UFP, Union des Forces de Progrès. 2011. "La Flambée des prix: Causes réelles et propositions." Nouakchott, March 5.

UGTG, Union Générale des Travailleurs de Guadeloupe. 2009. "Rapport de l'Autorité de la concurrence sur la grande distribution: Le point de vue d'Alain Plaisir." September 7.

Wallerstein, Immanuel. 1983. *Historical Capitalism*. London: Verso.

Weber, Max. 1978 [1922]. *Economy and Society*. Berkeley: University of California Press.

# 15

# The Price Is Not Right

## Financialization and Financial Crime

*Robert Tillman*

This chapter presents the argument that financialization, as a broad economic trend, has increased the opportunities for financial crime among firms both within and outside the financial services industry.[1] The growth of the financial services industry, the increasing dependence of many economies on financial services, an increasing focus on share value by firms, and dramatic increases in compensation within the financial services industry have all contributed to increases in the frequency and scale of financial crime in recent years. To illustrate these trends, three case studies are reviewed: (i) the manipulation of electricity prices by investment bank subsidiaries; (ii) the deliberate rigging of the London Interbank Offered Rate or "Libor"; and (iii) the fixing of foreign exchange (FX) rates by investment bank traders. The case studies involve efforts by financial-sector insiders to profit by manipulating the infrastructure of those markets, tinkering with the mechanisms by which prices and rates are set.

### Introduction

A series of large-scale financial scandals—the savings and loan crisis of the 1980s, the corporate accounting scandals of the early 2000s, and the global financial crisis that began in 2008—forced many criminologists and sociologists to rethink the fundamental nature and organization of white-collar crime

[1] This chapter draws on the arguments and materials presented in Robert Tillman et al. forthcoming.

and to take a closer look at the connections between white-collar crime, the economy, and financial institutions. The scope and scale of these fraud epidemics has led a number of researchers to conclude that they were symptomatic of larger shifts in the economy and in society. Analyzing the broader context of the savings and loan crisis of the 1980s, Calavita and Pontell (1991), for example, noted that previous studies of white-collar crime had focused on manufacturing enterprises that characterized industrial capitalism, whereas advanced economies such as the US economy are increasingly dominated by financial transactions. Therefore, they argued, "it seems likely that the qualitatively different 'production process' in finance capitalism will generate new forms of corporate crime in response to new sets of organizational pressures." Similarly, in their study of fraud in the small business health-insurance industry, Tillman and Indergaard (1999) argued that by the late twentieth century the economic terrain had been fundamentally restructured by corporations that had abandoned certain markets "where they once supplied products or services," such as health insurance, creating opportunities for new forms of white-collar crime. In a later study of corporate fraud, the same authors demonstrated that so-called "New Economy" firms, typified by companies such as Enron, took advantage of broader economic trends—including deregulation, a shift to network organization, and a shift among reputational intermediaries like lawyers and accountants to take on advocacy roles for their clients—to engage in a wide variety of fraudulent activities, the most common of which was financial statement fraud, in which investors were deceived about the true state of affairs at publicly held corporations (Tillman and Indergaard 2005).

The other aspect of these newer forms of financial crimes that has forced a reappraisal of their significance has been their costs, which in some cases are truly staggering. The savings and loan debacle, in which over 1,000 thrifts (building societies in the United Kingdom) had to be bailed out by the US government, eventually cost taxpayers over USD 125 billion. A recent analysis by three prominent economists put the costs of corporate securities fraud alone at USD 380 billion a year (Dyck et al. 2013). Economist Gabriel Zucman has estimated that 8 percent of the world's wealth—about USD 7.6 trillion—is held in secretive tax havens, beyond the reach of tax collectors and unusable for the public good (Zucman 2015). The costs of financial crime and its related economic dislocations are not only monetary but physical as well. A study published in British medical journal the *Lancet*, for example, estimated that the global financial crisis that began in 2008 resulted in an additional 260,000 deaths from cancer alone between 2008 and 2010 (Maruthappu et al. 2016).

The evidence suggests, then, that we have moved into a new era in which, unlike forms of white-collar crime studied by an earlier generation of scholars, contemporary financial crime threatens the stability of entire economies and the well-being of millions of individuals. It is no longer possible to think of white-collar and corporate crimes as "largely private matters" that do not threaten the social contract the way street crimes do, as the prominent political scientist James Q. Wilson once argued (Wilson 1975). What we need is a new understanding of the linkages between white-collar crime and financial institutions and broader economic changes. Or as Reurink, after an exhaustive review of the literature, recently put it: "what is needed to come to grips with the recent proliferation of financial crimes is a new theoretical framework; one that understands today's financial crimes as the dominant manifestations of white-collar crime in a historically specific form of finance capitalism" (2016: 35).

As a small contribution to this project, in this chapter I will present an argument about the impact that financialization, as a broad economic trend, and specific changes in financial institutions have had on the opportunities for financial crime. The essence of the argument is that over the past several decades those institutions that control the flow of money around the world have changed significantly, becoming more complex and more deeply embedded in the economies in which they operate and that "the increasing complexity of the global financial system has provided innumerable ways to fudge, fiddle, fix, hide, distort, and manipulate the intricate machinery that lies behind that system" (Tillman et al. forthcoming). The ability of financial-sector workers to manipulate that machinery has resulted in some of the high-profile, as well as some not so well-known, financial scandals that have surfaced in recent years, and in the second section of the chapter several of these scandals will be reviewed to illustrate the larger theoretical argument. The goal is not to present a comprehensive overview of financial crime but instead to provide a framework for understanding how diverse and seemingly unrelated financial crimes are in fact similar and linked by common underlying structures and sources.

## Financialization

Among the most important trends that have transformed the corporate landscape, and the financial services industry in particular, in recent years has been *financialization*, which can be defined broadly as "a pattern of accumulation in which profits accrue primarily through financial channels rather than through trade and commodity production" (Krippner 2005: 178). The broad scope of financialization is captured well in the following passage from journalist Rana Foroohar's book *Makers and Takers* (2016: 6):

> The financialization of America includes everything from the growth in size and scope of finance and financial activity in our economy to the rise of debt-fueled

> speculation over productive lending, to the ascendency of shareholder value as a model of corporate governance, to the proliferation of risky, selfish thinking in both our private and public sectors, to the increasing political power of financiers and the CEOs they enrich, to the way in which a "market knows best" ideology remains the status quo, even after it caused the worst financial crisis in seventy-five years.

Financialization can have many consequences, but one, to put it simply, is an economy based more on moving money around than on real production and substantive services. Financialization has also had a number of specific consequences for the financial services industry as well as non-financial companies, including:

(1) the financial services industry has come to dominate the economy to an unprecedented extent;
(2) many economies, both regional and national, have become increasingly dependent on financial services, which can skew policies in favor of those industries;
(3) firms within and outside the financial services industry have shifted their focus from improving the quality of their products or services to increasing the value of their stock; and
(4) levels of compensation in the financial services industry have dramatically increased, creating opportunities for individuals to amass large fortunes in relatively short periods of time (Tillman et al. forthcoming).

These trends have also altered the opportunity structures for white-collar crime and in what follows each is discussed in more detail.

### *Growth of the Financial Services Industry*

The late twentieth century saw a dramatic increase in the role of the financial services industry in the economies of the United States and other countries. By the end of the century the US economy had become so dominated by finance that economist/columnist Paul Krugman referred to it as "the monster that ate the world economy" (Krugman 2009). The monster metaphor was continued by journalist Matt Taibbi, who in a 2009 article referred to the investment bank Goldman Sachs as a "great vampire squid" (2009). The images conjured up by these words reflect real fears about the size and power of financial firms in American society.

This trend is clearly reflected in the economic data. In the early 1980s less than 10 percent of all domestic corporate profits came from the financial services industries. By the mid-2000s that proportion had jumped to 40 percent (Johnson 2009: 49). The expansion of finance is also reflected in wage data. During the 1950s wages paid to financial workers were, on average, about the same as those paid to workers in other sectors. By 2007, employees in the financial industries were receiving paychecks on average 181 percent higher than workers in other industries. These workers were part of the machinery controlled by "financial oligarchs" who, centered on Wall Street, "truly believe that they control the levers that make the world go round" (Johnson 2009: 50).

The dominance of the financial services sector is also reflected in the scope of its activities and the number of people it affects. In 1970, an average of 12 million shares were traded daily on the New York Stock Exchange. By 2000, an average of just over 1 billion shares were bought and sold every day. By the end of the twentieth century it was no longer just the upper classes who participated in the stock market. The proportion of Americans who owned stock either directly or through mutual funds or pension plans increased from 10 percent in 1970 to 48 percent in 2000 (Phillips 2002: 140). The primary beneficiaries of this growth were investment banks. Between 1999 and 2008, JP Morgan saw its assets increase from USD 667 billion to USD 2.2 trillion. At Goldman Sachs, assets grew from USD 250 billion in 1999 to USD 1.1 trillion in 2007 (Financial Crisis Inquiry Commission 2011: 65). This growth created so-called "too big to fail" institutions whose size made them essential to the financial infrastructure and gave them a choke-hold on the economy.

### *Economic Dependence on Financial Services*

As a result of this dramatic growth in the financial services industry many countries and cities are now highly dependent on finance to support their economies. Cities such as New York and London, which operate as global financial centers, exemplify this pattern. Before the financial crisis of 2008, taxes from Wall Street firms made up as much as 20 percent of all tax revenues in New York State (New York State Comptroller's Office 2012). While dropping immediately after the crisis began, by 2015 that proportion was back to 17.5 percent (New York State Comptroller's Office 2016). The relatively high wages paid in the securities industry show up in the fact that in 2010, 23.5 percent of all wages in New York City went to employees in that industry, despite the fact that they comprised only 5.3 percent of all private-sector workers in the city. In Britain and, in particular, London this dependence on finance is even greater. In 2007, financial services accounted for 8.3 percent of the United Kingdom's GDP and 18 percent of London's GDP (McKenzie 2009). In 2015, the financial sector accounted for 11 percent of all tax revenues in the United Kingdom (City of London Corporation 2015).

Because of this dependence, politicians in both of these countries have tended to be very protective of the financial sector, strongly resisting reform and opposing crackdowns on illegal practices. In 2009, when angry calls were heard in Washington to reduce the bonuses of executives at the bailed-out insurance giant AIG,[2] then New York governor David Paterson defended the company: "At the end of the day, when they shut those bonuses down, they were shutting New York State down. That's where we got our tax dollars" (Blain 2009). Political leaders in England took similarly defensive postures in 2012 when state and federal authorities in the United States accused British insurer Standard Chartered of violating American restrictions on doing business in Iran. John Mann, a Labour MP, saw in the regulatory action "an increasing anti-British bias by US regulators and politicians aimed at shifting financial markets from London to New York" (Rushe and Treanor 2012). These political responses to allegations of financial wrongdoing are examples of what Clift and Woll have called "economic patriotism," by which they mean: "economic choices which seek to discriminate in favour of particular social groups, firms or sectors understood by the decision-makers as insiders because of their territorial status" (Clift and Woll 2011). The implicit argument made by the apologists cited above is that the harms caused by financial malfeasance are greatly outweighed by the economic benefits they bring to society, or at least to the society in close geographical proximity to the misdeeds.

### *Financial Engineering*

As financial firms have come to dominate many economies, many non-financial firms have adopted their goals and methods, incorporating financial engineering strategies into their core business models. Foroohar described this trend concisely: "financial *thinking* has become so ingrained in American businesses that even our biggest and brightest companies have started to act like banks" (emphasis in original) (2016: 4). Indeed, a number of large non-financial companies have begun providing many services that once were only offered by retail banks, a trend that Olivier Godechot refers to as *bankarization* (2015: 4). The retailing giant Wal-Mart, for example, now offers its customers a full array of banking and money services, from check cashing to money transfers.

In this newer model an emphasis on research, product development, and increased efficiency is replaced with a predominant focus on maintaining the firm's stock price. To accomplish this goal, companies employ armies of lawyers and accountants in an effort to reduce their tax exposure, to buy

[2] President Obama blasted the company in public comments: "This is a corporation that finds itself in financial distress due to recklessness and greed." CNN, "Obama Tries to Stop AIG Bonuses: 'How do they justify this outrage?'" March 16, 2009. <http://www.cnn.com/2009/POLITICS/03/16/AIG.bonuses/>.

other companies, or to construct complex financial instruments and transactions that will boost their revenues or reduce their liabilities and ultimately boost their share price. From the perspective of many academics (mostly economists) and policymakers the focus on stock prices by publicly held firms was a positive trend, signaling the onset of an "investor revolution" in which shareholders would gain a larger share of profits and would exert more control over the firm's operations. An essential component of this new corporate orientation—what came to be known as the "shareholder value" model—was an effort to more closely align executives' interests with those of stockholders by making executive compensation increasingly dependent on share prices through the use of stock options and stock awards. The idea was that executives would be rewarded only if their performance created more value for shareholders.

But the academics who championed it did not foresee an unintended negative consequence of the model. Stock-based compensation schemes gave executives strong incentives to cheat, to engage in what many accounting professors refer to as "earnings management," but which almost everyone else would call "cooking the books." In these schemes executives seek to artificially increase revenues or to hide liabilities in an effort to improve the perception of their company's performance and the firm's share price. These tactics resemble "pump and dump" schemes (Tillman and Indergaard 2005). Corporate executives—aided by accountants, lawyers, and bankers—would "pump up" the firm's performance measures (for example, revenues and earnings) with false data, reap the rewards of the higher stock prices conveyed to them through bonuses and stock options, then "dump" their shares before market actors realized what was going on and the prices plunged. In the end, at companies such as Enron, executives walked away with huge amounts of money while shareholders were left holding nearly empty bags.

### *Big Money*

While most people have heard about the sky-high salaries paid to star traders and executives on Wall Street many fewer probably read a *Business Insider* magazine article that reported that in 2015 *summer interns* at investment banks were earning the equivalent of USD 85,000 a year (Crowe 2015). By itself this fact is not that important but it does reflect a significant shift in the financial services industry. Working on Wall Street or being employed as a trader in the Chicago Mercantile Exchange used to mean a steady, if not grand, income and a reasonable retirement package. But in the 1970s that began to change as remuneration in the financial sector began to skyrocket. This increase becomes more apparent when salaries in that industry are compared with those in another profession, engineering. Until the 1980s, highly educated finance workers and engineers were paid roughly equivalent amounts. But by 2005 finance workers were earning 35 percent more than similarly educated engineers (Philippon and Rashef 2012). As one would expect, in places such as New York City the difference in salaries for finance workers and everybody else was even more striking. By 2015, the average salary for employees in the securities industry in New York City was USD 404,800, nearly six times the average salary earned by other private sector employees in the city (New York State Comptroller's Office 2016).

This dramatic increase in the amount of funds flowing through the financial sector has altered both the opportunities and motivations for those who work there to engage in illegal activity. The influx of money fundamentally changed the "risk–reward equation" so that the potential gains from even small manipulations or misuses of information make financial crimes much more attractive than they once were (Stewart 2012). At hedge funds, for example, traders routinely engage in transactions worth millions of dollars and they come to understand that simply changing a few numbers or obtaining insider information about the health of companies can bring them tremendous rewards, with little fear of detection or punishment because the illegalities may be hidden in a mountain of high-speed trades. As financial markets become more complex and more opaque to outsiders, market players are able to exploit the inevitable loopholes and gaps in those systems to enrich themselves and their employers.

In short, the argument being presented here is that the increasing financialization of the economy, in the United States and elsewhere, has heightened the *criminogenic tendencies* of a number of industries, particularly the financial service industries; as opportunities for financial crime have increased, the potential rewards for illegal behavior have grown, and the possibility for detection and punishment remains low. This view is at odds with the traditional view of "market discipline" favored by economists since Adam Smith. In this view, financial markets function efficiently because they are guided by Smith's famous "invisible hand"; the collective wisdom and oversight of transactions by market participants ensures that the markets remain free of fraud and deception. Competition among participants creates a "market discipline" that ensures that no one has an unfair advantage. Those who cheat are brought into line through damage to their reputations which negatively impacts their position in the market.

In the next section I will present three case studies that illustrate how markets often do not conform to this idealized image but instead allow market participants to game the system. The three case studies focus on: (i) the manipulation of electrical energy prices by investment bank subsidiaries; (ii) the deliberate rigging of Libor; and (iii) the fixing of FX rates by investment bank traders. All three cases involve traders, with access to the complex machinery of the markets, working in collusion with their counterparts at rival firms to artificially manipulate and distort rates and prices in complicated schemes that, although implemented by the traders, were sanctioned by their superiors and ultimately benefited their employers. These were not, in other words, "rogue traders," but were agents acting on behalf of major market players who saw how gaps and inconsistencies in rules governing markets could be exploited for enormous profits.

## Three Schemes

### *Manipulating Markets for Electrical Energy*

In early 2001, the term "energy crisis" was given a new meaning when California began experiencing shortages of electricity, leading to "rolling blackouts"—planned reductions in the availability of energy utilities that resulted in power outages in certain communities. President-elect George W. Bush blamed the situation on environmental policies that restricted energy supplies. But the public would soon learn otherwise. Investigations in the aftermath of the crisis revealed how massive changes in the system of electricity production and distribution from a highly regulated system to a deregulated system in which electricity was bought and sold on electronic auction platforms created numerous opportunities for fraud and market manipulation. Traders at firms such as Enron were able to take advantage of a number of loopholes in the system—a system that Enron had a hand in creating—to make enormous profits at the expense of consumers.

By 2002, the electrical energy trading industry was declared all but dead by the media, with the big players such as Enron and Dynegy departing the market in disgrace. But, at the same time, new players were moving in; not energy companies but investment banks. In 2002, Swiss bank UBS purchased Enron's trading unit and within a few years was followed into the market by Wall Street powerhouses such as Bear Stearns, Goldman Sachs, Merrill Lynch, and Deutsche Bank. With all that had been revealed about the failures of the deregulated system one might think that policymakers would have plugged up all its holes, and they did, in fact, make some significant changes. But many opportunities for fraud remained.

The investment banks quickly began to apply the tactics of "arbitrage"—playing one market against another—to electrical energy markets. In California that market comprised several separate but related markets: a "day-ahead" market in which transactions involved "physical products" because they required the actual delivery of electricity, and a "financial products" market, in which transactions were, in essence, bets on the future direction of electricity prices (Federal Energy Regulatory Commission 2012a). Trades in this market typically consisted of "financial swaps." Both of these markets—for physical products and for financial products—were significantly influenced by prices established by the ICE (Intercontinental Exchange) daily price index. These were baseline prices calculated on the basis of all transactions conducted over specific periods of time.[3]

The relationship between these two markets was complicated but one of the flaws in the system allowed traders to make substantial profits in the market for financial swaps by artificially depressing or inflating the prices in the daily price index. In these strategies traders would intentionally lose money on a volume of transactions that was large enough to move prices in the physical products market in the desired direction but would improve their position in the financial swaps market. In other words, one could profit in one market by losing money in another.

This is exactly what the Federal Energy Regulatory Commission (FERC) claimed that traders at Barclays Bank did between 2006 and 2008 when they "engaged in a coordinated scheme during those product months to take the physical positions they had built and liquidate them in the cash markets—generally at a loss—to impact the ICE daily index settlements to benefit Barclays' related financial positions that settled against those indices" (*US Federal Energy Regulatory Commission* v. *Barclays Bank et al.*: 9). According to the Commission, using these tactics over a thirty-five-month period Barclays sustained losses of USD 4 million in the physical products market but achieved gains of USD 35 million in the financial products market (*Federal Energy Regulatory Commission* v. *Barclays Bank et al.*: 8–9).

To support their allegations against Barclays, FERC produced reams of trading data but they were also able to demonstrate that traders knew that they were illegally manipulating the market by reproducing email communications in which traders openly discussed and even boasted about their efforts to distort energy prices for a profit. For example, one trader informed another by email of his intention to "crap on" the day-ahead market to lower the daily index and benefit Barclay's position in financial swaps (Kelton 2012). Another trader bragged about manipulating prices on ICE at the Palo Verde trading location:

[3] In its complaint against Barclay, FERC described the daily price index in the following way: "One of the most commonly used indices and the relevant one for this case was the Intercontinental Exchange ('ICE') daily index. During the relevant time, much of the electricity trading in the western U.S. occurred on ICE... The ICE daily index was an index published by ICE each trading day based on the VWAP of all day-ahead fixed-price physical electricity transactions at a particular trading location... The ICE daily index was set by a methodology that calculates an index price based on the VWAP of all contributing volumes and prices traded on ICE. The volumes and prices that ICE used to calculate the daily index price were those trades that occurred in the day-ahead fixed-price physical market, a market commonly referred to as the 'cash' or 'dailies' market. In the dailies market, traders bought and sold electricity for physical delivery the following day at fixed prices (e.g., 25 MW/h of peak MIDC electricity for delivery the following day priced at $50 per MW/h)," *US Federal Energy Regulatory Commission* v. *Barclays Bank et al.*, 6.

"I totally f**kked with the Palo mrkt today... Was fun. Need to do that more often" (*US Federal Energy Regulatory Commission* v. *Barclays Bank et al.*: 39).

Investment bankers discovered other ways to game the electrical energy markets. The system in place in California, and in other states, was designed to increase competition and, at the same time, stabilize the market by means of various mechanisms that were supposed to reduce volatility and risk to market participants. One of these was what was known as "make-whole payments." How this mechanism operated was, like the larger market itself, extremely complex but it boiled down to this. Electrical energy generators could actually be paid for *producing electrical power at a loss* when their bid to produce electricity was so low it did not cover the costs of actually producing power. In California the formal mechanism through which this operated was called Bid Cost Recovery or BCR payments.

One of the investment banks that was quick to see the potential of this mechanism was JP Morgan, which in 2008 came into possession of two money-losing power plants in southern California. The plants quickly became profitable when JP Morgan, operating through a subsidiary, JP Morgan Ventures Energy Corporation (JPMVEC), implemented a "make money by losing money" strategy that relied on BCR payments. In 2013 FERC accused the firm of gaming the system, claiming that in an eight-month period beginning in August 2010, "JPMVEC collected market revenues of $21.9 million for these two plants while spending $29.5 million on gas and operating costs, for a loss at market rates of $7.6 million. But because of $34.6 million in BCR payments, the units generated profits on a marginal cost basis of $27 million over those months" (Federal Energy Regulatory Commission 2013).

JP Morgan eventually paid USD 410 million to settle the charges (Federal Energy Regulatory Commission 2013a). FERC also leveled market manipulation charges against several other investment banks involved in the electrical energy business, including Barclays, which was ordered to pay USD 453 million in penalties, and Deutsche Bank, which paid USD 1.6 million for illegal actions in California in 2010 (Federal Energy Regulatory Commission 2013b, 2013c).

The implications of investment banks being involved in the "real economy," such as commodities markets, was summed up by consumer activist Tyson Slocum as follows:

> When Wall Street banks engage in electricity trading, they often aren't interested in building value, hiring workers and introducing innovations. Instead, they seek to exploit or create loopholes to bend the market to their advantage. They're not interested in fair competition, but rather twisting the rules to maximize their profits at the expense of honest Americans.
>
> (Blair 2013)

### *Libor*

The same logic that led investment bankers to see the profits in rate rigging in electrical energy markets also led them to understand the value of manipulating interest rates, as was revealed in the ongoing Libor scandal. Indeed, many of the same investment banks were involved in both scandals. As in the electricity price schemes, the Libor scandal involved large financial institutions exploiting little-known technical mechanisms in the financial infrastructure for enormous profits. As journalist Matt Taibbi (2013) put it:

> The banks found a loophole, a basic flaw in the machine. Across the financial system, there are places where prices or official indices are set based upon unverified data sent in by private banks and financial companies. In other words, we gave the players with incentives to game the system institutional roles in the economic infrastructure.

Here again we see how financial complexity creates the opportunity for corruption and collusion on a grand scale.

As part of the machinery of the global banking system, Libor is a crucial baseline measure that affects nearly every aspect of the global financial system, from complex financial derivatives through mortgage rates to interest on student loans. Around USD 700 trillion in derivative contracts around the world are based on Libor. Banks not only lend money but also borrow money from each other and Libor is a measure of the average amount that banks have to pay each other for loans for set periods of time—for example, three months—for different currencies. Significantly, Libor is not based on actual transactions between banks but on estimates of interest rates submitted by major banks to the British Bankers Association in London every day. An average is calculated and that rate is then used by financial institutions globally to set a baseline for interest rates on all kinds of financial instruments.

In theory, Libor is an objective measure of the costs of borrowing money. In reality it is just another financial instrument that is vulnerable to manipulation and distortion by small groups of individuals in key positions in the economic infrastructure. This became apparent in June 2012 when the business press reported that Barclays Bank had reached an agreement with authorities in the United States and the United Kingdom to pay USD 450 million in fines and penalties to settle charges that it had manipulated Libor (Colchester and Eaglesham 2012). The allegations claimed that Barclays had manipulated the rate to achieve two purposes. One was to affect derivatives transactions in which the bank was involved. The other was to lower the bank's perceived borrowing costs to give a misleading impression of its financial health.

In the first type of scheme, derivatives traders and persons responsible for Libor submissions (submitters) were caught in email exchanges colluding to fix the daily Libor rate, as in the following.

> Friday, March 10, 2006:
> Trader: "Hi mate[.] We have an unbelievably large set on Monday (the IMM). We need a really low 3m [3-month] fix, it could potentially cost a fortune. Would really appreciate any help, I'm being told by my NYK [counterparts in New York] that it's extremely important. Thanks."
> Monday, March 13, 2006:
> Trader: "The big day has...arrived...My NYK were screaming at me about an unchanged 3m libor. As always, any help wd [would] be greatly appreciated. What do you think you'll go for 3m?"
> Submitter: "I am going 90 altho[ugh] 91 is what I should be posting."
> Trader: "I agree with you and totally understand. Remember, when I retire and write a book about this business your name will be in golden letters..."
> Submitter: "I would prefer this not be in any books!"
> (US Department of Justice 2012)

Barclays's three-month dollar Libor submission on March 13, 2006 was 4.90 percent, just as the trader had requested.

After the financial crisis began in 2008 banks were being scrutinized more carefully by regulators for weaknesses. One sign of weakness was increased borrowing costs, which would have indicated poor financial health which could have resulted in lower share prices. Investigators discovered emails from managers at Barclays stating that they were forced to submit low numbers to Libor because all the other banks were doing it and they did not want to appear to be paying higher rates than the others (US Department of Justice 2012).

Barclays was only the first large bank to become ensnared in the investigations of Libor cheating. By 2015, many of the world's largest banks were implicated in the schemes and punished with fines and penalties, including UBS, Royal Bank of Scotland, JP Morgan, Citigroup, and Deutsche Bank. A handful of traders have been prosecuted and convicted, but, as of this writing, no high-level banking executives have been charged with crimes.

Because banking customers were not directly involved it is difficult to gauge the costs of the Libor crimes. But it is important to recognize that many individuals and communities are affected by Libor and even small movements in the rate can have serious consequences. In the United States, cities, counties, and states invest in interest rate swaps based on Libor to help fund public works projects. When the Libor rates were artificially suppressed, they were forced to pay more for those projects. One of the cities in question, Philadelphia, filed a lawsuit in July 2013 against a number of large banks, asserting that they had "artificially and collusively suppressed Libor, which had the effect of secretly tilting the swaps in their favor, causing the banks to be substantially 'in the money' when they did not deserve to be, and effectively raising the losses to the City of Philadelphia" (*City of Philadelphia* v. *Bank of America* 2013: 20). The result exacerbated a severe budget crisis for the city's school district which was forced to lay off teachers and make cuts to music, language, after-school, and gifted student programs (Ward 2012: 3).

### *The FX Fix*

Revelations about the efforts by large international banks to manipulate Libor led to concerns that other key benchmark rates might also be vulnerable to deliberate rigging schemes. It did not take long for those fears to be realized. In May 2015, four of the largest banks in the world—Citigroup, JP Morgan Chase, Barclays, and Royal Bank of Scotland—agreed to plead guilty to US felony charges for their activities in manipulating FX rates over a number of years.[4] The FX rate-rigging schemes had much in common with the Libor manipulation scandal. In both cases, key benchmarks were determined by individuals who were also involved in transactions based on those benchmarks and had clear incentives to move those benchmarks in one direction or another. As with Libor, foreign exchange markets are huge, with USD 5.3 trillion changing hands every day. Many of the same banks were implicated in both the FX and the Libor scandals.

Foreign exchange rates move up and down throughout the day but, as with other markets, traders and investors need a benchmark rate to set the standards against which transactions can be evaluated. At 4 p.m. London time every weekday, the transactions for the most frequently traded currencies, including the US dollar and the euro, are monitored for 60 seconds and a median exchange rate is calculated or "fixed," and that becomes known as the "fix-rate." There are a number of ways that banks can profit from rigging the fix-rate. Banks buy and sell foreign currencies for clients and will often take a "buy" order at the daily fix-rate. If banks can buy the currencies at rates below the daily fix-rate then they stand to profit from the transaction. But this would require them to know what the daily fix-rate is going to be. One way they can do this is to collude with traders at other banks to submit buy and sell orders in the 60-second "fix" period so that the rate is driven up. Often times, this requires other traders to stand down, to not submit orders during the fix period.

Evidence of this collusion was found in numerous email communications between FX traders in which they openly discussed collaborative efforts to set

[4] A fifth bank, UBS, was also accused of forex manipulation but was not charged with criminal violations. However, it did agree to plead guilty to charges involving Libor manipulation. In her press conference announcing the charges Assistant Attorney General Janet Caldwell specifically cited the bank's violation of its Libor-related deferred prosecution agreement, stating: "UBS has a 'rap sheet' that cannot be ignored. Within the past six years, the department has resolved criminal investigations of UBS three times, resulting in non-prosecution or deferred prosecution agreements . . . Enough is enough." US Department of Justice 2015.

the rate. For example, in the exchange below, a trader from JP Morgan Chase (JPMC) is discussing with a trader at an undisclosed bank (Bank X) a plan to manipulate the 4 p.m. "fix rate" just before the fix period.

| | | |
|---|---|---|
| JPMC Trader: | 3:52:39 | tell u what |
| | 3:52:42 | let's double team it |
| | 3:52:45 | how much I got |
| Bank X Trader: | 3:52:46 | ok |
| | 3:52:47 | 300 |
| | 3:52:52 | u? |
| JPMC Trader: | 3:53:01 | ok ill give you 500 more |
| Bank X Trader: | 3:53:05 | wow |
| | 3:53:06 | ok |
| | 3:53:08 | ha |
| | 3:53:09 | cool . . . |
| JPMC Trader: | 3:53:20 | so we have 800 each |
| | 3:53:21 | ok |
| | 3:53:31 | but we gotta both do some at fix |
| | 3:53:36 | don't sell them all and take foot off haha |
| Bank X Trader: | 3:53:40 | i promise i will |
| JPMC Trader: | 3:53:47 | me too |

(Commodities Futures Trading Commission 2014)

As in the other case studies, while the collusive transactions were carried out by lower-level traders, their actions were fully sanctioned and encouraged by their superiors. At Barclays Bank, according to the New York State Department of Financial Services: "the misconduct at the Bank was systemic and involved various levels of employees . . . The culture within the Bank valued increased profits with little regard to the integrity of the market" (2015).

## Conclusion

This chapter began with an effort to view financial crimes in the context of the broader economic trend of financialization. Building on previous research I argued that financialization has had significant effects on the financial services industry and on non-financial firms. These changes include: (i) the increasing dominance of financial services in the economy; (ii) a growing economic dependence on financial services; (iii) a shift in non-financial firms to a focus on financial engineering and maintaining or increasing stock prices; and (iv) a dramatic increase in compensation for workers in the financial services sector. These trends, I argued, have enhanced the criminogenic tendencies present in the financial services, as well as other industries.

Next I presented three case studies that illustrate the criminological consequences of these larger economic shifts. The three case studies involve efforts by financial industry insiders to profit by manipulating entire markets by altering the infrastructure of those markets, tinkering with the mechanisms by which prices and rates are set. The analysis of these forms of financial crime has implications for both mainstream economic theories of markets and for economic sociology, which I will only briefly mention here.

Contemporary economic theories of financial markets rest on the assumption that these systems function efficiently because participants respond rationally to "signals" being emitted by the market, signals that provide information on which investment decisions can be made (Fama 1970). These signals—which include things such as interest rates, foreign exchange rates, and electrical energy prices—are assumed to have an objective quality, which, like measures of rainfall or the movement of glaciers, are unaffected by human behavior. The case studies presented in this chapter have shown that many of these "signals" are in fact social constructs, the practical accomplishments of individuals in specific social settings that are governed by their own norms of behavior. As in the movie *The Wizard of Oz*, in which the omnipotent Oz is revealed to be an old man behind a curtain pushing buttons and pulling levers, the majestic view (often promoted by mainstream economists) of financial markets as efficient perpetual motion machines is belied by the reality that they consist of real human beings making phone calls, sending emails, and texting one another, usually in pursuit of legitimate ends. But this reality also creates innumerable opportunities for these finance workers, usually at the behest of their superiors, to manipulate the marketplace.

This view of financial markets is consistent with the growing literature in the sociology of financial markets (Knorr-Cetina and Preda 2005). From this perspective, things like the daily price index for electricity, Libor rates, and foreign exchange fix-rates can be understood as "market devices." In Muniesa et al.'s (2007) formulation, these are defined as "the material and discursive assemblages that intervene in the construction of markets." These devices can include material objects such as cash registers and stock tickers, as well as financial instruments such as derivatives, all of which serve to organize markets by providing the means of conceptualizing markets and creating standardized calculations (Preda 2006). Measures of market activities—prices, ratings, indices—could be included in this conceptual framework. Fligstein and Roehrkasse recently suggested that the literature on "market devices," while important for economic sociology, has tended to see their constructive aspect, to assume that "they are relatively immune to manipulation and abuse." They argue that we should "expand analysis of market devices—to ask how their complexity gives market actors the ability to be fair or fraudulent" (Fligstein and Roehrkasse 2016). This chapter, hopefully, represents a very small step in this direction.

## References

Blain, Glenn. 2009. "Governor Paterson Says Bonuses Paid to Wall Street Financial Executives Were Good for State." *New York Daily News*, September 3.

Blair, Bridgette. 2013. "Get to Know Public Citizen." *Public Citizen News* 33(5).

Calavita, Kitty, and Henry N. Pontell. 1991. "'Other's People's Money' Revisited: Collective Embezzlement in the Savings and Loan and Insurance Industries." *Social Problems* 38(1): pp. 94–112.

City of London Corporation. 2015. *Total Tax Contribution of UK Financial Services Eighth Edition*. London: City of London.

Clift, Ben, and Cornelia Woll. 2011. "Economic Patriotism: Reinventing Control over Open Markets." *Journal of European Public Policy* 19: pp. 307–23. <http://www.cnn.com/2009/POLITICS/03/16/AIG.bonuses/>.

Colchester, Max, and Jeane Eaglesham. 2012. "Barclays Settles Rates Probe." *Wall Street Journal*, June 27.

Crowe, Portia. 2015. "Wall Street Interns Are Earning More Money than Ever This Summer." *Business Insider*, July 3.

Dyck, Alexander, Adair Morse, and Luis Zingales. 2013. "How Pervasive Is Corporate Fraud?" *Social Science Research Network*. <http://papers.ssrn.com/sol3/papers.cfm?abstract_id=2222608>.

Fama, Eugene. 1970. "Efficient Capital Markets." *Journal of Finance* 25(2): pp. 383–417.

Federal Energy Regulatory Commission. 2013a. "FERC, JP Morgan Unit Agree to $410 Million in Penalties, Disgorgement to Ratepayers." News release, July 30.

Federal Energy Regulatory Commission. 2013b. "FERC Orders $453 Million in Penalties for Western Power Market Manipulation." News release, July 16.

Federal Energy Regulatory Commission. 2013c. "FERC Approves Market Manipulation Settlement with Deutsche Bank." News release, January 22.

Financial Crisis Inquiry Commission. 2011. *The Financial Crisis Inquiry Report: Final Report of the National Commission on the Causes of the Financial and Economic Crisis in the United States*. Washington, DC: US Government Printing Office.

Fligstein, Neil, and Alexander Roehrkasse. 2016. "The Causes of Fraud in the Financial Crisis of 2007 to 2009." *American Sociological Review*, published online before print, June 23, doi: 10.1177/0003122416645594.

Foroohar, Rana. 2016. *Makers and Takers*. New York: Crown Publishers.

Godechot, Olivier. 2015. *Financialization Is Marketization!* Paris: Max Planck Sciences Po Center on Coping with Instability in Market Societies.

Johnson, Simon. 2009. "The Quiet Coup." *Atlantic Monthly* 303(4): pp. 46–50.

Kelton, Erika. 2012. "Barclays' Traders Show How Much Fun Wall Street Has Manipulating Markets." *Forbes*, November 11.

Knorr Cetina, Karin, and Alex Preda. 2005. *The Sociology of Financial Markets*. Oxford: Oxford University Press.

Krippner, Greta. 2005. "The Financialization of the American Economy." *Socio-Economic Review* 3(2): pp. 173–208.

Krugman, Paul. 2009. "Making Banking Boring." *New York Times*, April 10.

Maruthappu, Mahiben, Johnathan Watkins, Aisyah Maruthappu Mahiben et al. 2016. "Economic Downturns, Universal Health Coverage, and Cancer Mortality in High-Income and Middle-Income Countries, 1990–2010: A Longitudinal Analysis." *Lancet*, published online before print, May 25, doi: 10.1016/S0140-6736(16)00577-8.

McKenzie, Duncan. 2009. "Economic Contribution of UK Financial Services 2009." *ISFL Research*. <http://www.TheCityUK.com>.

Muniesa, Fabian, Yuval Millo, and Michel Callon. 2007. "An Introduction to Market Devices." *Sociological Review* 55(2): pp. 1–12.

New York State Comptroller's Office. 2012. "Street Business Declined in 2011, Industry Profits Down by Half from Prior Year." News release, February 29. <http://www.osc.state.ny.us/press/releases/feb12/022912.htm>.

New York State Comptroller's Office. 2016. "Wall Street Bonuses Decline in 2015." News release. <http://osc.state.ny.us/press/releases/mar16/030716.htm>.

Philippon, Thomas, and Ariell Rashef. 2012. "Wages and Human Capital in the U.S. Finance Industry." *Quarterly Journal of Economics* 127(4): pp. 1551–609.

Phillips, Kevin. 2002. *Wealth and Democracy: A Political History of the American Rich*. New York: Broadway Books.

Preda, Alex. 2006. "Socio-Technical Agency in Financial Markets." *Social Studies of Science* 36(5): pp. 753–82.

Reurink, Arjan. 2016. *From Elite Lawbreaking to Financial Crime: The Evolution of the Concept of White-Collar Crime*. MPIfG discussion paper 16/10. Cologne: Max Planck Institute for the Study of Societies.

Rushe, Dominic, and Jill Treanor. 2012. "City Fears that Wall Street Has the Square Mile in Its Sights." *Guardian*, August 11.

Stewart, James. 2012. "In a New Era of Insider Trading, It's Risk vs. Reward Squared." *New York Times*, December 7.

Taibbi, Matt. 2009. "The Great American Bubble Machine." *Rolling Stone*, July 9.

Taibbi, Matt. 2013. "Everything Is Rigged: The Biggest Price-Fixing Scandal Ever." *Rolling Stone*, April 25.

Tillman, Robert, and Michael Indergaard. 2005. *Pump and Dump: The Rancid Rules of the New Economy*. New Brunswick, NJ: Rutgers University Press.

Tillman, Robert, Henry Pontell, and William Black. Forthcoming. *Financial Crime and Crises in an Era of False Profits*. New York: Oxford University Press.

US Department of Justice. 2012. "Statement of Facts, U.S. Dept. of Justice and Barclays Bank PLC." <http://www.justice.gov/iso/opa/resources/9312012710173426365941.pdf>.

US Department of Justice. 2015. "Assistant Attorney General Leslie R. Caldwell Delivers Remarks at a Press Conference on Foreign Exchange Spot Market Manipulation."

News release, May 20. <http://www.justice.gov/opa/speech/assistant-attorney-general-leslie-r-caldwell-delivers-remarks-press-conference-foreign>.

Ward, Sharon. 2012. *Too Big to Trust? Banks, Schools and the Ongoing Problem of Interest Rate Swaps*. Harrisburg, PA: Pennsylvania Budget and Policy Center.

Wilson, James Q. 1975. *Thinking about Crime*. New York: Basic Books.

Zucman, Gabriel. 2015. *The Hidden Wealth of Nations: The Scourge of Tax Havens*. Chicago: University of Chicago Press.

## Legal Citations

*City of Philadelphia* v. *Bank of America Corporation et al.* Case no. 1:13-Cv-06020 (SDNY 2013) ("Complaint").

Commodities Futures Trading Commission. 2014. *In the Matter of J.P. Morgan Chase, USA before the Commodities Futures Trading Commission*. Docket no. 15-04 ("Order Instituting Proceedings").

Federal Energy Regulatory Commission. 2012a. *Barclays Bank PLC, Daniel Brin, Scott Connelly, Karen Levine, and Ryan Smith*. Docket no. IN08-8-000 ("Enforcement Staff Report and Recommendation").

Federal Energy Regulatory Commission. 2012b. *Barclays Bank PLC, Daniel Brin, Scott Connelly, Karen Levine, and Ryan Smith*. Docket no. IN08-8-000 ("Order to Show Cause and Notice of Proposed Penalty").

Federal Energy Regulatory Commission. 2013. 144 FERC 61,068 ("In Re Make-Whole Payments and Related Bidding Strategies") Docket No. IN11-8-000, 8.

*Federal Energy Regulatory Commission* v. *Barclays Bank*; Daniel Brin, Scott Connelly, Karen Levine, and Ryan Smith. Case 2:13-Cv-02093-TLN (EDCA 2013) ("Petition for an Order Affirming the Federal Regulatory Commission's July 16, 2013 Order Assessing Civil Penalties against Barclays Bank, Daniel Brin, Scott Connelly, Karen Levine, and Ryan Smith").

New York State Department of Financial Services. 2015. *In the Matter of Barclays Bank, PLC* ("Consent Order").

# Index

The manufacturer's authorised representative in the EU for product safety is Oxford University Press España S.A. of El Parque Empresarial San Fernando de Henares, Avenida de Castilla, 2 - 28830 Madrid (www.oup.es/en or product.safety@oup.com). OUP España S.A. also acts as importer into Spain of products made by the manufacturer.
Printed and bound by CPI Group (UK) Ltd, Croydon, CR0 4YY
14/09/2026
02216308-0012